Computer Communications and Networks

Series editors

A. J. Sammes, Cyber Security Centre, Faculty of Technology,
De Montfort University, Leicester, UK

Jacek Rak, Department of Computer Communications, Faculty of Electronics,
Telecommunications and Informatics, Gdansk University of Technology,
Gdansk, Poland

The **Computer Communications and Networks** series is a range of textbooks, monographs and handbooks. It sets out to provide students, researchers, and non-specialists alike with a sure grounding in current knowledge, together with comprehensible access to the latest developments in computer communications and networking.

Emphasis is placed on clear and explanatory styles that support a tutorial approach, so that even the most complex of topics is presented in a lucid and intelligible manner.

More information about this series at http://www.springer.com/series/4198

Zaigham Mahmood
Editor

Smart Cities

Development and Governance Frameworks

 Springer

Editor
Zaigham Mahmood
Debesis Education
Derby
UK

and

Shijiazhuang Tiedao University
Hebei
China

ISSN 1617-7975   ISSN 2197-8433   (electronic)
Computer Communications and Networks
ISBN 978-3-030-09551-2   ISBN 978-3-319-76669-0   (eBook)
https://doi.org/10.1007/978-3-319-76669-0

Printed on acid-free paper

This Springer imprint is published by the registered company Springer International Publishing AG
part of Springer Nature
The registered company address is: Gewerbestrasse 11, 6330 Cham, Switzerland

To

*Eyaad Imran Rashid Khan and
Zayb-un-Nisa Khan, the youngest in the
family and the most delightful*

Preface

Overview

A smart city is a new vision for urban development that brings together the various sectors of the society through the deployment of Internet of Things (IoT) and distributed computing technologies. The aim is to integrate and manage a city's resources and processes relating to transportation, health care, commerce, education, water and power, law enforcement, etc. as well as city's various departmental information systems. The suggestion is that the world cities are growing larger; new generations have entirely new priorities; hyper-globalization is revolutionizing how we build and deliver products and services; and technological innovation is accelerating at an exponential rate. Therefore, the ultimate objective is to develop smart living environments, improve living conditions of citizens, automate city services and processes, develop open and transparent systems, and, in general, build smarter and connected communities. Goal is to ensure that citizens' needs are met and they are technologically empowered to affect the city's functioning following a technologically led and citizen-centered-government approach.

Apart from the desire to use the technology for the sake of speed, openness, transparency, and effectiveness, there are currently a range of challenges that our cities face that drive the cities to urgently move to next levels of urbanization. These challenges include factors such as the following: rise in unemployment due to global economic downturn; pressures on housing sector due to growing demand, transportation, and health care due to increase in population; concerns about climate change; paradigm shift toward online entertainment and services; pressures on public finances and city resources due to increased awareness on the part of the general public; and the requirement to empower citizens to affect the working of local and federal governments. Fortunately, relevant computing technologies, social media offerings, distributed computing paradigms, mobile crowdsourcing, cyber-physical cloud computing, IoT frameworks, communication protocols, and device connectivity approaches are already well established to achieve citizens' empowerment to consume e-services provided by smart cities; and to allow city officials to interact directly with the community and monitor digital environments.

With this background, there is an urgent need for properly integrated solutions taking into account a number of related aspects including big data analytics and devices security; signaling and device detection; devices and data management; communication protocols and connectivity platforms; network bandwidth and topology; seamless connectivity and interoperability; and worldwide regulations and legal compliance.

In this context, this book aims to investigate development, management, governance, and monitoring approaches to building smart cities; and distributed computing environments therein. Majority of contributions in this volume focus on various aspects of related methodologies and approaches; device connectivity and communication; and security and interoperability. Thirty-two researchers and practitioners of international repute have presented latest research on frameworks, current trends, case studies, and suggestions for further enhancement of the IoT-based smart cities vision.

Hopefully, the current text, *Smart Cities—Development and Governance Frameworks,* will fill a gap with respect to smart living in smart environments and extend the existing body of knowledge in this field.

Objectives

The aim of this volume is to present and discuss the state of the art in terms of frameworks, methodologies, challenges, and solutions for IOT-based smarter living environments. The core objectives include the following:

- Capturing the state-of-the-art *research and practice* with respect to the issues and limitation of smart city environments;
- Presenting case studies illustrating approaches, best practices, examples, and practical solutions;
- Discussing corporate analysis and a balanced view of benefits and inherent barriers to smart city developments and management;
- Developing a complete reference for students, researchers, and practitioners of distributed computing systems and environments;
- Identifying further research directions and technological innovations in the context of distributed computing environments and IoT.

Organization

There are 13 chapters in this volume: *Smart Cities—Development and Governance Frameworks.* These are organized in three parts, as follows:

Part I: Frameworks and Models

This section has a focus on approaches and methodologies, relating to the next more advanced levels of urbanization. There are four chapters. In the first contribution, the authors present a recursive and layered approach to model large-scale resource management systems for self-sustainable cities. The second chapter discusses the security and privacy issues in relation to social, management, economy, and legal aspects of a smart city. The third contribution presents a novel architecture for hybrid vehicular wireless sensor networks, VANET-WSN, as a core component of smarter cities. The next chapter proposes a pricing mechanism for the management of natural resources, with particular emphasis on the energy sector, in the context of smarter living environments; case studies are also presented.

Part II: Challenges and Opportunities

This part of the book comprises five chapters that focus on issues and solutions. The first chapter discusses generic challenges of building intelligent distribute systems for smart cities. The next contribution focuses on building blocks for data and citizen-centric knowledge-based governance of smart cities and looks into the related IoT challenges. The third chapter in the section provides a holistic vision of smart city surveillance and fog computing paradigms including challenges and opportunities; a case study of urban traffic surveillance is also presented. The fourth contribution discusses issues and challenges relating to big data management and analytics relevant to smart grids. The final chapter considers risks and opportunities of electric vehicles adoption in smart city environments.

Part III: Examples and Case Studies

There are four chapters in this section that focus on ongoing research in relation to sustainability, illustrating several case studies. The first chapter looks at the design and sustainability approaches for building smart cities; the contribution explores smart city projects in four of the Japanese cities. The next chapter proposes a sustainable business model to implement smart city digital services in relation to smart city initiatives in Indian cities. The third contribution explores the challenges and opportunities in relation to smart city projects in Brazil; the authors discuss related factors such as collaboration, communication, sustainability, and automation. The final contribution of the book discusses the sustainability requirements for the provision of healthcare services, presenting several smart city scenarios.

Target Audiences

The current volume is a reference text aimed at supporting a number of potential audiences, including the following:

- *Communication Engineers, Software Developers,* and *Network Security Specialists* who wish to adopt the newer approaches to ensure the security of data and devices for seamless connectivity in the smarter cities environments.

- *Students* and *Lecturers* who have an interest in further enhancing the knowledge of technologies, mechanisms, and frameworks relevant to the smarter living environments from a distributed computing perspective.
- *Researchers* and *Practitioners* in this field who require up to date knowledge of the current practices, mechanisms, frameworks, and limitations relevant to the smart cities and Internet of Things vision.

Derby, UK   Zaigham Mahmood
Hebei, China

Acknowledgements

The editor acknowledges the help and support of the following colleagues during the review, development, and editing phases of this text:

- Prof. Zhengxu Zhao, Shijiazhuang Tiedao University, Hebei, China
- Dr. Alfredo Cuzzocrea, University of Trieste, Trieste, Italy
- Prof. Jing He, Kennesaw State University, Kennesaw, GA, USA
- Josip Lorincz, FESB-Split, University of Split, Croatia
- Aleksandar Milić, University of Belgrade, Serbia
- Dr. S. Parthasarathy, Thiagarajar College of Engineering, Tamil Nadu, India
- Daniel Pop, Institute e-Austria Timisoara, West University of Timisoara, Romania
- Dr. Pethuru Raj, IBM Cloud Center of Excellence, Bangalore, India
- Dr. Muthu Ramachandran, Leeds Becket University, Leeds, UK
- Dr. Lucio Agostinho Rocha, State University of Campinas, Brazil
- Dr. Saqib Saeed, University of Dammam, Saudi Arabia
- Prof. Claudio Sartori, University of Bologna, Bologna, Italy
- Dr. Mahmood Shah, University of Central Lancashire, Preston, UK
- Igor Tomičić, University of Zagreb, Pavlinska 2, 42000 Varazdin, Croatia
- Dr. Fareeha Zafar, GC University, Lahore, Pakistan

I would also like to thank the contributors to this book: 32 authors and co-authors, from academia as well as industry from around the world, who collectively submitted 13 well-researched chapters. Without their efforts in developing quality contributions, conforming to the guidelines, and meeting often the strict deadlines, this text would not have been possible.

Grateful thanks are also due to the members of my family—Rehana, Zoya, Imran, Hanya, Arif, and Ozair—for their continued support and encouragement. Every good wish, also, for the youngest and the most delightful in our family: Eyaad Imran Rashid Khan and Zayb-un-Nisa Khan.

Derby, UK   Zaigham Mahmood
Hebei, China
February 2018

Other Springer Books by Zaigham Mahmood

Data Science and Big Data Computing: Frameworks and Methodologies

This reference text has a focus on data science and provides practical guidance on big data analytics. Expert perspectives are provided by an authoritative collection of 36 researchers and practitioners, discussing the latest developments and emerging trends; presenting frameworks and innovative methodologies; and suggesting best practices for efficient and effective data analytics. ISBN: 978-3-319-31859-2.

Connected Environments for the IoT: Challenges and Solutions

This comprehensive reference presents a broad-ranging overview of device connectivity in distributed computing environments, supporting the vision of IoT. Expert perspectives are provided, covering issues of communication, security, privacy, interoperability, networking, access control, and authentication. Corporate analysis is also offered via several case studies. ISBN 978-3-319-70102-8.

Connectivity Frameworks for Smart Devices: The Internet of Things from a Distributed Computing Perspective

This is an authoritative reference that provides a focus on the latest developments on the Internet of Things. It presents state of the art on the current advances in the connectivity of diverse devices and provides in-depth discussion on the communication, security, privacy, access control, and authentication aspects of the device connectivity in distributed environments. ISBN: 978-3-319-33122-5.

Software Project Management for Distributed Computing: Life Cycle Methods for Developing Scalable and Reliable Tools

This unique volume explores cutting-edge management approaches to developing complex software that is efficient, scalable, sustainable, and suitable for distributed environments. Emphasis is on the use of the latest software technologies and frameworks for life cycle methods, including design, implementation, and testing stages of software development. ISBN: 978-3-319-54324-6.

Requirements Engineering for Service and Cloud Computing

This text aims to present and discuss the state of the art in terms of methodologies, trends, and future directions for requirements engineering for the service and cloud computing paradigm. Majority of the contributions in the book focus on requirements elicitation; requirements specifications; requirements classification; and requirements validation and evaluation. ISBN: 978-3-319-51309-6.

Software Engineering Frameworks for the Cloud Computing Paradigm

This is an authoritative reference that presents the latest research on software development approaches suitable for distributed computing environments. Contributed by researchers and practitioners of international repute, the book offers practical guidance on enterprise-wide software deployment relevant to the cloud environment. Case studies are also presented. ISBN: 978-1-447-15030-5.

Cloud Computing: Methods and Practical Approaches

The benefits associated with cloud computing are many; yet the dynamic, virtualized, and multi-tenant nature of the cloud environment presents numerous challenges. To help tackle these, this volume provides illuminating viewpoints and case studies to present current research and best practices on approaches and technologies for the emerging cloud paradigm. ISBN: 978-1-447-15106-7.

Cloud Computing: Challenges, Limitations, and R&D Solutions

This reference text reviews the challenging issues that present barriers to greater implementation of the cloud computing paradigm, together with the latest research into developing potential solutions. The book presents case studies and analysis of the implications of the cloud paradigm, from a diverse selection of researchers and practitioners of international repute. ISBN: 978-3-319-10529-1.

Continued Rise of the Cloud: Advances and Trends in Cloud Computing

This reference volume presents latest research and trends in cloud-related technologies, infrastructure, and architecture. Contributed by expert researchers and practitioners in the field, the book presents discussions on current advances and practical approaches including guidance and case studies on the provision of cloud-based services and frameworks. ISBN: 978-1-447-16451-7.

Cloud Computing for Enterprise Architectures

This reference text, aimed at system architects and business managers, examines the cloud paradigm from the perspective of enterprise architectures. It introduces fundamental concepts, discusses principles, and explores frameworks for the adoption of cloud computing. The book explores the inherent challenges and presents future directions for further research. ISBN: 978 1 447 12235 7.

User-Centric E-Government: Challenges & Opportunities

This text presents a citizen-focused approach to the development and implementation of electronic government. The focus is twofold: discussion on challenges of service availability and e-service operability on diverse smart devices; as well as on opportunities for the provision of open, responsive, and transparent functioning of world governments. ISBN: 978-3-319-59441-5.

Contents

Part I Frameworks and Models

1 Modeling Smart Self-sustainable Cities as Large-Scale Agent Organizations in the IoT Environment 3
Igor Tomičić, Bogdan Okreša Đurić and Markus Schatten

2 Cybersecurity System: An Essential Pillar of Smart Cities 25
Lata Nautiyal, Preeti Malik and Amit Agarwal

3 Towards Heterogeneous Architectures of Hybrid Vehicular Sensor Networks for Smart Cities 51
Soumia Bellaouar, Mohamed Guerroumi, Abdelouahid Derhab and Samira Moussaoui

4 Pricing Mechanisms for Energy Management in Smart Cities 71
Anulipt Chandan, Vidyasagar Potdar and Champa Nandi

Part II Challenges and Opportunities

5 Building Intelligent Systems for Smart Cities: Issues, Challenges and Approaches 107
Amrita Ghosal and Subir Halder

6 IoT Challenges in Data and Citizen-centric Smart City Governance 127
A. Sebastian, S. Sivagurunathan and V. Muthu Ganeshan

7 Smart City Surveillance at the Network Edge in the Era of IoT: Opportunities and Challenges 153
Ning Chen and Yu Chen

8   Big Energy Data Management for Smart Grids—Issues,
    Challenges and Recent Developments 177
    Vidyasagar Potdar, Anulipt Chandan, Saima Batool
    and Naimesh Patel

9   Risks and Challenges of Adopting Electric
    Vehicles in Smart Cities 207
    Vidyasagar Potdar, Saima Batool and Aneesh Krishna

Part III   Examples and Case Studies

10 Rising of Yokohama, Keihanna, Kitakyushu, and Toyota
    Smart Cities in the Land of the Rising Sun 243
    Somayya Madakam, Rajesh M. Holmukhe and Siddharth Tripathi

11 A Business Model for Digital Services for Smart
    Cities in India 263
    Chandrakumar Thangavel and Parthasarathy Sudhaman

12 Opportunities for Brazilian Smart Cities: What Is Realistic
    and What Is not 281
    Lucio Agostinho Rocha

13 Standards-Based Sustainability Requirements for Healthcare
    Services in Smart Cities 299
    Sofia Ouhbi, Ali Idri and José Luis Fernández-Alemán

Index 319

Contributors

Amit Agarwal University of Petroleum and Energy Sciences, Dehradun, India

Saima Batool School of Information Systems, Curtin Business School, Curtin University, Perth, Australia

Soumia Bellaouar Vehicular Networks for Intelligent Transport Systems (VNets) Group, Electronic and Computing Department, USTHB University, Algiers, Algeria

Anulipt Chandan National Institute of Technology, Agartala, India

Ning Chen Department of Electrical and Computing Engineering, Binghamton University, Binghamton, USA

Yu Chen Department of Electrical and Computing Engineering, Binghamton University, Binghamton, USA

Abdelouahid Derhab Center of Excellence in Information Assurance (CoEIA), King Saud University, Riyadh, Saudi Arabia

José Luis Fernández-Alemán Department of Informatics and Systems, University of Murcia, Murcia, Spain

Amrita Ghosal Department of Computer Science and Engineering, Dr. B. C. Roy Engineering College, Durgapur, India

Mohamed Guerroumi Vehicular Networks for Intelligent Transport Systems (VNets) Group, Electronic and Computing Department, USTHB University, Algiers, Algeria

Subir Halder Department of Computer Science and Engineering, Dr. B. C. Roy Engineering College, Durgapur, India

Rajesh M. Holmukhe Electrical Engineering Department, Bharati Vidyapeeth Deemed University College of Engineering, Pune, India

Ali Idri Software Project Management Research Team, ENSIAS, University Mohammed V, Rabat, Morocco

Aneesh Krishna Department of Computing, Curtin University, Perth, Australia

Somayya Madakam Information Technology Area, FORE School of Management, New Delhi, India

Preeti Malik Graphic Era University, Dehradun, India

Samira Moussaoui Vehicular Networks for Intelligent Transport Systems (VNets) Group, Electronic and Computing Department, USTHB University, Algiers, Algeria

V. Muthu Ganeshan Department of Computer Science and Applications, Gandhigram Rural Institute, Dindigul, India

Champa Nandi Tripura University, Agartala, India

Lata Nautiyal Graphic Era University, Dehradun, India

Bogdan Okreša Đurić Artificial Intelligence Laboratory, Faculty of Organization and Informatics, University of Zagreb, Varazdin, Croatia

Sofia Ouhbi FIL, Université Internationale de Rabat, Rabat, Morocco

Naimesh Patel Safeworld Systems Pvt Ltd, Ahmedabad, India

Vidyasagar Potdar School of Information Systems, Curtin Business School, Curtin University, Perth, Australia

Lucio Agostinho Rocha GPESI Research Group, Software Engineering, Federal University of Technology—Paraná, Dois Vizinhos, Brazil

Markus Schatten Artificial Intelligence Laboratory, Faculty of Organization and Informatics, University of Zagreb, Varazdin, Croatia

A. Sebastian Department of Computer Science and Applications, Gandhigram Rural Institute, Dindigul, India

S. Sivagurunathan Department of Computer Science and Applications, Gandhigram Rural Institute, Dindigul, India

Parthasarathy Sudhaman Department of Computer Applications, Thiagarajar College of Engineering, Madurai, Tamilnadu, India

Chandrakumar Thangavel Department of Computer Applications, Thiagarajar College of Engineering, Madurai, Tamilnadu, India

Igor Tomičić Artificial Intelligence Laboratory, Faculty of Organization and Informatics, University of Zagreb, Varazdin, Croatia

Siddharth Tripathi Marketing Group, National Institute of Industrial Engineering (NITIE), Mumbai, Maharashtra, India

About the Editor

Prof. Dr. Zaigham Mahmood is a published author of twenty-one books, seven of which are dedicated to e-government and the other fourteen focus on the subjects of cloud computing, data science, big data, Internet of things, smart cities, project management, and software engineering; including the textbook *Cloud Computing: Concepts, Technology & Architecture* which is also published in Korean and Chinese languages. Additionally, he is developing two new books to appear later in 2018. He has also published more than 100 articles and book chapters and organized numerous conference tracks and workshops.

He is the Editor-in-Chief of *Journal of E-Government Studies and Best Practices* as well as the Series Editor-in-Chief of the IGI book series on *E-Government and Digital Divide*. He is a Senior Technology Consultant at Debesis Education UK and a Professor at the Shijiazhuang Tiedao University in Hebei China. He further holds positions as Foreign Professor at NUST and IIU in Islamabad Pakistan. He has served as a Reader (Associate Professor) at the University of Derby UK, and Professor Extraordinaire at the North West University Potchefstroom South Africa. He is also a certified cloud computing instructor and a regular speaker at international conferences devoted to cloud computing and E-Government. His specialized areas of research include distributed computing, project management, and e-government.

Part I
Frameworks and Models

Chapter 1
Modeling Smart Self-sustainable Cities as Large-Scale Agent Organizations in the IoT Environment

Igor Tomičić, Bogdan Okreša Đurić and Markus Schatten

Abstract This chapter provides an overview of modeling techniques for large-scale systems in the Internet of Things (IoT) environment with a special accent on smart self-sustainable cities. The authors present a framework for modeling Large-Scale Multi-Agent Systems (LSMASs) including a graphical modeling language, and a tool, that aim to facilitate development of such systems in a recursive fashion. Smart self-sustainable cities in this chapter are modeled using this language that forms the basis for the Smart Self-Sustainable Human Settlements (SSSHS) framework developed by the authors. The SSSHS framework consists of several sustainability mechanisms which attempt to facilitate the self-sustainability of a human settlement by managing resources such as water, electricity, and heating, based on the current needs, production, and storage using a detailed agent-based methodology. By integrating these two frameworks (LSMAS and SSSHS), the authors show a recursive and layered approach that is able to model large-scale resource management systems in a hierarchical manner by using IoT technologies.

Keywords Smart cities · Internet of things · Large-scale multi-agent systems Modeling · Self-sustainability · Resources · Organizational modeling Sustainability mechanisms · Internet of everything

1.1 Introduction

According to Bowerman [5], a smart city ought to be *"the urban center of the future made safe, secure, environmentally green, and efficient because all structures - whether for power, water or transportation - are designed, constructed, and maintained, making use of advanced integrated materials, sensors, electronics, and*

I. Tomičić · B. Okreša Đurić (✉) · M. Schatten
Artificial Intelligence Laboratory, Faculty of Organization and Informatics,
University of Zagreb, Pavlinska 2, 42000 Varazdin, Croatia
e-mail: dokresa@foi.hr

© Springer International Publishing AG, part of Springer Nature 2018
Z. Mahmood (ed.), *Smart Cities*, Computer Communications and Networks,
https://doi.org/10.1007/978-3-319-76669-0_1

networks which are interfaced with computerized systems and comprised of databases, tracking, and decision-making algorithms". Thus, smart cities represent large-scale, complex, socio-technical, and socio-cybernetic systems which are inherently distributed in terms of interacting components and parallel in terms of interlacing processes. Smart cities are one of the important application domains of the Internet of Things (IoT), in which smart devices of various kinds cooperate to provide better services for its citizens [3]. An adequate formalism for modeling such systems is found in agent-based modeling, both in the context of engineering smart technologies and simulating social behavior.

Apart from being *smart*, for cities to be self-sustainable, they should be able to produce, manage, and consume their resources in an intelligent manner. Herein, we introduce the Smart Self-Sustainable Human Settlements (SSSHS) Framework (which we have already presented in [26]) that has demonstrated its efficiency in prolonging the period of self-sustainability in small-scale resource management experiments. SSSHS uses an agent-based approach in which resource producing, storing, and consuming units are represented as intelligent software agents that are able to negotiate resource use, depending on current needs of their users (e.g., inhabitants of a settlement).

In order to make this framework suitable for large-scale settings, we introduce additional techniques bound to organizational modeling of large-scale multi-agent systems (MASs) similar to the foundations which we have outlined in [21]. LSMASs need to be organized in a robust and scalable manner that would allow software agents in such systems to function and adapt to possibly complex environments they have to face. To establish such a complex organization, an adequate normative system, with an organizational structure consisting of organizational roles, has to be put in place, which agents can enact depending on current environmental and system-specific circumstances. We introduce a dynamic hierarchical structure based on a recursive definition of organizational units [17, 18], which represent the building blocks of (agent) organizations.

The rest of this chapter is organized as follows: first, in Sect. 1.2, we provide an overview of relevant literature; then in Sect. 1.3, we present the organizational metamodel that is used for modeling a smart city's resource management system in the form of an LSMAS. Afterward, the SSSHS framework is introduced in Sect. 4 in some detail. In Sect. 1.5, we provide a detailed description of modeling techniques for smart cities as a self-sustainable LSMAS, followed by analyses of an example scenario detailed in Sect. 1.6. Later, in Sect. 1.7, we discuss our findings, and, in Sect. 1.8, we draw conclusions and provide guidelines for future research.

1.2 Literature Overview

Organizational models for MASs have been developed based on features of human organizations from their initial phase, yet only recently have researchers become interested in exploring the meaning of organizational features in LSMAS. An interesting overview of the existent models for organizational modeling of MAS in general, although some of those are applicable to LSMAS as well, was given in [7]. The models described in the mentioned paper were evaluated against a set of modeling dimensions for agent organizations. We have presented an improvement of those dimensions, making them more susceptible to the modern ideas which encourage development of LSMAS, presented in the form of a set of perspectives of organizational modeling, in [18]. The organizational metamodel used in this chapter is being built based on these perspectives [14, 15].

Agent-based modeling approaches proved to be adequate for modeling the IoT domain [4, 19, 25, 26], especially when considering the potential interoperability issues that may be derived from heterogeneous set of devices, communication protocols, networks, data formats, etc. IoT systems are, by definition, distributed and intelligent, which is equivalent to most definitions of MAS. In the domain of smart cities, which can be viewed as large-scale IoT systems, the use of agent-based modeling and implementation techniques becomes an even greater necessity. Due to the mere scale of such systems, organizational design of agent organizations seems to be an adequate toolset to approach such systems.

Several recently published papers describe research on smart buildings and smart grids in cooperation with agents and IoT concepts, some of which employ the idea of swarm [11], some deal with user intention models [29], some work on coordination of agents of energy management systems [22], and some are considering energy systems using ontology-based systems of agents [2]. Also, Roscia et al. [16] discuss a model of the Intelligent Distributed Autonomous Smart City (IDASC) by using MASs and IoT, and elaborate on an infrastructure and architecture of a multi-agent system for a smart city model, concluding with a conceptual, cross-domain model of a smart city. Clearly, the intention of this chapter differs from already published work in details such as dealing with self-sustainability emerging from individual agents' interaction, and their mutual cooperation and communication which is translated to higher aggregation levels, i.e., groups of individual agents are considered as well.

The IoT initiative has often been referenced in the context of sustainability, energy efficiency, and environmental issues, especially in the context of the Environmental IoT (EIoT) domain. For example, Vlacheas et al. [27] consider the key issues that might prevent the IoT from supporting the sustainable development of smart cities: the heterogeneity among connected objects and unreliability of associated services. The authors propose the cognitive management framework—a framework that allows selection of individual devices (agents) for the specific task to be performed in the given spatiotemporal context in an effort to address those issues. The work presented herein deals with setting up the adequate roles (inside an imposed normative organizational structure), which can then be enacted by specific agents. From this perspective, the work of [27] is complementary, but with a different intention.

An agent-based simulator that attempts to create dynamic behavior is presented in [12]. The simulator deals with heterogeneous devices that have producing and/or consuming roles within the simulation, and are able to act in an autonomous manner and collaborate with each other. The main focus of the simulation carried out by the authors was to reproduce a residential scenario of energy consumption, with appliances having only two possible states (ON and OFF). The appliances considered herein use our proposed SSSHS approach and have the possibility of operating time manipulations together with several modes of consuming operations (delayed, advanced, default, savings, and off), which enables more possibilities in terms of managing self-sustainability.

Another approach to observing dynamics of resource exchange (namely renewable electric energy) was described in [13]. The authors introduce the idea of an exchange of electricity and a novel digital currency they called NRGcoin. Their work focuses on the negotiation and exchange process of renewable electricity as the only resource being exchanged, as opposed to mechanics of individual units working with various resources as presented in this chapter. The idea of introducing a special currency for energy exchange, along with specific behavior of included housing unit agents, is noteworthy though, since it presents one of the possible ways of negotiation interaction of various housing units of a system. Furthermore, their model helps in regulating consumption and production, and managing electricity storage.

1.3 Large-Scale Multi-agent Systems: An Organizational Metamodel

The idea of organization is not a new concept in the world of MAS, and it seems to be crucial to LSMAS. The first thoughts about the organizational modeling of a MAS were derived from the domain of human organizations and the set of concepts used to describe organizations of humans. Since humans can be abstracted as agents, as far as their position and significance in an organization is concerned, and their interaction can be formalized, it is apt to speak of copying features of human organizations to MAS. Furthermore, it is argued [6, 9] that LSMASs benefit from some organizational features and constraints, since having a defined code of conduct can help utilize individual agents' features, strengths, and group commitment, along with overcoming their temporal limitations and skill constraints.

There are two dominant perspectives on organization as a concept in MAS, and subsequently LSMAS, that are mutually not excludable [1, 8]. Organization can be observed as a concept imposed on the given system (organization centered MAS), thus being devised by an agent outside of the goal system, and then cast upon it, imposing on it authority and order. This approach constrains the agents of the system using an already devised set of rules and other organizational features. Such an approach can comprise agents that can perceive the given organization. Furthermore, such agents can influence the organization to change, if such a change is needed based on the state of the environment and the whole system. Therefore, the agents can change the organizational features of the system, if the proposed change can make it easier to achieve a group goal. On the other hand, emerging organization is about a bottom-up approach to the idea of organization—organizational constraints are results of individual agents' interactions. Instead of a given organization, organizational features of such a system grow based on agents' perception of the environment and their reactions. The emerging organization is therefore more open to change, and the constraints it introduces on the system are more natural, being derived from the system itself. It is argued that LSMAS benefit the most from the combination of both, slightly favoring the cast-upon approach. Although the emerging organization approach seems more natural for an LSMAS primarily because of the decentralized feature of MAS, the imposed-upon organization allows the agents to act faster [28]. On the other hand, emerging MAS organizations can be more robust and adaptive, since their behavior depends exclusively on their mutual interactions with the environment they are situated in.

A number of MAS models have tackled the problem of organization when dealing with artificial autonomous agents, but there are only a few of them specializing for LSMAS [7]. Therefore, we have proposed a novel LSMAS organizational metamodel featuring human organizational concepts in recent research [14, 15, 18], one that would introduce additional organizational concepts into modeling LSMAS, in particular organizational dynamics, and is currently in an early stage of development. The current results can be used to model a system though, as is shown further in this section using the metamodel as a work in progress.

The metamodel is aiming to introduce an enhanced experience for users modeling LSMAS with organizational features. In its final version, the metamodel is envisioned to support modeling of organizational features including organizational structure, normative elements, and organizational dynamics. The idea of the metamodel stems from the research and guidelines we set in [18, 20], where a set of organization modeling perspectives is presented that is deemed as useful for the modern research of LSMAS. The metamodel is being developed with general use in mind, with intentions of allowing developers of various LSMAS domains to use it effectively. Domains such as the IoT and smart cities can be abstracted using the idea of LSMAS, and are therefore adequate for modeling using the metamodel described herein.

The metamodel uses a recursive approach similar to that of holons and holarchy [1]. For example, the basic element of the metamodel is an organizational unit which represents either an individual agent or a group of organizational units [18]. A similar approach is applied to various other elements of the metamodel (for example, roles and objectives).

One of the features of the finished metamodel allows the user to generate programming code for the modeled system. The generated code provides the developer with essential code for creating the modeled system based on the metamodel. Following are the elements included in the current version of the metamodel, aimed at describing an LSMAS:

- Organizational Unit: An organizational unit is the concept that models the actors of the system—individual agents and groups of agents. An organizational unit plays roles, conducts actions, and achieves goals, following the norms of the system.

- Role: The role element serves as a way of representing sets of norms of the modeled system. Every organizational unit can play a certain set of roles which dictate actions and behaviors available to the given organizational unit and constraints that have to be respected by the organizational unit playing a particular role.
- Individual Knowledge Artifact: Individual knowledge artifacts are the way of modeling knowledge available to individual agents. This knowledge is not universally accessible, i.e., each individual can access their knowledge artifact, unless stated otherwise.
- Organizational Knowledge Artifact: Since roles are elements of the system rather than elements of individual agents, roles have access to artifacts containing knowledge concerning the system, along with various norms and other organizational features of the modeled system.
- Objective: The objective element is used for modeling various kinds of goals of the system. Objectives are defined recursively as well; therefore, an objective can consist of several subobjectives until the basic level is reached.
- Process: Each role provides the organization unit playing the given role with a set of actions. Various combinations of these actions are designated as processes that serve a purpose of achieving a specific goal. There is a strong connection between objectives, processes, and roles, since processes make various roles applicable to specific objectives.

There are a number of modeled elements for connecting the stated class-like elements of the metamodel. These are primarily used to designate various types of relations between the elements included in the metamodel. Various relations are possible, and some of which are listed below:

- Being a part of: since one of the more interesting aspects of organization for this metamodel is the formation of groups of organizational units, a very important connection represents grouping of various elements.
- Available roles for enacting: each organizational unit can, at a given point in time, play a certain role. When it is enacting a role, the organization unit is enhanced with applicable actions, knowledge, and constraints.
- Accessible knowledge artifacts: the general idea is that organizational units can access individual knowledge artifacts, and roles have access to organizational knowledge artifacts, since the first describe individual agent (or group of agents) and the latter are concerned with the system.
- Serving a process: each role has a set of actions at their disposal. A group of actions from one or more roles that can be conducted in order to achieve a particular objective is called a process.
- Relevance for an objective: it is important to specify for which objective each process is useful, since such a description makes it possible for an agent to easily find a role suitable for the obstacle or an objective the agent is faced with.

1.3.1 A Simple Example

A simple example useful for showing the general idea of how the metamodel can be used is presented here, for the sake of clarifying the basics of the metamodel. It should be noted here again that the metamodel is a work in progress and will be changed for the better in the near future.

This example is based on the recipeWorld idea [10] comprising factories (service agents), orders (service-seeking agents), and recipe parts (services). For more in-depth description, please refer to the original paper.

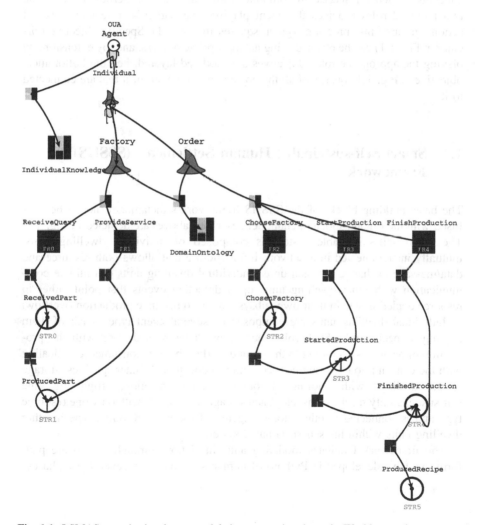

Fig. 1.1 LSMAS organizational metamodel showcase using the recipeWorld example

Figure 1.1 shows the basic model of the recipeWorld, developed using the described metamodel, comprising the core elements of recipeWorld. An individual agent situated in the system fashioned after the recipeWorld idea is represented using an organizational unit element of the metamodel (stick figure in Fig. 1.1), in its individual state. Such an individual agent has access to individual knowledge artifact (black-yellow in Fig. 1.1) comprising individual knowledge of or about the given agent. Only two roles (blue hats in Fig. 1.1) are present—one for factory agents (service providers) and one for order agents (service seekers). Since the services are bound to individual agents, they are specified as a part of the agent's individual knowledge. Both roles have access to an organizational knowledge artifact (black-blue in Fig. 1.1), which defines language used in the system, basic concepts needed for successful communication, and their properties. Each of the two modeled roles provides the agent playing that particular role with a set of actions grouped into processes (green squares in Fig. 1.1). Specific objective (circular in Fig. 1.1) can be reached using an appropriate process, and, by extension, by playing the appropriate role. Objectives are modeled layered, i.e., the bottommost objective in Fig. 1.1 consists of all the objectives on the left of it that are connected to it.

1.4 Smart Self-sustainable Human Settlements (SSSHS) Framework

The basic building blocks of the SSSHS framework's metamodel (not to be confused with the organizational metamodel described above) are depicted in Fig. 1.2. The smart self-sustainable system is composed of individual dwelling units, mutually interconnected in a network infrastructure that allows both resource and data/message exchange between units. Individual dwelling units can initiate communication with other dwelling units upon detecting events that point either to resource depletion within their own subsystems or to resource production overflow.

Individual dwelling units are composed of several agent types, each of them playing a specific role. Such roles include producer role, dealing with the production of resources according to the input data distribution; consumer role, dealing with the consumption of resources according to consumer's inner specifics; storage roles, dealing with storing resources, communication, triggering the self-sustainability mechanisms; etc. Each storage agent deals with only one resource type and is connected to other storage agents of the same resource type in other dwelling units within the self-sustainable system.

The framework facilitates modeling and simulation (through a software platform, we have developed in Python) of human settlements in several key phases:

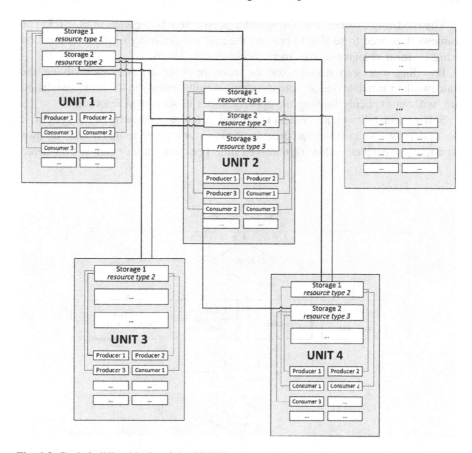

Fig. 1.2 Basic building blocks of the SSSHS metamodel (adopted from our previous work [24])

1. Defining temporal granularity of the simulation (a second, a minute, an hour, a day, 4 days, 2 weeks, a month, etc.), i.e., the smallest time unit that enables changes in the simulation namespace.
2. Defining the total duration of the simulation.
3. Implementing scenario context by instantiating model's entities (producer, consumer, and storage agents).
4. Defining the inner states of the included agents (setting the relevant parameters of agents according to available data and context, thus tuning their behaviors).
5. Implementing a multi-agent system by defining mutual relationships of agents, thus creating a network of agents that can communicate, negotiate, make offers, etc.
6. Setting the relevant input data from the environment that would affect the included agents and their behavior during the simulation run.
7. Initiating the simulation run, analyzing the results produced by the framework, tweaking, and optimizing the model according to those results.

The modeling process from the modeler perspective is depicted in Fig. 1.3. The framework proved to be able to prolong the self-sustainability of the settlement by using its inner resource management mechanisms [24–26].

Dwelling units can manage one or more resource types, thus enabling the framework to simulate one or more resources simultaneously in the same simulation run, without explicitly limiting the upper number of simulated resources.

Self-sustainability in this context is defined as a binary property of the system; if the system is able to cover resource demands in any given moment with its own production capacities within the observed time period, such a system is considered

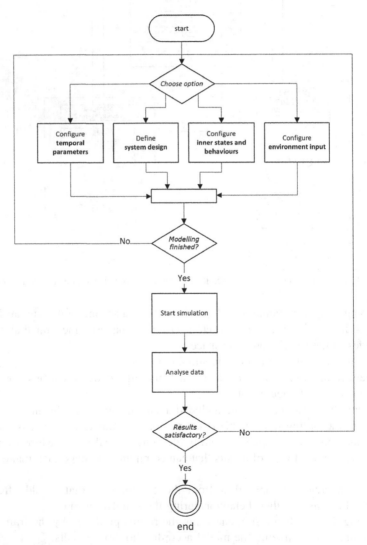

Fig. 1.3 The SSSHS modeling process illustration (adopted from [23])

self-sustainable for this time period. Contrariwise, if the system is not able to maintain this resource autonomy, it is considered not self-sustainable, and thus unable to function off-grid. If the simulation results show that the latter is the case, further analysis of the system and model optimizations are needed in an effort to make the system self-sustainable. The SSSHS framework offers verbose simulation output data which might point to the key factors that impede self-sustainability.

Preserving self-sustainability in any given moment within the simulation runtime is facilitated by the SSSHS framework's self-sustainability mechanisms. Two major scenarios are considered when dealing with the intermittent resource production and consumption.

- In the first scenario, production rates may overflow the storage capacities within a dwelling unit, risking a loss of resources because of the inability of the unit to store this excess of produced resources. This same excess might be critically needed in one or more of the other units, or simply distributable among other units, with priority queue based on the individual's storage levels for the given resource. The SSSHS framework triggers the upper resource level alert when detecting a possible resource overflow, and mechanisms such as advancing consumption operating times, restoring default consumption rates, and offering and distributing surplus resources to other units are able to handle such events, preventing the overall loss of resources.
- In the second scenario, dwelling units may lack the production rates that would handle the increasing demand for a resource. In this scenario, a dwelling unit might completely run out of a resource, rendering the system as not self-sustainable. The SSSHS framework is equipped to deal with such scenarios by utilizing its lower threshold mechanisms such as activating the consumers' savings modes, manipulating the consumers' operating times, or initiating a negotiation process that has the potential to result in a resource transfer from other dwelling units. Figure 1.4 depicts the self-sustainable mechanisms' activities managed by the SSSHS framework based on the detected simulation events throughout the main system roles.

The "resource negotiation" is an inter-dwelling mechanism that calculates the client's needed resource value which would bring its resource level above the lower threshold zone, and then requires a service from other agents, or servers, to initiate the resource transfer if the agreement is made between them. After the client sends its offer, the server calculates its own resource capacities by inspecting its current inner state and decides on the counteroffer it is willing to send to the client. If the counteroffer is greater than zero and resource transfer costs are acceptable, the negotiation process is initiated. If the resource transfer costs are not acceptable, or the agreement is achieved but the counteroffer does not provide sufficient resource quantity, the client sends further requests to other agents, sequentially, until its resource levels are above the defined threshold.

The SSSHS negotiation process from the client perspective is depicted via finite state machine in Fig. 1.5.

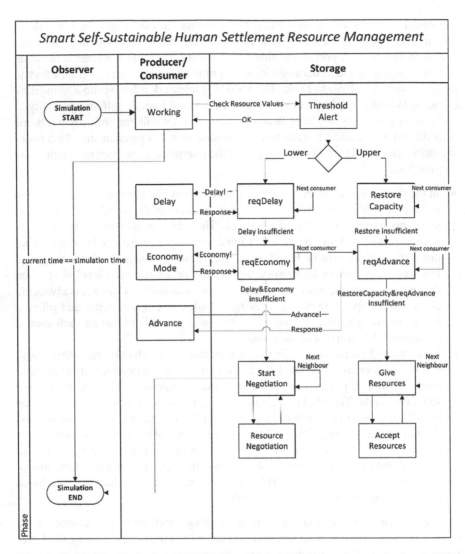

Fig. 1.4 The activity diagram of the SSSHS framework (adopted from our previous work [26])

1.5 Modeling Smart Cities as LSMAS

The described SSSHS metamodel defines a self-sustainable system as a collection of organizational units comprising an organization of individual agents enacting various roles including consumer, producer, and storage. These work in unison and try to maintain self-sustainability through balancing loads of produced, stored, and consumed resources. Individuals within an SSSHS dwelling unit are agents that

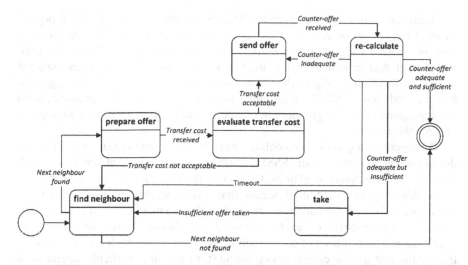

Fig. 1.5 A finite state machine of the SSSHS negotiation process (adopted from [24])

cooperatively work not to fail the main objective of the organization (the dwelling unit)—maintaining self-sustainability.

So far, the SSSHS framework has been used to model small-scale settlements and might be cumbersome to be used in large-scale settings directly due to a number of reasons. First, the framework assumes that various agents in a dwelling unit, as well as the dwelling units themselves, are mutually connected with resource exchange and communication pipelines in the form of a full graph. While this might be possible in small settlements, it is nearly impossible for the case of cities. Second, the used negotiation and sustainability mechanisms prescribe communication of an individual unit with all other agents in order to share resources when needed, which is impractical. To solve the first issue, we introduce organizational units in a recursive hierarchical structure. Producer, consumer, and storage agents are grouped in organizational units on a number of levels: apartment, house, building, building block, neighborhood, part of city, city, etc. Only organizational units on the same level are connected by a full resource and communication graph which reduces the number of needed connections dramatically. Also, to solve the second issue, organizational units in need of sharing resources query and negotiate only with other units on the same level, thus reducing the number of exchanges messages dramatically as well. To connect the various levels, we introduce a dynamic leader role: each organizational unit has a leader–negotiator which, in case a resource sharing issue cannot be solved on the current level, is entitled to negotiate and query other leaders on the next level. This leader–negotiator unit also has to manage self-sustainability mechanisms, as defined in the SSSHS framework, on its upper level to provide information (like manipulation of operating times, for example) from one level to another.

Figure 1.6 shows such an extended SSSHS system using the LSMAS organizational metamodel described earlier. The basic unit of the SSSHS, the dwelling unit, is modeled using an organizational unit (stickman on Fig. 1.6) on its individual level. Aggregation of such individual agents is modeled using organizational units named building, neighborhood, and settlement, in a rising level of aggregation, i.e., individual SSSHS agents representing dwelling units (for example, flats) are aggregated (joined or grouped) into building units which are in turn aggregated into neighborhoods.

The described approach to modeling stems from the joined ideas of SSSHS and the organizational metamodel. SSSHS observes units as special constructs built from several other lower level units. Coupled with the organizational metamodel, it is possible to upgrade the SSSHS idea so that various levels of aggregated units act just as the individual units do. This idea is described in more detail in [18]. Briefly, and applied to SSSHS, it can be described as follows. A dwelling unit is an organizational unit. If a set of organizational units is coupled with a set of roles for those units, and specific criteria of organizing (for example, a particular objective of maintaining self-sustainability, or a particular mission, and similar), then that set is an organizational unit. This observation makes it possible to apply SSSHS ideas to organizational units on various levels of aggregation. In other words, it makes it possible to model a system comprising aggregated dwelling units, i.e., building units, and work with them as if they were basic dwelling units, thus making them

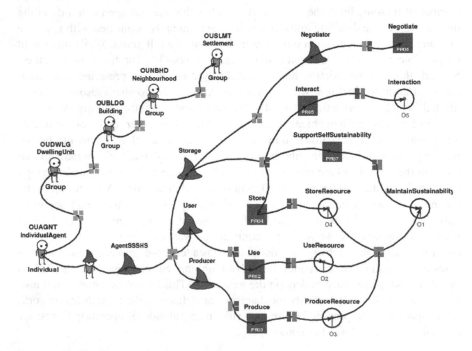

Fig. 1.6 SSSHS elements of the chapter modeled using the LSMAS organizational metamodel

able to play SSSHS roles and strive to continually reach the main goal of maintaining self-sustainability. Furthermore, it is possible to raise the level of aggregation and observe neighborhood units (aggregated building units) as organizational units, and let them play SSSHS roles, just as the organizational units on lower levels of aggregation did. A big challenge arises here though, which is concerned with communication between units belonging to different aggregation units.

Basic SSSHS units are modeled as standalone units, meaning that, as mentioned in Sect. 1.4, they strive to produce, use, and store enough resources for themselves in order to be free from the wider environment, and to be able to survive off the grid. The challenge present in levels of aggregation arises from the need for the means of communication between various aggregated units. For example, it is defined by the SSSHS framework that storage units take care of the coordination and communication, but if several dwelling units are to be aggregated into a single building unit, in an environment already consisting of several building units comprising dwelling units, and this building unit strives to maintaining self-sustainability, which of the included dwelling units will be responsible for interunit communication with other building units? In other words, how will building units communicate with each other and exchange resources, thus maintaining self-sustainability? Furthermore, should another level of aggregation be introduced, where neighborhood units are created comprising a number of building units, how will they communicate between each other?

The answer to these questions is devised in the form of a new role that is meant to work as a negotiator of an aggregated unit. Since the storage role contains all the actions necessary for the process of interaction and communication in general, it is thought to be only fitting to create this new role as a part of the storage role. Furthermore, such a view is in compliance with the general description of the SSSHS framework insomuch as storage units continue to take care of one resource only. For example, a storage unit working with resource named electricity communicates with other such storage units in other aggregated units. Together, storage units of an aggregated unit coordinate into knowing the state of a given resource in the given aggregated unit. Normative elements of an organization are responsible for assigning negotiation role to specific storage units, and ascertaining that there is only one such unit at any given point in time. For the sake of understanding, an example scenario is given in the following section.

Another important problem is the problem of transferring resources on higher levels of aggregation. For example, on a neighborhood level, the amounts of resources to be shared are probably much larger than on individual levels, exceeding storage capacities of individual storage units. Thus, another line of hierarchy has to be introduced to aggregate individual lower level storage units into virtual larger storage units. This also implies the need to extend the current resource sharing protocols of the SSSHS framework with an additional mode of operation, in which a storage negotiator unit can instruct lower level storage units to transfer or receive resources from a higher level. In this way, greater levels of a given resource can be shared between higher level units when needed (in peak consumption of production times for example).

Additional clarification is needed on Fig. 1.6, which shows SSSHS example modeled using the organizational metamodel described earlier in this chapter. As mentioned earlier in this section, an individual agent can be aggregated into units of higher aggregation level. Each individual unit can play one of the SSSHS roles (blue hats in Fig. 1.6). Playing a role provides the given individual with actions necessary for undertaking the process (green squares in Fig. 1.6) associated with the given role. Processes are usually connected to objectives (circular in Fig. 1.6) they can help fulfill. Following the stated, one can see in Fig. 1.6 that, for example, an individual unit (stick figure in Fig. 1.6) can play three different roles, one of which, the Storage role, through its negotiator sub-role, provides the given agent with actions needed to undertake process named negotiate that contains actions necessary for the resource negotiation process. It is worth noting here that some of the stages of aggregation can be changed depending on the specific situation, i.e., some of them can be further detailed or skipped entirely (for example, it is not necessary to consider building aggregation level if DwellingUnits are houses, or it is not necessary to take into account neighborhood aggregation level if the settlement in question comprises only a couple of DwellingUnits).

1.6 Example Scenario

To clarify the model described in the previous section, consider the following (simplified) example scenario:

> A (smart self-sustainable off-grid) city consisting of 3 buildings, each building having 5 flats, each flat having a (smart) photovoltaic system, a (smart) battery unit, and a (smart) refrigerator enacting the roles of producer, storage, and consumer, respectively (see Fig. 1.7 for an illustration).

Let us assume that this city is organized into three organizational levels: (1) flat level (each individual flat is an organizational unit with the battery unit as its negotiator), (2) building level (each building's flats are an organizational unit with the flat on the ground floor as its negotiator), and (3) city level (consisting of all three buildings, with the first building being the negotiator). Note that, on the city level, the actual negotiator is the battery unit from the ground floor in the first building, which is enacting a role on two higher levels.

Due to geographical location, the first building has the best orientation to the sun, while the other two buildings' PV panels end up in the shadow of the first building earlier during the day. In this way, the battery units of the first building are charged longer, thus coming to a point where they cannot store any additional electricity. Let us assume that the battery unit on the fourth floor of the first building is the first to reach full charge and initiate negotiation to share its surplus energy to battery units on the same level—the units in the first building. For a short period of

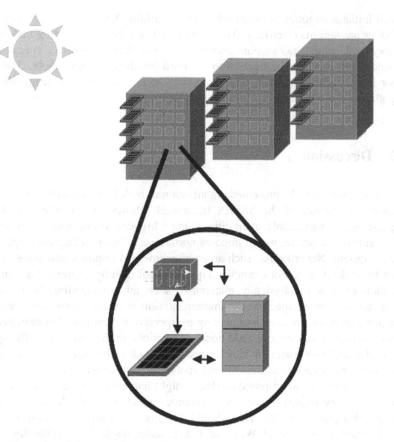

Fig. 1.7 Illustration of the example scenario

time, these units can receive additional electricity from the PV panel above them, but soon, one after another, become fully charged. At that point, the negotiator on the ground floor initiates negotiation on a higher level (building level) and finds that building two has enough space to take care of surplus electricity coming from the first building's PV panels. The electricity from these panels is first redirected to the ground floor of the first building (negotiator), then to the ground floor of the second building (second negotiator), and finally distributed by the negotiator of the second building among the battery units in the flats above.

Let us further assume that, due to low production, charge runs low in all battery units in building three. For example, the refrigerator in flat on floor 2 of the third building schedules that it will need additional energy in the following period, which exceeds the current level of its respective battery unity. The battery unit (negotiator) first initiates negotiation with the battery units on the same level (flat level) and gets informed that none of the battery units in building three has enough spare electricity to share. It informs the negotiator on this level (the battery unit on the ground floor), which initiates negotiation on a higher level (building level) and finds that the first building has surplus electricity. The negotiator from the first building instructs the battery unit, which has surplus energy in its building, to redirect energy to the ground floor, and then redirects it to the third building's ground floor. The negotiator from the third building then redirects it to the second floor, from where the negotiation was initiated.

1.7 Discussion

As one can see from the presented organizational model, as well as the example, the proposed extension of the SSSHS framework allows for flexible modeling of large-scale self-sustainable smart cities using a higher level of abstraction, namely, organizational structure, which imposes normative roles on the agents employed in such a system. Nevertheless, such an architecture also imposes new questions that have to be dealt with. For example, a question not directly addressed herein is the question of how to physically materialize such an organization. While from a computer science perspective the implementation is merely a (possibly wireless) computer network, from an engineering perspective the proposed system becomes harder to realize and imposes additional constraints on the function of the system, since physical movement of various resources has to be achieved. This implies additional infrastructure and additional spatiotemporal constraints.

For example, in the proposed model, it might happen that some appliance in one part of the city requires water as a resource, which is available only in a quite distant other part of the city. How should this amount of water be transported from one location to the other? While such a transfer might be feasible for smaller distances, or even for greater distances for certain types of resources like electricity, for resources such as water, heat, or oil (especially in smaller amounts) this is not the case. Also, even if such a transport is feasible (and cost effective), the question of how much time is needed to transport such a resource can impose additional constraints onto the system.

From this discussion, it becomes obvious that additional constraints have to be put in place in regard to negotiation, including careful design of organizational levels. A possible solution is to define feasibility zones for each agent and each type of resource. For example, one might define that a feasibility zone for the resource type water reaches only to all agents which are in a certain temporal reach (e.g., the certain amount can be transported within a given time limit). Other possibilities might include distance/proximity limits, channel type limits, or level limits (e.g., negotiate only on n levels from the current one).

Further constraint of the current model is that modeling of other types of interactions, beyond resource management, has not been included into it explicitly. While this hierarchical structure might function in some types of interactions, for other types of interactions, which require greater dynamics, like adaptive smart flats with ambient intelligence [19], it might be too rigid. Nevertheless, such interactions can be modeled using different types of organizational forms (like the learning organization, for example), which can function in parallel to the current defined model, since agents only get additional roles to enact.

1.8 Conclusion

In this chapter, we have extended the SSSHS framework with additional organizational concepts (namely, organizational structure and normative roles) to allow modeling of self-sustainable smart cities with special regard to resource management, using our LSMAS organizational metamodel that is still under development. We have described the current state of the LSMAS metamodel and showed its practical applicability in modeling complex multi-agent organizations.

By introducing a hierarchical structure into the SSSHS framework and by defining the role of negotiator, we have shown that it becomes feasible even for large-scale systems like smart cities. Additionally, we have provided an example scenario which aims on better depicting the various interactions that might take place in such a system. In the end, we have discussed the implications of the proposed model, and identified a number of spatiotemporal constraints, namely, feasibility zones, that have to be imposed on the model to become feasible for certain types of resources.

Our future research will focus on further enrichment of the provided models through the introduction of the proposed feasibility zones, as well as large-scale simulations of various scenarios to identify possible additional bottlenecks and problems with the model. Another line of research might be the introduction of learning techniques for smart devices in residential buildings as outlined in [19], through possible inclusion of additional organizational design techniques.

Acknowledgements This work has been supported in full by the Croatian Science Foundation under the project number 8537.

References

1. Ahmed Abbas H (2015) Organization of multi-agent systems: an overview. IJIIS 4:46. https:// doi.org/10.11648/j.ijiis.20150403.11
2. Anvari-Moghaddam A, Guerrero JM, Rahimi-Kian A, Mirian MS (2016) Optimal real-time dispatch for integrated energy systems: an ontology-based multi-agent approach. In: 2016 IEEE 7th international symposium on power electronics for distributed generation systems (PEDG). IEEE, pp 1–7
3. Atzori L, Iera A, Morabito G (2010) The internet of things: a survey. Comput Netw 54:2787–2805. https://doi.org/10.1016/j.comnet.2010.05.010
4. Ayala I, Amor M, Fuentes L (2012) An agent platform for self-configuring agents in the internet of things. In: Infrastructures and tools for multiagent

5. Bowerman B, Braverman J, Taylor J et al. (2000) The vision of a smart city. In: 2nd international life
6. Corkill DD, Lander SE (1998) Diversity in agent organizations. Object Mag 8:41–47
7. Coutinho LR, Sichman JS, Boissier O (2009) Modeling dimensions for agent organizations. In: Dignum V (ed) Handbook of research on multi-agent systems: semantics and dynamics of organizational models. IGI Global, pp 18–50
8. De Wolf T (2004) Emergence and self-organization: a statement of similarities and differences. In: Proceedings of the 2nd international workshop on engineering self-organizing applications, pp 96–110
9. Dignum V (2009) Handbook of research on multi-agent systems: semantics and dynamics of organizational models. https://doi.org/10.4018/978-1-60566-256-5
10. Fontana M, Terna P (2015) From agent-based models to network analysis (and return): the policy-making perspective. Working Paper Series 07
11. Hurtado LA, Nguyen PH, Kling WL (2015) Smart grid and smart building inter-operation using agent-based particle swarm optimization. Sustain Energy Grids Netw 2:32–40. https://doi.org/10.1016/j.segan.2015.03.003
12. Karnouskos S, Holanda TN de (2009) Simulation of a smart grid city with software agents. In: 2009 third UKSim European symposium on computer modeling and simulation. IEEE, pp 424–429
13. Mihaylov M, Razo-Zapata I, Rădulescu R, Jurado S, Avellana N, Nowé A (2016) Smart grid demonstration platform for renewable energy exchange. In: Demazeau Y, Ito T, Bajo J, Escalona MJ (eds) Advances in practical applications of scalable multi-agent systems. The PAAMS collection. Springer International Publishing, Cham, pp 277–280
14. Okreša Đurić B (2017) A novel approach to modeling distributed systems: using large-scale multi-agent systems. In: Mahmood Z (ed) Software project management for distributed computing. Springer International Publishing, Cham, pp 229–254
15. Okreša Đurić B (2016) Organizational metamodel for large-scale multi-agent systems. In: de la Prieta F, Escalona MJ, Corchuelo R, Mathieu P, Vale Z, Campbell AT, Rossi S, Adam E, Jiménez-López MD, Navarro EM, Moreno MN (eds) Trends in practical applications of scalable multi-agent systems, the PAAMS collection. Springer International Publishing, Cham, pp 387–390
16. Roscia M, Longo M, Lazaroiu GC (2013) Smart City by multi-agent systems. In: 2013 international conference on renewable energy research and applications (ICRERA). IEEE, pp 371–376
17. Schatten M (2012) Active graph rewriting rules for modeling multi-agent organizational dynamics. In: 1st international internet & business conference
18. Schatten M (2014) Organizational architectures for large-scale multi-agent systems' development: an initial ontology. In: Omatu S, Bersini H, Corchado JM, Rodríguez S, Pawlewski P, Bucciarelli E (eds) Distributed computing and artificial intelligence. 11th international conference. Springer International Publishing, Cham, pp 261–268
19. Schatten M (2014) Smart residential buildings as learning agent organizations in the internet of things. Bus Syst Res J. https://doi.org/10.2478/bsrj-2014-0003
20. Schatten M, Grd P, Konecki M, Kudelić R (2014) Towards a formal conceptualization of organizational design techniques for large scale multi agent systems. Proc Technol 15:576–585. https://doi.org/10.1016/j.protcy.2014.09.018
21. Schatten M, Ševa J, Tomičić I (2016) A roadmap for scalable agent organizations in the internet of everything. J Syst Softw 115:31–41. https://doi.org/10.1016/j.jss.2016.01.022
22. Stavropoulos TG, Rigas ES, Kontopoulos E, Bassiliades N, Vlahavas I (2014) A multi-agent coordination framework for smart building energy management. In: 2014 25th international workshop on database and expert systems applications. IEEE, pp 126–130
23. Tomičić I (2016) Agent-based framework for modeling and simulation of resource management in smart self-sustainable human settlements. Doctoral dissertation

24. Tomicic I, Schatten M (2016) A case study on renewable energy management in an eco-village community in Croatia–an agent based approach. Int J Renew Energy Res (IJRER) 6:1307–1317
25. Tomičic I, Schatten M (2015) Towards an agent based framework for modeling smart self-sustainable systems. Interdisc Description Complex Syst 13:57–70
26. Tomičić I, Schatten M (2016) Agent-based framework for modeling and simulation of resources in self-sustainable human settlements: a case study on water management in an eco-village community in Croatia. Int J Sustain Dev World Ecol 23:504–513. https://doi.org/10.1080/13504509.2016.1153527
27. Vlacheas P, Giaffreda R, Stavroulaki V, Kelaidonis D, Foteinos V, Poulios G, Demestichas P, Somov A, Biswas A, Moessner K (2013) Enabling smart cities through a cognitive management framework for the internet of things. IEEE Commun Mag 51:102–111. https://doi.org/10.1109/MCOM.2013.6525602
28. Weyns D, Haesevoets R, Helleboogh A (2010) The MACODO organization model for context-driven dynamic agent organizations. ACM Trans Auton Adapt Syst 5:1–29. https://doi.org/10.1145/1867713.1867717
29. Yang K, Cho S-B (2016) Towards sustainable smart homes by a hierarchical hybrid architecture of an intelligent agent. Sustainability 8:1020. https://doi.org/10.3390/su8101020

Chapter 2
Cybersecurity System: An Essential Pillar of Smart Cities

Lata Nautiyal, Preeti Malik and Amit Agarwal

Abstract From smartphones to smart cities, the world has changed in nearly every aspect. Modern cities are seen as a collection of certain important components and entail dimensions such as the quality of life and socioeconomic developments. Smart cities are an attempt to develop cities that are well-organized, maintainable, secure, technology-driven, and a convenient place to live. In this context, smart cities also encounter a number of challenges especially with regard to legal complications, environment, and other regulatory matters that underpin the policy prospects. There are a number of crucial factors that are vital for the development and management of smart cities. These factors have been used to craft a framework that imparts a more upgraded idea of the smart city initiatives. The relevant pillars or factors refer to social, management, economy, and legal dimensions. Additionally, the technologies and smart devices used in smart cities that capture all manner of data raise the questions of security and privacy. Confidentiality can be endangered and ruptured by a large number of practices which are generally treated as intolerable; however, these are part of operations in a smart city ecosystem. This chapter discusses the security issues in great detail and also provides some solutions to security in smart cities.

Keywords Smart city · ICT-Driven city · Digital city · Intelligent city Cybersecurity · Technological factors · Security of smart city

2.1 Introduction

Today, we are turning to an era where everything is getting smarter, from smartphones to smartwatches and even our dwellings are getting smarter. A smart city can be described as a city that deploys the advancements in communication and

L. Nautiyal · P. Malik
Graphic Era University, Dehradun, India

A. Agarwal (✉)
University of Petroleum and Energy Sciences, Dehradun, India
e-mail: preetishivach2009@gmail.com

information technology and the use of smart devices of all nature to carve an urbanized infrastructure. A smart city provides services for the city and its citizens that cover all the various dimensions of modern civilization including efficient water management, primary health care, renewable and clean energy, smart grids, intelligent road safety, e-governance, wireless Internet access, efficient waste recycle, transportation, education, artificial intelligence-aided public safety, and real estate in a more productive and comprehensive manner.

Only ten percent of the global population resides in top 30 metropolises with 600 cities holding the quarter of it [1]. Presently, half of the world population is living in cities. Despite the fact that cities engross just two percent of the earth's landmass, urban human takes in more than three-quarters of world's natural resources. In the present scenario, half of the world population is said to be urbanized as residing in cities. The planet is at the verge of getting urbanized as a whole. The rise in toll of urban people requires attention as it brings out some challenges with it such as problems in waste management, shortage of resources, and pollution.

Human health hazards, traffic overload, downfall in infrastructures [2–4], and rise in rapid urbanization throw another set of challenges and apart from technical, physical, and material there are social and organizational problems, which demands attention to diverse stakeholders, over interdependence, competing values, and political complexity. Hence, the problem of rapid urbanization gets crucial [5–7]. The extreme urge to urbanization has to be dealt with proper insight and stable consideration as to curb it to become a crisis. Necessity as the mother of invention is a popular idiom and it implements on smart city crisis too. There is a need for smart cities as migration from rural to urban area is seen to be increasing at a much faster rate.

The problem of rapid urbanization can be solved with the smart city approach but we have to keep this in mind that smart city is an outcome of synergizing the innovations in Information and Communication Technology (ICT), urban town planning, and management policies. The policy management prospect of innovation and technology has to be weaved up with the practical implementation of technology in order to come up with a sustainable user welfare smart city. The task is not just technological per se, but how to design and use technology and management for the real benefit of people's well-being.

While majority of authors describe smart cities in terms of technological developments, they ignore the essential town planning and urban development policies. Amidst all the hue and cry for smart city establishments, we have to understand the fact that a smart city is not just a product of innovation in ICT, and it needs a huge consideration over policy and planning for the managerial side of technology.

In this chapter, we discuss the nontechnological facets of smart cities while integrating it with technology. The chapter is organized as follows. The next section discusses the conceptualization of smart city; Sect. 2.3 presents essential pillars of a smart city, viz., social, management, economy, and legal dimensions. Section 2.4 is dedicated to discussing security in smart cities. Section 2.5 includes information security in smart cities and Sect. 2.6 presents security from governance, social, and economic perspective. Section includes technological factors. Growth of cyber threats and security challenges is presented in Sects. 2.8 and 2.9. Finally, the last section concludes the chapter.

2.2 Conceptualization of Smart City

Though there have been a lot of emphases on explaining the concept of smart city, the general description is often vague. Some of the literature refers to case studies, while others explain technological advances in terms of smart power back up, smart grids, smart health care, smart road safety system, smart water management system, etc. But there is no clear definition that describes the features of smart city in a broader sense. To facilitate this, it is useful to dig into the past compositions given by various authors. The following sections elaborate on this further.

2.2.1 Past: ICT-Driven City, Efficient City, Cyber City, Digital City, and U-City

The era of smart cities came into existence as of 1994, in Netherlands, when the term Digital City (DDS) was first coined as a virtual public domain [8]. That interval of time is prominently recognized for the boom in growth and popularity of Internet-based applications. Numerous researchers began to focus on ICT and smart intelligent devices. Some researchers, for example, those at the Brookhaven National Laboratory disclosed the concept of the next big thing: efficient smart cities. Till late 1999, when Internet get commercialized and became a necessity, the concepts of ubiquitous computing, U city, and cyber city were proposed, and eventually in 2000 the idea of smart city was brought into existence.

Korea leads the way in development of U cities as post-ubiquitous computing, in 1998. Mark Weiser, the chief technologist of the Xerox Palo Alto Research Center, came up with a desktop model of human–computer interaction. Korean government has put the concept of U City in use for many development projects since 2005.

A ubiquitous city (U City) is a hybrid of ubiquitous computing within an urban environment. It can be explained as a unification of information systems with social systems, where all the devices and services are connected with wireless fidelity, sensors, and RFID tags [9]. Anthony Townsend, a research director at the Institute for the Future in Palo Alto, and a former Fulbright scholar in Seoul visualize U City as an exclusively Korean idea [10].

2.2.2   Present: Intelligent City, Knowledge City, Smart City

These days, the notion of smart city has become prevalent, though it has resemblance to U-City. The only way to differentiate between the two ideas is through the degree of intelligence. Smart city is known as a post-ubiquitous city. Well U city is a city which has artificial intelligence, facilitated by information technology to render basic facilities. Latest smart city is an extension of U city post-telecommunication revolution, in which humans can stay in touch connection of individuals to the city with human neural network. Smart cities follow people interaction and communication irrespective of their location. The importance of two assets namely social and ecological capital paints smart city in a totally different color among its other counterpart technology-driven urban cities. Moreover, smart city is not fundamentally stands on the ground of hard concrete infrastructure, i.e., physical capital but it also relies on the intellectual and social capital made available by quality of knowledge communication and social infrastructure [11]. Smart city is not a stagnant concept; it is changing with time, adapting according to the needs, and hence its implementation on initial stage is hard and complex. Another explanation of smart city is a city which is equipped with all the smart systems interacting with each other through smart communication system, latter is a boon from innovations in the ICT.

2.2.3   Future: MESH City—Sense, Soft, and Warm
Technology City

In modern terms, smart cities can be termed as MESH cities [12], referring to the following:

- M for Mobile (mobile networks that support them provide the data, real-time information, conduit to supply feedback about a city, its users, and its systems),
- E for Efficient (about sustainability achieved through effective usage, monitoring and management of energy, traffic, etc.),
- S for Subtle (invisible and non-intrusive systems, easy-to-handle modern systems for citizens),
- H for Heuristics (Heuristics-based consistent improvement, which conforms to the system self-reflexing, self-adapting, and citizen-oriented).

Futuristic ICT will be a combination of the soft as well as warm techniques. Artificial intelligence will provide the feature of emulating human emotions [13]. Future of smart cities can be visualized as cities having a blend of sense, soft, and warm technology. Lee and Hancock [14] categorize the facts of smart city by subjective view on them. Three distinctive categories are given in Table 2.1. According to these practical and academic interpretations of a smart city, there is none which gives a general fit to all idea of a smart city. Based on the several kinds of conceptual schemas given above to define smart city framework, this paper presents a universal set of components that are required to decode the concept of smart city projects.

As explained above, the concept of smart city is still evolving; it will take a substantial amount of time to conceptualize itself firmly [15, 16]. The concept has been put to use everywhere in world with different naming classifications, semantics, and context. A variety of adjectives have been extensively used in the place of word smart, viz., intelligent, hi-tech, digital, etc. Some has even replaced the use of the word smart with modern urbanization, if it is urbanized it has to be smart. Referring smart cities as an urban labeling phenomenon [16] for better understanding of the fact that is why there is a need of a conceptual research in this field. Table 2.1 shows some of the working definitions that currently exist in the literature.

Giffinger et al. [17] consider smart as performing in a forward-looking way. The forward-looking development for smart city projects issues like awareness, flexibility, transformability, and strategic behavior, synergy, individuality, and self-decisiveness [17]. The Harrison et al. study [19] depicts it as an equipped, intelligently interconnected city. Instrumentation empowers seizure and assimilation of real-time data with the help of sensors, kiosks, meters, personal devices, cameras, smartphones, incorporated medical devices, web, and other likewise data-acquisition systems, with social networks as human sensor network.

Table 2.1 Working definitions of a smart city	A city soundly performing in a forward-looking way in terms of economy, governance, mobility, ecologically created on the smart composition of endowments and activities of self-decisive, independent, and responsible citizens [17]
	A city which supervises and integrates specific conditions of all of its critical infrastructures comprising roads, bridges, tunnels, rails, subways, airports, seaports, network communications, water, power, and buildings, can better modify its resources, plan, and draft its maintenance acts and optimizing its services to citizens [18]
	A city linking the physical infrastructure to the IT infrastructure to the social infrastructure, to the business infrastructure to gain the summed up intelligence of the city [19]
	A city endeavoring to make itself smarter, i.e., more sustainable, efficient, equitable, and livable [20]
	A city fusing ICT and Web applications and technology with other organizational, design and planning efforts to hasten up the bureaucratic operations and assist to mark novel, innovative solutions to city management, with the improvement in sustainability index [3]
	It makes use of smart computing technologies to build critical infrastructure elements and services for the city, which includes city administration, education, efficient healthcare, public safety measures, entrepreneurship, real estate, transportation, as well as impeccable, interconnected, and reliable [4]

Interconnection encompasses the integration of data through an enterprise computing system and the communication of processed data to different city services. Intelligence relates to ability to the take improved operational decisions by taking inputs from complex analytics, optimization, data modeling, and visualization in operational processes. The Natural Resources Defense Council [20] elucidates smarter in the urban context as more sustainable, efficient, and livable. Toppeta [3] recommends the betterment in sustainability and livability. Washburn et al. [4] envisage a smart city as an assemblage of smart computing technologies collaborated with components of infrastructure and services. Smart computing specifies a brand new progeny of integrated chips, hardware, and software network technologies that hand carry IT systems and real-time applications with advanced analytics to enhance business processes [4].

After having an overall comprehensive look at the smart city concepts, it can be viewed as a huge organic system possessing properties of a system, working with many interdependent subsystems, i.e., all subsystems within a system strive to obtain a common objective. Dirks and Keeling [21] decipher smart city as the organic integration of systems. The interaction between a smart city's core systems has taken into account to make the system of systems smarter. No system operates in isolation. In this sense, Kanter and Litow [22] consider a smarter city as an organic whole—a network and a linked system. While systems in industrial cities were mostly skeleton and skin, postindustrial smart cities are analogous to organisms that develop an artificial nervous system, which prepares them to behave in intelligent manner [23]. The novel intelligence of cities, therefore, is situated in the increased efficient digital telecommunication networks (the nerves), ubiquitously embedded intelligence (the brains), sensors and tags (the sensory organs), and software (the knowledge and cognitive competence).

2.3 Pillars of a Smart City

There are a number of crucial factors that are vital for the comprehensive determination of developing smart cities. These factors have been used to craft a framework that imparts a more upgraded idea of the smart city initiative. The four pillars or factors are, namely, social, management, economy, and legal dimensions.

Institutional infrastructure refers to activities relating to governance, planning, and management of a city. ICT has provided a new aspect to this system molding it in user-centric, efficient, responsible, and transparent way. Physical infrastructure confers to its stock of cost-productive and intelligent physical foundation, for example, the urban portability system, fast broadband, wireless system, the lodging and housing stock, clean and renewable energy, water supply system, sewerage and sanitation utility, efficient waste management system, water seepage system, and so on which are incorporated through utilization of innovation. Social infrastructure refers to components that promote growth of human and social capital, like education, healthcare, recreation, etc. It also includes creative arts, children's parks, and gardens. Economic infrastructure denotes to developing sound infrastructure that provides new employment opportunities and entices capital investments. The growth of smart cities and uprising demand for data communications will lead to huge acquisition and analysis of data. This analysis then expedites intelligence and gives insight on how to deal critical situations. The analysis and knowledge inferences of big data will activate the call for information security at all phases.

2.3.1 Social

The residents of a smart city can also play a significant part in developing the design of the smart city as it has been considered that the concept of smart cities is purely founded on smart communities. The citizens can establish talks and exchange information and facts with one another in groups that is a clear manifestation of the fact that smart cities are made on the grounds of smart communities. In recent scenario, it has been observed that smart city residents have taken many initiatives by getting informed through the fast and easily accessible information through Internet and it helped them to address the problems and share the opinions and solutions with their community or in a larger platform, i.e., in a group of intellectuals striving to reach solution, both in face-to-face and remote situations using data, models, scenarios all made available by the contemporary ICT [24]. It has been found that present kinds of interactions are responding to novel ICT but still remain inactive and passive. Recent media and the web revolution are giving this type of participation a new edge and platform for increasing the liquidity of this interaction as both data and approaches to provide solution are being shared [25]. It is also important to consider the social condition of the citizen of a city if that city needs to be considered as smart city. If the city is smart only in economical perspective, then that city would not be considered as smart. The emphasis is also given on balancing the need of several resident communities. Projects of smart cities touch the different facets of its citizens and also have an impact on the quality of life of citizens and aim to foster more aware, educated, and informed citizens. Also, the citizens of smart city can actively participate in the governance and management of the city. The citizen's role is so imperative that they can influence the success or failure of the project. The engagement of all citizens is necessary. It is not about a group of people who are enthusiast. It touches all the daily chores and everyday life of all citizens. Social media also has its parts to play in smart city initiatives.

As the smart city is about rebuilding and enhancing facilities, communication is a critical factor in engaging people by showing them the enormous value of data. The media now has become the game changer of the society as it becomes the prime supplier of information. It executes as the reservoir and significant broadcaster of information. It actually becomes the mirror of our society and influences the lives of all classes of people living in a society driven by information and technology. It also plays a role of a guardian in society to keep track of all the activities of government or public or industry. Internet has made information readily available to all the classes of society, and now it is momentarily to reach out to latest updates.

2.3.2 Management

To manage a smart city, the governance has to be smart and it becomes one of the prime challenges for smart city management. Restricted transparency, fragmented accountability, unequal city division, and improper management of resources are some of the inseparable salient features of regular governance. A radical step has to be taken to switch from regular governance to e-governance which is very essential for the efficient management of the smart cities. Smart governance invites active political involvement, citizen services, and efficient utility of e-government. Authors in [26] have proposed some impactful elements and challenges for e-government initiatives which can be elongated to the smart city governance as most smart city startup moves get propulsion from governments and supplemented by the extensive use of technology to assist and render their services to citizens in better manner. Being ICT as the pioneer of smart cities, e-governance is the force to accentuate the decision-making process, improve public policy-making, and enhance public governance. E-administration encourages people to include thoroughly in each of the aspects explained above. Internet and Web is the most generally utilized channel of correspondence individuals, and in this way smart city citizens can consolidate the requirements and wishes of the diverse target gatherings and address them in the best way. ICT can improve procedures in democracy and open doors for people and groups to connect with the government. Internet empowers noteworthy interest, as it weakens the limitations forced by topography, in capabilities or different components. It additionally empowers access to data by people and gatherings that had not been incorporated earlier. Smart administration is a vital norm for a smart city that is accomplished with and by good citizen participation adorned with private/public partnerships [27]. Smart governance can be achieved by smart and intelligent administration of infrastructure that promotes service integration and collaboration, communication, and information exchange [28].

2.3.3 Economy

One of the key factors in smart city initiative is economy. A significant pointer to predict growing smart city competition is the capability of the city as an economy-enhancing engine [27]. Operational aspect of a smart economy comprises factors from economic competitiveness as entrepreneurship, trends, innovation, manufacturing, productivity, and flexibility of the labor market and their assimilation to national and global market. If a city is able to proliferate the capital economically with innovations going on, it can be called an intelligent city. The amount and graph of profit occurred mentions the economic growth of the city. Smart cities encourage profit too though the economic growth of the smart city is presumed to be constant as of short lifespan of ICTs. Smart city projects supports business as economic enhancing platform and make way to flow capital. Economic income growth in smart city must be constant because of the short life cycle of ICTs. The criterion of government aids and invasion in smart city projects is vital to check the strength of corporate players. Business has been recognized as one of the prime systems of smart cities by [29], which encircle several systems as citizens system, business and transportation system, networking and communication system, and clean water management and energy system. The motives of smart city development are not only to alleviate the problem of rapid urbanization but to enhance and develop information technology initiative and lay down an idea to change by business development actions [30]. Preparing a platform for industrial and business development is mandatory for a smart city [31]. Smart city initiatives are going to provide a lot of business supporting activities which includes employment to many, business capital flow, workforce improvement, and improved productivity.

2.3.4 Legal

Expansion of smart cities is not possible without any kind of legitimate and legal compliances. Governments and other political bodies affect the operation of smart city initiative a lot. Smart city development is highly influenced by political as well as legal bodies [32]. Governments and policy drafting entities should draft policies that patronize the development of smart cities [33]. The legislation and regulatory issues related to development part of smart city should be dealt with less troubled legal proceedings. Pro-active measures should be called out for implementation and management of smart city induced by enforcing laws and policies that help to support growth and development. Innovations in policy drafting are as important as the need for new innovations. Though there are no measures taken in policy drafting for managing innovations [34], policies being drafted must be in accordance with both technical and nontechnical necessities of urban development and growth [35, 36].

Smart cities encounter a number of challenges in regard to legal complications, environment, and nature regulatory matters that master the policy prospects [26]. Rules and regulations shall be taken into account while opting for any kind of decision [37]. A good understanding of law and legislations is much needed to exercise the benefits of ICT in an appropriate way. Smart cities have to be supervised with considerably drafted policies and guidelines. To simplify the coordination and working between management, administration and local governing bodies' proper principles and policies are very essential [16, 38, 39].

2.4   Security of a Smart City

Smart cities can build profitability and efficiencies for peoples; yet, they have a significant issue when security is thought little of. As local governments seek after smart activities, understanding the maximum capacity of these digitally associated groups begins with actualizing cybersecurity, best practices starting from the earliest stage [40, 41]. The idea of smart cities is intense as its vision incorporates administration and association of the entire city by using embedded technology. These are standardized as the cities that observe and integrate status of all their infrastructures, management, administration, citizen and communities, wellness, education, and natural environment through information and communication technologies (ICT). Various highly advanced integrated technologies such as sensors, electronic, and network connected with computerized system including database, tracking, and decision-making algorithm are required to design, construct, and maintain the smart city [42]. As urbanization is attaining the significant growth, there is a need of incorporating a smarter approach in dealing with several issues relating to economic restructuring, ecological consequences, management issues, and public sector problems. With the increase in the speed of change, the obstacles of modern cities are becoming difficult. This demands organizational changes particularly concentrating on the most recent innovations and communication through Internet.

The word global village appears to be exceptionally lucid with the intelligent city as modernization is reliant on most recent advances and internetwork. The idea is also persuaded by the organizations promoting and selling their products like GPS, iPad, smartphones, and other innovations [43]. The smart city, hence, anticipates smarter development. It is believed that appropriate investments in formulating the systems of a city by using embedded technologies will help in vast growth in economic system as well [44]. There are certain pioneering cities such as Barcelona, Amsterdam, Masdar, Singapore, and France that are considered as the role model and next-generation smart cities [45]. The universal idea of a smart city and its major components is given in Fig. 2.1.

A list of a number of new and upcoming ICTs that are the most important part of a competent smart city are the Internet of Things (IoT), smartphone technology, RFID (Radio Frequency Identification System), smart meters, semantic web, linked data, ontologies, artificial intelligence, cloud computing, collective intelligence, smart apps, and biometrics. The IoT is defined as the connection of material objects combined with computational devices, software, electronics, smart sensors, and connectivity so that it can be used to attain higher measure and service by exchanging data with the maker, operator, and other connected devices. Each object is uniquely different through its embedded computing system but is able to function within the infrastructure of Internet. The backbone of smart city is embedded technology for which the concept of IoT plays an important part in the growing of ideal and safe smart city. The IoT is considered as a major research and innovation idea that leads to a lot of opportunities for new services by interconnecting physical

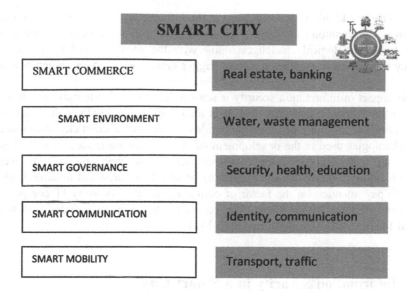

Fig. 2.1 Components of a smart city

and virtual worlds with a huge amount of electronics distributed in different places including houses, vehicles, streets, buildings, and many other environments [46].

The concept of smart cities is characterized by the fact that it is solely relies on embedded systems, smart technologies, and the IoT. In general, the dependent of smart city on information technology and embedded infrastructure leads to facilitate the standard of living of its citizens.

The development of smart cities comes across a number of hurdles like socioeconomic and political issues but the greatest barrier is the technical issues. In technical problems, the issue of security and privacy covers an important part along with the other issues like system interoperability and cost-efficient technology [47]. The issues of security and privacy of information are covered under the area of information security. The main aim of information security is to protect the information from attacks, viruses, frauds, and many other vicious activities that may cause harm either to the information, or the need of information in the technologically embedded smart cities. The security has become extremely important and a vital prerequisite to consumer acceptance in the infrastructures of smart cities because the networks will be inclined to a large range of malicious attacks, and the internal and external parties are not trusted [48]. As the concept of smart cities is still in developing phase, the need to find out the most important requirements of information security with respect to the use of various technologies is crucial.

It is also important to focus on aspiring smart cities in order to identify the correct requirements, and limitations as well as to identify the achievements and flaws in information security. The information security of smart city is very important as these cities are exposed to malicious attacks which can alter or damage the whole infrastructure and communication systems. Alternatively, the main aim of a smart city would not be accomplished if the information is not properly secured. Moreover, the attention should also be paid on privacy in a smart city environment. Other two technological challenges along with the security challenges refer to privacy of systems that gather data and trigger emergency response when needed [49].

The impact of information security is not on the technical side only, and it also impacts the economic concerns [50]. It is also important to address the issues of information security for a better economic development of a smart city. As most of the technologies used in the development of smart cities are related to IoT, cloud computing, real-world user interfaces, smart sensors, smartphones, semantic web, etc., it is highly required for smart cities to be ideally secured and reliable. It also needs to pay attention on the factor of commercialization as many IT companies have new solutions for the smart cities as well. The example includes launch of Global Intelligent Urbanization by Cisco [51].

2.5 Information Security in a Smart City

The topic of security and privacy of information in a smart city has always attracted the attention of researchers. The reason is that the information security should be present in an unfailing manner in smart cities in order to ensure the continuity of vital services like health care, governance, and energy/utility. Several factors such as governance factors, social/economic factors, and most importantly economic factors are taken under consideration in order to distinguish the issues in information security in a smart city.

The IoT has been the key enthusiasm of the researchers as it is the center technology on which the smart cities are being created and kept up [52]. For instance, in [48], the key concerns regarding security and privacy are presented, keeping in the context of technological standards; the paper particularly concentrates on Machine-to-Machine (M2M) standard solutions that are helpful in better implementation of IoT in a smart city. One of the most important factors that play key role in developing a smart city is big data which is concerned with the production of large datasets in a smart city and is an inevitable phenomenon including national consensuses, government records, and other information about the citizens [53]. Such data can be used by the smart cities in order to extract useful information and real-time analysis and ubiquitous computing. The author in [54] explains that along with providing various opportunities for smarter life, big data also brings itself challenges of security and privacy. The challenges include lack of tools for management of big data, third-party data sharing, threats in growing public databases, data leakage, and concerns over digital security.

In [49], the cybersecurity challenges are taken into consideration. Here, mainly the authors concentrate on two main challenges, security and privacy. A mathematical model is proposed in which the interaction between people, IoT, and servers which are vulnerable to information security threats is considered. One of the primary concerns regarding the proposed work is that though the mathematical and graphical model for the IoT, people, and servers is given stating that it will help in locating the problems in security and privacy, the methodology to do so is not discussed. Moreover, Bohli et al. [55] presented a distributed framework for IoT applications, which promises security, trust, and privacy in information delivery. The advantage of using distributive framework is that it can address certain information security issues of IoT applications that play a key role in building a smarter city.

The authors in [56] mainly focus on the stakeholders related to information security. The identification and classification of stakeholders of a smart city help in addressing the security problems in smart city in a better way. In this paper, onion model approach is proposed and all the concerned stakeholders regarding the security and privacy of information are identified by using this model. The authors proposed that by identifying all the stakeholders, the security requirements and issues are identified in a better way and a comprehensive framework to deal with these issues has also been presented.

In [57], the authors considered the role of smart software in relation of information security. The main focus is on discussing the role of smart software in developing a smarter city along with paying attention to the limitations regarding security issues.

A number of security software models are also discussed. The issue of security problems in sensing and querying in urbanization is presented in [58]. An encryption scheme to deal with the issues of data integrity and privacy is proposed.

Another concept of smart grids and their importance in smart city is discussed by authors in this paper. Smart grids are considered an integral component of a smart city as they provide the services of very novel and efficient energy supply chain and information management [59] In [60], the authors discuss the information security issues in a smart grid. Various requirement and models of information security are discussed and compared regarding the concerned issues with methodologies by authors.

In [61], the author discusses the relationship between anonymity and security and then realizing the need of balance between anonymity and security in smart grids. In this, author proposes a new concept for designing Internet so that security issues are handled in a better way. The reconstituting of Internet proves to be an interesting idea as author believes that redesigning and creation of multiple Internets with attempt to have a balance and anonymity can create a difference.

The paper [62] focuses mainly on China and various issues that can come across in developing a smart city in China. It also discusses the main application systems for a smart city and many hurdles that come across in developing a smart city are discussed in detail. It has been found that author paid less attention to information security issue and is not discussed in detail. Suciu et al. [63] propose a new solution for security by introducing the concept of cloud computing. It has been discussed that better security can be achieved by defining the platform of cloud computing and IoT properly for a smart city. In order to achieve that, they have proposed a framework for the information that can be automatically managed by the distributed cloud computing services. There is also a requirement of focusing on the privacy issues of a common citizen of a smart city. For example, in [64], authors discuss and analyze the privacy issues of citizens of a smart city. This includes five important dimensions: identity privacy, query privacy, location privacy, footprint privacy, and owner privacy, and a 5D model is proposed to consider these five issues. It is shown by the authors that by using their model, privacy-aware smart city is achievable.

In [65], Galdon-Clavell and Gemma question the credibility of a smart city mainly considering various problem areas in the implementation of smart cities, including security and privacy in context of individuals as well as institutions and governments. They proposed a smart solution which says that it is important to understand the problem area efficiently and then only smart cities can be constructed. Another author focuses on the issue of privacy in [66] where the authors concentrate on the problem areas in trace analysis and mining for the smart cities and found that though data mining and trace analysis play a vital role in smart cities, it is a challenging task to be done, keeping in mind the privacy concerns and usage of limited and relevant data only.

2.6 Security Concerns in Terms of Governance, Social, and Economic Perspectives

It is necessary to identify the main requirements in a smart city in the context of information security, in order to develop a better understanding of the problem areas. Moreover, the knowledge of core requirements will also help to identify the correct and feasible solutions to those problems. The information security in smart city is mostly dependent on three factors: governance, socioeconomic, and technological factors. The main responsibility of these factors is to influence and identify the information security issues in a smart city. The ICT technologies play an important role and work together to form a smart city. They not only implement the whole infrastructure of a smart city and provide solutions to information security problems but also trigger new concerns and problems regarding security, privacy, protection, and resilience.

It is recognized that the governance factors and socioeconomic factors are dependent on the technological factors as they are implemented in smart city via technology. These factors come together to influence the information security issues in a smart city, which can again be managed through technology as it is a major driving force in this scenario. So the function of technology in security management and the issues of information security in implementation of all the technology require the primary concern. However, we cannot ignore other two factors along with technology factor as in order to identify the core information security requirements, there is need to study the governance, social, and economic factors as well. In this section, these factors are discussed in terms of information security.

2.6.1 Governance Factors

Various governance factors that influence and trigger the security issues include utility, health sector, infrastructure, education, transport, etc. The biggest concern for the researchers is attacks and frauds which can be introduced by improper implementation of the smart city while smart city promises to provide all the ways to maintain whole infrastructure and management issues. These malicious attacks and frauds can be problematic to the main purpose of smart cities. In fact, they could cause more issues than advantages they promise.

Need for Security Testing

An important aspect is brought into picture by Cesar Cerrudo, the Chief Technology Officer at the security research firm IOActive Labs [67]: the governance authorities that are the customers of technology firms do not bother to test the security of the systems they buy. Their emphasis appears to be on testing the functionality of the technology, and they do not pay attention to the security testing. So the awareness among the authorities to have a genuine concern over security issues is a key requirement.

Threats to Critical Infrastructures

Another of the most essential and vital areas is critical infrastructure where changing a solitary procedure in a basic framework can cause defer or loss of basic services [68]. The main critical infrastructures include health care, industry, and telecommunication. The implementation of critical infrastructures in smart cities mainly includes IoT and smart grids. So the possible threats to these two technologies should be taken into consideration.

Moreover, big data integrity and resilience generated by critical systems are two factors that can pose big problems as big data needs to be properly stored, managed, and protected. This has also become the responsibility of a smart city's critical infrastructure to handle and maintain its security, resilience, and data integrity [69]. Therefore, there is urgency for the critical infrastructure to be safe from malicious attacks that may cause crucial damage to smart cities and their promised services. The most important type of critical infrastructure is health sector as it is also related to the life of patient which can be on a risk if critical information is altered by attacker [70]. Thus, there is a need for very secure encryption system for health information systems in a smart city.

Smart Mobility, Security, and Privacy Requirements

Privacy concerns also arise due to smart mobility as chances of personal information disclosure are possible in various phases such as collecting, publishing, and utilizing trace data. Here, localization techniques include GPS, GSM, Wi-Fi, Bluetooth, and RFID because central servers do not need to know device IDs [71]. Trace analysis and data mining techniques are used by some of the smartphone apps that provide services of smart mobility. Moreover, the information sent and received from devices used in smart mobility infrastructure may subject to malicious attacks cause wrong traffic reports in satellite navigation systems [72]. Hence, the importance of optimized use of ICT technology keeping in mind the security and privacy threats is identified by analyzing the problems in smart mobility domain.

Energy and Utility Optimization

Energy and utility services are more and more dependent on smart grids that make use of communication technologies in both directions for efficient energy management. Cloud computing likewise offers features that can ensemble easily for smart grid software platforms [71]. Security and privacy of data is the highest priority issue for utilities and user both [72]. In addition, the problem of security proliferates when it is implemented with cloud infrastructure. An appropriate methodology should be there to save energy and utilities from scams and malicious attacks. A report by [69] proposed that one can use Public Key Infrastructure (PKI) and managed PKI to confront security issue in smart grids. The next section discusses this issue in detail.

2.6.2 Social and Economic Factors

In smart cities, people get assistance with their social issues through technology that offers elementary platform services for urban development, backup, and communal management. This makes smart cities a one-step service system [62]. Furthermore, smart cities offer services to improve economics, banking, and business events for a smarter financial growth. The economic and social factors in case of smart cities are like communication, banking, and finance. These factors also open to security and privacy attacks. The following section presents these issues in detail.

Challenges in Smart Communication

The communication sector of smart cities is open to a number of attack, viruses, scams, and confidentiality attacks. Telecommunication area is part critical infrastructure in smart cities. There are various governance financial activities that are carried out over telecommunication and network. Hence, smart cities require some kind of secure and authenticated environment for this type of activities. Besides, M2M communication also offers some services to the residents of smart cities [73]. Hence, this type of communication also attracts the researcher in the field of security in smart cities. In the current era, people mainly communicate with each other with the help of smartphones and tablets. This area also leads to new pressures on the security field. Their privacy and security of information should also be considered. It is obvious that the more we use some technology, the more it becomes prone to attack [74]. All ICT technologies like cloud computing, Bluetooth, wireless networking, and IoT have their own role in smart cities.

Therefore, security related to these techniques should be taken into account while designing the structure of smart cities.

Individual Privacy

The information of an individual citizen of the smart city should be confidential. People of smart city communicate with each other and use the services in number of ways by using modern technology that is connected using network and system. These heterogeneous networks and system are on the target of the hackers and attackers. These attackers and hackers intrude in the confidential information of an individual and deprive individuals of their rights [64]. While considering an individual's right of privacy, one thing that must be taken into account is social networking. And this depends on the information provided by the individual and the method in which it can be utilized by the hacker or attacker. The providers of social networking provide adequate data to identify an individual's profile [75].

Banking, Finance, and Business

The basic elements of smart cities are smart banking, economics, and business. However, whereas the smart cities offer increase in economy, banking, and business sector, these fields are also prone to attacks as one can attack for gaining financial gain. An attacker or a hacker can also negatively interfere with the economy of a society or the entire city.

2.7 Technological Factors

Technology is an essential element that makes a smart city provides functionalities that it is intended to provide. One can say that smart cities solely depend on technology to provide the service to its citizen and government. Financial growth, banking, business, and smart governance are the promises that a smart city provides to its citizen by using technology. All of these promises are good but along with these services one thing that has to be considered is security and privacy of individual. In reality, without the services like security and privacy a smart city is not so smart.

The IoT includes a large number of eminent and heterogeneous devices, and allows free access to information for different online facilities for smart cities. IoT has enormous importance in the development and maintenance of smart cities. Some IoT architectures are specially designed for smart cities like urban IoT [76]. European countries are working on several projects that are designated to tackle the research challenges in various aspects of IoT. SmartSantander is an example that has been developed for smart cities.

Radio Frequency Identification (RFID) Tags

RFID tags RFID tagsare used in different components of smart city. RFID tags are used in the environment [77], industry [78], and mobility [79]. It has conveyed noteworthy benefit to many fields as well. This technology is also prone to security threats and attacks [80]. Authors in [81] studied that one can steal sensitive information through RFID tags and can create problem with respect to information privacy and confidentiality. Information leakage may also cause the problem of data integrity. Here are a few other related issues:

- **Abuse of Tags** [81]: RFID tags are small in size that makes them cost efficient. These tags can be embedded into different functions; hence, the cost of implementing security into system is very less due to its size. An unauthorized user can use these RFID tags. RFID tags and readers communicate with each other by using Electronic Product Code (EPC) and this EPC is again viable to attacks by the attacker. Tag detachment is also a problem in using RFID tags [82].
- **Tag Killing**: An attacker may also delete or kill the tags by using physical destruction and make them useless [82]; then, the reader of the tag would not be able to recognize the RFID tag. This type of attacks is carried out by the DoS type of attacks. One thing that has to be noted is that tag killing may also be used for improving the privacy issue of a system [81].
- **Tag Cloning**: Cloning a tag means creating a copy of tag. Unauthorized copy of the tag can be created and the data in the tag may be misused. The copied data is relocated onto the tag of the attacker.
- **Threats to Readers**: Disruption of the reader is also a big challenge in using RFID tags. An attacker can control the reader and he can be damaged by using electromagnetic waves to disrupt the data of the RFID tag [81].
- **Threats to Privacy**: One can track an RFID tag without the knowledge of the user [81]. Furthermore, the EPC of tags is unique that makes the tracking of tags easier. Traceability and credentials of tags lead to leakage of personal information of an individual. Therefore, tracking the tags is also a major issue [38]. Along with tag tracking, location privacy should also be considered.
- **Signal Interference**: RFID system can adopt two frequency ranges: low frequency (125 kHz, 225 kHz, 13.65 MHz) and high frequency (433 MHz, 915 MHz, 2.45 GHz, 5.8 GHz) [37]. Hence, the two frequencies from adjacent band may interfere each other. This situation may lead to data integrity in the communication between RFID tag and RFID reader.
- **Jamming**: Jamming causes the disturbed communication. It can affect the integrity of the system communication. This attack is performed by strong aerial at substantial distance and inactive means like shielding [82].
- **Threats to Communication**: RFID tag and RFID readers communicate with each other through wireless network. And these wireless signals can be easily attacked by the attacker to modify, search, and block the signal [81]. Therefore, the communication should be properly secured by using encryption and

authentication mechanism. In wireless communication, one can perform either active or passive attack [83, 84]. Even wired communication also has some security concern.

Smart Grids

Smart grids are an essential factor in the development of smart cities and in the management of energy in smart cities. Smart grids are essentially sensors and communicating networks like instruments that are used to communicate [59]. In such situation, information is prone to threats. According to research by [85–87], following are the major threats that need to be considered when developing smart cities:

- **Threat to Network Availability**: DoS is a kind of network availability attack. This type of attacks introduces some kind of delay in the network services.
- **Threat to Data Integrity**: Data integrity is basically concerned with the mechanism to stop modification of data through replay, delay on injection, etc. Major goal of data integrity attack is information of customer or information regarding network operation.
- **Threats to Information Privacy**: Privacy is fundamental right of an individual. Hence, communication in smart grid should take care of privacy of a person.
- **Threats to Devices**: One can change battery of smart meters or even he/she can damage or modify the smart meter.
- **Proposed Solution for Smart Grids**: The proposed must include the integrity of meter data and maintenance of meter securely [86, 87]. TCP/IP is nice for Internet. For authentication, various standards of encryption are there that can be used. PKI is also better for security in smart cities.

Biometrics

Biometric is a technique that identifies an individual's unique behavior and features. The characteristics of two types: physical and behavioral. Sensors are used in this technology for authenticating an individual [88]. Bill Maheu [89] stated that approximately every year 3.7 dollar can be saved by implementing biometric services in smart cities. Following are the key areas that can be secured by using biometric techniques [89]: health, education, institutions, utilities, fuels, and general security.

Smartphones

Smartphones are also the key component of IoT infrastructure in a smart city. These provide access to number of services that also assist in maintenance of smart cities. The major security threats to smartphones are as follows [74]:

- Malicious smart applications,
- Botnets and Spyware,
- Threats from Bluetooth,

- Location and GPS,
- Threats through Wi-Fi, and
- Threats through social networks.

2.8 The Growth of Cyber Threat

Cyber threats are becoming an issue of serious concern. Cybersecurity now needs a synchronized effort among the related organizations, government agencies, and advanced academics with cutting edge insight into the future of technology. Cyber criminals can cause harm and steal information. They are practicing on new technologies for getting over the safety measures of their identified organizations. This is being done to extract IPs and they are doing this for abrasion, deteriorate, disorganize sensitive data, and withdraw intellectual property.

With the passing of time, cyberattacks are on the increase, both in numbers and sophistication. Because of the increase in attacks, it is hard to tell what type of risk will arise in the coming years. The experts have already forecast that by 2020, individuals could be getting payments for distributing or sharing of their private data and hackers could be manipulating markets in the favor through financial intelligence gathering. Despite this uncertainty, there is a great need to be more cautious about the types of security controls needed.

2.9 Security Challenges in Smart Cities

Confidentiality is a basic right of every citizen which is also secured by national laws in distinct ways. Privacy concerns involve the right of mandating personal privacy including common practices with concern to access or displaying of information pertaining to oneself via cyber. Sensitive information can relate to data that should be secured from illegal access to safeguard the privacy or security of an individual or institution.

Smart city automation traps confidential data directed to broaden the quantity, limits, and distinguishable pieces of data that are originated about an individual or places. Privacy risks can be reduced and safeguarded by various techniques some of which are well known, for example, the following:

- **Surveillance**: Close observation, recording, and watching a suspected spy or a criminal.
- **Aggregation**: Clustering of distinct perspective of data of an individual to recognize a sequence of operations.
- **Data leakage**: Shortage of data protection methods may cause leakage or unauthorized access of privileged data.

- **Extended usage**: Data usage for a longer time span other than mentioned intentions without the subject knowledge.
- **Insecure hardware**: The topmost leading worries of smart cities relate to the equipment, infrastructures, etc. are unsafe and not evaluated randomly. Due to shortfall in uniformity of IOT devices, the sensors are inclined toward hacking. Prominent personal hacks the sensors to fill up with unreal data, which causes abnormal behavior like system failures and shutdown.
- **Larger Attack Surface**: Smart city enterprise applies composite, networked assembly of framework to handle ample number of services. Devices attached to the network are open to be attacked by the hackers. Trading off a single device makes it accessible to hack the whole network. The liability of a system is declined by few matter of contention which includes weak security, encryption, poor servicing, cascade effect, and human errors.
- **Bandwidth Consumption**: Large number of sensors would create pool of data and bring the server down if they try to communicate to a single server at once. Not enciphered links use to communicate with the server may lead to security breakdown. Other wireless communications are influenced by the excessive consumption of bandwidth from billions of devices.
- **Application risk**: Applications have increased the incorporation of various devices in our day-to-day routine. Ranging apps from social networking to efficient gadgets to games, apps have increasingly driven the smartphone revolt and completed it as advanced and accessible as today. Apps show the existence of its usefulness but apparently are bound to developer's imagination; it encourages the idea of Bring Your Own Device (BYOD) in the industry.

Since the corporates allow their staffs to bring and use their personal devices, and use the same to connect to work-related devices and information, it seems impossible to avoid the main security risks due to the following:

- **Malicious Apps (Malware)**: A number of apps are more on the devices than the chances that some of them may contain malware code or virus.
- **App Vulnerabilities**: Apps delivered or created by the association may have less security assurance to take over corporate data.
- **Simple bugs with huge impacts**: Even a minor bug can have great impact. As smart cities may run on a huge number of systems and devices managing critical services, a small bug can deteriorate its performance. For instance, in November 2013, Bay Area Rapid Transit (BART), major software glitch, service was shut down by a technical problem involving track switching; it affected 19 trains with about 500–1000 passengers on board.

2.10   Conclusion

Nowadays, we are entering into an era where *things of use* are becoming more intelligent and *smarter* than ever. A smart city can be defined as a city that deploys the services of the existence scientific advancements in communication and information technology to carve an urbanized infrastructure and services for the city which covers all the essential aspects of modern civilization, viz., efficient water management, primary health care, renewable and clean energies, smart grids, intelligent road safety, e-governance, wireless Internet access, efficient waste recycle, transportation utilities, education, artificial intelligence-aided public safety, and real estate in a more productive, useful, and comprehensive manner.

The information security in a smart city, that is highly important, is mostly dependent on three factors: city governance, socioeconomic dimensions, and technological dependence. The main responsibility of these factors is to identify and resolve the information security issues in a smart city. Here, the ICT technologies play the important role and work together to form a smart city. They not only implement the whole infrastructure of a smart city and provide solutions to information security problems, but also trigger new concerns and problems regarding security, privacy, protection, and resilience.

The ultimate mission of the smart cities is to brave innovative creativity by the governments and commercial sector to initiate the financial progress and develop day-to-day quality of life by empowering local development and connecting latest technology to benefit the residents. Smart energy, small buildings, ease of mobility, and data and personal security are some of the key parameters of smart cities. Technologies used in smart cities capture data relating to various forms of privacy and significantly raise the volume and increase the protection of data being generated about people and places. Confidentiality can be endangered and ruptured by a large number of practices which are generally treated as intolerable; however, these are part of operations in a smart city ecosystem. This chapter discusses the security issue in great detail and also provides some solutions to security in modern smart cities.

References

1. Dobbs R, Smit S, Remes J, Manyika J, Roxburgh C, Restrepo A (2011) Urban world: mapping the economic power of cities. McKinsey Global Institute
2. Borja J (2007) Counterpoint: intelligent cities and innovative cities. Universitat Oberta de Catalunya (UOC) Papers: E-journal on the knowledge society, no 5. Available at http://www. uoc.edu/uocpapers/5/dt/eng/mitchell.pdf
3. Toppeta D (2010) The smart city vision: how innovation and ICT can build smart, "livable", sustainable cities. The Innovation Knowledge Foundation. Available from http://www. thinkinnovation.org/file/research/23/en/Toppeta_Report_005_2010.pdf

4. Washburn D, Sindhu U, Balaouras S, Dines RA, Hayes NM, Nelson LE (2010) Helping CIOs understand "smart city" initiatives: defining the smart city, its drivers, and the role of the CIO. Forrester Research, Inc., Cambridge, MA
5. Dawes SS, Cresswell AM, Pardo TA (2009) From "need to know" to "need to share": tangled problems, information boundaries, and the building of public sector knowledge networks. Public Adm Rev 69(3):392–402
6. Rittel HWJ, Webber M (1973) Dilemmas in a general theory of planning. Policy Sci 4: 155–169
7. Weber EP, Khademian AM (2008) Wicked problems, knowledge challenges, and collaborative capacity builders in network settings. Public Adm Rev 68(2):334–349
8. Van den Besselaar P, Beckers D (2005) The life and death of the great Amsterdam digital city. Lect Notes Comput Sci 3081:66–96
9. Lee Y (2013) Ubiquitous (smart) city. In: Proceedings of EU Parliament seminar on smart (ubiquitous) city consortium, p 3
10. O'connel P (2005) Korea's high-tech Utopia, where everything is observed. The New York Times
11. Caragliu A, Del Bo, Nijkamp P (2011) Smart cities in Europe. J Urban Technol 18(2):65–82
12. Komninos N (2011) MESH cities. Research report on digital cities, cyber cities. www.urenio. org
13. Shin J (2012) ICT Leadership toward human-centered technology. Korea IT Times, 24 Sept 2012
14. Lee J, Hancock M (2012) Toward a framework for smart cities: a comparison of Seoul, San Francisco and Amsterdam. Research Paper, Yonsei University and Stanford University
15. Boulton A, Brunn SD, Devriendt L (2011) Cyberinfrastructures and "smart" world cities: physical, human, and soft infrastructures. In: Taylor P, Derudder B, Hoyler M, Witlox F (eds) International handbook of globalization and world cities. Edward Elgar, Cheltenham, UK. Available from http://www.neogeographies.com/documents/cyberinfrastructure_smart_world_cities.pdf
16. Hollands RG (2008) Will the real smart city please stand up? City 12(3):303–320
17. Giffinger R, Fertner C, Kramar H, Kalasek R, Pichler-Milanović N, Meijers E (2007) Smart cities: ranking of European medium-sized cities. Centre of Regional Science (SRF), Vienna University of Technology, Vienna, Austria. Available from http://www.smartcities.eu/download/smart_cities_final_report.pdf
18. Hall RE (2000) The vision of a smart city. In: Proceedings of the 2nd international life extension technology workshop, Paris, France, September 28. Available from http://www.osti.gov/bridge/servlets/purl/773961-oyxp82/webviewable/773961.pdf
19. Harrison C, Eckman B, Hamilton R, Hartswick P, Kalagnanam J, Paraszczak J, Williams P (2010) Foundations for smarter cities. IBM J Res Dev 54(4):1–16
20. Natural Resources Defense Council (2017) What are smarter cities? Available from http://smartercities.nrdc.org/about
21. Dirks S, Keeling M (2009) A vision of smarter cities: how cities can lead the way into a prosperous and sustainable future. IBM Global Business Services, Somers, NY. Available from ftp://public.dhe.ibm.com/common/ssi/ecm/en/gbe03227usen/GBE03227USEN.PDF
22. Kanter RM, Litow SS (2009) Informed and interconnected: a manifesto for smarter cities. Harvard Business School General Management Unit Working Paper, pp 09–141. Available from http://papers.ssrn.com/sol3/papers.cfm?abstract_id=1420236
23. Mitchell WJ (2006) Smart city 2020, Metropolis. March 20. Available from http://www.metropolismag.com/story/20060320/smartcity-2020
24. IFF (2011) 2020 Forecast: the future of cities, information, and inclusion: a planet of civic laboratories. Technology Horizons Program, Palo Alto, CA 94301. Available at http://www.iftf.org/
25. Brail RK (ed) (2008) Planning support systems for cities and regions. Lincoln Institute of Land Policy, Cambridge, MA

26. Gil-García JR, Pardo TA (2005) E-government success factors: mapping practical tools to theoretical foundations. Gov Inf Q 22(2):187–216
27. Giffinger R, Fertner C, Kramar H, Kalasek R, Pichler-Milanoviü N, Meijers E (2007) Smart cities: ranking of European medium-sized cities. Centre of Regional Science (SRF), Vienna University of Technology, Vienna, Austria. Available from http://www.smartcities.eu/download/smart_cities_final_report.pdf
28. Odendaal N (2003) Information and communication technology and local governance: understanding the difference between cities in developed and emerging economies. Comput Environ Urban Syst 27(6):585–607
29. Dirks S, Keeling M, Dencik J (2009) How smart is your city? Helping cities measure progress. IBM Global Business Services, Somers, NY. Available from ftp://public.dhe.ibm.com/common/ssi/ecm/en/gbe03248usen/GBE03248USEN.PDF
30. Cairney T, Speak G (2000) Developing a 'smart city': understanding information technology capacity and establishing an agenda for change. Centre for Regional Research and Innovation, University of Western Sydney, Sydney, Australia. Available from http://trevorcairney.com/file_uploads/cgilib.30886.1.IT_Audit.pdf
31. Bronstein Z (2009) Industry and the smart city. Dissent 56(3):27–34. Available from http://www.communitywealth.org/_pdfs/articlespublications/cross-sectoral/article-bronstein.pdf
32. Mauher M, Smokvina V (2006) Digital to intelligent local government transition framework. In: Proceedings of the 29th international convention of MIPRO, Opatija, Croatia, 22–26 May 2006. Available from http://www.mmcconsulting.hr/Download/2008/03/07/Mauher_M_Digital_to_Intelligent_City_Transition_Framework.pdf
33. Eger JM, Maggipinto A (2010) Technology as a tool of transformation: e-Cities and the rule of law. In: D'Atri A, Saccà D (eds) Information systems: people, organizations, institutions, and technologies. Physica-Verlag, Heidelberg, pp 23–30
34. Hartley J (2005) Innovation in governance and public services: past and present. Public Money Manag 25(1):27–34
35. Yigitcanlar T, Velibeyoglu K (2008) Knowledge based urban development: the local economic development path of Brisbane. Australia. Local Econ 23(3):195–207
36. Mahler J, Regan PM (2002) Learning to govern online: federal agency internet use. Am Rev Public Adm 32(3):326–349
37. Bakici T, Almirall E, Wareham J (2016) A smart city initiative: the case of Barcelona. J Knowl Econ 4(2):135–148
38. Vasseur J (2010) Smart cities and urban networks. In: Vasseur J, Dunkels A (eds) Interconnecting smart objects with IP: the next internet. Morgan Kaufmann, Burlington, MA, pp 360–377
39. Ebrahim Z, Irani Z (2005) E-government adoption: architecture and barriers. Bus Process Manag J 11(5):589–611
40. The United Nations (2017) Our common future: the Brundtland report 1987. Available at: http://www.un-documents.net/our-common-future.pdf
41. Aoun C (2013) The smart city cornerstone: urban efficiency. http://www.digital21.gov.hk/eng/relatedDoc/download/2013/079%20SchneiderElectric%20(Annex).pdf
42. Bowerman J, Braverman J, Taylor H. Todosow, Von Wimmersperg U (2000) The vision of a smart city. In: 2nd international life extension technology workshop, Paris, 2000
43. Kunzmann KR (2014) Smart cities: a new paradigm of urban development. Crios 4(1):9–20
44. Dirks, Gurdgiev C, Keeling M (2010) Smarter cities for smarter growth: how cities can optimize their systems for the talent-based economy. IBM Institute for Business Value
45. Forbes (2015) Top five smart cities in the world. http://www.forbes.com/sites/peterhigh/2015/03/09/the-top-five-smartcities-in-the-world, accessed 03 Apr 2015
46. Komninos N, Schaffers H, Pallot M (2011) Developing a policy roadmap for smart cities and the future internet. In: eChallenges e-2011 conference proceedings, IIMC International Information Management Corporation
47. Naphade M, Banavar G, Harrison C, Paraszczak J, Morris R (2011) Smarter cities and their innovation challenges. Computer 44(6):32–39

48. Bartoli, Hernandez-Serrano J, Soriano M, Dohler M, Kountouris A, Barthel D (2011) Security and privacy in your smart city. In: Proceedings of the Barcelona smart cities congress. Int J Adv Comput Sci Appl (IJACSA) 7(2), 2016
49. Elmaghraby S, Losavio MM (2014) Cyber security challenges in smart cities: safety, security and privacy. J Adv Res 5(4):491–497
50. Anderson R (2001) Why information security is hard-an economic perspective. In: Proceedings 17th annual computer security applications conference, ACSAC 2001. IEEE, pp 358–365
51. Cisco (2015) Cisco intelligent urbanisation. http://www.urenio.org/2009/03/13/ciscointelligent-urbanisation/, accessed 22 Apr 2015
52. Dohler M, Vilajosana I, Vilajosana X, LLosa J (2011) Smart cities: an action plan. In: Barcelona smart cities congress
53. Kitchin R (2014) The real-time city? big data and smart urbanism. GeoJournal 79(1):1–14
54. Schmitt C (2014) Security and privacy in the area of big data. National consortium for data science, white paper
55. Bohli J-M, Langendorfer P, Skarmeta AF (2013) Security and privacy challenge in data aggregation for the iot in smart cities. River Publisher Series in Cmoounications, p 225
56. Khan Z, Pervez Z, Ghafoor A (2014) Towards cloud based smart cities data security and privacy management. In: Utility and cloud computing (UCC), 2014 IEEE/ACM 7th international conference
57. Sen M, Dutt A, Agarwal S, Nath A (2013) Issues of privacy and security in the role of software in smart cities. In: IEEE 2013 international conference on communication systems and network technologies (CSNT). IEEE, 2013, pp 518–523
58. Wen M, Lei J, Bi Z (2013) SSE: a secure searchable encryption scheme for urban sensing and querying. Int J Distrib Sens Netw 9(12)
59. Clastres (2011) Smart grids: another step towards competition, energy security and climate change objectives. Energy Policy 39(9):5399–5408
60. Ling PA, Masao M (2011) Selection of model in developing information security criteria on smart grid security system. In: 9th IEEE international symposium parallel and distributed processing with applications workshops (ISPAW), pp 91–98
61. Goel S (2015) Anonymity vs. security: the right balance for the smart grid. Commun Assoc Inf Syst 36(1):2
62. Su K, Li J, Fu H (2011) Smart city and the applications. In: 2011 international conference on electronics, communications and control (ICECC). IEEE, 2011, pp 1028–1031
63. Suciu G, Vulpe A, Halunga S, Fratu O, Todoran G, Suciu V (2013) Smart cities built on resilient cloud computing and secure internet of things. In: 19th international conference on control systems and computer science (CSCS). IEEE, 2013, pp 513–518
64. Martinez-Balleste, Perez-Martınez PA, Solanas A (2013) The pursuit of citizens' privacy: a privacy-aware smart city is possible. Commun Mag IEEE 51(6):136–141
65. Galdon-Clavell G (2013) (not so) smart cities?: the drivers, impact and risks of surveillance-enabled smart environments. Sci Public Policy 40(6):717–723
66. Gang Pan WZSL, Qi G, Wu Z (2013) Trace analysis and mining for smart cities: issues, methods, and applications. IEEE Commun Mag 121:2013
67. The Guardian (2015) Why smart cities need to get wise to security and fast. http://www.theguardian.com/technology/2015/may/13/smart-citiesinternet-thingssecurity-cesar-cerrudo-ioactive-labs, accessed May 2015
68. Abouzakhar N (2013) Critical infrastructure cybersecurity: a review of recent threats and violations
69. Symantec (2013) Transformational smart cities: cyber security and resilience. Executive Report
70. Solanas C, Patsakis M, Conti I, Vlachos V, Ramos F, Falcone O, Postolache PA, Perez-Martınez R, Di Pietro DN, Perrea et al (2014) Smart health: a context-aware health paradigm within smart cities. IEEE Commun Mag 52(8):74–81

71. Simmhan Y, Kumbhare AG, Cao B, Prasanna V (2011) An analysis of security and privacy issues in smart grid software architectures on clouds. In: 2011 IEEE international conference on cloud computing (CLOUD). IEEE, 2011, pp 582–589
72. Polonetsky J, Wolf C (2009) How privacy (or lack of it) could sabotage the grid. Smart grid news
73. Wan J, Li D, Zou C, Zhou K (2012) M2M communications for smart city: an event-based architecture. In: 2012 IEEE 12th international conference on computer and information technology (CIT). IEEE, 2012, pp 895–900
74. Leavitt N (2011) Mobile security: finally a serious problem? Computer 44(6):11–14
75. Gross R, Acquisti A (2005) Information revelation and privacy in online social networks. In: Proceedings of the 2005 ACM workshop on privacy in the electronic society. ACM, 2005, pp 71–80
76. Zanella, Bui N N, Castellani AP, Vangelista L, Zorzi M (2014) Internet of things for smart cities. IEEE Internet Things J 1(1):22–32
77. Luvisi Lorenzini G (2014) Rfid-plants in the smart city: applications and outlook for urban green management. Urban For Urban Green 13(4):630–637
78. Zhu X, Mukhopadhyay SK, Kurata H (2012) A review of RFID technology and its managerial applications in different industries. J Eng Technol Manag 29(1):152–167
79. Ramos, Lazaro A, Girbau D (2014) Multi-sensor UWB time-coded RFID tags for smart cities applications. In: 2014 44th European microwave conference (EuMC). IEEE, 2014, pp 259–262
80. Xiwen S (2011) Study on security issue of internet of things based on RFID. In: IEEE 2012 fourth international conference on computational and information sciences (ICCIS). IEEE, 2012, pp 566–569
81. Nie X, Zhong X (2013) Security in the internet of things based on RFID: Issues and current countermeasures. In: Proceedings of the 2nd international conference on computer science and electronics engineering, Atlantis Press, 2013
82. Mohite S, Kulkarni G, Sutar R (2013) RFID security issues. Int J Res Technol 2(9). ESRSA Publications
83. Aggarwal R, Das ML (2012) Rfid security in the context of internet of things. In: Proceedings of the first international conference on security of internet of things, ACM, 2012, pp 51–56
84. Babar S, Stango A, Prasad N, Sen J, Prasad R (2011) Proposed embedded security framework for internet of things (iot). In: 2011 2nd international conference on wireless communication, vehicular technology, information theory and aerospace & electronic systems technology (wireless VITAE). IEEE, 2011, pp 1–5
85. Lu Z, Lu X, Wang W, Wang C (2010) Review and evaluation of security threats on the communication networks in the smart grid. In: Military communications conference, 2010-MILCOM 2010. IEEE, 2010, pp 1830–1835
86. Yan Y, Qian Y, Sharif H, Tipper D (2012) A survey on cyber security for smart grid communications. Commun Surv Tutor IEEE 14(4):998–1010
87. Liu J, Xiao Y, Li S, Liang W, Chen C (2012) Cyber security and privacy issues in smart grids. Commun Surv Tutor IEEE 14(4):981–997
88. Rathgeb, Uhl A (2011) A survey on biometric cryptosystems and cancelable biometrics". EURASIP J Inf Secur 2011(1):1–25
89. How connectivity and biometrics are making cities safer. http://smartcitiescouncil.com/article/how-connectivity-and-biometricsare-making-citiessafer, accessed 31 May 2015

Chapter 3
Towards Heterogeneous Architectures of Hybrid Vehicular Sensor Networks for Smart Cities

Soumia Bellaouar, Mohamed Guerroumi, Abdelouahid Derhab and Samira Moussaoui

Abstract Smart cities are increasingly playing a fundamental role in managing the city's asset. Smart transportation is an important building block of a smart city as it can efficiently resolve many issues related to the traffic on the road. Vehicular ad hoc networks (VANETs) in smart cities may ensure wide inter-vehicle communication and disseminate data and safety-related information. VANETs have their specific characteristics such as long lifetime battery energy, high mobility, and large storage capabilities. In certain circumstances, VANETs may not ensure timely detection of road events and connectivity between vehicles due to their low density, high mobility, or low deployment of roadside unit (RSU) infrastructure. Wireless sensor networks (WSNs) are equipped with low processing and low storage capabilities but they ensure high detection of events. To overcome VANETs limitations, and as VANET and WSN have complementary characteristics, the combination of VANET and wireless sensor network (WSN) technologies into one hybrid architecture enables to identify new aspects and fields of intelligent transportation systems and may offer new services for the smart cities. In this kind of hybrid network, sensor nodes have small size and can be deployed densely inside the road to monitor traffic, roads status, and weather conditions. This chapter describes the hybrid vehicular sensor networks and discusses their deployed applications, communication paradigms, challenges, and existing architectural solutions. Moreover, a heterogeneous VANET-WSN architecture is proposed and open issues and future directions are discussed to help stimulating future studies in this emerging research field.

Keywords Hybrid vehicular sensor network · VANET · Wireless sensor network
WSN · Cloud computing · IoT · Smart city

S. Bellaouar (✉) · M. Guerroumi · S. Moussaoui
Vehicular Networks for Intelligent Transport Systems (VNets) Group,
Electronic and Computing Department, USTHB University, Algiers, Algeria
e-mail: sbellaouar@usthb.dz

A. Derhab
Center of Excellence in Information Assurance (CoEIA), King Saud University,
Riyadh, Saudi Arabia

© Springer International Publishing AG, part of Springer Nature 2018
Z. Mahmood (ed.), *Smart Cities*, Computer Communications and Networks,
https://doi.org/10.1007/978-3-319-76669-0_3

3.1 Introduction

With the growth of population and economic development inside urban environments, the daily life problems of citizens become more complicated. Thus, the smart cities are increasingly becoming an effective approach to solve these problems, and hence the number of digital devices (sensors, actuators, and smart appliances) as well as connected vehicles on the road is growing day by day to manage the city for better decision-making.

One of the main goals of smart cities is to minimize their transportation problems, which caused congested roads and accidents. Vehicular ad hoc networks (VANETs) aim to solve these issues by improving the vehicle mobility and having more safe smart cities. Moreover, wireless sensor networks (WSNs) are considered as a fundamental infrastructure to provide services for smart cities. Their versatility and their diverse usage help to measure and collect a lot of data that may enhance the daily life of the smart city's citizens. Initially, the development of vehicular technologies focused on building efficient and safer roads [1]. But nowadays, due to the huge development of wireless technologies and their application in vehicles, it becomes possible to use hybrid wireless vehicular sensor network. This network aims to reduce pollution and congestion, prevent accidents, and ensure easier communication among vehicles and infrastructures and safer roads. For instance, sensors and embedded systems are used on an automated highway system. This system makes the experience of driving less burdensome with fewer accidents, especially on long trips by making the highway itself part of the driving experience and integrating roadside technologies that allow using the system more efficiently [2].

Motivation

The development of smart cities is based on deploying smart technologies such as: sensors, smart vehicles, and technological devices on roads, which might lead to several issues in the smart city like the deployment cost and the integation of different technologies. This can influence the main objectives of developing a smart city such as safety and quality of living. Hence, by taking the heterogeneous environment into account, a study of numerous deployments of WSNs in smart transportation for smart cities needs to be explored. Sensor services for gathering specific data are utilized in VANET-WSN, regarding the monitoring and supervising of each cyclist, vehicle, parking lot and air pollution control [3]. Vehicular wireless sensor network can provide monitoring systems and infrastructures with more efficiency, lower cost and better safety.

Consequently, the vehicular wireless sensor network contributes in managing cities and improving the different features of human life by creating cost-effective services with more efficiency, and reducing traffic congestion, accidents, and pollution. Thus, this network helps to ensure citizens' safety to improve the quality of their lives through different applications. Therefore, the main contributions of this chapter are as follows:

- We identify the architectures and systems of hybrid vehicular wireless sensor networks.
- We provide a classification of different vehicular wireless sensor network applications for smart city, as well as a taxonomy classification of these networks with respect to: architecture, information, and access technologies.
- We propose a multilayer and heterogeneous architecture for hybrid vehicular wireless sensor networks.
- We discuss the main open issues of wireless sensor vehicular networks and identify possible future directions.

Chapter Organization

In the rest of this chapter, we outline the requirements of smart cities in Sect. 3.2. In Sects. 3.3 and 3.4, we present the requirements of smart transportations in smart cities and we present the communication technologies used by the connected vehicles. In Sect. 3.5, we identify the objectives of VANET-WSN in smart city and discuss their applications and their implementation challenges. In Sects. 3.6 and 3.7, we describe architectures and systems of VANET-WSN and discuss the existing testbed platforms and simulation environments. In Sect. 3.8, we give a short description of our proposed multilayer VANET-WSN architecture. In Sect. 3.9, we present the remaining open issues and outline possible future research directions with an architecture that we propose. Section 3.10 concludes the chapter.

3.2 Requirements of Smart Cities

Nowadays, the way of living, communication and habits of citizens have changed. The digital technology is included in our environment, social and economic life to provide a high quality of life. A smart city requires some already clear items for urban environments such as smart health care, smart water distribution, smart transportation and there will surely be others in the future. The main components composing the smart urban environments are as follows [3, 4]:

- **Smart health care**: To monitor patients' health parameters and truck ambulance through sensor devices. These systems identify the status of the patients and the location of the ambulance in order to provide real-time information on the patient's health and faster decision-making.
- **Digital signage systems**: These help to provide advertising services where the customers can buy the ticket of concert posters via the billboard.
- **Smart grids systems**: To maximize the energy efficiency by providing the necessary amount of electricity depending on the demand.
- **Smart urban lighting systems**: These adjust the intensity of the light depending on the presence of people on the street with minimum energy wastage.

- **Smart city maintenance systems**: To notify the City Council of any damages in the urban elements through notifications sent from the citizen's smart phones, in order to repair the damage faster.
- **Transportation and vehicular traffic networks**: To provide a considerable source of data in smart cities. The citizens and the government can significantly use the traffic data by employing a proper analysis. The vehicular traffic information is used to identify mainly traffic congestion and accidents. This information allows analyzing the traffic and notifying the officers, but in order to generate large amount of information, it requires high-capacity communication infrastructure. The smart transportation can provide the following functionalities:
- **Smart parking systems**: These aim at finding parking spaces and guide drivers to the exact location. They allow reducing air pollution.
- **Intelligent public transport systems**: To control and manage public transportation networks, maintain their performance, and provide passengers and decision-makers with up-to-date information about trips and network operating conditions.
- **Traffic management systems**: To manage the traffic lights and inform drivers about the best route to take in order to reduce congestion.
- **Smart taxi applications**: That allow finding and booking the closest taxi without the human intervention.

3.3   Requirements of Smart Transportation Networks

Nowadays, vehicles have the capabilities to communicate and share useful information with each other or with the roadside unit (RSU) under a network known as VANETs [5]. This network has been developed to provide security, information service and comfort (video, Music, internet access, etc.) for drivers and passengers. The demand of existing and emerging smart transport applications is increased, while the number and requirements transport components are continuously growing. Therefore, the wireless vehicle sensor network deployed in a smart city must provide flexible, efficient, and easy to use services. It requires less effort/time consumption as well as a minimum of interaction [6]. The main requirements that should be considered in the deployed transport system for smart cities are as follows:

- **Fault-tolerant systems**: The smart devices and systems participating in the smart city environment must be available. In some situations, when an accident or a natural disaster occurs, the system must work to propagate important information about the situation and damage. Moreover, the transport systems must be able to decrease or eliminate peaks in resource request.
- **Energy Efficiency of communication**: The problem of energy consumption does not exist in VANETs. In a smart city, the transport system is heterogeneous. We can find collaboration between several systems and technologies in

order to perform a specific task. For this reason, the development of lightweight communication protocols can ensure more energy-efficiency related to new technologies and achieve sustainability and quality of communication. Also, the transport system must implement fast and reliable communication protocols to enable real-time interactions between the smart roads and the smart vehicles.

- **Security and safety mechanisms**: The architecture of smart transport must provide adequate security mechanisms to prevent a hacker from taking control of the vehicle and compromising the decision-making solutions. In addition, the security mechanism must consider the real-time contextual factors and ensure adaptive planning travel and monitoring systems based on current traffic situation.

3.4 Communication Technologies for Connected Vehicles

Wireless communication is important for vehicles as it allows sharing and exchanging necessary information between vehicles to make decisions, and which might influence the behavior of motorists or drivers.

The detection devices are implemented on the vehicles or on the roads. They offer several designs of connected vehicles in smart transportations. The VANET provides a wireless communication between moving vehicles based on a dedicated short range communication (DSRC) for low overhead operation 802.11p with a maximal bit rate of 27 Mb/s. It is achieved through a wireless medium WAVE family 1609 stack [7]. Vehicle can communicate with other vehicles by establishing vehicle-to-vehicle communication (V2V) or communicate with RSU next to the road by forming vehicle-to-infrastructure communication (V2I). These wireless communications have limited bandwidth. However, the data traffic, which is required by some devices such as HD camera and 3D imaging, is continuously growing [8].

In a smart city, there is a lot of wireless devices deployed for several purposes all over the city (on roads, buildings, etc.). For that, other types of communications can be used in smart transportation. Existing works attempt to integrate commercial WiFi, Bluetooth, ZigBee, WiMax, LTE (4G), and the five generation (5G) into vehicles. They allow longer range communication and high throughput that could not be supported by the primary communication DSRC. The vehicles can communicate with the sensors deployed on the road (at the edge of the road, in the middle of the road, according to an urban grid, etc.) using, in general, the Zigbee 802.15.4 technology to exchange different information [7]. This vehicle-to-sensor communication allows the interaction between vehicles and WSN which means that the vehicles must be equipped with different communication interfaces not only with 802.11p. In addition, vehicles can communicate with pedestrians using 3G or WIFI access technologies. This communication aims to find mechanisms to ensure pedestrian safety [9]. The smart cities allow vehicles to interact with the environment, i.e., roads, residential buildings, market places, and collaborate with different systems such as smart healthcare systems and cloud computing systems. These offer more computing capabilities and more specified services related to smart transportation. However, embedding the vehicles with these devices might increase the deployment cost, which requires making a compromise between the benefits offered by the communication technology and its corresponding deployment cost.

3.5 VANET-WSN

3.5.1 Definition

Hybrid VANET-WSN (V-WSN) network is a VANET, which is extended by deploying wireless sensor nodes along the road especially on highways. Sensors act as access points (APs), monitor, and control traffic flow in real time and detect incident on roads [10]. The main objective of this network is to improve transportation safety and relieve the difficulty of communication in this network.

In the context of smart city, sensors are deployed in city zones for large fields and applications, so hybrid V-WSN network can collaborate and communicate with other networks with different technologies (3G, LTE, etc.), as shown in Fig. 3.1.

3.5.2 Objectives

The vehicular wireless sensor network deployed in a smart city must provide flexible, efficient, and easy to use services. This leads to identify the following main objectives:

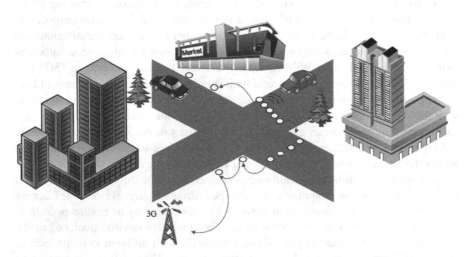

Fig. 3.1 Hybrid V-WSN network

- Deploy services to the users on the road through various applications [11].
- Set up and maintain a communication networking among vehicles without any central base station [12].
- Ensure an optimal and efficient way of communication to enable real-time interactions.
- Provide adequate security and reliability mechanisms to prevent incidents.
- Provide reliability and timeliness solutions by considering the delay requirement and real-time contextual factors.
- Ensure collaboration and cooperation between smart transportation systems and others smart systems such as social and economic networks.

3.5.3 Applications

Many transport infrastructures, bridges, and tunnels have collapsed due to natural disasters or because of poor maintenance. For example, in 2007, the bridge in Minneapolis killed 13 and injured 145 people. In 2008, this bridge was rebuilt using a sensing system to collect data regarding structural behavior and corrosion [13]. Smart road applications need more than vehicle devices. Smart and reliable unmanned aerial vehicles (UAVs) are recently used in smart roads to automate road infrastructure components. UAVs can be equipped by DSRC interfaces to enable wireless communication under VANETs [14]. For example, a set of UAVs replaces a road support team. It could fly around the location of an incident to provide basic support or report the situation of the traffic.

Several IT functions have been integrated into the vehicles to give a wide variety of applications and services. As shown in Fig. 3.2, applications and services in the V-WSN networks can be classified as follows:

Monitoring/Management Applications

These are based on the exchange of information related to the state of the road. Monitoring bridges are a successful application of smart roads. For example, the six-lane, 2.9 km Charilaos Trikoupis Bridge in Greece is outfitted with 100 sensors that monitor its condition. After opening it in 2004, the sensors detected vibrations in the cables holding the bridge, which led engineers to install additional weight to dampen the cables [13]. Moreover, monitoring airflow to visibility and gases (CO, CO_2, NO_2, O_2, SH_2, and PM-10) inside tunnels are some parameters to monitor air tunnels quality [13].

Security Applications

These are the most important applications in smart transportation because road accidents cause death, especially among young people. Road safety is significantly improved thanks to alert messages exchanged between fixed or mobile entities of the network. Safety applications can use UAVs such as flying accident report agent

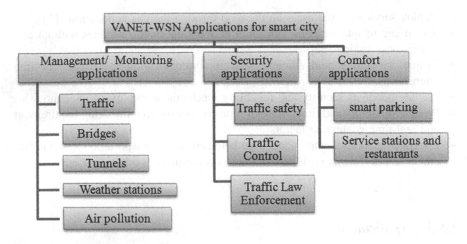

Fig. 3.2 Hybrid basic classification of V-WSN application

or flying police eye. When a traffic accident occurs, UAVs might help the rescue team to reach the accident scene within the shortest time [14].

Comfort Applications

These allow accessing the Internet, suggesting popular spots, hotels, and shopping malls for tourists or citizens. An intelligent navigation services application allows recommending the best route to drivers by considering some parameters such as: the least time-consuming route and the most energy-saving route [15]. Moreover, smart parking applications minimize the amount of time spent by the individual to look for parking [16].

3.5.4 Issues and Challenges

Smart V-WSN technologies in smart cities need to cope with population growth while ensuring long-term sustainability with optimized operation cost, and be resilient to disasters and failures. A design and operation challenge is to have a good mix of smart technologies. So, the vehicular wireless sensor networks are rather sufficiently smart to be sustainable for years. The challenges for building smart V-WSN are the following:

Heterogeneous Wireless Networks Designs

The optimal deployment of heterogeneous wireless sensors in the road requires careful consideration and design of appropriate protocols such as fast and reliable MAC access protocol and data forwarding mechanisms. This allows to guarantee timely transmission of critical messages and to deal with the high redundancy of the transmitted information.

Interoperability Among Heterogeneous Wireless Networks

The architecture, resource allocation, mobility management, quality of service (QoS) provisioning, and security of deployed systems need a uniform conception to enable communication among different wireless networks. It is required to pay considerable attention to address this challenge in the future.

Cost

The financial cost is related to the design, the network operations and the cost of deploying such a smart technology. The progress of science and technology would make the smart technology cheaper in the future and would not impose additional taxes on citizens [17].

High Energy Consumption

The energy consumption rate of resource-constrained devices in smart city is significantly high. In the future, and with the growing number of citizens, the energy consumption rate of communication technologies will still be considered as high. Future V-WSN devices must ensure control and optimization of renewable energy sources.

Security and Privacy

Users request high level of privacy and security guarantees in order to participate to such a system. These requirements represent major concerns that need to be addressed to encourage larger participation of users of mobile devices to the mobile sensing applications [18]. Security includes enhanced emergency- response services, and automated messages for alerting drivers and pedestrians and real-time information on available roads. While authenticating the vehicle, the privacy related to identity and location information must be kept private.

Efficiency

Higher efficiency of V-WSN systems can reduce the operational cost and improve sustainability of the smart transportation. Any smart city design needs to take these potential disasters and failures into consideration, so that the city can quickly recover from such situations [17].

3.6 Architecture of V-WSN

VANET provides a wide variety of communication architectures, especially with the emerging of some technologies such as IoT, cloud computing, smart grid, and UAV. The most known communication classifications are VANET communications in-vehicle domain, ad hoc domain, and infrastructure domain [19] or geocast/

broadcast, multicast, and unicast approaches [20], and one-hop or multi-hop communication [21]. We classify the V-WSN architecture based on the used concept as explained below.

V-WSN Architecture

A recent trend consists of using WSN in VANET applications to improve driving safety and traffic efficiency. The deployment of sensors on selected roads is serious issue. The authors in [10] considered the deployment of a minimal number of APs (i.e., RSUs and sensors) along the two sides and the median island of the road considering a two lanes which represent the road as a grid.

Depending on the application type and requirements, the proposed communication architecture differs from one another in V-WSN network. For traffic monitoring application, the proposed architecture [20], which was implemented in two cities of South Africa [22], consists of WSN sensors, RFID scanner, and TMC.

For effective and efficient vehicle-sensor and sensor–sensor interactions, we distinguish several propositions. The sensor nodes can have two types: the regular sensor node and the AP sensor node. Regular nodes are deployed between two adjacent APs to sense and relay messages, APs have extra responsibilities of discovering and communicating with vehicles, and managing the network, which is based on two types of clusters: Vehicle clusters and sensor clusters (Regular nodes between two APs form cluster). Usually in this hybrid network, the vehicle nodes have two communication interfaces: WIFI IEEE 802.11 interface and ZigBee IEEE 802.15.4 interface [23], but we can that find sensor nodes have a ZigBee IEEE 802.15.4 interface and the sink node has two interfaces: a IEEE 802.11p interface and a ZigBee IEEE 802.15.4 interface for communication WSN-sink-vehicle while vehicle nodes have IEEE 802.11p interface [24].

The cooperation between WSNs and VANETs permits to extend the transmission range of ad hoc nodes. Vehicles store road information in the WSN's sink when they pass through WSN. Other cars obtain the information stored (e.g., weather conditions, location of accidents, possible building, etc.) from the WSN's sink [25]. The same idea was used for pollution-free monitoring system using a hybrid V-WSN and LTE-M technology. This technology is deployed on moving buses, and Zigbee wireless sensors are deployed on the bus stations as fixed nodes. When buses stop on the stations, the modules of LTE-M can collect air data from Zigbee wireless sensors directly or the sensors transmit the data to the sink node of the cluster. Then, the sink node feeds a database or either using direct USB or Ethernet. The data collected are sent to the cloud where they are analyzed [26].

Reference Architecture of V-WSN

For an effective distribution of tasks, the subsystems have been devised into the following systems [27]: *Sensing subsystem, distribution subsystem, decision-making subsystem, and the execution subsystem.* These are presented in Fig. 3.3.

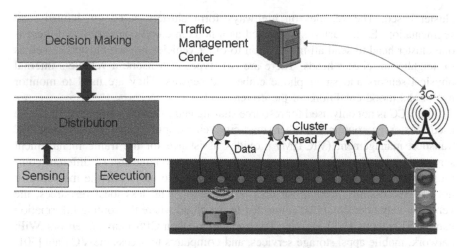

Fig. 3.3 Reference architecture for WSN-based ITS applications (adopted from [27])

- *The sensing subsystem* is composed of all the devices responsible of sensing information relative to road and traffic state.
- *The distribution subsystem* allows exchanging information between different parts of the system.
- *The decision-making subsystem* plans the necessary actions in order to achieve the objectives of the application. It can be a centralized traffic management control (TMC), which is a decision-making center, WSN nodes, or other devices.
- *The execution subsystem* performs actions that foster changes in the traffic flow.

Vehicular Cloud Computing

The new paradigm vehicular could computing (VCC) is based on mobile cloud computing. It has attracted researchers in order to provide more road safety and more traffic applications for smart city. VANET clouds are divided into three architectural frameworks named vehicular clouds (VCs), vehicles using clouds (VuC), and hybrid vehicular clouds (HVC) [28]. We distinguish permanent cloud and temporary cloud for VANETs [29]. The permanent VANET-Cloud presents the conventional cloud while the temporary VANET-Cloud sub-model consists of VANET computing resources and passenger devices. VANET-Cloud groups infrastructure components into three layers: Client layer, communication layer, and cloud layer. *Client layer* consists of general end users; *Communication layer* consists of several communication devices and networks: Internet gateways, wireless networks such as VANETs, WSN, 3G/4G networks, and *cloud layer* (a permanent and temporary cloud) refers to the VANET-Cloud services [29]. We can also notice that another V-CLOUD architecture is divided into three layers: in-car vehicular cyber-physical system, vehicle-to-vehicle network (V2V), and vehicle-to-infrastructure (V2I) network layers. The communication architecture is cluster based. The vehicles on highways form clusters based on defined road segmentation. Each cluster is organized as a node in cloud computing and there is one cluster head to send all information to other vehicles in each cluster as well as to neighboring cluster heads. There are two types of sensors: a vehicle's internal physical sensors and smart phone embedded sensors. They are used to monitor health and mood conditions of the driver.

The VCC is not only used for resource sharing and intensive computing, it can be used for storage, routing and other smart city vehicle applications. For instance, VC transport management (VICTiM) provides assistance for the traffic management services, mechanisms for the storage of the information and use of different communication protocols, which calculate the efficiency to propagate the messages or not. To successfully accomplish data broadcasting with less local resources, the vehicular networks should be connected to the cloud where the routing information using RST equipped with internet. The user can use their GPS, camera, sensors, WiFi network, mobile apps, storage services, and computers to access the VC data [30].

The cloud can also be used in smart parking application where the architecture system consists of three layers: A sensor layer, a communication layer, and an application layer. At the application layer, an information center provides cloud-based services. At the communication layer, various wireless technologies provide connection between the application and the sensor layer, based on the ABC&S communication paradigm [31]. Also dissemination protocol for VANET, such as cloud computing-based message dissemination protocol for VANET (ClouDiV), combines the use of cloud computing infrastructure and cloud structure based on OnBoard computers of vehicles. ClouDiV uses a proactive approach, which is applied by each data center in order to discover fresh and updated routes, and use a reactive approach, which is performed by each vehicle aiming to find the nearest data center [32].

VANET and IoT

A novel concept of a universal network framework including all the existing heterogeneous networks is being strongly experienced and shaped due to the highly growing number of things; IoT is revolutionizing many new research and development areas. Internet of Vehicle (IoV) is one of the revolutions brought by IoT. Communications in IoT can be considered as a hybrid communication because large number of things can communicate with different ways and technologies.

Each vehicular communication of IoV is enabled using a different wireless access technologies (WAT). The communication architecture includes vehicles, RSUs, and a range of communication devices, which makes the architecture more complex. The realization of heterogeneous vehicular network architecture is a challenging task.

The major network elements of IoV network model are the cloud, connections, and the clients. Several networks are integrated into the IoT architecture such as the social networking, which brings the Social Internet of Vehicles (SIoV) paradigm. In this social network, every node establishes social relationships with other objects in an autonomous way. Social relationships can be established among the vehicles in

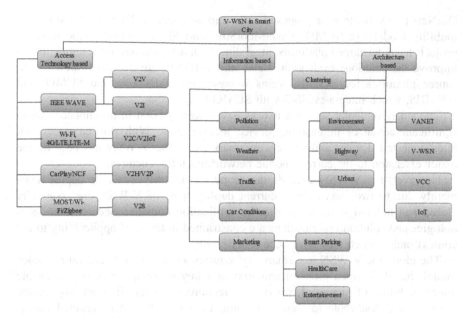

Fig. 3.4 Classification of V-WSN in smart city

order to provide useful and trustworthy information and services to the vehicles. These relationships can be either static between vehicles belongs to the same automaker or dynamic between vehicles comes through V2V communications [33].

The evolution of research and technologies allowed the construction of smart cities and the Internet of things which can deal with challenges of VANET communications and their architectures. We present a classification of VANETs architecture.

In Fig. 3.4, we propose a classification of V-WSN model in smart cities. There are different classification criteria considered in vehicular wireless sensor for smart city model. We distinguish three possible classes, architecture based, information based, and access technology based. Each service designed in V-WSN must support the hybrid network model.

3.7 Testbeds of V-WSN

A coherent smart vehicular wireless sensor framework is required to support heterogeneous domains of smart city and the specific requirements of information and communication technology (ICT).

Existing simulation systems can be used to evaluate the performance of the developed V-WSN protocols in smart city due to the inaccessibility or the high cost of the needed resources. Many researchers use simulators such as ns-2, ns-3, and

OmNet++ to validate their proposed ideas and approaches. They used a vehicular mobility model like SUMO, VanetMobiSim, and SIDRA TRIP. Some research projects have developed platforms integrating both network and traffic simulators to improve the solutions evaluation. Veins and iTETRIS are the most known open source platforms for V-WSN. Veins is based on OMNeT++ and SUMO, and iTETRIS, which integrates NS-3 with SUMO [18].

The smart vehicular sensor networks have recently risen in prominence due to significant advances in enabling device technologies. With this emergence of interconnected devices and services in smart cities, the V-WSN has become the major extension to the current mobile networking infrastructures.

However, the V-WSN exceeds the scope of currently available deployments mainly due to two issues. First, current deployments of V-WSN are essentially closed and tailored solutions to specific application domains. Second, new technologies and solution optimizations are constrained in terms of applicability to the context under which they have been tested.

Therefore, the V-WSN in a smart city requires an agreed architectural reference model, based on open protocol solutions and key enabling services that enable interoperability of deployed smart city resources across different application domains and contribute to their integration to a globally interconnected infrastructure. Some projects target experimental test facility for the research and experimentation of architectures to evaluate scientific research under real-world operational conditions as shown in Table 3.1. In [34], the researchers designed a mobile sensor computing system called CarTel. It is a mobile-embedded computer combined with a set of sensors. CarTel nodes collect, process, deliver, and visualize data from sensors located on mobile units. CarTel has been deployed on six cars, running on a small scale in Boston and Seattle for over a year. It has been used to analyze commute times, analyze metropolitan Wi-Fi deployments, and for automotive diagnostics.

Another testbed for vehicular mesh networking was presented in [35], called HarborNet. It is based on cloud data, and has been deployed in the seaport of Leixões in Portugal. It allows controlling network and collecting data from moving trucks, cranes, two boats, and roadside units. In [36], the researchers built a VC testbed called VCbots. The latter contains major hardware components: robot vehicle on board, mini cloud, remote cloud, and management server. It allows reconfigurable testing environment without any assistance of infrastructure. The common architecture of these testbeds is shown in Fig. 3.5. Table 3.1 presents a comparison between these testbeds.

3.8 Heterogeneous V-WSN Architecture System

To leverage the functionalities of V-WSN networks in smart cities, we propose a new hybrid vehicular architecture model called heterogeneous VANET-WSN architecture. The latter integrates several technologies and concepts such as cloud

Table 3.1 Comparison of some sensor vehicular testbeds

Testbed	Nodes	Communication	Data	Operations	Cases studies
CarTel	Mobile (equipped with GPS)	Wireless (WiFi, Bluetooth) or mobile phone flash memories, or USB keys	Heterogeneous	Traffic monitoring, environmental monitoring, civil infrastructure monitoring, automotive diagnostics, geo-imaging, data muling	Commute time road traffic, traffic hot spot heuristics, wide-area Wifi measurement
HarborNet	Trunks, cranes, tow boats, patrol vessels (all equipped with GPS), and roadside units, connected to the optical fiber backbone of the sea port, and cloud-based data	Wireless (IEEE 802.11p/wave, Wi-Fi interface (IEEE 802.11a/b/g/n) 3G interface)	Heterogeneous	Control of experiments via IEEE 802.11p links and/or the cellular backhaul, delay-tolerant operation, performance measurement (received signal strength indicator (RSSI), packet delivery ratio (PDR) and the bandwidth)	The network coverage offered by the vehicular mesh network and three roadside units, the dynamics of the connections established by trucks via the vehicular mesh network
VCbots	Robot vehicle (VC-truck, VC-van, 1VC-sedan, VCcompact)	Wireless WiFi, LTE, IEEE 802.11p/wave)	Heterogeneous	Group-based message dissemination for road hazard avoidance, platooning, cross coordination	Vehicle cooperation application (implement a platooning algorithm)

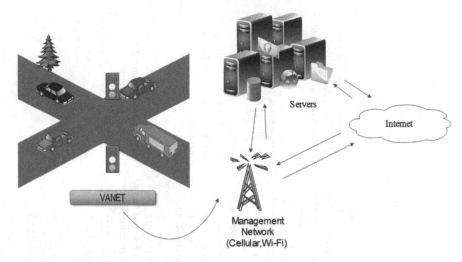

Fig. 3.5 System architecture of hybrid V-WSN framework

computing and IoT, which allows the heterogeneity of communication and expansion of the architecture in the future.

The important features of VANET-WSN architecture are worth being deeply studied. First, the proposed VANET-WSN architecture is designed to be generic compared to the ones described in Sect. 3.6. So, it supports and fits any type of VANET-WSN application. Second, it encompasses different concepts and systems. VANET-WSN allows collaboration and coordination with other systems for different purposes. For instance, when an accident occurs, vehicles share the accident position in social and personal network, so citizen avoids taking the paths that lead to the accident location. Third, it is coherent with the concept of a smart city, as it improves the citizen's quality of life by setting traffic management and allowing emergency services to reach the incident with minimum delay.

This model gathers, on one hand, the advantage of the conventional VANET, and on the other hand, it uses the computing resources of smart city devices, which can be permanent or temporarily available in the area. The temporary devices are vehicles, passengers, taxis, and bus companies. The permanent devices can be sensors deployed on roads or on buildings. This architecture is based on four layers as depicted in Fig. 3.6.

Users Layer

The users are static or mobile and could be considered as computing resource entities, which help the others to perform their service requests. They could be vehicles, passengers, and pedestrians which can establish its request through smart phone, onboard computer, GPS, Wi-Fi, etc.

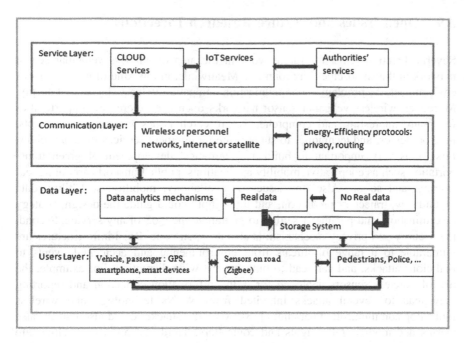

Fig. 3.6 Heterogeneous V-WSN base layer architecture

Data Layer

It applies some mechanisms that analyze and filter data on real and non-real data in order to specify the type of communication in the next layer. Also, it allows storing some important data temporary.

Communication Layer

This layer ensures a connection between users. It consists of several communication devices such as Internet, wireless networks (VANETs, WSN, 3G/4G, 5G), cellular base station, road base station, satellite, private networks, etc. Furthermore, this layer must fix security and routing protocols according to the technology used for communication.

Services Layer

This layer refers to the software and hardware delivered as services. Services proposed to the customer can be divided into three kinds of services: cloud computing services, authorities' services, and IoT services. Cloud computing services as conventional cloud can be software, platform, and infrastructure. Authorities' services can be on-site as police intervention and remotely. IoT services refer to all IoT component services, which can interact with the vehicular wireless sensor network.

3.9   Open Issues and Future Research Directions

Several directions exist for future work in the area of wireless vehicular sensor network in the smart cities environment. Meanwhile, in this kind of heterogeneous environment, the problem of communication compatibility has to be studied deeply. Moreover, wireless vehicular sensor networks open even more new opportunities for many interesting and comprehensive research issues targeting at concepts, methodologies, and techniques to support the requirement services for smart cities. First, it is very important to build a systematical development of green transportation such as cooperative mobility applications, public transport carpooling, car sharing, and so on. Also, the issues of availability, mobility, scalability, data redundancy, trajectory prediction, and throughput could guide the design, strategy determination, and parameter setting to guarantee the QoS of any service. Second, the security and privacy mechanism is also an open issue. Road infrastructures are vulnerable to a range of threats from environmental and accidental events to malicious attacks, and can lead to outages and wide disruption. For example, the use of wireless sensors deployed for traffic information collection and reporting may lead to several attacks inherited from WSNs technology and wireless multi-hop communication paradigm [18]. Also, the attacker could also launch false alarms and modify traffic lights and controllers. Third, the proposed architecture system still lacks an incentive and decision-making mechanism such as a mechanism that encourages users to participate in data sharing and choose the best services. One practical direction is to allow interoperability (of multiple technologies), standards, and latency of network architecture. The framework of vehicular wireless sensor system also produces several promising research directions. It must take into consideration various characteristics, including smart transport strategy and the performance evaluators, infrastructures, legal and regulatory policies and services models. The objectives of such a framework are to identify new challenges, quantify benefits, and evaluate performance [37].

3.10   Conclusion

The hybrid vehicular wireless sensor network in smart city is a recent paradigm that integrates VANET and WSN. It creates smart environments and may offer new services in smart cities. It helps drivers and users to reduce congestion and pollution, prevent accidents and improve road safety in smart cities.

This chapter provides a classification of different VANET-WSN applications for smart city, as well as a taxonomy classification of VANET-WSN network with respect to architecture, information, and access technologies. It presents also relevant tools and testbeds. Also, it proposes an architecture system for heterogeneous vehicular wireless sensor network and discusses open issues for the development of this network. It is expected that some research areas such as: heterogeneous communication, green hybrid VANET-WSN for smart cities, cooperative mobility applications, electric vehicle charging applications carpooling, car sharing, and on-demand taxi applications will draw more attention in the future.

References

1. Khekare GS, Sakhare AV (2013) A smart city framework for intelligent traffic system using VANET. Paper presented at the international multi-conference on automation, computing, communication, control and compressed sensing (iMac4s)
2. Prabhu B, Antony AJ, Balakumar N (2017) A research on smart transportation using sensors and embedded systems. Int J Innovative Res Comput Sci Technol, 5(1). ISSN: 2347-5552
3. Talari S, Shafie-khah M, Siano P, Loia V, Tommasetti A, Catalão JP (2017) A review of smart cities based on the internet of things concept. Energies 10(4):421
4. Germany Telefónica IoT Team (2013) 10 features that the city of the (near) future will have. https://iot.telefonica.com/blog/features-smart-city-future. Accessed 24 Oct 2017
5. Umer T, Rehmani MH, Ding ZG, Kim B-S, Khan SU (2017) IEEE access specialtion editorial: resource management in vehicular adhoc networks: energy management, communication protocol and future applications. IEEE Access 5:7839–7842
6. Schlingensiepen J, Nemtanu F, Mehmood R, McCluskey L (2016) Autonomic transport management systems—enabler for smart cities, personalized medicine, participation and industry grid/industry 4.0. In: Intelligent transportation systems–problems and perspectives. Springer, pp 3–35
7. Gerla M (2012) Vehicular cloud computing. Paper presented at the 11th annual Mediterranean ad hoc networking workshop (Med-Hoc-Net)
8. Delmastro F, Arnaboldi V, Conti M (2016) People-centric computing and communications in smart cities. IEEE Commun Mag 54(7):122–128
9. Anaya JJ, Merdrignac P, Shagdar O, Nashashibi F, Naranjo JE (2014) Vehicle to pedestrian communications for protection of vulnerable road users. Paper presented at the intelligent vehicles symposium proceedings, 2014 IEEE
10. Lin C-C, Deng D-J (2015) Optimal two-lane placement for hybrid VANET-sensor networks. IEEE Trans Ind Electron 62(12):7883–7891
11. Korichi A, Lakas A, Fekair MEA (2016) An efficient QoS-compliant routing scheme for VANET. Paper presented at the 5th international conference on electronic devices, systems and applications (ICEDSA) 2016
12. Ur Rehman S, Khan MA, Zia TA, Zheng L (2013) Vehicular Ad-Hoc networks (VANETs)-an overview and challenges. J Wirel Netw Commun 3(3):29–38
13. Spain Libelium Ecosystem (2013) Smart roads—wireless sensor networks for smart infrastructures: a billion dollar business opportunity. http://www.libelium.com/smart_roads_wsn_smart_infrastructures/. Accessed 23 Oct 2017
14. Menouar H, Guvenc I, Akkaya K, Uluagac AS, Kadri A, Tuncer A (2017) UAV-enabled intelligent transportation systems for the smart city: applications and challenges. IEEE Commun Mag 55(3):22–28
15. Pan G, Qi G, Zhang W, Li S, Wu Z, Yang LT (2013) Trace analysis and mining for smart cities: issues, methods, and applications. IEEE Commun Mag 51(6):120–126
16. Eckhoff D, Zehe D, Ivanchev J, Knoll A (2017) Smart city-to-vehicle—measuring, prediction influencing. ATZelektronik worldw 12(2):60–63
17. Mohanty SP, Choppali U, Kougianos E (2016) Everything you wanted to know about smart cities: the internet of things is the backbone. IEEE Consum Electron Mag 5(3):60–70
18. Djahel S, Doolan R, Muntean G-M, Murphy J (2015) A communications-oriented perspective on traffic management systems for smart cities: challenges and innovative approaches. IEEE Commun Surv Tutor 17(1):125–151

19. Al-Sultan S, Al-Doori MM, Al-Bayatti AH, Zedan H (2014) A comprehensive survey on vehicular ad hoc network. J Netw Comput Appl 37:380–392
20. Mbodila M, Ekabua O (2013) Novel model for vehicle's traffic monitoring using wireless sensor networks between major cities in South Africa. Paper presented at the proceedings of the international conference on wireless networks (ICWN)
21. Sanguesa JA, Fogue M, Garrido P, Martinez FJ, Cano J-C, Calafate CT (2016) A survey and comparative study of broadcast warning message dissemination schemes for VANETs. Mob Inf Syst 2016:1–18
22. Mbodila M, Obeten E, Bassey I (2015) Implementation of novel vehicles' traffic monitoring using wireless sensor network in South Africa. Paper presented at the IEEE international conference on communication software and networks (ICCSN)
23. Qin H, Li Z, Wang Y, Lu X, Zhang W, Wang G (2010) An integrated network of roadside sensors and vehicles for driving safety: concept, design and experiments. Paper presented at the IEEE international conference on pervasive computing and communications (PerCom)
24. Xia R, Ye C, Zhang D (2010) Vehicle to vehicle and roadside sensor communication for intelligent navigation. Paper presented at the 6th international conference on wireless communications networking and mobile computing (WiCOM)
25. Tripp Barba C, Ornelas Aguirre K, Aguilar Igartua M (2010) Performance evaluation of a hybrid sensor and vehicular network to improve road safety. Paper presented at the proceedings of the 7th ACM workshop on performance evaluation of wireless ad hoc, sensor, and ubiquitous networks
26. Jamil MS, Jamil MA, Mazhar A, Ikram A, Ahmed A, Munawar U (2015) Smart environment monitoring system by employing wireless sensor networks on vehicles for pollution free smart cities. Proc Eng 107:480–484
27. Losilla F, Garcia-Sanchez A-J, Garcia-Sanchez F, Garcia-Haro J, Haas ZJ (2011) A comprehensive approach to WSN-based ITS applications: a survey. Sensors 11(11): 10220–10265
28. Hussain R, Son J, Eun H, Kim S, Oh H (2012) Rethinking vehicular communications: merging VANET with cloud computing. Paper presented at the IEEE 4th international conference on cloud computing technology and science (CloudCom)
29. Bitam S, Mellouk A, Zeadally S (2015) VANET-cloud: a generic cloud computing model for vehicular ad hoc networks. IEEE Wirel Commun 22(1):96–102
30. Kumar NA, Raj EGDP (2015) VCS-RSCBAODV: vehicular cloud storage concepts for RSCBAODV protocol to reduce connection breakage in VANET. Adv Comput Sci Int J 4 (3):147–153
31. Ji Z, Ganchev I, O'Droma M, Zhao L, Zhang X (2014) A cloud-based car parking middleware for IoT-based smart cities: design and implementation. Sensors 14(12):22372–22393
32. Bitam S, Mellouk A (2015) Cloud computing-based message dissemination protocol for vehicular ad hoc networks. Paper presented at the international conference on wired/wireless internet communication
33. Nitti M, Girau R, Floris A, Atzori L (2014) On adding the social dimension to the internet of vehicles: friendship and middleware. Paper presented at the IEEE international Black Sea conference on communications and networking (BlackSeaCom)
34. Hull B, Bychkovsky V, Zhang Y, Chen K, Goraczko M, Miu A et al (2006) CarTel: a distributed mobile sensor computing system. Paper presented at the proceedings of the 4th international conference on embedded networked sensor systems
35. Ameixieira C, Cardote A, Neves F, Meireles R, Sargento S, Coelho L, Costa R (2014) Harbornet: a real-world testbed for vehicular networks. IEEE Commun Mag 52(9):108–114
36. Lu D, Li Z, Huang D, Lu X, Deng Y, Chowdhary A, Li B (2016) VC-bots: a vehicular cloud computing testbed with mobile robots. Paper presented at the proceedings of the first international workshop on internet of vehicles and vehicles of internet
37. Khatoun R, Zeadally S (2016) Smart cities: concepts, architectures, research opportunities. Commun ACM 59(8):46–57

Chapter 4
Pricing Mechanisms for Energy Management in Smart Cities

Anulipt Chandan, Vidyasagar Potdar and Champa Nandi

Abstract The power supply network, Smart Grid, is one of the most critical infrastructures which help to realize the vision of Smart Cities. Smart Grids can provide a reliable and quality power supply with high efficiency. However, the demand for electricity fluctuates throughout the day, and this variable demand creates power instability leading to an unreliable power supply. The inherent difficulties can be addressed to a certain extent with demand-side management (DSM) that can play a vital role in managing the demand in Smart Grids and Microgrids, by implementing dynamic pricing using Smart Meters. This chapter reviews relevant challenges and recent developments in the area of dynamic electricity pricing by investigating the following pricing mechanisms: Time-of-Use Pricing, Real-Time Pricing, Critical Peak Pricing, Day-Ahead Pricing, Cost Reflective Pricing, Seasonal Pricing, and Peak Time Rebate Pricing. We also discuss four real-world case studies of different pricing mechanisms adopted in various parts of the world. This chapter concludes with suggestions for future research opportunities in this field.

Keywords Smart Grids · Renewable energy sources · Energy measurement
Energy management · Demand-side management · Energy conservation
Load management · Energy efficiency · Energy storage · Distributed energy
resources · Appliance scheduling

A. Chandan
National Institute of Technology, Agartala, India

V. Potdar (✉)
School of Information Systems, Curtin University, Perth, Australia
e-mail: Vidyasagar.Potdar@cbs.curtin.edu.au

C. Nandi
Tripura University, Agartala, India

© Springer International Publishing AG, part of Springer Nature 2018   71
Z. Mahmood (ed.), *Smart Cities*, Computer Communications and Networks,
https://doi.org/10.1007/978-3-319-76669-0_4

4.1 Introduction

The increasing demand for electricity and limited fossil fuels has given rise to
Demand Response (DR)-based electricity markets via Smart Grids. By means of
DR, customers can manage or control their demand according to the pricing signals
received from the utility company. Alternative sources of electrical energy generation such as wind, solar, geothermal, biogas, etc., are contributing to meet the
growing demand. However, these sources are less reliable, which is a major issue
[1–3]. Hence, electricity generation is not enough to meet the energy demand,
which creates a gap between demand and supply. One way to address this challenge
is to increase the generation capacity of existing power plants, but this requires a
great deal of capital investment and also affects the environment. The other option
is to optimize the existing capacity to reduce the gap, thereby fulfilling the demands
of all users.

With advancements in technology, improvement in the quality of life, rapid
economic growth and industrialization, the demand for electricity has increased
significantly. According to the World Energy Council report [4], the consumption
of electrical energy will increase to 20% in 2030, up from 18% in 2014. The
increasing demand can be met by either increasing production or demand-side
management (DSM). There are various issues which need to be managed effectively
in order to reduce the gap between demand and supply. One of these issues is the
peak-to-average load ratio. DR is an important tool for reducing the
peak-to-average load ratio. DR can be realized via the DSM technique [5, 6] that
can improve the power grid reliability by dynamically changing electricity consumption or rescheduling it with the implementation of dynamic tariffs [7]. Hence,
DSM plays a vital role in realizing the grand vision of interconnected smart cities
and Smart Grids.

In the literature, peak load management (or reducing the peak-to-average load
ratio) is the most sought-after objective in demand response programs. The demand
for electrical energy during peak periods can be met by establishing new generating
stations, energy storage, or by demand response. However, setting up a new conventional power generating station just to meet the peak demand is not a practical
solution because it is expensive and will be used only during peak demand periods.
Further, it is not environmentally friendly as it produces harmful greenhouse gases.
Alternative power generating sources such as wind, solar, etc., can be used to meet
the power demand during peak periods, but they are not reliable as their generation
can vary according to environmental conditions, weather, geographical location,
etc. Hence, DR becomes an important method of reducing the peak-to-average load
ratio and it can be achieved by means of dynamic pricing.

Dynamic pricing of electricity is one of the most valuable tools for DSM as
customers have the opportunity to participate in day-to-day operations of the
electricity grid by shifting their load during off-peak periods in response to the
dynamic tariff of electrical energy like Time-of-Use [8, 9] and other incentive-based
pricing strategies such as Real-Time Pricing, Critical Peak Pricing, Day-Ahead

Pricing, Seasonal Pricing [10], Cost Reflective Pricing [11], and Peak Time Rebate [12, 13]. In the traditional grid, it was difficult to apply various dynamic pricing strategies as it was not possible to track the consumption of electrical energy at different periods; however, with the adoption of smart meters in Smart Grids, it can now be easily and reliably achieved.

Several studies in the literature have examined DSM [14, 15], but none of them have comprehensively considered the challenges associated with different pricing strategies. This chapter examines various challenges and reviews the recent developments in the area of dynamic electricity pricing. The following pricing mechanisms are investigated in detail—Time-of-Use Pricing, Real-Time Pricing, Critical Peak Pricing, Day-Ahead Pricing, Cost Reflective Pricing, Seasonal Pricing, and Peak Time Rebate Pricing. Further, we also include four real-world case studies of dynamic pricing mechanisms adopted in various parts of the world. This chapter concludes with suggestions for future research directions in this field.

4.2 History of Power Grids

The earliest electrical network was simple and localized consisting of few generating units and a distribution network. Thomas Edison designed the first electrical network in New York City on Pearl Street in 1882. It had a 100-V generator with a few hundred lamps in the neighborhood [16]. At that time, the demand for electricity was increasing rapidly and to fulfill this demand, new generation capacity was necessary, along with long-distance transmission and distribution capability. To meet this demand, investment in new infrastructure began which led to the larger and more complex electrical networks that we see today. Managing this complexity became a new challenge and the concept of grid evolved to address this issue. The grid comprised three entities namely: electricity generation, electricity transmission, and electricity distribution.

The power industries which began as regulated industries had the following characteristics: monopolistic franchise, obligation to serve, regulation oversight, least cost operation, regulated rates, and assumed returns [17]. In such a regulated market structure, the generation, transmission, and distribution of electricity were all controlled by a single entity [18].

During the 90s, the power industries faced significantly high demand that led to increased operational efficiency brought about by companies changing their inefficient systems and irrational tariff policies [19]. This resulted in the deregulation of the power industry which led to the establishment of the following entities: GenCo (generating company), TransCo (transmission company), DisCo (distribution company), ResCo (retail energy service company), and ISO (independent system operators) [20]. Deregulation of the power industry opened up the power sector and introduced competition in the electrical industry. One of the major outcomes of deregulation was increased reliability and secure operation of the power grid [21].

Increased competition, as a result of deregulation, resulted in unprecedented demands for electrical power, which required optimal utilization of the available resources. Hence, power companies began implementing SCADA systems (Supervisory Control and Data Acquisition) which provided some control but still lacked real-time control of the distribution network [22].

In a traditional hierarchical grid, the power plants are positioned at the top of the hierarchy and the consumers toward the bottom, and the flow of information is unidirectional. This system has several drawbacks such as: (1) voltage and frequency instability due to dynamic nature of the load, (2) difficulties in demand-side management, (3) integration of distributed generation is not possible [23], (4) electricity consumption occurs at the same time as generation, and (5) storage of electricity is expensive, so unused electricity is wasted.

To address these challenges, a real-time infrastructure is required to monitor and control the system. To obtain a complete and efficient control of the overall system, additional feedback is required from the consumer side, which makes the real-time monitoring of the distribution network very important. Advancement in information and computing technology makes it possible for the utility to receive these real-time inputs to the grid [24]. This is a realization of Smart Grid. A future grid or Smart Grid is a grid that is integrated with information and communication technology (ICT) with advanced dynamic control [25]. Smart Grids are described in the following section.

4.3 Traditional Grids to Smart Grids

In 1997, Vu et al. [24] introduced the term *Smart Grid* for the first time. They referred to a Self-Managing and Reliable Transmission Grid as Smart Grid. However, it was not until the 2003 North East blackout in the USA that it became popular. Massoud Amin in 2004 also referred to the term Smart Grid [26].

Modernization of the existing power grid is referred to as Smart Grid. Smart Grids are built on top of the existing grid infrastructure by effectively utilizing information technology, internet of things (IoT) and smart algorithms for efficiently managing components like sensors, relay, energy management system (EMS), SVC (Static Var Compansator), Supervisory Control and Data Acquisition (SCADA), etc.

As mentioned earlier, the traditional grids have the following characteristics: (1) they are unidirectional, meaning that power flows only from one end to the other; (2) the generation happens centrally, (3) consumers are required to pay fixed tariffs, and (4) consumers rely on a traditional electricity meter, which shows only the total amount of energy consumed, but does not provide a breakdown of when the consumption occurred. Smart Grids address these limitations by means of three innovations:

- Smart Grids modernize existing power systems through an advanced control system, for example installing advanced sensors like PMU (phasor measurement unit) to monitor network parameters in real time, facilitate remote monitoring of the entire network, and use self-healing designs [27]
- Smart Grids enable end users to monitor and control their daily consumption and the associated costs, thereby giving some degree of autonomy in energy management [12]
- Smart Grids enable the integration of distributed energy resources (DER) in the existing grid effectively, thereby increasing the overall generation capacity and reliability of the whole power system [27].

The basic idea behind the Smart Grid is a two-way digital communication and advanced sensor network which creates an adaptive feedback loop [22]. In a traditional grid, the flow of information is unidirectional; whereas in the Smart Grid, it is bidirectional between the utilities and smart meters, which is termed "Advanced Metering Infrastructure (AMI)" [28]. With the help of smart meters, utilities can inform the end consumer about tariffs, thereby empowering the latter to have control of their overall consumption. Whereas from the utility perspective, analyzing the data gathered from smart meters helps to better manage the demand. However, this should be done in a trustworthy environment to protect consumer privacy [23]. Consumers' privacy, cybersecurity, and the price of smart meters are just some of the issues which need to be addressed in order to make Smart Grid more resilient and reliable [29].

Smart Grids have evolved over time. The *first generation* of Smart Grid used computational intelligence such as fuzzy logic and neural networks in the power system, adopting a neural network approach for security assessment and the development of automated meters [30]. The *second generation* of Smart Grid focused on global control of the grid, stability of the system, self-healing, and dynamic pricing [30]. The *third generation* focused on optimal power flow which ensured global optimization of the grid by applying various optimization techniques such as approximate dynamic programming, dynamic stochastic optimization [30]. The *fourth generation* of Smart Grid is concerned with sustainable development, better demand response management with renewable energy source integration in the grid, including more storage in the grid using plug-in hybrid vehicles (PHEV) integration, battery storage, and mobile/distributed generation using PHEVs [27].

The future of smart distribution grid is the Microgrid, which is regarded as a small-scale energy zone with small-scale energy resources such as photovoltaic cells (PV), fuel cells, wind turbines, and battery storage [31]. The operation of a Microgrid can be either standalone or connected to the grid [32]. However, there are various challenges to implementing Microgrid in reality; some are technical (such as power quality, reliability, overall network efficiency, and interconnection of network [33]) and others are nontechnical (such as demand response management, prosumer management, education about the technology, and consumer privacy [29]). Microgrids play an important role in shaping the future energy grids with renewable sources that can meet the local demand as well as supply extra power to other Microgrids. Besides, Microgrid networks provide a more reliable power supply to the consumer in a smart city.

4.4 Smart Grids and the Vision of Smart Cities

The World Urbanization Prospects report published in 2014 stated that an additional 2.5 billion people will become part of the urban population by 2050, 90% of whom will be in Africa and Asia. It further states that the world's urban population will rise to 66% by 2050 [34], which will put a significant load on cities' existing infrastructure, thereby impacting on future sustainable development [35, 36]. The infrastructure of cities will need to be modified in order to sustain the pressure of an ever-increasing population. Cities need to be remodeled into smart cities where people can enjoy modern facilities with ease.

In a smart city, the basic civic infrastructure needs to be managed more effectively and in a streamlined manner. This includes the management of water, energy, transport, and health services. The underlying objective is to ensure that cities of the future do not compromise the environment as a result of socioeconomic progress. Information and communication technology is the backbone of the cities of the future.

The energy demands of a smart city are high because most modern utilities such as induction cooktops, air conditioners, air purifiers, heaters, etc., run on electricity. Infrastructures including public communication networks and healthcare services also depend on electricity. Hence, the energy infrastructure is one of the most important and critical urban infrastructures to support the realization of a sustainable smart city. Therefore, the Smart Grid is appropriate for the power infrastructure of smart cities.

A Smart Grid allows a smart city to exploit local power generation to meet the immediate needs of the city and manage the load in such a manner that the critical load required for hospitals, fire stations, police, and the like will not be affected during an outage and, if affected, the self-healing nature of the Smart Grid will restore the supply very quickly. Smart Grids also enable smart cities to manage the total load and local renewable energy source more efficiently. They help smart cities to achieve ambitious environmental goals. The smart metering infrastructure of Smart Grids enables smart cities to meet power demands and harness more local energy with net metering very easily and effectively. Hence, Smart Grids are one of the fundamental infrastructures necessary to realize a dream of smart cities.

As already mentioned, smart cities need huge amounts of electrical energy, and therefore require demand-side management. By means of dynamic pricing methods, the Smart Grid facilitates demand-side management. Several dynamic pricing methods are proposed in the literature, which will be discussed in the next section.

4.5 Dynamic Pricing Mechanisms

Many experimental and empirical studies have been conducted to discover the effect of peak load pricing to reduce peak load [37]. But only a handful of program types have been developed and only a few utilities really use demand response (DR) as a day-to-day tool in grid and energy management due to engineering complexity, capital investment, etc. [38].

DR programs are designed to flatten the load profile of the consumer either by reducing consumption during peak hours or by shifting the load to off-peak times. Demand response can be either dispatchable or non-dispatchable [14]. Dispatchable DR programs allow the utility to control the user load during peak times, whereas non-dispatchable DR programs provide incentives or time-varying pricing schemes to reduce the load. Time-varying pricing or dynamic pricing is a simple and effective mechanism for demand response.

Dynamic pricing is a time-varying electricity pricing mechanism designed to provide an economic incentive for consumers to participate in demand management via "demand participation" or "demand response". It is used as an economic tool that manages demand by informing the consumer about the electricity price in the near future. Customers can use this information to modify their load and participate in demand response [29]. One of the most important aspects of demand response is the two-way communication between the utility and the consumer, which is made possible by the Smart Grid infrastructure.

Customers can actively participate in the operation of the grid. They can participate in the DR programs, consider the information they receive about the electricity price, and make wise decisions regarding their daily electricity consumption [8]. A non-dispatchable demand response program using dynamic pricing method can be easily implemented in the Smart Grid network.

The various dynamic pricing schemes which are available for demand response are Time-of-Use (TOU), Real-Time Pricing (RTP), Critical Peak Pricing (CPP), Day-Ahead Pricing [14, 29, 39]. These are now discussed in the subsequent sections.

4.5.1 Time-of-Use (TOU) Method

The TOU pricing scheme is based on the variation in the cost of electricity depending upon the time of use. For instance, during peak time usage, tariffs are higher, and are lower during off-peak times. However, with a flat rate tariff, a set rate is charged for the use of electricity regardless of the time of day. With TOU pricing, a different rate is fixed for different time slots over a day. Ideally, TOU should shift the load from peak time to off-peak time. The TOU time-varying scheme is generally preferred by the retail market because of its simple structure

[8]. However, despite its simple structure, utilities face several challenges when implementing it in a real system. These challenges are discussed below.

Challenges

The TOU pricing method is one of the most important economic methods employed in DR (demand response) programs. This pricing scheme is a static time-varying pricing scheme, which is easier and cheaper to implement by the utility. It looks like a very simple strategy for DR but there are various difficulties which are associated with it and need to be addressed before implementing it in the retail energy market. The main difficulty faced by utilities is the existing traditional meter, which is unable to capture energy consumption data at specific times. So, it is difficult to implement this scheme in a system that still has traditional meters. If these were replaced with smart energy meters, utilities could easily apply the TOU tariff [40]. However, these replacements are costly for the utility, and customers have concerns regarding privacy. Another challenge faced by utilities is the design of TOU pricing, which includes a subset of challenges such as designing TOU with uncertainties in generation and demand, designing under different market structures or designing with localized generation integrated into the grid. Different market structures need different TOU designs [8]. In other words, a specific market structure requires a specific design. For instance, in some places, the need for a heating system is considered when designing a TOU scheme, whereas in other places, a heating system is not required due to the different climatic condition. Another challenge is the establishment of an optimal pricing strategy, which will maximize the utilities' profits as well as offer monetary and social benefits to consumers. Another subset of TOU design challenges, which is found in Smart Grids, is the presence of several distributed energy resources (DER). These energy sources play a vital role in shaping the future source of clean energy. So, when designing a TOU tariff scheme, these sources should be considered in order to make the TOU pricing more effective. A summary of the aforementioned challenges is presented in Table 4.1. Recently, several researchers have proposed various means of overcoming these challenges. These recent developments are covered in the following section.

Recent Developments

As discussed in the previous section, there are various challenges, which impede the smooth implementation of TOU pricing. Researchers around the world have proposed various methods for overcoming these challenges.

The design of a TOU scheme plays a vital role in the success of TOU pricing in the retail market. Ferreira et al. [8] designed a TOU tariff using stochastic optimization, considering uncertainty in price fluctuations of electricity demand, with quadratic constraints. The proposed approach showed increment in social welfare and improvement in load factor. Celebi and Fuller [41] examined TOU pricing under different marketing structures and proposed a multifirm, multi-period equilibrium model to forecast future TOU rates. In designing their model, the researchers used the variational inequality (VI) problem approach. The advantage of

Table 4.1 Challenges and recent developments in TOU pricing

Challenges	Designing with uncertainties in generation and demand [7]
	Designing under different market structures [37]
	Designing with localized generation integration in grid [43]
	An optimal pricing strategy to maximize benefits for consumers and utility [38]
	The inclusion of distributed sources in tariff design [41]
Recent developments	Quadratic programming and stochastic optimization techniques used to design tariff with uncertainties in demand and generation [7]
	A multifirm, multi-period equilibrium model to forecast future TOU prices [37]
	A game theory approach used to find the optimal TOU pricing [38]
	A multi-agent simulation system proposed to analyze the effect of the TOU pricing on the behavior of large customers [39]
	A DR algorithm with photovoltaic generation proposed which requires minimal sensors, and does not require forecasting of solar resources [43]

this approach, compared with the complementarity approach, is the type of variable required for the solution. The VI approach requires only primal variables, whereas the complementarity problem approach requires both primal and dual variables. Their findings showed that the customer benefits from TOU pricing compared to the flat rate under a different market structure. Yang et al. [42] used the game theoretic approach to find the optimal TOU pricing. They proposed multi-stage game models between utility companies and consumers, whereby the utilities seek to maximize their profit and the consumers seek cost reductions and an uninterrupted power supply. They studied the responses of consumers to the TOU pricing scheme. Their studies showed that in the residential sector, the consumers shift their load from peak time to off-peak times. Commercial customers were not very responsive during office hours, that is, their consumption did not decrease significantly. Of the three sectors—residential, commercial, and industrial—the industrial customers were more flexible in changing their load according to the TOU rate. Ali et al. [43] proposed a price-based demand response scheme with a two-part tariff based on time-of-use (TOU) pricing within a Microgrid. They formulated the load scheduling problem in a Microgrid as a combinatorial optimization problem. In this two-part tariff, one part concerns the TOU pricing and the other part penalizes customers if they exceeded the specified maximum demand limit. This is more effective in reducing the total demand. The TOU pricing strategy also assists utilities with the management of profit and risk.

After designing a TOU, the effectiveness of TOU pricing needs to be determined with different scenarios. Jia-hai [44] designed a multi-agent simulation system to analyze the effectiveness of the TOU pricing on the behavior of large customers and the change on system load simultaneously. They found that, if the price difference between the flat rate and the TOU rate was less than 15%, then customers did not shift their load; however, if the price difference was between 15 and 45%, then the customers were likely to change their load linearly with the price difference, and if the difference is more than 45%, then again customers were unresponsive to price. Consumers responded to the price fluctuation by decreasing their load if there was a significant difference in cost. However, this simulation model was limited to a small number of large customers. Pallonetto et al. [45] developed a rule-based algorithm for a TOU tariff for a residential building with the following objectives: (1) minimize energy consumption, (2) minimize carbon emissions, and (3) maximize monetary benefit to the consumer in a Smart Grid with a renewable energy source. They studied two different cases: thermal energy storage and zonal temperature control. Their analysis showed an annual reduction of consumer electricity consumption by up to 15.9%, carbon emission reduction by 27%, and a greater utilization of power generated by a renewable energy source at grid scale. The TOU pricing scheme can help to reduce harmful greenhouse gases, thereby protecting the environment. Optimal utilization of a renewable energy source can be achieved through the TOU scheme.

In the Smart Grid, the presence of DER has an effect on TOU pricing and, therefore, on demand response because of the bidirectional flow of energy and net metering system. Leger et al. [46] formulated a DR algorithm with photovoltaic generation for the Smart Grid based on net energy flow shown in a smart meter. This DR approach is interesting because it requires minimal sensors, does not require the forecasting of solar resources, and requires minimum input from the user side which leads to the automated implementation of demand response using TOU pricing. Johnson et al. [47] analyzed the performance of bifacial PV (photovoltaic) array energy output during summer. They analyzed the power output from a PV array by orienting it in different directions. Then the total energy cost was analyzed according to two different rates: TOU and flat rate tariff. They performed an experiment during summer by keeping the PV array facing west, and determined whether or not customers could benefit from the reorientation of the PV array. With the TOU pricing scheme, the cost of energy is high during the afternoon in summer. If the reorientation of PV panels can generate more power during this period, then consumers can benefit financially as they use less energy from the grid. However, the findings indicated that the reorientation of the array did not result in any significant cost savings.

The acceptance of the TOU by residential consumers depends upon how it will affect them. Torriti [48] studied the impact of TOU in the residential sector. He studied the peak shifting in residential areas in Northern Italy. His study showed that a significant level of load shifting takes place for morning peaks, but issues regarding evening peaks were not resolved. His studies also indicated that the average consumption of energy per user increased after the implementation of TOU pricing. Average consumption increased but payments made by consumers decreased due to the lower tariff during off-peak periods when more energy was used. Dehnavi and Abdi [49] suggested a DR program that combined dynamic economic dispatch with TOU pricing. In economic load dispatch, the generation unit is scheduled optimally to reduce the fuel cost subjected to constraints. They integrated both the problem of economic load dispatch and the design of TOU pricing into a single optimization problem and used the meta-heuristic imperialist competitive algorithm to find the optimal solution. Their study showed that there was a reduction in fuel cost after the application of TOU pricing; moreover, network reliability was improved, and customers' electricity bills were reduced.

Torriti [50] used a stochastic model to analyze the TOU dataset of Trento in Northern Italy. His analysis showed that there is an unstable relationship between the consumption of energy and TOU pricing, and that future consumption can be predicted by weather conditions and active occupancy. This study had significant implications for the TOU pricing scheme in Italy as it was based on nonvoluntary participation, thereby demonstrating the consequence of large-scale implementation of the TOU tariff. The new tariff scheme needs to be communicated effectively to end users so that they can actively participate in demand response. The new tariff scheme needs to be communicated via a number of channels including the new tariff being printed on the bill, mobile phones, television advertisements, radio, and newspapers.

TOU pricing is the first demand response price incentive program to be implemented in various countries worldwide. Numerous researchers have proposed several techniques such as quadratic programming, stochastic optimization, combinatorial optimization, MILP, etc., to address the problems faced by utilities when implementing TOU pricing. A summary of recent developments is presented in Table 4.1.

4.5.2   Real-Time Pricing (RTP) Method

RTP is a dynamic pricing scheme which follows the spot price of electricity in the wholesale market. The wholesale market is a power market, where the electricity is sold for re-sale purpose and a uniform biding strategy is used to set the spot price (real time) of electricity. Based on the spot price in the wholesale market, the hourly rate of RTP for retail consumers is fixed by the utility [51]. In this pricing method, the price signal is released a day ahead or an hour ahead. It has been one of the most researched topics in dynamic pricing in recent times as the smart metering infrastructure has been rolled out in several countries around the world [3, 52–54]. It has also attracted numerous researchers globally who have attempted to find effective and efficient methods for the practical implementation of RTP schemes.

RTP is different from TOU (time of use) in several ways. TOU is a predefined tariff block pricing strategy; that is, the cost of energy varies from time to time during a whole day, and this variation is announced by the retailer before the billing cycle. However, with RTP, the tariff is announced by the retailer a day or an hour before. The fixed tariff structure of TOU over a long period makes it static in nature, but the RTP changes after an hour or a day which makes it a dynamic scheme. Due to the static nature of TOU, it is not very effective in addressing the peak load problems [39]. On the other hand, the RTP is dynamic in nature and it can adjust the tariff within a short period of time. Hence, it is more effective in dealing with peak load reduction. Since the RTP is linked to the wholesale price, it is able to reflect fluctuations in the wholesale market price, which cannot be done by the TOU. Evidently then, the RTP has several advantages over the TOU pricing, but there are also various challenges, which make difficult to implement it in reality. The challenges associated with RTP are discussed below.

Challenges

There are several issues related to RTP implementation and its impact on the consumers and the utility, which should be carefully considered before it is implemented. One of the most important of these is the design of the RTP scheme itself. RTP schemes should be designed in such a way that they offer a win–win situation for both consumer and utility. Demand profile and consumer satisfaction are important factors which need to be considered when designing an RTP tariff structure, because consumers have to change their consumption behavior according to the pricing signal they receive from the utility company on a daily or hourly basis. The utility company needs to communicate the tariff to the end consumer in real time via different communication media. There are several technologies available that can facilitate this communication including an in-home display unit, smart meters, e-mail, SMS, energy orbs (globes that light up green, yellow or red) which show a different colored light to indicate peak, medium peak, off-peak hours, etc. However, it is likely that the consumer will not be available to make a decision when a price signal arrives (e.g., consumer is away from a computer/mobile device or in a meeting for instance). This scenario has two adverse impacts: first, the consumer may have to pay more if the pricing signal is high and second, the utility company cannot reduce the peak demand even with RTP implementation. This can be a challenging task for both the consumers and the utility. Hence, consumers may be reluctant to shift to RTP schemes. There is also a possibility that they may change utility providers if they find that RTP is inconvenient. Hence, RTP schemes need to be designed so that they not only benefit the consumer, but also motivate them to be part of a new paradigm. One such approach is to implement automated load management systems that can be programmed to react to RTP signals in real time according to customer preferences in order to derive the maximum benefit from RTP and to address some of the other issues. However, designing an effective automated load controller is a challenge in itself because each household appliance needs to communicate with the controller for effective control. Other than design challenges, the economic impact on the consumer and the utility needs to be thoroughly analyzed, and the RTP's social impact on the consumer needs to be determined. Other than the aforementioned issues, several other critical challenges need to be overcome such as the implementation of RTP without demand-side management, and price forecasting that includes models for short-term and long-term forecasting, i.e., daily versus hourly forecasting. Variation in pricing poses another problem: understanding how consumers respond to pricing structures, and whether they accept or ignore the pricing signals. If the customers ignore the pricing signals (i.e., they consume power even if the price signal is considered high by the utility company), what can be done to manage peak

Table 4.2 Challenges and recent developments in RTP pricing

Challenges	Designing RTP based on forecasted spot price of the wholesale market [52]
	Designing based on analysis of real-time data [54]
	Designing with load uncertainty at consumer end [55]
	Analysis of the economic impact on consumer without demand-side management [61]
	An optimal pricing strategy to maximize utility profit [58]
Recent developments	A least-square support vector machine (LS-SVM) method used to forecast spot price of the wholesale market [52]
	A new real-time pricing scheme proposed which was based on price components with instantaneous data analysis [54]
	An iterative stochastic optimization approach to design an RTP which includes load uncertainty at the consumer end [55]
	A versatile convex programming demand response optimization for automatic load management of various types of loads in the smart home [57]
	A non-cooperative game among the consumer and search for the unique equilibrium in demand response for demand-side management [59]

demand? In this situation, real-time smart meter data can be analyzed to design real-time and adaptable pricing structures to ensure the effective management of peak demand. Alternatively, penalty schemes can be explored as a mechanism to manage peak demand. Consumer privacy is an issue related to smart meters because the energy use pattern and smart meter data can be hacked and may be used by an unauthorized person for unlawful activities. All these issues need to be addressed in order to effectively implement the RTP. A summary of the various challenges associated with RTP is presented in Table 4.2.

Recent Developments

The design of an RTP scheme is important for both the consumer and the utility. Much research has been conducted in recent times to make it more realistic to implement RTP schemes on a large scale by addressing some of the abovementioned challenges. Numerous researchers have proposed several techniques to address these problems using various methods such as convex optimization, least-square support vector machines, genetic algorithm, stochastic optimization, etc., and these are briefly articulated below.

Real-time price forecasting: Real-time price (RTP) forecasting is a challenging task as there are so many variables that need to be considered when designing a RTP forecasting model. For example, a statistical model for forecasting real-time retail prices would require inputs such as hourly or daily wholesale market prices, weather conditions, local generation availability, renewable generation capacity, customer demand profile, etc. Furthermore, such models can be tailored for short-term or long-term forecasting. Oldewurtel et al. [55] applied least-square support vector machines (LS-SVM) for regression to compute short-term tariff forecasts for the wholesale market based on past spot price and grid load levels. This price forecast data have been used to design an RTP for retail customers, which reflects the wholesale price. Their studies showed that within the proposed tariff regime, the peak electricity demand of buildings can be significantly reduced.

Determine price based on consumer responsiveness to price: Kim and Giannakis [53] designed a strategy to determine RTP pricing based on consumer responsiveness to price, using an online convex optimization framework to find the real-time pricing structure with two feedback structures: (1) partial information (i.e., load data) that is known to the utility and (2) full information (i.e., aggregate load and price fluctuations) that is known to the utility.

Reducing the peak-to-average ratio: Reducing the peak to average ratio is an important factor that needs to be considered when designing an RTP scheme. Qian et al. [56] proposed a two-stage optimization technique to design an RTP scheme for the Smart Grid to reduce the peak-to-average ratio. On the one hand, users react to price to maximize their financial benefit; on the other hand, utilities try to formulate an RTP with forecasted user reaction to maximize their profits. The researchers' simulation result showed that the proposed algorithm can effectively reduce the energy usages peak.

Real-time data analysis for price determination: Vivekananthan et al. [57] proposed a new real-time pricing scheme which was based on price components with instantaneous data analysis and after the data has been analyzed in real time, the information about price and the appropriate load adjustment is sent through a smart meter to an in-home unit display. With this information, consumers can easily identify their critical load for possible adjustment.

Impact on price due to uncertainty: In practice, users' responsiveness to price is uncertain particularly when they have been equipped with an automated energy consumption scheduling (ECS) device. Samadi et al. [58] designed two real-time pricing algorithms based on finite-difference and simultaneous perturbation methods using an iterative stochastic optimization approach which includes the load uncertainty at the consumer end. In the presence of large consumers, these algorithms converge much faster because they do not involve direct user interaction. This study showed that the proposed algorithm can reduce the peak-to-average ratio.

Energy management controller: The energy consumption pattern of residential area varies considerably. For future smart cities, each home must be equipped with an energy management controller.

Load Management: Load management is one of the crucial aspects of the RTP pricing scheme as it fluctuates hourly or daily. Hence, there is a need for load management which has to be done with the help of a smart control device because manual load management in the RTP scheme is very difficult. A smart meter makes it easier to communicate with the load end and therefore the load management in houses is easier in smart cities.

Load Management Strategy: In [59], a load management strategy is proposed under a Smart Grid paradigm. This strategy is based on RTP pricing and the use of different household appliances and electric vehicles in a typical smart house. With the help of a smart meter, the consumer can manage the load which can include the charging of electric vehicles, washing machine use, etc. Under the RTP scheme, the proposed model enabled users to reduce their electricity bill by 8–22% for a typical summer day. Hence, load management enables consumers to reduce their electricity bill and helps the utility with its demand response.

Types of loads and Automatic Load Management: Tsui and Chan [60] categorizedvarious types of loads in a smart home like schedule load (which need to be switched on and off at a particular time to save energy), battery-assisted load, and model-based load. The authors formulated a versatile convex programming for demand-response optimization of automatic load management of various types of loads in a smart home. From the perspective of the utility, the consumers' response is important while designing the tariff structure.

Combined Load Management for Community-based RTP: In [52], the author proposed a new architecture for the smart home community. To reduce the peak-to-average power ratio, RTP has been used between the home community and the utility. In this RTP scheme, the charge for electricity at the end of a day is calculated according to the combined loads of the entire community. Combined load scheduling for the community is required in this scheme.

RTP for Profit Maximization for Utility: Meng and Zeng [61] proposed a decision-making scheme for a retailer and its customers based on the Stackelberg game. They modeled a one-leader, N-follower Stackelberg game between the electricity retailer and its customers. The author designed an efficient energy management system to maximize the consumer benefit. Whereas for the utility side, they designed an optimal RTP rate that took into consideration the responses from customers in order to maximize the benefits for the utility. Their findings indicated that the retailer benefitted from the proposed RTP pricing algorithm.

Energy control: In [62], the author formulated a non-cooperative game for the consumers and searched for a unique equilibrium in demand response which is aligned with the Nash equilibrium. The Nash equilibrium is a set of strategies where no consumer has an incentive to change its strategy unilaterally given the strategies of the other consumers. To find the Nash equilibrium of this game, the authors proposed an energy control algorithm which could be used to control the energy consumption of the consumers. Their study indicated that there is a reduction in the peak load, the daily load and the peak-to-average ratio with RTP feedback.

Energy storage device: In the RTP pricing scheme, an energy storage device enables consumers to maximize their savings by optimally utilizing the storage device. The storage device needs to be charged and discharged in such a manner so that it will reduce the consumers' bills. In [63], the author developed a new optimization model to find the best storage size and control process for the charging and discharging. However, the maintenance and replacement cost of the storage facility is not viable within the current RTP pricing structure where there is not much difference between maximum and minimum prices each day.

RTP without DSM: Campillo et al. [64] studied the impact of RTP on customers. Customers without a demand-side management facility were considered in this study. The authors determined the theoretical impact by analyzing the data for the previous 7 years from 2000 to 2007 obtained from a smart metering infrastructure, and compared these data with data for two different pricing strategies: RTP and fixed pricing. They studied data for 400 households, which they divided equally into two consumer groups: one used district heating and other used electricity to run ground-source heating. Their studies showed that customers who had not changed their consumption pattern benefitted after shifting from a flat rate tariff to an RTP tariff.

Load Curtailment and Load Shift: Althaher and Mutale [65] investigated the impact and benefit to residential consumers who used the automatic demand response system under real-time pricing. Although the authors proposed a scheme for load curtailment and load shift, more work needs to be done to make the real-time pricing more user-friendly. The other concern regarding this scheme is that it requires a great deal of data in order to accurately forecast the RTP price, thereby raising the issue of customer privacy which must be protected in every manner possible.

As the electrical industry moves towards sustainability, the integration in the grid of a renewable energy source becomes increasingly important. A renewable energy sources such as solar–photovoltaic cells, wind energy farm other distributed generation (DG) source is an important source of energy for smart cities. These sources of power generation are not as reliable as the conventional sources because their availability depends on natural environmental factors such as weather, wind speed etc. Therefore, the demand response system plays vital role in bridging the gap between demand and supply. In [66], the author proposed a stochastic unit commitment model for the integration of wind power into grid. The given optimization technique is used to realize higher wind power generation under various possible wind condition. This technique could also deal with the wind power uncertainty economically. The proposed stochastic optimal model with RTP could be helpful to integrate large-scale wind power.

The previous discussion showed that there have been many developments in the field of RTP pricing. Researchers explore various aspect of the RTP like profit maximization for consumer and for utility, optimal energy storage utilization, optimal DG utilization with RTP, consumer privacy, etc. Consumer privacy is one of the concerns which need to be explored more for effective implementation of RTP in real market. Structure of RTP is complex, hence special emphasis is needed to be put on consumers education. A brief summary of recent developments is presented in Table 4.2.

4.5.3 Critical Peak Pricing

Critical peak pricing (CPP) is another pricing strategy employed for demand response which is slightly different from TOU and RTP. CPP increases electricity prices to punitive levels at peak hours on critical days announced beforehand [67].

As mentioned earlier, the TOU has a predefined block for the pricing mechanism; that is, the pricing for the different intervals of time is fixed for a certain duration (like a month) that makes TOU static in nature, whereas the real-time pricing changes after an hour or a day which makes the RTP a dynamic pricing scheme. But in certain cases, TOU pricing scheme is not sufficient to reduce the peak because consumers can shift their load to create a peak at another time, and the energy consumption may increase [48].

Critical peak pricing (CPP) incorporates some of the characteristics of both RTP and TOU and solves the problem faced by the utilities to implement the TOU and RTP pricing schemes. The CPP based on the TOU pricing scheme has a simple structure and can also reduce the peak demand by identifying a peak event and increasing the electricity cost for the duration. Although it is less dynamic, it can handle peak demand effectively. The various challenges facing the implementation of CPP in the retail market are discussed below.

Challenges

CPP programs are based on the TOU structure but include critical events which can be called by the utility at a very short notice. However, CPP programs are limited to calling peak events no more than 50 or 100 times [39]. CPP can be seen as a modified version of TOU because the peak event called is based on a system constraint, not on consumer demand behavior. Some of the features of RTP are available in the CPP scheme. For example, the retail price CPP can vary with the wholesale market price during peak periods. In RTP, the information related to the electricity price can be declared an hour before, whereas with CPP, it must be declared a day before the peak event [68]. Therefore, there are more constraints in CPP than in RTP. Although the CPP structure is simple, there are challenges associated with this scheme which need to be overcome before it is fully implemented. One of the challenges is the price during peak times which needs to be adjusted so that consumers will reduce their consumption and utilities can manage the demand as well as make a profit [69]. If the prices are very high, then customers will be reluctant to shift to this new tariff; if the prices are low, then customers will not respond to price and therefore the demand will not decrease during peak time. Hence, the design of optimal pricing for peak times is one of the critical challenges, in addition to the rate and frequency of calling the peak event. Other challenges are related to the magnitude and characteristics of demand responses of consumers to the CPP from various sections of society such as high-end users, low-end users, etc. [70]. With the automatic demand controller, the household load can effectively deal with the peak pricing, although automatic controllers are not so common. Therefore, consumers need to control their load manually which is not possible in some instances. Informing consumers about a peak event is done via different communication channels. However, sometimes consumers do not receive the information or may receive it after a delay, which means that they cannot react to the peak price and ultimately are financially disadvantaged. Therefore, the utility should ensure that the information reaches the consumer on time. Another challenge is consumer education, since the consumers' need to know how to control the

Table 4.3 Challenges and recent developments in CPP pricing

Challenges	Finding optimal peak rate which will maximize utility's profit [64]
	Find the minimum number of event days during CPP [65]
	Analysing the impact on people's lifestyles [33]
	Finding the optimal duration of peak event [65]
	Determining the target consumer who will respond more readily to CPP [66]
Recent developments	Deterministic dynamic programming used to solve the events scheduling problem [64]
	Profit index used for revealing the effect on utility's profit with variation in CPP parameters [64]
	Descriptive statistics and graphics used to analyze and know residential demand response [65]
	Analysis of the impact of CPP on energy demand and disadvantages for consumers [33]
	Design of zonal tariff with CPP for more efficient demand response [69]

appliance manually in order to reduce the peak demand. These challenges are summarized in Table 4.3.

Recent Developments

The design of the CPP is crucial as it has more constraints compared to RTP and TOU. Park et al. [71] designed a CPP with the objective of maximizing the utility's profits by taking into consideration the consumers' response to dynamic pricing. The number of events, their duration, and peak rate are some of the important factors to consider when designing a CPP scheme. In the CPP pricing scheme, the optimal peak rate (OPR) is the optimal price during peak periods. As the optimal peak rate increased, the consumer response decreased. The authors used the profit index which is an additional benefit that the utility can derive from the triggering of a critical event. By using the profit index, the effects of parameters such as critical peak price, peak event, and duration of peak event on the profit of the LSE (least square error) can be analyzed. A minimum number of peak events needs to be triggered by the utility in the CPP pricing scheme in order to benefit financially, unlike the uniform pricing scheme. The length of the peak duration influences the consumer response to the CPP pricing [40]. The shorter the duration of the peak time, the better will be the response compared to the longer duration. During a peak, customers can curtail their consumption by reducing space heating and cooling systems.

Residential consumers' average consumption of electricity is reduced significantly under the CPP pricing scheme [68]. In this study, the authors divided consumers into two different groups: one group was charged according to CPP with base TOU pricing, and the other group was charged TOU. The study was conducted using four different cost structures during the peak period, and demonstrated that in all four cases, the consumers who followed the CPP scheme consumed less. It shows the effectiveness of CPP in reducing consumption. This reduction varies depending on whether the consumers are high-end or low-end users in response to the TOU pricing scheme, the high-end users significantly reduced their energy consumption, whereas low-end users saved significantly more on their annual electricity bills [69].

In [70], Herter and Wayland analyzed the data for the summer months only (1 July–30 September 2004) from 483 households who took part in the CPP experiment, which was conducted in California. In this pilot study, the participants were divided into twelve strata, according to climate zone and building type. Findings of the analysis indicated that the CPP events were successful at reducing load during peak periods. Their analysis also showed that there were significant load increases just after the notification of an event day has been sent to consumers and also just after the event ends. This indicated that much of the load reduction during the CPP period results from load shifting by participating households.

CPP can be implemented by forming groups of consumers (zones) who will voluntarily participate in a CPP scheme and in return expect some type of incentive from the utility. This pricing scheme is known as a zonal tariff. The design of a zonal tariff scheme requires the effective coordination of the supplier and network operators [72]. The authors concluded that with this pricing scheme, a demand-side resource could be created, which would be able to offer load reduction based on dispersed customers.

Dynamic pricing may have an adverse impact on people's lifestyles. Kii et al. [37] examined the impact of CPP on people of different ages. They conducted a survey in which the participants were given choices in terms of the appliances that they wanted to switch off during the peak hours (e.g., the air conditioner, refrigerator, etc.) but unique option among various choices is going out or staying at home during the peak time. This study will assist with the development of future smart cities. Their study indicated that the CPP may have a more negative impact on older people. Moreover, population density directly affects the demand for electricity. If the population density increases by 10%, then demand will decrease 0.047 and 0.021% for the households with residents who are able to go out and average households, respectively.

The CPP program has a simply structured variable pricing scheme, which can efficiently deal with peak loads. The findings of various case studies which have been done in different electrical markets show that CPP is more effective than TOU pricing. The recent developments in this pricing area are presented in Table 4.3.

4.5.4 Day-Ahead Pricing (DAP)

In the TOU pricing scheme, the tariff structure is fixed by the utility a month before or more. Therefore, consumers know the tariff in advance and can shift their load which produces a new peak [48]. With the CPP that is based on TOU, information related to a peak event must be sent to the consumer a day ahead of the event. This is because for both dynamic pricing systems, the base price is fixed at the start of the billing cycle, and in the case of CPP, the peak event is decided only one day before it occurs, with a limited number of peak events in a year. Hence, the utility has little control over the daily load. In RTP, the rate is varied hourly and therefore it is more uncertain, which makes it less attractive to the consumer [73]. The day-ahead pricing scheme in which the tariff is fixed a day ahead is beneficial for both the consumer and the utility. Seasonal Pricing Consumers and many enterprise customers prefer day-ahead, time-dependent pricing. In comparison, the day-ahead pricing is much more attractive to residential consumers because they can plan their activities in advance according to the day-ahead price [73] and schedule their appliances accordingly.

Challenges

The day-ahead pricing is most prominent from the consumer as well as from utility point of view compared with other dynamic pricing schemes. Consumers can schedule their activities well beforehand, and the utility can fix the tariff to benefit financially and maintain the constant load profile. It also helps the utility to reduce the cost of purchasing the electricity from the wholesale market. Day-ahead pricing is looking very promising for demand response, but there are several issues associated with it. The first and most important challenge is the designing of a forecasting model [74]. Energy price forecasting has been done by analyzing the various input parameters such as the forecasted energy demand, available supply, local weather, etc. So, the forecasting of the energy price a day ahead is a challenging task and needs a robust and effective model [75]. Another challenge for the utility is that it needs to inform consumers about the day-ahead pricing. The utility needs to send the information to consumers so that they can schedule their appliances. Since the pricing is declared a day ahead, there is a chance of peak during low price time. If consumers change their load during off-peak periods, the utility may incur a financial loss. Hence, there is the need for an optimal day-ahead price to maximize the benefit for the utility [76]. These are several challenges which need to be overcome in order to obtain the maximum advantage from day-ahead pricing. A summary of these challenges has been presented in Table 4.4.

Recent Developments

For day-ahead pricing, forecasting is important. Several methods are available for forecasting the day-ahead price of electricity. Joe-Wong et al. in [73] developed an algorithm to determine the day-ahead pricing in order to minimize the cost incurred

Table 4.4 Challenges and recent developments in day-ahead pricing

Challenges	Forecast the day-ahead price [70]
	Optimal day-ahead pricing for minimizing the cost to utility [69]
Recent developments	Artificial neural network for day-ahead price forecasting [70]
	An algorithm to estimate the response of the consumer to the day-ahead pricing [72]

by the service provider, and maximize revenue. Their algorithm also estimates the response of the consumer to DAP in a Smart Grid environment. Consumers respond to DAP by reducing their load during high price times. With the day-ahead pricing scheme, there is a significant reduction in the peak consumption and therefore there is a reduction in the peak-to-average ratio.

Another method for day-ahead price forecasting is the artificial neural network. The relationship between input data (weather condition, demand, and supply) and target parameters (reducing peak load, maximizing utility benefit) for price forecasting is nonlinear in nature. The artificial neural network is a common technique that can deal with nonlinearity. The day-ahead price forecasting using the artificial neural network with a clustering algorithm is presented in [74]. It is a robust forecasting scheme which includes the tradition generation unit, self-producer, retailer, and aggregators. The ANN (artificial neural network) model for load forecasting using only historical price values has not demonstrated reliable performance in this study, although the researchers designed a cascade ANN network to reduce errors. Their results indicated that the cascaded neural networks were the optimal model. The authors also designed a hybrid forecasting model comprising a two-stage process where the clustering tool was combined with the cascaded ANN. The efficiency of the hybrid model was no better, but it produced fewer errors than the cascade neural network.

Price forecasting is one of the challenging tasks. There is only a limited number of forecasting methods available for load forecasting. The price time series method used to forecast the day-ahead price is volatile and is influenced by a diverse set of parameters such as weather conditions, hydrocapacity, fossil fuel prices, etc. Therefore, a novel computational intelligence is required based on models for load forecasting. A summary of recent developments is presented in Table 4.4.

4.5.5 Other Pricing Incentive Schemes for DR

Apart from the dynamic pricing mechanisms for demand response discussed above, the literature includes various other pricing mechanisms used for demand response programs. Some of them are cost reflective pricing [11], season pricing [10], and peak time rebate [12, 13].

Cost Reflective Pricing: A cost reflective tariff reflects the cost of supplying electricity which includes the spot price in the wholesale market, transmission network costs and future expansion costs. In other words, the cost reflects the true cost of supplying electricity.

Seasonal Pricing: The demand for electricity varies from season to season because electrical appliance requirements differ from one season to another. Electricity generation varies seasonally due to the availability of other energy sources. For example, in summer, less electricity can be generated by a hydropower plant because of the reduced amount of water. Demand management is required to bridge the gap between demand and supply during different seasons. This can be achieved by adopting seasonal variable pricing which will vary according to the season.

Peak Time Rebate (PTR): Dynamic pricing schemes such as TOU, RTP, DAP pricing, and CPP are all based on the restructuring of electricity tariff. The peak time rebate is given to consumers who help the utility by reducing their consumption during peak times. Consumers may choose whether or not to reduce their load: if they reduce it, they receive the rebate; if not, they will pay a flat rate. In this pricing scheme, the consumers have not been forced indirectly to reduce the peak load by increasing the tariff during a certain period. This benefits the customers, but the utility has to wait for the consumers' response.

Challenges

The most challenging task is to design a pricing scheme that will benefit both the consumer and the utility. Designing a cost-reflecting scheme with integrated renewable energy sources, and that considers network cost, is one of the challenges faced when implementing a cost reflecting the price. Various factors influence the customers' response to cost-reflective tariffs, so it is necessary to find which factor has the greatest influence on consumers, and how consumers will respond if there are any changes to this factor.

A seasonal pricing scheme varies according to the season. So, the challenge here is to design an optimal seasonal pricing scheme which will effectively reduce the gap between demand and supply during a particular season. When designing the seasonal pricing, weather data needs to be considered in order to accurately forecast the seasonal price.

Peak time rebate (PTR) relies on rewarding the customers during the peak time based on their load reduction. Accordingly, any load that can be shifted to off-peak periods looks like a gain. PTR scheme heavily depends on consumer base load (CBL). So, the method to find the consumer base load is important while designing the rebate pricing scheme. Consumer response to this pricing scheme is important from the utility perspective. Hence, consumers must be informed of the benefits that they can receive. Other challenges include the ways by which consumers can receive information about the peak time and rebate they will receive if they reduce their load during peak time. The above challenges are summarized in Table 4.5.

Recent Development

An electrical distribution network has two essential costs: network operational cost and network development cost. The network development cost includes the cost of expanding the network. In a deregulated competitive market where coordinated generation and network planning is replaced by pricing, economic efficiency which can be achieved by sending the pricing signal to the end user, can influence their energy consumption behavior according to their location. The authors of [11] developed a cost reflective pricing scheme for a distribution network with distributed generation. In developing this pricing scheme, they took network security into consideration. They proposed a pricing framework which included the network planning cost, fixed cost, and other factors that had a simple structure. The authors

Table 4.5 Challenges and recent developments in seasonal, PTR, and cost reflective pricing

Challenges	Designing seasonal pricing scheme [9]
	Designing zonal tariff with distributed generator [10]
	Designing PTR including human behavior [11]
	Designing a method to find CBL, which will benefit all stakeholders by an optimal incentive scheme [12]
	How PTR program is different for the residential customer compared to industrial customer [12]
Recent developments	Cost reflective pricing scheme for distribution network with distributed generation [10]
	Energy consumption reduction by incorporating carbon tax with electricity price [9]
	A price elasticity-based DR model to simulate the response of customers [11]
	Economic analysis of PTR program [11]
	Analysis of the impact of CBL performance on PTR programs offered to residential customers [12]

created a price zone in the distribution network because creating a unique charge for each and every node in a network would be impractical. The effective technical and economic integration of DG (distributed generation) into various zones of power systems has reduced the cost reflective price.

Hung et al. in [9] studied the seasonality of electricity consumption by Taiwanese consumers. Most of the peak demand occurred during the summer months. The regulated summer rates were higher than those for the non-summer months. Their studies confirmed that in the residential sector, there was greater electricity demand in summer. They found that price fluctuations during the summer season were lower than those of non-summer months due to the consistently high temperatures. Their results suggest that energy consumption and CO_2 emissions can effectively be reduced during non-summer months if the carbon tax is considered in combination with the electricity price, since in Taiwan, the electricity price is lower in the non-summer months and higher in the summer months. By combining the carbon tax with electricity price, the government of Taiwan is able to smooth the electricity expenditure of households over the course of a year.

An incentive-based demand response program is different from a price-based program. From the policy perspective, the PTR (Peak Time Rebate) program is more appealing than other programs because it requires minimal changes to existing systems and produces a favorable result if it is designed optimally. In [12], Mohajeryami et al. studied the effect of behavioral characteristics in the design of demand response programs. Loss aversion is one of the behavioral characteristics of human beings. Its effect on the customers' perception of the different programs was also examined by authors. They also examined the impact of two dynamic programs (PTR and RTP) on demand response. They proposed a model which can be used by utilities for profit maximization and can be used to design a more efficient dynamic pricing scheme. They have examined two PTR cases to test the proposed model. The first PTR case took loss aversion into consideration, while the second PTR case did not. The first RTP case performed better than the PTR; whereas the second PTR case performed better than the RTP. Their study showed that loss aversion had no effect on the consumers' selection of an appropriate dynamic pricing program. As shown in this study, in DR programs, behavioral impacts have to be taken into the consideration more seriously. The findings indicated that behavioral characteristics cannot be ignored when one of two competing programs is being selected.

In [13], the authors studied the relationship between accuracy of customer baseline (CBL) calculation and efficiency of the peak time rebate (PTR) program for residential customers. The authors analyzed the economic performance of PTR for residential customers. The CBL calculation method to predict the consumer load profile on event days is an important means of calculating the efficiency of PTR. Hence, the authors analyzed the accuracy and bias metrics of CBLs and explained how these metrics translate into financial losses for utility and customers. They used exponential moving average and regression methods and their adjusted forms to calculate the CBL. This CBL was used to determine the economic performance of the PTR. Their study showed that the utility paid at least half of its revenue as a rebate just because the CBL had not been calculated accurately.

There are several pricing mechanisms that have not been extensively used for demand response. Several pilot tests have been conducted with these programs, but these are very limited in number. These programs need to be explored more for effective demand response output. In future, these programs could be combined with TOU, RTP to design more effective dynamic programs for demand response. A summary of the recent developments is presented in Table 4.5.

4.6 Case Studies

In the literature, various pricing schemes have been proposed by researchers across the globe. But there are doubts about the consumer response to dynamic pricing and this is one of the impediments to the full-scale rollout of dynamic pricing. The various experiments were conducted to study consumer responses to various dynamic pricing strategies, and determine their usefulness in a demand response program. Four case studies are presented here.

Day-Ahead Pricing Experiment: Belgium

A pilot experiment study of day-ahead pricing in the Belgium market was conducted from September 2013 to July 2014 [77]. A total of 240 residential consumers participated in this experiment, 186 of whom were equipped with smart appliances such as smart domestic hot water buffers and electric vehicles. The remaining 54 families participated in a manual dynamic pricing scheme. Analysis of consumer consumption profiles showed that there were very limited to no behavioral changes.

The experiment analysis showed a significant shift of the flexible load like washing machine, dishwasher, etc., from peak hours to off-peak hour, i.e., to the lower price periods. But this significant shift of flexible loads had an impact at the national level, whereas the physical impact on the local distribution grid was limited. Another finding was the high variation in energy consumption and load flexibility in the groups of pilot participants.

A questionnaire was administered before and after the experiment to determine the users' acceptance of the dynamic pricing. Analysis shows that for complex pricing schemes that require frequent price consultation, an automated response by means of smart appliances is preferable to the manual response.

TOU/CPP Pilot Study: British Columbia

A pilot study was conducted in a Canadian province, British Columbia, which experiences a severe winter peak. The study was intended to determine the relative kW response of the participants who had the TOU/CPP electricity tariff [78]. Relative kW response is defined as the percentage change in the customer's hourly kW due to exposure to time-varying pricing.

The data were collected from November 2007 to February 2008 for 1717 single-family homes, 411 of which were allocated to the control group and the rest to the treatment group. Hourly kW data collected from the control group of customers with the flat rate tariff and the treatment group of customers with the TOU/CPP rates, triggered by a 1-day advanced notice.

Remotely activated load control devices were considered in this pilot study to automatically reduce water heating and space heating load during CPP events. Analysis of this study shows that TOU pricing yields statistically significant evening peak kW reductions of 4–11%. An additional evening peak kW reduction of about 9% could be achieved via CPP. This can be further increased to 33% through remotely activated load control of space heating and water heating. The result shows that an optional TOU rate design can effectively reduce residential peak demands.

CPP and Peak Time Rebate (PTR) Experiment: Michigan

Consumers energy (CE) conducted a pilot experiment in Michigan known as the personal power plan (PPP) from July 2010 through September 2010 [79]. A total of 921 residential customers participated in this experiment. This PPP pilot project was conducted by dividing the customers into two groups. The first group was subject to time-varying rates, whereas the second group was subjected to their existing rate but they received information about peak times and peak pricing.

The CE created a price information only (PIO) consumer group to determine whether consumer behavior changed after information had been received. Two dynamic pricing strategies, i.e., CPP and peak time rebate (PTR) both of which were layered atop a TOU rate, were used to study consumer responses. During the pilot study, a total of 6 days were announced as critical peak days and the participants were informed about each one day ahead.

During the PPP period, the control group customers faced the inclining block rates structure in which tariff varied according to total consumption. The treatment customers were given one of the rates: CPP, PTR, or PIO. CE customers showed the same price responsiveness to the equivalently designed PTR and CPP rates. This pilot study showed that there was a reduction in critical peak period usage by the entire treatment group. There was no significant difference between the CPP (15.2%) and PTR (15.9%) treatment groups. Consumers in the PIO group also reduced their usage by 5.8%. However, the total monthly consumption remained unchanged for both the CPP and the PTR groups as the daily variations were statistically insignificant. This indicated that, although there was a reduction in peak demand for the CPP and PTR groups, this did not have any statistically detectable load building or load conservation impact.

The pilot study also involved two control groups. A randomly selected group of 228 consumers, who were unaware of the pilot program were placed in the first group. The second group comprised the remaining 92 consumers who knew that the utility would observe their daily usage patterns. This was done to study any changes in human behavior as a result of participants knowing that they are being monitored by a utility. This is known as "Hawthorne bias". Their study showed that the consumption pattern of both groups remained unchanged. Therefore, there is no definitive evidence of a Hawthorne effect in the PPP pilot program.

CPP Field Experiment: Kitakyushu and Kyoto

A field experiment was conducted by the Japanese Ministry of Economy, Trade, and Industry (METI) in four cities in Japan (Yokohama, Toyota, Kyoto and Kitakyushu) to examine the effect, on residential electricity demand, of dynamic pricing and smart energy equipment.

In [80], the authors analyzed experimental data for the summer of 2012 in two cities—Kitakyushu and Kyoto. The Kitakyushu experiment had 182 participants and the Kyoto experiment had 681 participants. The participants were paid 12,000 yen (USD 105) to participate in this experiment; moreover, a smart meter and in-home display were installed in their homes for free.

Electricity consumption data were collected from the smart meters at 30-minute intervals. Of the 182 households, 112 were randomly selected for the treatment group. Consumers in the treatment group had a time-of-use price schedule on nonevent days. A CPP day was announced one day ahead, with the critical peak price shown on the home display unit.

Critical peak prices for the two cities are slightly different. This study showed that the CPP of higher marginal prices led to larger reductions in consumption, but the rate of incremental reductions diminishes with increases in price. This study also showed a slight increase in consumption during off-peak hours. Consumers increased their consumption by 4–5% during the off-peak hours in the Kitakyushu experiment, whereas in the case of Kyoto, the consumption increased by 3–4%.

In the Kyoto experiment, a warning-only treatment group of consumers was formed. In this group, consumers received day-ahead notices about the CPP event in the same way that consumers in the dynamic pricing group did. However, they were told that their price would not change. The warning-only treatment group reduced their consumption by 3% which is small compared to that of the dynamic price consumer group. However, this demonstrated that informing consumers about the peak time will help to reduce the peak demand, which is an interesting finding.

4.7 Future Research Directions

In this chapter, we discussed several dynamic pricing schemes such as TOU RTP, CPP, day-ahead pricing, etc. Each of these schemes has some unique characteristics and addresses some aspect of energy consumption management. Although this area has received much research attention, there are still numerous open research issues that need investigation in the future, as briefly discussed below.

Open Research Directions in TOU (Time of Use)

Designing the smart house controller with the TOU pricing for smart home is an important field for research. An algorithm is needed for the efficient use of a storage device and a renewable energy source in order to reduce the customer's electricity bill. There is a need to analyze the effects of the TOU program in terms of voltage improvement and frequency control. A smart device in the home will reduce electricity costs for the consumer, but on the other hand, it will decrease the utility's revenue. Therefore, what is needed is a TOU tariff that maximizes utility profits.

Open Research Directions for RTP (Real-Time Pricing)

The establishment of an RTP tariff is a task that requires intensive effort because, of all the dynamic pricing systems, RTP is the most complex. Consumer wants and needs vary from person to person, so an RTP scheme needs to be aligned with individual consumer requirements and preferences. The responsiveness to the pricing is another method that can be used for the design of RTP pricing. Another research opportunity in RTP is use of the recurrent neural network for solving DSM (demand-side management) optimization problems. Design of RTP with imperfect information from any side either customer or generation side needs to be explored more in future. The distributed generation systems such as rooftop PV (photovoltaic) cells will play a vital role in future DR (demand response) program, so there is need to design RTP with feed-in tariffs from rooftop PVs. Privacy constraints should be taken into account when designing and implementing an efficient RTP scheme.

Open Research Directions in CPP (Critical Peak Pricing)

Various communication modes (e.g., by mail, email, telephone, social media, etc.) should be used to deliver information related to event day and critical peak time prices. The synchronizing of all communication modes is required for the efficient and effective information system. A forecasting model needs to be designed that can forecast data with minimal error. A CPP price model needs to be developed which includes the pre-established load variability from the consumer end.

Open Research Directions in DAP (Day-Ahead Pricing)

A two-sided pricing mechanism needs to be developed. The first side of the mechanism enables the consumer to sell to the utility the power generated locally using renewable sources such as a photovoltaic cell, etc. The other side of price mechanism is where the utility sells the electricity to the user. A DAP forecast model needs to be developed incorporating a new computational intelligence technique that takes into account other clustering algorithms. The DAP forecast model needs to integrate renewable energy sources, but take into account the uncertainties associated with them.

General Open Research Directions

The smart meter data collected may breach the privacy of the consumer. Hence, consumer privacy is another important issue which needs to be considered when designing a pricing scheme. Consumer privacy has not received much attention in the design of dynamic pricing scheme like TOU, RTP, CPP, PTR, day-ahead pricing, etc. However, consumer privacy is a serious concern and it must be protected. Their is a need to developed secure pricing model which assure their is no privacy breach of the consumer and if it happened they must be compensated.

Web and mobile applications need to be developed to assist customers with decision-making regarding the Smart Grid technologies, and ensure a higher penetration of DR (demand response) programs.

Most of the strategies proposed to date are based on either the varying price or price incentive method. However, all these schemes require that customers accept the terms and policies established by the utility company. These give the utility company the right to set the rate for the various pricing schemes; therefore, once the consumers have chosen a tariff schedule, they will have to pay according to that scheme. This allows the utility to increase the tariff during the peak period so as to increase its profits. Hence, consumers are helpless as they cannot shift their critical load to an off-peak period and will, therefore, have to pay more. With the implementation of the smart meter infrastructure, it is easier to obtain data from the consumer end, and consumers can easily track their consumption level. Consumers know their consumption pattern and thus can manage their load accordingly. Hence, future electricity prices should be established in such a way that the interests of both consumer and supplier are protected.

The amount of data collected from the smart meter will be enormous, and the handling of this data will be challenging. Although this huge amount of data will make it easier to forecast prices, what is required is a model designed to make use of this rich data in order to produce reliable price forecasts.

4.8 Conclusion

The electrical infrastructure is one of the critical infrastructures of future smart cities. A Smart Grid supplies the power to smart cities. Demand response is an integral part of Smart Grids, and one of the methods used for demand response is dynamic pricing. Demand-side management will play a crucial role in reducing the peak load in smart cities. In this chapter, we explore various dynamic pricing schemes such as TOU, RTP, CPP, PTR, and day-ahead pricing, which can be used for the demand response program, and which are very effective. This chapter has discussed the various challenges and issues related to the practical implementation of these dynamic pricing schemes. These challenges need to be studied in greater depth in order to find effective solutions to ensure the efficiency of a demand response program. Several case studies have been included in this chapter to demonstrate the effectiveness of these programs. This chapter has also included suggestions for future work on dynamic pricing.

References

1. Katz J, Andersen FM, Morthorst PE (2016) Load-shift incentives for household demand response: evaluation of hourly dynamic pricing and rebate schemes in a wind-based electricity system. Energy. https://doi.org/10.1016/j.energy.2016.07.084
2. Ye B, Ge F, Rong X, Li L (2016) The influence of nonlinear pricing policy on residential electricity demand—a case study of Anhui residents. Energy Strategy Rev 13–14:115–124. https://doi.org/10.1016/j.esr.2016.09.001
3. Tang Q, Yang K, Zhou D et al (2016) A real-time dynamic pricing algorithm for smart grid with unstable energy providers and malicious users. IEEE Internet Things J 3:554–562. https://doi.org/10.1109/JIOT.2015.2452960
4. World Energy Scenarios (2016) The grand transition. http://www.worldenergy.org/publications/2016/world-energy-scenarios-2016-the-grand-transition/. Accessed 19 Dec 2016
5. Steen D, Carlson O (2016) Effects of network tariffs on residential distribution systems and price-responsive customers under hourly electricity pricing. IEEE Trans Smart Grid 7:617–626
6. Kim J-Y, Lee MH, Berg N (2016) Peak-load pricing in duopoly. Econ Model 57:47–54. https://doi.org/10.1016/j.econmod.2016.04.012
7. Moura PS, De Almeida AT (2010) The role of demand-side management in the grid integration of wind power. Appl Energy 87:2581–2588
8. de Sá Ferreira R, Barroso LA, Lino PR et al (2013) Time-of-use tariff design under uncertainty in price-elasticities of electricity demand: A stochastic optimization approach. IEEE Trans Smart Grid 4:2285–2295
9. Hu F-N, Tang Y-D, Zou Y (2007) The mechanism of the TOU price based on the Bi-linkage of purchase and sale prices. Zhongguo Dianji Gongcheng Xuebao Proc Chin Soc Electr Eng 27:61–66
10. Hung M-F, Huang T-H (2015) Dynamic demand for residential electricity in Taiwan under seasonality and increasing-block pricing. Energy Econ 48:168–177. https://doi.org/10.1016/j.eneco.2015.01.010

11. Mutale J, Strbac G, Pudjianto D (2007) Methodology for cost reflective pricing of distribution networks with distributed generation. In: 2007 IEEE power engineering society general meeting. IEEE, pp 1–5
12. Mohajeryami S, Schwarz P, Baboli PT (2015) Including the behavioral aspects of customers in demand response model: real-time pricing versus peak-time rebate. In: NAPS 2015. North American power symposium. IEEE, pp 1–6
13. Mohajeryami S, Doostan M, Asadinejad A (2016) An investigation of the relationship between accuracy of customer baseline calculation and efficiency of peak time rebate program. In: PECI 2016 IEEE. Power energy conference at illinois. IEEE, pp 1–8
14. Balijepalli VSKM, Pradhan V, Khaparde SA, Shereef RM (2011) Review of demand response under smart grid paradigm. In: 2011 IEEE PES innovative smart grid technologies—India (ISGT India), pp 236–243
15. Haider HT, See OH, Elmenreich W (2016) A review of residential demand response of smart grid. Renew Sustain Energy Rev 59:166–178. https://doi.org/10.1016/j.rser.2016.01.016
16. Schewe PF (2007) The grid: a journey through the heart of our electrified world. National Academies Press
17. Lai LL (2001) Power system restructuring and deregulation: trading, performance and information technology. Wiley
18. Bhattacharya K, Bollen M, Daalder JE (2012) Operation of restructured power systems. Springer Science & Business Media
19. Nwaeze ET (2000) Deregulation of the electric power industry: the earnings, risk, and return effects. J Regul Econ 17:49–67
20. Abhyankar AR, Khaparde SA (2013) Introduction to deregulation in power industry. Rep. Indian Institute of Technolgy Mumbai
21. Vittal V (2000) Consequence and impact of electric utility industry restructuring on transient stability and small-signal stability analysis. Proc IEEE 88:196–207
22. Farhangi H (2010) The path of the smart grid. IEEE Power Energy Mag 8:18–28
23. Gungor VC, Sahin D, Kocak T et al (2012) Smart grid and smart homes: key players and pilot projects. IEEE Ind Electron Mag 6:18–34. https://doi.org/10.1109/MIE.2012.2207489
24. Vu K, Begouic MM, Novosel D (1997) Grids get smart protection and control. IEEE Comput Appl Power 10:40–44
25. Guo Y, Pan M, Fang Y (2012) Optimal power management of residential customers in the smart grid. IEEE Trans Parallel Distrib Syst 23:1593–1606
26. Amin M (2004) Balancing market priorities with security issues. IEEE Power Energy Mag 2:30–38
27. Fang X, Misra S, Xue G, Yang D (2012) Smart grid—the new and improved power grid: a survey. IEEE Commun Surv Tutor 14:944–980
28. Chen TM (2010) Smart grids, smart cities need better networks [Editor's note]. IEEE Netw 24:2–3
29. Cavoukian A, Polonetsky J, Wolf C (2010) Smartprivacy for the smart grid: embedding privacy into the design of electricity conservation. Identity Inf Soc 3:275–294
30. Werbos PJ (2011) Computational intelligence for the smart grid-history, challenges, and opportunities. IEEE Comput Intell Mag 6:14–21
31. Nikmehr N, Ravadanegh SN (2015) Optimal power dispatch of multi-microgrids at future smart distribution grids. IEEE Trans Smart Grid 6:1648–1657
32. Lasseter RH, Paigi P (2004) Microgrid: a conceptual solution. In: 2004 IEEE 35th annual power electronics specialists conference, 2004. PESC 04. IEEE, pp 4285–4290
33. Ipakchi A, Albuyeh F (2009) Grid of the future. IEEE Power Energy Mag 7:52–62
34. Nations U (2014) World urbanization prospects: the 2014 revision, highlights. Department of Economic and Social Affairs. Population Division, UN
35. DESA U (2015) World population prospects: the 2015 revision, key findings and advance tables. Working Paper
36. Curiale M (2014) From smart grids to smart city. In: 2014 Saudi Arabia Smart Grid Conference (SASG). IEEE, pp 1–9

37. Kii M, Sakamoto K, Hangai Y, Doi K (2014) The effects of critical peak pricing for electricity demand management on home-based trip generation. IATSS Res 37:89–97. https://doi.org/10.1016/j.iatssr.2013.12.001
38. Jang D, Eom J, Kim MG, Rho JJ (2015) Demand responses of Korean commercial and industrial businesses to critical peak pricing of electricity. J Clean Prod 90:275–290. https://doi.org/10.1016/j.jclepro.2014.11.052
39. Borenstein S, Jaske M, Rosenfeld A (2002) Dynamic pricing, advanced metering, and demand response in electricity markets. Center for Study Energy Markets
40. Herter K, McAuliffe P, Rosenfeld A (2007) An exploratory analysis of California residential customer response to critical peak pricing of electricity. Energy 32:25–34. https://doi.org/10.1016/j.energy.2006.01.014
41. Celebi E, Fuller JD (2012) Time-of-use pricing in electricity markets under different market structures. IEEE Trans Power Syst 27:1170–1181
42. Yang P, Tang G, Nehorai A (2013) A game-theoretic approach for optimal time-of-use electricity pricing. IEEE Trans Power Syst 28:884–892
43. Ali SQ, Maqbool SD, Ahamed TI, Malik NH (2013) Load scheduling with maximum demand and time of use pricing for microgrids. In: 2013 IEEE global humanitarian technology conference: South Asia satellite (GHTC-SAS). IEEE, pp 234–238
44. Jia-hai Y (2006) Customer response under time-of-use electricity pricing policy based on multi-agent system simulation. In: 2006 IEEE PES power systems conference and exposition, pp 814–818
45. Pallonetto F, Oxizidis S, Milano F, Finn D (2016) The effect of time-of-use tariffs on the demand response flexibility of an all-electric smart-grid-ready dwelling. Energy Build 128:56–67. https://doi.org/10.1016/j.enbuild.2016.06.041
46. Leger AS, Sobiesk E, Farmer A, Rulison B (2014) Demand response with photovoltaic energy source and time-of-use pricing. In: 2014 IEEE PES T&D conference and exposition. IEEE, pp 1–5
47. Johnson J, Hurayb W, Baghzouz Y (2013) Economic evaluation of energy produced by a bifacial photovoltaic array in the era of time-of-use pricing. In: 2013 International conference on clean electrical power (ICCEP). IEEE, pp 348–352
48. Torriti J (2012) Price-based demand side management: assessing the impacts of time-of-use tariffs on residential electricity demand and peak shifting in Northern Italy. Energy 44:576–583. https://doi.org/10.1016/j.energy.2012.05.043
49. Dehnavi E, Abdi H (2016) Optimal pricing in time of use demand response by integrating with dynamic economic dispatch problem. Energy 109:1086–1094. https://doi.org/10.1016/j.energy.2016.05.024
50. Torriti J (2013) The significance of occupancy steadiness in residential consumer response to time-of-use pricing: evidence from a stochastic adjustment model. Util Policy 27:49–56. https://doi.org/10.1016/j.jup.2013.09.005
51. Nazar NSM, Abdullah MP, Hassan MY, Hussin F (2012) Time-based electricity pricing for demand response implementation in monopolized electricity market. In: 2012 IEEE student conference on research and development (SCOReD). IEEE, pp 178–181
52. Anees A, Chen Y-PP (2016) True real-time pricing and combined power scheduling of electric appliances in residential energy management system. Appl Energy 165:592–600. https://doi.org/10.1016/j.apenergy.2015.12.103
53. Kim S-J, Giannakis GB (2014) Real-time electricity pricing for demand response using online convex optimization. In: 2014 IEEE PES innovative smart grid technologies conference (ISGT). IEEE, pp 1–5
54. Mohsenian-Rad A-H, Leon-Garcia A (2010) Optimal residential load control with price prediction in real-time electricity pricing environments. IEEE Trans Smart Grid 1:120–133
55. Oldewurtel F, Ulbig A, Parisio A, et al (2010) Reducing peak electricity demand in building climate control using real-time pricing and model predictive control. In: 2010 49th IEEE conference on decision and control (CDC). IEEE, pp 1927–1932

56. Qian LP, Zhang YJA, Huang J, Wu Y (2013) Demand response management via real-time electricity price control in smart grids. IEEE J Sel Areas Commun 31:1268–1280

57. Vivekananthan C, Mishra Y, Ledwich G (2013) A novel real-time pricing scheme for demand response in residential distribution systems. In: IECON 2013-39th annual conference on IEEE industrial electronics society. IEEE, pp 1956–1961

58. Samadi P, Mohsenian-Rad H, Wong VW, Schober R (2014) Real-time pricing for demand response based on stochastic approximation. IEEE Trans Smart Grid 5:789–798

59. Lujano-Rojas JM, Monteiro C, Dufo-López R, Bernal-Agustín JL (2012) Optimum residential load management strategy for real-time pricing (RTP) demand response programs. Energy Policy 45:671–679. https://doi.org/10.1016/j.enpol.2012.03.019

60. Tsui KM, Chan S-C (2012) Demand response optimization for smart home scheduling under real-time pricing. IEEE Trans Smart Grid 3:1812–1821

61. Meng F-L, Zeng X-J (2014) An optimal real-time pricing for demand-side management: a stackelberg game and genetic algorithm approach. In: 2014 international joint conference on neural networks (IJCNN). IEEE, pp 1703–1710

62. Ma K, Hu G, Spanos CJ (2014) Distributed energy consumption control via real-time pricing feedback in smart grid. IEEE Trans Control Syst Technol 22:1907–1914

63. Dufo-López R (2015) Optimisation of size and control of grid-connected storage under real time electricity pricing conditions. Appl Energy 140:395–408. https://doi.org/10.1016/j.apenergy.2014.12.012

64. Campillo J, Dahlquist E, Wallin F, Vassileva I (2016) Is real-time electricity pricing suitable for residential users without demand-side management? Energy 109:310–325. https://doi.org/10.1016/j.energy.2016.04.105

65. Althaher SZ, Mutale J (2012) Management and control of residential energy through implementation of real time pricing and demand response. In: 2012 IEEE power and energy society general meeting. IEEE, pp 1–7

66. Liu X, Wang B, Li Y (2013) A transmission-constrained stochastic unit commitment model with real-time pricing for high wind power integration. In: 2013 IEEE PES Asia-Pacific power energy engineering conference (APPEEC). IEEE, pp 1–6

67. Wang Y, Li L (2016) Critical peak electricity pricing for sustainable manufacturing: modeling and case studies. Appl Energy 175:40–53. https://doi.org/10.1016/j.apenergy.2016.04.100

68. Kato T, Tokuhara A, Ushifusa Y et al (2016) Consumer responses to critical peak pricing: Impacts of maximum electricity-saving behavior. Electr J 29:12–19. https://doi.org/10.1016/j.tej.2016.02.002

69. Herter K (2007) Residential implementation of critical-peak pricing of electricity. Energy Policy 35:2121–2130. https://doi.org/10.1016/j.enpol.2006.06.019

70. Herter K, Wayland S (2010) Residential response to critical-peak pricing of electricity: California evidence. Energy 35:1561–1567. https://doi.org/10.1016/j.energy.2009.07.022

71. Park SC, Jin YG, Song HY, Yoon YT (2015) Designing a critical peak pricing scheme for the profit maximization objective considering price responsiveness of customers. Energy 83:521–531. https://doi.org/10.1016/j.energy.2015.02.057

72. Andruszkiewicz J, Lorenc J, Michalski A, Borowiak W (2016) Opportunities of demand flexibility bidding in result of critical peak pricing implementation for low voltage customers in Polish power system. In: 2016 13th international conference on European energy mark (EEM). IEEE, pp 1–5

73. Joe-Wong C, Sen S, Ha S, Chiang M (2012) Optimized day-ahead pricing for smart grids with device-specific scheduling flexibility. IEEE J Sel Areas Commun 30:1075–1085

74. Panapakidis IP, Dagoumas AS (2016) Day-ahead electricity price forecasting via the application of artificial neural network based models. Appl Energy 172:132–151. https://doi.org/10.1016/j.apenergy.2016.03.089

75. Amjady N, Daraeepour A (2009) Design of input vector for day-ahead price forecasting of electricity markets. Expert Syst Appl 36:12281–12294

76. Doostizadeh M, Ghasemi H (2012) A day-ahead electricity pricing model based on smart metering and demand-side management. Energy 46:221–230. https://doi.org/10.1016/j. energy.2012.08.029
77. Vanthournout K, Dupont B, Foubert W et al (2015) An automated residential demand response pilot experiment, based on day-ahead dynamic pricing. Appl Energy 155:195–203. https://doi.org/10.1016/j.apenergy.2015.05.100
78. Woo C-K, Horowitz I, Sulyma IM (2013) Relative kW response to residential time-varying pricing in British Columbia. IEEE Trans Smart Grid 4:1852–1860
79. Faruqui A, Sergici S, Akaba L (2013) Dynamic pricing of electricity for residential customers: the evidence from Michigan. Energy Effic 6:571–584
80. Ida T, Ito K, Tanaka M (2013) Using dynamic electricity pricing to address energy crises: evidence from randomized field experiments. In: 36th annual national Bureau of economic research summer institute. Proceeding EEE

Part II
Challenges and Opportunities

Chapter 5
Building Intelligent Systems for Smart Cities: Issues, Challenges and Approaches

Amrita Ghosal and Subir Halder

Abstract The concept of smart cities is gaining popularity and momentum due to their ability of providing improvised living for humans along with preserving the environmental factors. Implementing the concept of smart cities needs the incorporation of several technologies such as the Internet of Things (IoT) and Information and Communication Technology (ICT). Such technologies pave the way for a better development and efficient governance of smart cities. In this context, many real-life applications' studies ranging from food management to Intelligent Transport System (ITS) management have been or being undertaken by researchers. For example, one is motivated to take up the factor of ITS as this is an integral part of such smart cities and enhanced travel within such cities. The need for ITS has generated numerous issues ranging from serious traffic jams to maintenance of roads. It has been realized that the relationship between vehicles, road networks and people can be made stronger by utilizing better transportation infrastructure along with advanced information technologies. Thereby, the ultimate objective is to build related management and governance system that are more efficient, convenient, safe and intelligent than existing systems. Smart cities are fast emerging as possible solutions for making the transport systems more intelligent and eco-friendly. This motivates us to take up this survey work that compiles a study on the different aspects of smart cities that has been considered till now. This current contribution presents the issues and approaches of different technologies employed for smart cities. We also provide the different architectural approaches and the related concerns. The survey wraps up with open issues for smart cities that can be taken up as research work for future.

Keywords Internet of Things · Intelligent system · Smart city Wireless sensor networks · Challenges

A. Ghosal (✉) · S. Halder
Department of Computer Science and Engineering,
Dr. B. C. Roy Engineering College, Fuljhore, Durgapur, India
e-mail: ghosal_amrita@yahoo.com

© Springer International Publishing AG, part of Springer Nature 2018
Z. Mahmood (ed.), *Smart Cities*, Computer Communications and Networks,
https://doi.org/10.1007/978-3-319-76669-0_5

107

5.1 Introduction

Recent years have seen a surge in technological advancement coupled with human population growth and needs. To make human life more comfortable and secure along with sustainability of the environment, the concept of smart cities has been developed. The definition of smart city has evolved with time. One such definition coined by the authors in [1] regards a smart city as *a synthesis of hard infrastructure (or physical capital) with the availability and quality of knowledge, communication and social infrastructure*. The latter form of capital is decisive for urban competitiveness. Previous definitions of smart city also included the idea of the *wired city* [2]. The advent of smart cities will definitely improve the quality of human life if handled with proper guidance and technology. Internet of Things (IoT) plays a vital role in smart city development by amalgamating the capability of the physical world and the intellect of the computational world. The aim is to expand the abilities of things in the real city and reinforce the practicality of functions in the real world. IoT provides a wider range to researchers for development of sustainable smart cities. Ideally, smart cities are those that monitor and combine the status of their infrastructures, management, governance, people and communities, health, education and natural environment using Information and Communication Technologies (ICT). The design, construction and maintenance of smart city is done by using highly advanced integrated technologies, that include sensors, electronics and networks which are linked with computerized systems comprised of databases, tracking and decision-making algorithms [3]. The rapid growth in urbanization, the need for economic restructuring, environmental issues, governance issues and public sector problems require to be dealt with a smarter approach. The challenges faced by modern cities are becoming complicated as they try to cope up with the speed of frequent changes. To overcome this hindrance, the need for organizational changes generally focusing on the latest technologies and communication through Internet has become the need of the hour.

It is accepted that current ICT forms the core part of an effective smart city that include IoT, smartphone technology, radio-frequency identification system (RFID), smart metres, semantic web, linked data, artificial intelligence, cloud computing, collective intelligence, software, smart applications and biometrics [4]. The IoT is the network of physical/tangible objects integrated with computational devices, software, electronics, smart sensors and connectivity so that it can be used to achieve greater value and service by exchanging data with the maker, operator and other connected devices [5]. Each thing is unambiguously distinctive through its embedded computing system but is able to inter-operate within the infrastructure of the Internet. The concept of IoT plays a crucial role in the development of ideal and secure smart city, as a smart city is solely dependent on the embedded technology. The IoT is considered as a major research and innovation idea that leads to a lot of opportunities for new services by interconnecting physical and virtual worlds with a huge amount of electronics distributed in different places including houses, vehicles, streets, buildings and many other environments [6].

The development of ICT is for increasing the efficiency of energy systems, the delivery of services ranging from utilities to retailing in cities, and to improve communications and transportation. The smart city models are designed keeping in mind their functioning in real time using sensed data received at regular intervals along with use of intelligent laboratories for facilitating their monitoring and design. With time new ICT is being developed that is essentially network dependent and facilitates enormous interactions among several domains. A portion of the coordination process must incorporate the ways of citizens where they are able to couple their personal knowledge with those of experts who are entrusted with developing these technologies. This comes with the concern for privacy and security which are prime factors to sustain the challenge for the smooth functioning of smart cities. The need for information security arises for a better economic development of a smart city. The major components of a smart city include smart economy, smart environment, smart governance, smart people, smart mobility and smart living as depicted in Fig. 5.1 [7].

The application domains that need implementation in smart cities include the following [8]:

- Resource utilization and management: This is related to natural resources as well as energy, water monitoring and management.
- Transportation: It deals with ICT utilization for transportation management that includes intelligent transportation products and mobility.

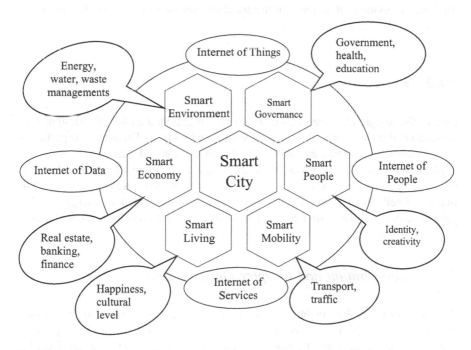

Fig. 5.1 Major components of a smart city

- Urban infrastructure: It refers to structural and building management with the ICT.
- Living: Living includes quality of human life, education, health and safety in urban environment.
- Government: This refers to governmental functions such as e-democracy, public e-service delivery, accountability, transparency and administration's efficiency within the city.
- Economy: It covers areas that reflect domestic product in city, innovative spirit, employment and e-business.
- Coherency: Coherency addresses the social issues such as digital divide, social relations and ICT connectivity.

5.1.1 Characteristic of Smart Cities

A model for smart city has been created for measuring a city with respect to areas such as economy, people, mobility, governance, environment, etc. This model helps to get a better idea about the existing conditions of the city and also the areas that need to be developed in order to make the city a smart one [9]. It consists of the following six characteristics, namely, smart economy, smart people, smart governance, smart mobility, smart environment and smart living. A brief idea about the different components that make up the six characteristics of a smart city [10, 11] is provided in Fig. 5.1.

5.1.2 Key Issues

Due to the unique characteristics of smart city mentioned earlier, the design, construction and maintenance of intelligent system is highly challenging. The particular requirements for building an intelligent system generally depend on the nature of applications, constraints imposed by hardware and network infrastructure. Based on these, some of the specific and unavoidable issues that the designer must face while building intelligent system are public safety, health care, transport, energy, etc. We provide a detailed discussion of key issues and inherent challenges in Sect. 5.4.

5.1.3 Contribution and Chapter Organization

A smart city is an ultra-modern urban area that addresses the needs of businesses, institutions and especially citizens [12]. Smart cities are fast emerging as possible solutions for making the transport systems more intelligent and eco-friendly.

Though smart cities are facing many problems during their development, including socioeconomic and political issues, but the most important hurdle here is the technical issues. In technical problems, along with the other issues like system interoperability and cost-efficient technology, the concern of security and privacy is very important. All these factors motivate us to take up this survey work. Initially, we define the need for smart cities along with the inherent challenges faced by them. We also review the different architectural approaches for smart cities. Further, we provide detailed description of the real-life implementation of such existing schemes. Finally, we give an insight into the possible directions for future work in smart cities.

This chapter has been organized as follows. In Sect. 5.2, we briefly discuss the various architectures that were proposed for undertaking the works on smart cities. In Sect. 5.3, we study existing works on real-life applications ranging from food management to energy management and finally transport management. Section 5.4 presents a summary of the key issues and challenges in building intelligent systems for smart city. Section 5.5 draws possible open research issues. Finally, Sect. 5.6 concludes this chapter.

5.2 Architectural Approaches for Smart City Development

This section gives a brief description of the various architectures that were proposed in course of time for development of smart cities [13]. It includes works that deal with architectural layers, Service-Oriented Architecture (SOA), Event Driven Architecture (EDA), IoT and also combined architectures.

5.2.1 Architectural Layers

Architectural layers use a structure for developing services and applications in smart city by dividing them into pieces (referred to as layers) for ease of modification and adjustment. There is a physical and logical separation of every layer from the others. This feature of architectural layers is the reason behind its large-scale acceptance by researchers. A number of works that have incorporated architectural layers concept for smart cities are briefly discussed below.

In one of the earlier works, Ishida [14] proposed a three layer architecture for smart cities. The author's comparison between the smart cities of America online, Amsterdam, Helsinki and Kyoto was one of the first in this field. The first layer referred to as the information layer comprises the data collected from real time sensors and files from the Internet which are combined together using Geographical Information Systems (GISs). The second layer is the interface layer which is responsible for creating a virtual environment of the cities through 3D spaces and 2D maps. The final layer is the interaction layer where agent systems are used for communicating with each other.

In another interesting work, the smart city of Trikala in Greece was developed by Anthopoulos et al. [15], where the architecture is made up of five layers. The first as well as the fifth layers are user layers that consist of the stakeholders of a smart city, i.e., the designers of the services and the end users. The infrastructure layer is the second layer consisting of technologies, platforms and networks that are needed to create and offer the services. The third layer is named as the information layer that contains the necessary data such as geospatial data needed for operations in smart cities. The fourth layer is named as the service layer that consists of the application provided for the city and allows for interaction between citizens and organizations.

In contrast, Su et al. [16] proposed three stages for the building of smart city. The first stage is the manufacture of public infrastructure while the second stage is the manufacture of public platform. The second stage consists of network infrastructure, cloud computing platform and Wireless Sensor Networks (WSNs). Finally, the third stage is the manufacture of application systems such as, some basic applications like construction of wireless city, smart home, etc.

Recently, Carretero [17] developed a self adaptive system for smart city using an architecture named ADAPCITY. It provides heterogeneous devices with the capability of reacting effectively in different environments. Also, this system has the ability of immediate recovery as well as updates and creates new operations. Here, the architecture is divided into four layers. First layer, the physical layer, consists of the state and behaviour of the devices and objects. Second layer, the grid layer, is responsible for the process, storage and communication among the data coming from the physical layer. Third layer, the management layer makes use of statistics, data mining and prediction techniques for managing the processed data from the grid layer. The final layer is the control layer that includes the provided services, taking into consideration the desires of the account users and optimization measurements.

Different from earlier works, Vilajosana et al. [18] proposed a generic architecture by combining the common features of several existing platforms. The bottom layer of the platform named as capillary network layer consists of sensors and actuators needed for data collection, data warehouses for storage of historical, real time and metadata. The service layer receives the incoming data from the capillary network layer. It then processes, combines and secures the received data. It manages different types of data, such as big, open and streaming data and also provides analytics services. The last layer is the application layer where the data are analyzed and converted into useful information, which is eventually provided to people through predefined interfaces.

Apart from the aforesaid works based on architecture, IBM has also defined the structure of smart city based on three layers, viz. perception, network and application. The perception layer is responsible for recognizing the device and gathering of data using sensors, GPS, RFID, etc. The second layer is the network layer that processes the data obtained by the perception layer using components related to the intelligence and communication capabilities of the network. While the third layer which is the application layer examines and evaluates the total amount of data through advanced technologies, such as cloud computing and fuzzy techniques.

5.2.2 Service Oriented Architecture (SOA)

In SOA, the primary objective is collection, communication and interaction between services. The communication between different services in a computer system is implemented by data exchange among them. Every interaction is considered to be unconstrained as services are unrelated, loosely coupled and self-sufficient.

In one state-of-the-art work, Anthopoulous et al. [19] developed a common architecture for smart cities based on SOA, named as enterprise architecture. It contained information regarding urban development and service delivery in such environments. The enterprise architecture combines the logical and physical architectures. The authors developed this architecture keeping in mind the drawbacks of the architecture that was used for developing Trikala as a smart city. This architecture was used to overcome the problems faced by Trikala.

5.2.3 Event Driven Architecture (EDA)

In EDA, creation, identification utilization and response to events are handled. The events that are dealt here with are generally uncommon and are related to uncertain modifications and asynchronous conditions. This architecture produces results that invoke production of notification of events. For example, a change is detected by the sensors and the events resulting from this change are processed by the system. This architecture can also be combined with SOA. For example, in one work [20], Filipponi et al. designed the SOFIA project by combining the architectures EDA and SOA. This project was developed for monitoring cities for security threats and also for detecting emergency and abnormal situations.

5.2.4 Internet of Things (IoT)

In IoT, a number of heterogeneous devices are connected to the Internet and they identify themselves using IP addresses and protocols. Here, the devices are embedded with sensors and actuators and are wirelessly connected to the internet. IoT provides for connectivity and communication between the sensors to facilitate various applications for users. IoT-based architecture has played a prime role in the coming up of smart cities. Some of the works that have dealt with IoT in smart cities are described as follows.

An infrastructure for smart city termed as smart city critical infrastructure is developed by Attwood et al. [21]. The purpose of this infrastructure is protecting critical infrastructures from failure or assists the system to recover and continue functioning if a failure was inevitable. For operating all the functions mentioned previously, sensor actuator networks are very much essential. These actuator networks connect themselves to IoT for collecting data needed by the smart city. The basic elements of smart city critical infrastructure developed by researchers such as smart cities systems annotation and aggregation service, critical response reasoning instance, sensor actuator network overlay state management, etc.

In [22], Asimakopoulou and Bessis concentrated on disaster management using crowdsourcing techniques to create smart buildings. Crowdsourcing technology is used for detection of emergency events and hazards by citizens using APIs in their mobile phones. The authors also proposed other technologies such as grid computing to integrate heterogeneous resources, cloud computing to enable access to these resources and pervasive computing to collect and handle data from devices.

In another work, Wang et al. [23] demonstrated the use of world wind geographic software developed by NASA for reconstructing a city. The software is an open-source platform that allows visualization, simulation and interaction in all living sectors of a smart city. The two main components of this technology are data collection and visual display. The data are collected through IoT, network analysis and web map services.

Samaras et al. [24] developed a smart city platform SEN2SOC for implementation in the SmartSantander City of Spain. The objective was to increase the interaction between sensor and social networks using the system of natural language generation (NLG) for improving the standard of living of the citizens and visitors in a smart city. The architecture of SEN2SOC platform is component based and includes mobile and web applications, sensor and social data monitoring, statistical analysis and interface. The NLG system is embedded in the platform and has the capability of receiving information from sensors and converts it into messages that can be easily understood by humans.

In [25], a smart parking system is proposed by Horng. The proposed system enables the people in locating parking spaces easily and quickly, which eventually helps in reduction of fuel congestion and air pollution. The proposed smart parking system uses WSNs for searching the presence of vehicles near a parking space. In smart parking system, an internal recommendation mechanism of the specific place informs the Parking Congestion Cloud Centre (PCCC). The PCCC transmits these data to the cloud server. The user ultimately receives the required information through his/her mobile device, which also acts as a sensor for the cloud server at the same time.

Besides the above-mentioned architectures, some works are undertaken by combining the features and technologies of the different architectures mentioned above. Examples of such architectures include combinations of IoT-AL [26], IoT-SOA [27, 28], IoT-SOA-AL [29], IoT-EDA [30], etc.

5.3 Real Life Applications

In this section, we provide a brief description of some state-of-the-art works that have been implemented in smart cities in various application areas such as food management, energy management, etc. For example, in food management, work on smart food supply is discussed. Likewise, in energy management, the works dealing with the concept of integrating renewable energy with conventional energy systems for reducing energy consumption are discussed. This is followed by smart transport systems where works considering traffic safety applications to smart parking are discussed.

5.3.1 Food Management

This section describes the works undertaken by researchers to solve real life problems that form a part of smart city with respect to food management.

In [31], the authors studied a case for tracking the origin of food supply chain that forms an important IoT application for smart cities. The food supply chain in modern cities has seen a rapid growth with increasing demands of human beings. In this respect, IoT serves as a platform for monitoring and managing food supply chain. Finally, the authors proposed a smart sensor data collection mechanism for monitoring, analyzing and managing the food industry in cities. In particular, the proposed data collection mechanism is used for tracing the contamination source and thereby backtracking the infected food in the markets.

5.3.2 Energy Management

Energy management is a prime aspect that needs to be taken care of while designing of smart cities. Considering the current scenario, the objective of the applications used in smart cities should promote use of renewable energy for their operations. Also, one must pay attention to conservation of energy for which energy utilization should be reduced. Given below are two works that have proposed mechanisms for energy preservation in smart cities.

In [32], authors have proposed the design of a Sustainable Energy Microsystem (SEM) that aims to integrate different subsystems that function independently such as dispersed generation from renewable and combined heat and power units, recharging of plug-in hybrid and electric vehicles used for surface mobility etc. Here, the authors try to move beyond the idea of smart grids and look for solutions that will make it possible for a better integrated management of energy flows between different subsystems that will form an integral part of smart city. The SEM is conceptualized as a flexible energy hub used for supplying and storing many energy carriers. Therefore, this work actually proposes new tools that are aimed at optimizing the design and the e-governance of SEM. Here, the new tools are integrated based on complexity science and risk analysis. Also, reliability and quality are assured by proposing new technologies for service optimization and reconfiguration. The authors have also tried to devise mechanisms using the new technologies for minimizing the infrastructure vulnerabilities. Further, they have analyzed the control of interdependencies among the infrastructures and also between the environment and the infrastructure. Finally, organizational problems and human factor impacts on SEM control and management are studied in the work.

In another work [33], the authors have proposed solutions through the project DC4Cities that aim to optimize the share of local renewable power sources while operating data centres in smart cities. Basically, data centres are important functionaries in smart cities as they perform the dual function as IT service providers and energy consumers. A major challenge for future smart cities is that of integrating intermittent renewable energy sources into the local power grid with an objective of IT-based low carbon economy. The authors have proposed methods for power management options between the data centre and the smart city together with internal adaptation strategies. Finally, the authors have implemented the proposed mechanism and evaluated the same through simulation.

5.3.3   Transport Management

Intelligent transport systems are a fundamental part of smart city [34] without which the operation of such a city would be incomplete. Intelligent transport systems include applications related to traffic safety, traffic law enforcement, traffic control and smart parking. In Fig. 5.2, reference architecture of a typical WSN-based ITS is shown. It is worth noting that the architecture has four main subsystems, namely, sensing, distribution, decision-making and execution. Each of these subsystems may carry out their work independently. The discussion given below highlights some of the works done in intelligent transport system area.

Traffic safety applications have been dealt with in [35, 36] that monitor the presence of traffic or animals within a safety zone as defined by the application. The objective of traffic applications is to deal with prevention of accidents. The sensor devices are made to work proactively for alerting drivers against some possible dangers such as the presence of obstacles, animals, bad road conditions or vehicles driving in the wrong direction. These devices communicate among themselves for warning the drivers of events that are not within their sight, thereby averting any major accident. These sensor devices function using a particular approach or a

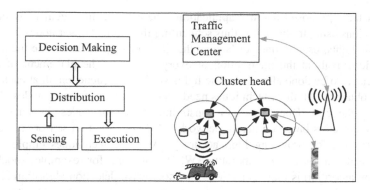

Fig. 5.2 Architecture of a WSN-based ITS

combination of both approaches. In the first approach, when a static sensor node detects the arrival of a vehicle, it activates the remaining static nodes for obtaining the conditions of the road that follows. The second approach makes the road information available to the nodes prior to the vehicles reaching them. This means that whenever any required data is obtained, it is transferred to a particular area so that they are collected by the passing vehicles later on. The second approach is very much applicable for detecting non-ephemeral events. In [37], the authors have suggested placing static sensor nodes at the beginning of every road that makes it possible for all vehicles to know beforehand the conditions of the road that were gathered by previous vehicles. The authors in [38] have combined WSNs and Vehicular Ad hoc Network (VANET) for implementing this technique. Here, WSN monitors the road and VANET circulates the information to other vehicles travelling on roads without WSNs or to distant static sensor nodes for warning drivers of absence of other vehicles.

In other works (e.g. [39, 40]), the authors use techniques for detecting speed limit breaches that form a part of traffic law enforcement application by collaborating between two sensor nodes. Here, cameras are used which trigger when such a speed violation is detected and the photographs are sent to Traffic Management Centre (TMC) where they are processed and stored. Also, it is possible to warn the drivers by using Variable Message Signs (VMSs) before issuing any fine. In [40], detection of illegal parking is handled by placing sensor nodes that take a picture of the number plate of the vehicle that has created this issue. In another work [41], the authors have used techniques for findings of post accident investigation. The post-accident investigation is necessary for determining the responsibilities after an accident.

In [42], the authors use traffic guidance applications such as path planning that are needed for determining the best urban scenarios. Here, sensor nodes are used for monitoring small-to-medium size road networks and estimate the time cost of each road segment for obtaining the optimum path in a particular direction. Also, the authors have proposed another application where traffic management is done at intersections using traffic lights, thus scheduling the traffic. Sensor nodes are placed on traffic lights, usually one per lane so that it is possible to determine the number of traffic arrivals at the intersection of every segment. The placement of sensor nodes can also be done after the traffic lights so that the queue length at each traffic light is obtained. All these techniques need a small number of sensor nodes, thereby reducing the cost. Due to certain constraints of sensor nodes, in some works acoustic detectors based on neural networks [43] and vibration sensors in vehicles [44] are used for providing high accuracy. As these techniques employ costly mechanisms, a purely collaborative WSN solution, for example shockwave detection algorithm is more suitable [45]. Shockwave detection algorithm is based on the fact that when an accident occurs, two shockwaves are generated in the traffic flow. One of the shockwave's propagates in the opposite direction of traffic while the other travels in the direction of traffic. In [46], the authors have implemented this method by placing sensor nodes along the road for estimating traffic volume and detecting potential shockwaves that are validated by adjacent nodes.

The lack of parking spaces in cities is a major concern which results in illegal parking, congestion due to low speed driving and long searching times for finding empty parking space by drivers. To reduce this problem for drivers, several smart parking systems have been developed which guide drivers to vacant parking spots (PGIS—Parking Guidance Information System) and enable smart payment and reservation options. For the deployment of smart parking systems, WSNs are a much better substitute against more expensive wired sensors. In [47], the authors proposed applications for detecting parking spaces using WSNs that detect the distribution of vacant parking lots where sensor nodes are placed at the entrance of each floor. In [48–50], the authors have used WSN that is deployed in a grid layout manner over the parking area. Here, the sensor nodes perform the task of vehicle detection that leaves or enter the parking area. WSNs are also used for on street parking applications where it is not cost effective to use VMS (Variable Message Sign) or other informative panels in the streets just for parking purposes. Thus, on-street parking systems depend on smart vehicles that are incorporated with On Board Units for receiving parking information.

5.4 Issues and Challenges of Building Intelligent Systems for Smart Cities

In this section, we provide an insight into the several issues and challenges that may be faced while designing, constructing and implementation of intelligent systems for smart cities.

5.4.1 Issues

There are a number of issues related to building intelligent system for smart cities, both of technical and social nature. Some of the specific technical issues are as follows:

- Public safety: Information analysis to be done in real time for reducing crime and act quickly to threats faced by the public.
- Health care: More improvised connections and advanced analytics for interpreting a large amount of data collected is required for providing better healthcare.
- Transport: Integrating all transport modes with each other, removing congestion and enabling issuance of new avenues are areas to be taken care of while designing the factor of transport in smart cities.
- Connectivity: In smart cities all businesses, citizens and systems should be provided with high speed connectivity for the smooth running of all applications in such cities.
- Energy issue: Areas should be explored where energy from conventional systems can be procured that can be utilized for operating the various applications in smart cities. Also, people should be made aware of their individual energy consumptions and devise mechanisms for reducing such consumptions.
- Water: Raising awareness to reduce wastage of water as well as analyze the entire ecosystems that will help to estimate the amount of water supply to homes, industries and any other organizations.

5.4.2 Challenges

Like any emerging field, smart cities also face several genuine challenges that need to be addressed while developing such cities. Some of the challenges are briefly discussed below:

- Implementation cost: The development of smart cities involves technologies that are incurring a huge cost. Many cities that have tried to implement technologies with the ultimate objective of making the city 'smart' have invested lots of money. For example, the bus system in Copenhagen, Denmark, costs €125 million annually [12].
- High energy consumption: The sustaining of the technologies needed for the running of smart cities requires high energy that can be a major challenge for the upcoming of smart cities.
- Privacy and security: Privacy and security will play a very vital role for smart cities. The people in smart cities will use smart city services with their smartphones and computers that are connected through networks. Also, in the context of smart cities, enabling technologies for sensing applications makes the

communication networks highly vulnerable to threats related to cybersecurity and cyber vandalism. So handling these security issues related with the functioning of smart cities is a real challenge that needs utmost attention.

- Integration of technologies: Smart cities are fast emerging as a possible solution for brighter future prospects. While information and communication technologies are being used for development of such cities in terms of materials and infrastructure, the same technologies are also used for the planning of smart cities that involve the usage of computations and data. Therefore, a vital challenge is to demonstrate how the technologies utilized for the above mentioned developments are interoperable so that cities can really be termed as smart ones.
- Traffic management system: Challenges in WSNs used in smart cities for traffic management systems range from the need for a highly reliable and fast MAC access protocol to data forwarding mechanisms for ensuring critical message transmissions that carry information regarding emergency situations on roads.
- Mobility: In smart cities, it is very much essential to guarantee uninterrupted service to mobile users while shifting between different access networks. This is important so as to enable flawless running of applications in smart cities.
- Scalability: The limitations with respect to restrictions in storage, bandwidth and computational abilities that act as an hindrance to service providers while handling a large number of users should not come in the way of proper functioning of the different services applicable to smart cities.
- Fault tolerance: This is a real challenge while designing smart cities as information and communication technologies should be implemented in such a way such that they are highly resilient to system failures.
- Upgradation: This feature is true for the development of any technology and likewise for smart cities too. Upgrading a smart city will incur a huge cost as such a city is very much dependant on communication and technologies, thereby posing a tough challenge.

5.4.3 State-of-the-Art Solutions

In this section, a brief description of the various key issues that were addressed in recent past for the development of intelligent systems for smart cities is provided.

In [51], Suryadevara et al. developed a low cost, flexible, robust and data driven intelligent system for determining the wellness of elderly persons living alone in a smart home. The system model comprises of two modules, viz. WSN and intelligent home monitoring software system. These modules are vested with the task of collecting sensor data and performing data analysis for detection of changes in the behavioural pattern of the elderly. Based on the behavioural pattern of the elderly person, the healthcare service providers provide accurate assistance to the elderly persons. The authors have tested the models at several elderly homes and the results are found to be convincing. Similar to [51], a WSN based intelligent elderly care monitoring system was designed by Dasios et al. [52]. Initially, the system monitors and records various environmental parameters such as temperature, humidity and light intensity to gather daily activity like moving, sitting and sleeping of the elderly person. If any significant deviation from the normal activity pattern of an individual is detected, the system issues automated alarms to authorized persons.

In [53], Semertzidis et al. proposed a real-time traffic monitoring system using visual sensor networks. The proposed system consists of a number of visual sensor nodes and personal computers. The visual sensor node captures imagery data and sends them to the personal computer for processing and subsequent recognition and tracking of any car. An intelligent vehicle speed controlling system is proposed in [54]. In the proposed system, RFID is used for communication between vehicle and traffic signs in order to control the vehicle speed. In another work [55], Magpantay et al. implemented and deployed a WSN for the monitoring of usage of electric energy in smart buildings. Here, WSN is developed using the Granular Radio Energy (GRE) sensing node. The GRE sensing node consists of a micro-controller, a radio, a battery and a giant magnetoresistive magnetic field sensor. The authors have implemented these GRE sensing nodes based WSN in smart building for reducing energy consumptions and have obtained effective results. Similar to [55], an intelligent energy monitoring system called EnerISS (Energy Integrated urban planning & managing Support System) is developed by Kim et al. [56]. In EnerISS, a WSN is used to collect energy usage data from the buildings. The collected energy usage data coupled with location information (i.e. GIS data) are stored in EnerISS database. Finally, based on the rules generated from the interaction between the consumer and producer, EnerISS takes in-time decision for efficient energy supply management.

In [57], Metje et al. proposed an intelligent water pipeline monitoring system based on WSNs. In the proposed system, sensor nodes are used to monitor specifically three parameters, namely, vibration, pressure and sound. By monitoring these parameters, the system successfully detects a leakage in the pipeline.

5.5 Future Directions

There have been a number of researches on building intelligent system for smart cities, however, there are some important open issues that remain unresolved or have not been explored extensively. This section provides an insight into the research areas of building intelligent systems for smart cities where very little has been done till date. Areas where further improvements can be done are also described briefly:

- Cloud platform usage for development: Using the cloud computing platform in smart cities can be one of the areas that need to be explored in future as cloud services can further improve life in smart cities. This can be achieved by using big data driven dispatch of police or traffic details, coordinated public works scheduling, municipal repairs, etc., for ensuring public safety and security. Thus the challenge of managing big data in smart cities using cloud services is an upcoming area of immense interest for researchers.

- Incorporating IoT in a broader prospect: Though IoT has become a part and parcel for the proper functioning of smart cities, still a lot of work remains to be done for deeper utilization of IoT in such cities. IoT plays a very important role in obtaining valuable information from real world data. The services of IoT fall in a very wide domain. More role of IoT in smart cities can be investigated.
- Securing interoperability: Many technologies that use state-of-the-art security within city functions such as lighting, transportation, etc., allows free movement of data within them. Therefore, intelligent communication can be ensured between such technologies. It is thus necessary for securing interoperability between such systems that can be taken up as a prospective research work.
- Data management: In smart city, data plays an important role. A large amount of data will be produced by smart cities, thus handling and understanding them will be an important challenge. Further, to store this huge amount of data one needs a big amount of storage. Addressing these challenges require greater synergy between the application viewpoint and implementation.

5.6 Conclusion

In the near future, it is perceived that the services of smart cities will be indispensable. Nevertheless, a lot of work still needs to be done and more refinement in existing structures are necessary. Considering all these factors we have gone forward with this survey where the general concept of smart cities together with the issues and challenges are discussed. Also, how intelligent systems such as transport form an integral part are demonstrated by discussing works that have been taken up by researchers. In general, the major components of smart cities include smart commerce, smart infrastructure, smart environment, smart governance, smart communication and smart mobility. The development of smart cities is vulnerable to several issues such as socioeconomic, political and the most important being technical issues. The technical issues involve system interoperability and cost efficient technology, thereby making it necessary to give importance to security and privacy issues. Security is a prime factor in smart cities as the networks that form an integral part of the functioning of such cities are susceptible to malicious attackers. As the concept of smart cities is still in the development phase, it necessitates for identifying the core need of information security in various technologies. Finally, we discuss the future areas that need to be explored in the smart city sector to wrap up this survey.

References

1. Caragliu A, Bo CD, Nijkamp P (2011) Smart cities in Europe. J Urban Technol 18(2):65–82
2. Dutton WH, Kraemer KL, Blumler JG (1987) Wired cities: shaping the future of communications. Macmillan Publishing Co. Inc., Indianapolis, IN
3. Bowerman B, Braverman J, Taylor J, Todosow H, Wimmersperg UV (2000) The vision of a smart city. In: Proceedings 2nd international life extension technology workshop, 28
4. Batty M, Axhausen KW, Giannotti F, Pozdnoukhov A, Bazzani A, Wachowicz M, Ouzounis G, Portugali Y (2012) Smart cities of the future. Eur Phys J Spec Top 214(1): 481–518
5. Arasteh H, Hosseinnezhad V, Loia V, Tommasetti A, Troisi O, Shafie-khah M, Siano P (2016) Iot-based smart cities: a survey. In: Proceedings of 16th international conference on environment and electrical engineering, pp 1–6
6. Komninos N, Schaffers H, Pallot M (2011) Developing a policy roadmap for smart cities and the future internet. In: Proceedings international conference on eChallenges, pp 1–8
7. Ijaz S, Shah MA, Khan A, Ahmed M (2016) Smart cities: a survey on security concerns. Int J Adv Comput Sci Appl 7(2):612–625
8. Anthopoulos LG (2015) Understanding the smart city domain: a literature review. In: Transforming city governments for successful smart cities, pp 9–21
9. Giffinger R, Gudrun H (2010) Smart cities ranking: an effective instrument for the positioning of the cities? ACE: Archit City Environ 4(12):7–26
10. Fertner C, Giffinger R, Kramar H, Meijers E (2007) City ranking of European medium-sized cities. Centre of Regional Science, Vienna UT
11. Lombardi P, Giordano S, Farouh H, Yousef W (2012) Modelling the smart city performance. Eur J Soc Sci Res 25(2):137–149
12. Khatoun R, Zeadally S (2016) Smart cities: concepts, architectures, research opportunities. Commun ACM 59(8):46–57
13. Kyriazopoulou C (2015) Smart city technologies and architectures: a literature review. In: Proceedings international conference on smart cities and green ICT systems, pp 1–12
14. Ishida T (2000) Understanding digital cities. In: Proceedings international conference on digital cities: experiences, technologies and future perspectives, LNCS 1765, pp 7–17
15. Anthopoulos LG, Tsoukalas IA (2006) The implementation model of a digital city: the case study of the digital city of Trikala, Greece: eTrikala. J e-Government 2(2):91–109
16. Su K, Li J, Fu H (2011) Smart city and the applications. In: Proceedings international conference on electronics, communications and control, pp 1028–1031
17. Carretero J (2012) ADAPCITY: a self-adaptive, reliable architecture for heterogeneous devices in smart cities. In: European commissions-ICT proposers
18. Vilajosana I, Llosa J, Martinez B, Domingo-Prieto M, Angles A (2013) Bootstrapping smart cities through a self-sustainable model based on big data flows. IEEE Commun Mag 51(6):128–134
19. Anthopoulos L, Fitsilis P (2010) From digital to ubiquitous cities: defining a common architecture for urban development. In: Proceedings 6th international conference on intelligent environments, pp 301–306
20. Filipponi L, Vitaletti A, Landi G, Memeo V, Laura G, Pucci P (2010) Smart city: an event driven architecture for monitoring public spaces with heterogeneous sensors. In: Proceedings 4th international conference on sensor technologies and applications, pp 281–286
21. Attwood A, Merabti M, Fergus P, Abuelmaatti O (2011) SCCIR: smart cities critical infrastructure response framework. In: Proceedings developments in E-systems engineering conference, pp 460–464
22. Asimakopoulou E, Bessis N (2011) Buildings and crowds: forming smart cities for more effective disaster management. In: Proceedings international conference on innovative mobile and internet services in ubiquitous computing, pp 229–234

23. Wang R, Jin L, Xiao R, Guo S, Li S (2012) 3D reconstruction and interaction for smart city based on world wind. In: Proceedings international conference on audio, language and image processing, pp 953–956
24. Samaras C, Vakali A, Giatsoglou M, Chatzakou D, Angelis L (2013) Requirements and architecture design principles for a smart city experiment with sensor and social networks integration. In: Proceedings 17th Panhellenic conference on informatics, pp 327–334
25. Horng GJ (2015) The adaptive recommendation mechanism for distributed parking service in smart city. Wirel Pers Commun 80(1):395–413
26. Wang Y, Zhou Y (2012) Cloud architecture based on near field communication in the smart city. In: Proceedings 7th international conference on computer science & education, 2012, pp 231–234
27. Andreini F, Crisciani F, Cicconetti C, Mambrini R (2011) A scalable architecture for geo-localized service access in smart cities. In: Proceedings future network and mobile summit, pp 1–8
28. Hu M, Li C (2012) Design smart city based on 3S, IoT, grid computing and cloud computing technology. In: Proceedings internet of things workshop, CCIS 312, pp 466–472
29. Xiong Z, Zhengand Y, Li C (2014) Data vitalization's perspective towards smart city: a reference model for data service oriented architecture, In: Proceedings 14th IEEE/ACM international symposium on cluster, cloud and grid computing, pp 865–874
30. Wan J, Li D, Zou C, Zhou K (2012) M2M communications for smart city: an event-based architecture. In: Proceedings 12th international conference on computer and information technology, pp 895–900
31. Zhang Q, Huang T, Zhu Y, Qiu M (2013) A case study of sensor data collection and analysis in smart city: provenance in smart food supply chain. Int J Distrib Sens Netw, article ID 382132, pp 1–12
32. Brenna M, Falvo MC, Foiadelli F, Martirano L, Massaro F, Poli D, Vaccaro A (2012) Challenges in energy systems for the smart-cities of the future. In: Proceedings international energy conference and exhibition, pp 755–762
33. Klingert S, Niedermeier F, Dupont C, Giuliani G, Schulze T, Meer HD (2015) Renewable energy-aware data centre operations for smart cities the DC4Cities approach. In: Proceedings international conference of smart cities and green ICT systems, pp 1–9
34. Losilla F, Sanchez AJG, Sanchez FG, Haro JG, Haas ZJ (2011) A comprehensive approach to WSN-based ITS applications: a survey. Sensors 11(11):10220–10265
35. Birk W, Osipov E, Eliasson J (2009) iRoad—cooperative road infrastructure systems for driver support. In: Proceedings 16th ITS world congress, pp 1–12
36. Qin H, Li Z, Wang Y, Lu X, Zhang W, Wang G (2010) An integrated network of roadside sensors and vehicles for driving safety: concept, design and experiments. In: Proceedings international conference on pervasive computing and communications, pp 79–87
37. Kong F, Tan J (2008) A collaboration-based hybrid vehicular sensor network architecture. In: Proceedings international conference on information and automation, pp 584–589
38. Weingärtner E, Kargl F (2007) A prototype study on hybrid sensor-vehicular networks. In: Proceedings 6th GI/ITG KuVS Fachgespräch wireless sensor networks, pp 1–4
39. Yoo S, Chong PK, Kim D (2009) S3: school zone safety system based on wireless sensor network. Sensors 9(8):5968–5988
40. Bohli JM, Hessler A, Ugus O, Westhoff D (2008) A secure and resilient WSN roadside architecture for intelligent transport systems. In: Proceedings 1st ACM conference on wireless network security, pp 161–171
41. Chang YS, Juang TY, Su CY (2008) Wireless sensor network assisted dynamic path planning for transportation systems. In: Proceedings international conference on autonomic and trusted computing, LNCS 5060, pp 615–628
42. Shuai M, Xie K, Ma X and Song G, (2008), An on-road wireless sensor network approach for urban traffic state monitoring. In: Proceedings 11th international conference on intelligent transportation systems, pp 1195–1200

43. Harlow C, Wang Y (2002) Acoustic accident detection system. ITS J-Intell Trans Syst J 7(1):43–56
44. Mateo RMA, Lee Y, Lee J (2009) Collision detection for ubiquitous parking management based on multi-agent system. In: Proceedings international symposium on agent and multi-agent systems: technologies and applications, LNAI 5559, pp 570–578
45. Gazis DC (2002) The origins of traffic theory. Operations Res 50(1):69–77
46. Chowdhury M, Wang KC, Fries R, Ma Y, Bagaria D (2007) Distributed wireless sensor network system for transportation safety and security. In: Proceedings defense and security symposium, pp 653807–653807
47. Lee S, Yoon D, Ghosh A (2008) Intelligent parking lot application using wireless sensor networks. In: Proceedings international symposium on collaborative technologies and systems, pp 48–57
48. Benson JP, O'Donovan T, O'Sullivan P, Roedig U, Sreenan C, Barton J, Murphy A, O'Flynn B (2006) Car-park management using wireless sensor networks.. In: Proceedings 31st IEEE conference on local computer networks, pp 588–595
49. Srikanth SV, Pramod PJ, Dileep KP, Tapas S, Mahesh U, Patil S, Chandra B (2009) Design and implementation of a prototype smart PARKing (SPARK) system using wireless sensor networks. In: Proceedings international conference on advanced information networking and applications, pp 401–406
50. Yoo S, Chong PK, Kim T, Kang J, Kim D, Shin C, Sung K, Jang B (2008) PGS: parking guidance system based on wireless sensor network. In: Proceedings 3rd international symposium on wireless pervasive computing, pp 218–222
51. Suryadevara NK, Mukhopadhyay SC, Wang R, Rayudu RK (2013) Forecasting the Behavior of an Elderly using Wireless Sensors Data in a Smart Home. Eng Appl Artif Intell 26 (10):2641–2652
52. Dasios A, Gavalas D, Pantziou G, Konstantopoulos C (2015) Wireless sensor network deployment for remote elderly care monitoring. In: Proceedings 8th ACM international conference on PErvasive technologies related to assistive environments, pp 61–64
53. Semertzidis T, Dimitropoulos K, Koutsia A, Grammalidis N (2010) Video sensor network for real-time traffic monitoring and surveillance. IET Intell Transp Syst 4(2):103–112
54. Pérez J, Seco F, Milanés V, Jiménez A, Díaz J, Pedro T (2010) An RFID-based intelligent vehicle speed controller using active traffic signals. Sensors 10(6):5872–5887
55. Magpantay P, Paprotny I, Send R, Xu Q, Sherman C, Alarcon L, White R, Wright P (2014) Energy monitoring in smart buildings using wireless sensor networks. In: Proceedings 3rd international conference on smart systems devices and technologies, pp 78–81
56. Kim SA, Shin D, Choe Y, Seibert T, Walz SP (2012) Integrated energy monitoring and visualization system for smart green city development. Autom Constr 22(2012):51–59
57. Metje N, Chapman D, Cheneler D, Ward M, Thomas A (2011) Smart pipes—instrumented water pipes, can this be made a reality? Sensors 11(8):7455–7475

Chapter 6
IoT Challenges in Data and Citizen-centric Smart City Governance

A. Sebastian, S. Sivagurunathan and V. Muthu Ganeshan

Abstract Internet of Things (IoT) environment is affecting all spheres of human life and society. Increasing number of handheld devices, low-cost internet access, constant strive for innovation, enormous inherent business value, comfort, efficiency, and automation have made IoT environment highly dominant. Over the years, many efforts have been made to implement IoT connectivity frameworks in relation to development of smart cities, including development of smart energy, smart transport, smart healthcare and so on. However, not much attention has been given to the smart city governance. In this context, resolution of IoT challenges in data and citizen-centric smart city governance is a welcome effort in the right direction. In this chapter, we discuss in detail the nature of data and citizen-centric smart city governance and describe the challenges and solutions in such connected environment. We present the building blocks of data and citizen-centric smart city governance for creating knowledge centers (kc) for various city governance services, with a view that knowledge-based governance will bring the much-needed efficiency, transparency, trust, and sustainability.

Keywords Internet of things · IoT · Smart city · Governance · Knowledge centre Social IoT · Citizen-centered governance

6.1 Introduction

Internet of Things (IoT) can be defined as "the pervasive presence around us, of a variety of things or objects such as Radio-Frequency Identification (RFID) tags, sensors, actuators, mobile phones, etc., which through unique addressing schemes, are able to interact with each other and cooperate with their neighbors to reach common goals" [1]. Cisco defines Internet of Everything (IoE) as the "convergence

A. Sebastian · S. Sivagurunathan (✉) · V. Muthu Ganeshan
Department of Computer Science and Applications,
Gandhigram Rural Institute, Dindigul, India
e-mail: sebastinsj@gmail.com

© Springer International Publishing AG, part of Springer Nature 2018
Z. Mahmood (ed.), *Smart Cities*, Computer Communications and Networks,
https://doi.org/10.1007/978-3-319-76669-0_6

of people, process, data, and things that bring about unprecedented disruption" [1]. This ecosystem of interconnected things and the technology that manage them have enormous business value. For example, the whole annual economic impact caused by the IoT is estimated to be in the range of \$2.7–\$6.2 trillion by the year 2025. Healthcare applications and related IoT-based services that enable medical wellness, prevention of diseases, diagnosis, treatment, and monitoring services to be delivered efficiently through electronic media are expected to create about \$1.1–\$2.5 trillion annually by the global economy by 2025 [2]. National Informatics Centre (NIC) foresees that by 2025, internet nodes may reside in everyday things like food packages, furniture, paper documents, wearable devices, home appliances, automobile parts, and more. It means, popular demands combined with advancing technology would permeate every aspect of human life [3]. Hence, IoT is an all-encompassing term for a network backbone that will host billions of devices and sensors that communicate intelligently. Figure 6.1 explains the components of IoT technology stack.

Efforts to deploy IoT technology in agriculture, forest preservation, supply chain management, industrial automation, smart home, etc. are fast catching up. The number of research articles published and research carried by technology delivering companies and many smart city projects around the world suggest that IoT technology is implemented most in smart city initiatives. The reason behind this is that the cities are becoming the focal point of economic prosperity, employment opportunities, and conducive ambience for business activities. Most government departments are also situated in cities. Better infrastructure for health care, education, entertainment, and transport too, add people's attraction to cities. Today, cities have become iconic symbols of progress and development. According to the global health observatory, urban population accounted for more than half of the total global population as of 2009 and will be more than 60% by 2030. The UN World Economic and Social Survey 2013 suggested Africa, Asia, and other developing regions will be housing an estimate of 80% of the world's urban population in the coming years [4]. Therefore, in the coming years, smart city management will be one of the indicators of development and technical advancement of a nation. Focus Group on Smart Sustainable Cities (FG-SSG) define smart city as an innovative city that uses Information and Communication Technologies (ICTs) and other means to improve the quality of life, efficiency of urban operation and services, and competitiveness, while ensuring that it meets the needs of present

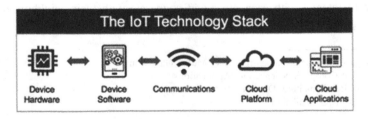

Fig. 6.1 IoT technology stack

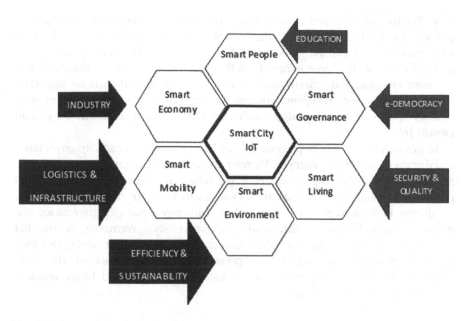

Fig. 6.2 Components of a smart city

and future generation with respect to economic, social, and environmental aspects [4]. A city can be classified as *smart* when safety, enhanced public services, and health monitoring systems become available to any citizen, wherever he is located. All these require precise design, develop and deployment, and maintain public-private infrastructures based on advanced and integrated materials, sensors, electronics, computer systems, and databases [5]. There are six components associated with different aspects of urban life, as shown in Fig. 6.2.

Based on the IoT connected environment, there are many smart city initiatives currently taking place around the world. These include: PlanIT Valley (Portugal), Neapolis (Cyprus), Skolkovo Innovation Center (Russia), Cyberport Hong Kong (China), Songdo International Business District (South Korea), Cyberjaya (Malaysia), Masdar City (Abu Dhabi, UAE), King Abdullah Economic City (KAEC) in Saudi Arabia, Gujarat International Finance Tec-City (GIFT) in India, and Infocomm Development Authority (IDA) of Singapore [4].

Primarily, smart city management comes under city government. Many of the smart city government activities such as delivery of citizen utility services, data and information sharing among various government entities, efficient response to emergency situations, decisions for many maintenance services, dissemination of information regarding health to public, etc. come under city government. Hence, city government holds the key for the efficient use of IoT technology for citizen's well-being and economic growth. Smart city governance is an infrastructure mechanism to help smart city government perform its services. IoT environment for smart city governance can bring efficiency, innovation, leadership, transparency, cost-effective and sustainable future. It is a common perception that what makes a city smart is the technology that efficiently delivers government services. In actuality, the success of technology lies in the hands of smart citizens. In this regard, we aim to look at the IoT environment from the point of smart city governance based on smart city data and citizens themselves. Citizen participation is an important aspect of governance. Therefore, governance is responsible to infuse smartness in citizens by providing quality education, moral values, and opportunities for overall growth [6].

In this chapter, we aim to propose data and citizen-centric smart city governance and discuss related IoT challenges. Remaining sections are organized as follows. In Sect. 6.2, we elaborate the various concepts related to smart city governance and provide justification for data and citizen-centric smart city governance. In Sect. 6.3, we discuss in detail various IoT approaches to manage smart city governance and propose data and citizen-centric model for smart city governance. Section 6.4 discusses IoT challenges in data and citizen-centric smart city governance; solutions are also presented. In Sect. 6.5, important quality indicators of data and citizen-centric smart city governance are listed. Conclusion and future research areas are discussed in Sect. 6.6.

6.2 Internet of Things Environment for Smart City Governance

Smart City governance can be defined as the ability of different sectors of government to provide government information and services to citizens by electronic means quickly and accurately, with minimum cost and less effort at any time and through a single site on the internet [7]. In other words, it may be said that a city government is the body of representatives that govern and control the city at a given time. Governance is the set of rules and laws framed by the government that are to be implemented through these representatives. data and citizen-centric smart city governance can use IoT environment for efficient delivery of government services, exchange of information, business transactions, and the integration of various stand-alone systems. It aims at the services between government-to-customer (G2C), government-to-business (G2B), government-to-government (local), and government-to-government (central, G2G) [7]. IoT technology will be part of the broadband highway that will deliver a wide range of governance and citizen services. Smart city governance empowers citizens through hassle free and transparent governance. At the heart of this transformation will be digitizing of government processes, supporting database and cloud infrastructure to simplify, improve, and optimize the various governance operations.

IoT technology for smart city governance also helps the government to assess the impacts technologies have on the practice and administration of governments and their relationships between public servants, wider society, not for profits

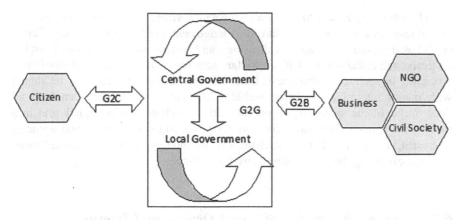

Fig. 6.3 Smart city governance relations

organizations (NGO), and corporate entities [8]. SMART governance refers to the process of government functioning to bring about smart, moral, accountable, responsible, and transparent governance [9]. Figure 6.3 is a smart city governance conceptual model to improve the interaction between G2C, G2B, G2G, and NGO, which aims to increase the administrative effectiveness and efficiency in the governance operations.

In this way, the strategic objective of IoT technology for smart city governance is to support and simplify governance, where stakeholders like citizens, civil society organizations, private companies, government lawmakers, and regulators on networks can take active participation in nation building [8]. We aim to analyze factors that make IoT environment suitable for smart city governance. They are: connected environment for connected government, growth rate of Internet access, growing number of smart devices, people's awareness on the role of government, advancements in ICTs, and effort toward sustainable growth.

6.2.1 Connected Environment for Connected Government

In a traditional city governance model, government services reach citizens in a hierarchical or top-down manner. Judgment, decisions, and policies are made at the top level and carried out by the lower ranks. They do manual reporting which result in time delay, slow process, etc. Add to this, various departments of the government such as health, education, public welfare, legal, etc. work in isolation. Additionally, not only departments but many cities and states in a country also act in isolation. Though citizen welfare is the focus of all government departments in a city, their interactions are not collective and helpful to reach a common goal. Each department in a city collects citizen-related data and maintains their own welfare related activities.

IoT technology is able to create a connected environment between departments and states resulting in citizen welfare knowledge centre (KC). In Knowledge Centre (KC)-based approach, governance decisions, and policies are no more top-down but collective and collaborative. Citizen welfare activities can be carried out timely and efficiently in such an environment. Data collected from smart city can be shared with parties interested in citizen welfare. Efficient data analytics can help all departments of the smart city to provide citizen welfare services quick and in a time-bound manner. This paves the way for participation of citizens and agencies interested in citizen welfare. Therefore, IoT technology with its connected environment can bring the best in smart city governance.

6.2.2 Increased Number of Smart Devices and Internet Access

The demand for IoT technology for smart city governance has its roots in the increased number of smart devices and easy access to cheap Internet services. Although in smart city governance, digital adoption is slow around the world, the numbers of people accessing digital services are increasing. The easy access to mobile connectivity and the business models of e-commerce are attracting users to prefer online services. For example, a network of almost 6000 UK online centers is established to allow people to access and familiarize with the online services. Figure 6.4 provides figures for world population, connected devices across the world and connected devices per person for the years 2003, 2010, 2015 and 2020. The values of connected devices and population are in billions. We can see that in the year 2020, the connected devices will reach 50 billion and the population

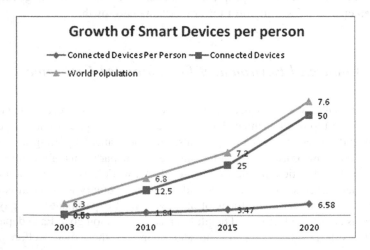

Fig. 6.4 Growth chart of smart devices with population

7.6 billion making 6.58 connected devices per person. Rapid growth of smart devices and Internet has led governments in both developing and developed countries to use technology for efficient and effective service to the citizens. Besides fast delivery of services, government services can be extended to all geographical segments in the country round the clock, all days in a year.

Along with efficient smart city governance, sharing of data across the government departments enable the policy makers to improve the quality of their decisions. Creating kc information database about development related activities facilitate the planners to make a holistic plan of city infrastructure such as location of hospitals, community health clinics, educational institutions, recreational avenues, etc. [9]. A careful planning of smart city governance can fully reap the benefits of IoT technology and connected environment.

6.2.3 IoT Technology: Government Performance Indicator

State of the art smart city facilities involve not only huge financial capital but also high maintenance cost. Therefore, pressure is mounting on the city governments to reduce the operating cost. At the same time, awareness level of citizens about the role of government is increasing. As a result, citizens expect an improved service from the city government with more flexibility, efficiency, and without any premium rate for the additional services. Service delivery mechanisms are undergoing fundamental change and moving toward citizen-centric governance. Growing number of digital citizens also means increase in common man's skill level in using the digital technology. Day by day, digital citizens are moving from passive consumers of government services to active consumers. In smart city governance set up, the performance of the city government can easily be assessed, the loopholes easily identified and digital citizens can closely monitor and suggest if and when changes are needed. Framing city governance policies and stakeholder relationships are strengthened by smart city governance analysis.

6.2.4 Convergence of Network Technologies and City Governance

The IoT European Research Cluster (IERC) definition states that "IoT is a dynamic global networking infrastructure with self-configuring capabilities based on standard and interoperable communication protocols where physical and virtual things have identities, physical attributes, and virtual personalities and use intelligent interfaces, and are seamlessly integrated into the information network" [10]. IoT environment is made not of a single technology but convergence of many technologies. Thus, IoT provides solutions based on the integration of information technology: hardware and software used to store, retrieve, and process data and communication technology for communications between individuals and groups. The rapid convergence of information and communication technology is taking place at three layers of technology innovation: the cloud, data and communication networks, and devices [10].

As a result of convergence, IoT applications require that industries and business houses adapt to converging IoT environment. This convergence will create new opportunities for startup, which in turn will benefit the users with enriched user experience. In addition, handling sheer number of things and objects that will be connected to the IOT, newer technological attempts such as cognitive technology, contextual intelligence, content, and context-aware applications, and fuzzy controlled systems that may reach the edges of the network through smart devices, make future of smart city governance bright. Hence, IoT is not only a network of computers, but it has evolved into a network of networks, where devices of all types and sizes, vehicles, smartphones, home appliances, toys, cameras, medical instruments, and industrial systems, all connected, all communicating, and sharing information at all time. This will benefit smart city governance in a big way.

6.3 IoT Approaches to Smart City Governance

As discussed in Sect. 6.2.4, the IoT connected environment brings device manufacturers, ICTs, DBMS, and Cloud under one umbrella. Many manufacturers bring out new products to meet the demanding needs at different layers of the IoT network. There are also many existing city governance models touching distinct stages of smart city governance. Smart city governance in developed countries has evolved considerably and moved to higher stages; however, the reality appears somewhat different. There is little empirical evidence that state–citizen interaction occurs as the models predict; users of government portals may visit to access specific information, or transact, or communicate with the state [12]. Therefore, designing a smart city governance model with focus on citizen interaction as well as data-driven is a felt need. Data from smart city operations as well as citizen interaction become the building blocks of our suggested smart city governance model. Efficient management of smart city data (collection, aggregation, analysis, judgment, and decision) with citizen interaction will be the right way to build smart city governance. Academicians and industry personals have proposed various approaches to manage smart city governance. Each approach addresses specific Smart City governance challenge. Our objective is to propose Data and Citizen-centric smart city governance. In this section, we discuss few approaches to smart city governance such as Business Model (BM), Service Oriented Approach (SOA), Role or Attribute-Based Approach (RBA), Context or Content-Aware Approach (CAA) and discuss in detail proposed Data and Citizen Centric Approach (DCA).

6.3.1 Business Model (BM)

Global technology vendors and business houses such as CISCO, IBM, MICROSOFT, AMAZON, INTEL, etc. are investing heavily in IoT market. This is because the growth of IoT is also attributed to the business value it generates for the future. IoT network due to its decentralized sensing and actuation capabilities also generate volume of data. So Cloud, Big Data Analytics, Data Mining, etc. are promising areas for revenue generation. Added to these, IoT has also enabled access to digital channels and communication pathways by people, institutions, and business houses resulting in increasing amount of commercial activities such as online purchases, digital money transactions, cloud-based services, online applications, and information services. So business houses are forced to revamp operations to support this new digital model. Since access to goods, products, and services are no longer limited by geography, markets have expanded drastically, presenting significant opportunities. According to a recent McKinsey Global Institute report, the IoT has the potential to unleash as much as $6.2 trillion in new global economic value annually by 2025. The firm also projects that 80–100% of all manufacturers will be using IoT applications by then, leading to potential economic impact of as much as $2.3 trillion for the global manufacturing industry alone [11].

IoT business model uses the opportunity of converging technologies toward value creation and new business opportunities. These business opportunities are realized by deploying smart city initiatives. Smart city deployments such as smart homes, smart transport, smart health, smart meter, etc. are focused on using IoT technology for profit. Therefore, the focus is more on developing tiny devices with more capability and efficient methods to collect, store, and retrieve data resulting in better business value. In BM approach, user's interest takes a back seat [12]. In a way, the value of a user depends on the profit margin. In the long run, smart city governance BM will fail because of lack of citizen welfare and participation. Citizens also express isolation and resentment to such city governance model.

6.3.2 Service Oriented Approach (SOA)

SOA is a better model than BM. In SOA, the IoT environment for smart city governance is arranged based on the type of service they provide to citizens. We can categorize the type of data as Data gathering service, Communicating and Transporting Service, Cloud & BIG DATA Service, Data Management Service, Applications Service, and Security Service. Figure 6.5 explains the SOA architecture. In this approach, Data Management and Security services are common to all service layers. Other services work within their layer and interact with layers adjacent to them. SOA solves IoT challenges in smart city governance such as identity, scalability, and authentication. Each service unit can be further divided

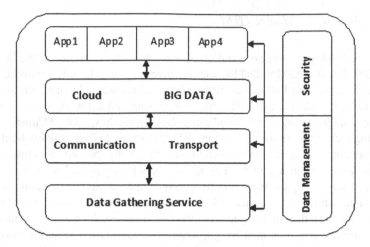

Fig. 6.5 Service-oriented architecture

into subunits and each subunit has privileges within their service domain. In this way, SOA architecture is able to handle medium-size IoT smart city governance.

In a smart city governance scenario, SOA is reasonably successful in delivering citizen welfare services. However, the limitation of SOA is that it focuses more on the integrity of the IoT network. Any modification on any of the layer is a huge task and also customized solutions to new applications are difficult. It can handle smart city governance to a certain level but as user interface increases it fails in the aspects of participatory government, collective intelligence, and less interaction with various stakeholders of city governance. It promotes the use of ICTs and smart technologies in governance space but cares little for the user's capabilities and aspirations.

6.3.3 Role or Attribute-Based Approach (RBA)

SOA helps to improve delivery of city governance services but it performs poorly on access control of resources and services. To handle these, Role or Attribute-based Approach (RBA) provides a better approach to enable scalable, manageable, effective, and efficient access control systems to the IoT-connected environment. IoT is basically resource-constrained network system. Devices are constrained in processing ability, memory, bandwidth, and power. Therefore, management of constrained resources is still a big challenge. RBA is more into securing the resources and network from attacks. Each user in RBA is assigned with roles or attributes-based access, authentication, and authorization to use network resources. RBA-based security is also considered. Once again, the entire network is structured in a hierarchy of roles or attributes with related privileges. RBA also is very helpful in maintaining privacy of the user as the focus of access is based on role or attribute. RBA is better than SOA in terms of scalability and security. In this way, RBA is able to provide access and security to users as well as services in smart city governance scenario.

6.3.4 Context/Content-Aware Approach (CAA)

IoT integration of sensory, computing, and communication devices generates more data. This gives rise for metadata, i.e., the ability to extract content or context from generated data. This ability to extract content becomes more crucial and complex when data becomes voluminous (i.e., BIG DATA). Complexity can be reduced through the integration of cognitive principles in the extraction of content from data and can serve as a foundation toward creating overall awareness of a current situation. This then gives the system the ability to respond to changes within its situational environment, with little or no direct instruction from users and therefore, facilitate customized, dependable, and reliable service creation.

CAA is capable of managing operations in smart city governance. In CAA, device, user, service, and network contexts are extracted and analyzed in order to create virtual networks, select heterogeneous access networks, and implement trust in IoT services. It also supports edge diversity, i.e., interconnectivity of various IoT services and end devices with different network technologies, for instance, Wi-Fi, LTE, ZigBee, and Bluetooth Smart, etc. By virtualizing the physical network, bandwidth reservation, QoS support, flow control, and load, balancing could be realized for different IoT services [13]. Therefore, CAA with its ability to extract content can efficiently respond to the demands of smart city governance. Smart city governance that deals with emergency response system, supply-demand equations and preemptive preparations for coming events can be well handled by CAA. But in CAA, data and citizen input are poorly utilized.

6.3.5 Data and Citizen-centric Approach (DCA)

The above-mentioned approaches address IoT challenges in smart city governance such as identity, scalability, resource management, privacy, and security. However, in all approaches, the focus is on safeguarding the integrity of network architecture. So the focus of smart city governance was also managing smart city governance infrastructure. But what makes IoT technology relevant and popular in smart city governance is not so much the architecture but creation of knowledge hidden behind these voluminous data. What makes IoT environment and city governance smart is the possibility of knowledge creation (kc) for different needs of the smart city. In this regard, data and citizen-centric IoT environment for smart city governance is the need of the hour. Data and citizen-centric smart city governance has immense potential to meet challenging smart city applications such as smart transport, smart home, smart business, smart health, smart electricity and water, smart parking, and many more. The idea of smartness lies in the inherent knowledge that is hidden beneath acquired city data. The data volume is directly proportional to the size of the smart city governance network. In this way, kc for various smart city services will be the first step in meeting data and citizen-centric approach.

Knowledge creation (kc) process eventually is developed in to Knowledge Centres (KCs). The creation of Knowledge Centre (KC) for smart city governance involves not only data but also citizens. As IoT technology is becoming popular, citizens are awakening to the resourcefulness of citizens with their handheld smart devices. The real live data of the smart city can be obtained from citizens themselves. In DCA, citizens are also sensors (data gatherers). Weather forecast, emergency relief operations, traffic updates, market analysis, delivery of government services, citizen database, etc. can be obtained from citizens themselves. This mode of participatory data collection from citizens will be more authentic, fault tolerant, and above all citizens will own the IoT vision as their own.

6.3.5.1 Data and Citizen-centric Smart City Governance

Data and citizen-centric smart city governance model is presented in Fig. 6.6. This model has four layers: Sensing Layer, Network layer, Data and Service Management Layer, and Application Layer. Sensing Layer consists of devices such as Sensors, Actuators, RFID tags, Meters, Video devices, and citizens. The function of sensing layer is to sense the physical reality, aggregate and transmit the data to the network layer. Network Layer deals with both routing and transporting acquired data to the next layer. This is done via communication medium such as wired, wireless, mobile communications (2G/3G/4G/LTE), GPRS, bluetooth, Wi-Fi, WiMAX, NFC, ZigBee, etc. Framing, header compression mechanisms, secure connection, etc. are also handled here. The data and service management layer is special to data and citizen-centric model. This layer has three parts: Data Analytics, Storage, and Knowledge Centre (KC). The received data are aggregated at the border router or gateway at the sensing layer. Eventually, aggregated data are stored in Cloud for data analytics using advanced techniques in data mining and big data. The result is the creation of KC which is useful to make appropriate decision followed by desired action. This is explained in detail in Fig. 6.7. The application layer provides interface for users to interact with the system. The security system provides security to all the layers at various degrees.

6.3.5.2 Data Aggregation

In the coming years, handling IoT data will be a big challenge. Every knowledge creation (kc) exercise involves managing big data. At the sensing level, all kinds of data such as integer, Boolean, audio, and video images are generated. Each type of

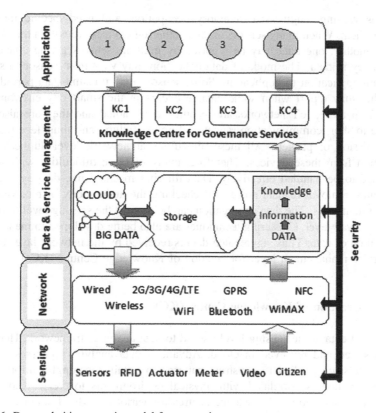

Fig. 6.6 Data and citizen-centric model for smart city governance

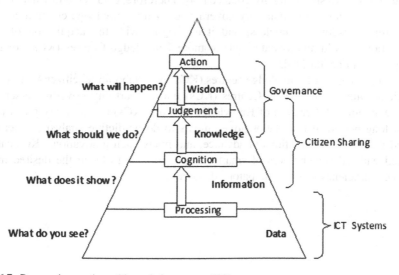

Fig. 6.7 Process in creation of knowledge centre (KC)

data has varying length, size, memory occupation, and need-specific mode to transmit them. When many sensors or data gathering devices are within the vicinity of one another, one data may be reported by multiple sensors giving chance for redundancy in data. The mode of data collection may vary from sensor to sensor and from application to application. Some sensors may transmit data periodically and other may report when some change occurs in the smart city environment. Apart from these, IoT networks are resource constrained and they are also susceptible to short communication ranges and power failure; and thus, face frequent retransmission of packets. All these difficulties at network level duplicate data generation from these devices. Therefore, many of these difficulties with sensed data need to be handled effectively. Data filtering mechanisms, data aggregation techniques, removal of data noise, and checking the authenticity of received data are important tasks. The data aggregation can be done at the sensing level or border router gateway level. Clustering techniques are also being developed to manage the aggregation of data. Thus, aggregated data is received by the network layer to data and service management layer for creation of Knowledge Centres (KCs).

6.3.5.3 Creation of Knowledge Center (KC)

Aggregated data at the sensing level are fed to data analytics framework. Here, the data is stored and retrieved in cloud. Advanced data analytic processes or data mining tools are applied to construct patterns to obtain meaningful information. This information is correlated with physical environments to create Knowledge Centre (KC). Creation of knowledge centres for various needs of smart city governance can be achieved. Repeated knowledge creation with citizen experience brings wisdom to smart city governance [14]. Therefore, data is the raw material for data and citizen-centric smart city governance. While knowledge creation changes over time, wisdom is timeless, and it all begins with the acquisition of data. Collection of voluminous data leads to more Knowledge Centres (KCs) for right judgment and action [15].

Hence, creation of knowledge centres (KCs) is collaborative, citizen-centric, and efficient. Due to Knowledge Centres (KCs) many smart city governance services can be automated. Creation of Knowledge Centres (KCs) in smart city governance for a long period of time helps governments to do predictive analysis, better prepared for untoward situations in advance, and many such innovations. KCs can be shared with all stakeholders of smart city governance to bring the desired transparency, efficiency, and participatory democracy.

6.4   IoT Challenges in Data and Citizen-centric Smart City Governance

IoT technology has inherent challenges like standardization, heterogeneity, scalability, security, and interoperability. As the size of the network increases, these challenges become more complex. IoT environment for smart city governance, with voluminous data, hyper-connectivity, and network complexity can severely affect the integrity, efficiency, security, and life span of the network. In this section, we discuss in detail IoT challenges our proposed model data and citizen-centric smart city governance would face and suggest solutions to manage them. The IoT challenges for smart city governance are: Data Management, Data Reusability, Identity, Privacy, and Cybersecurity. To meet these challenges, trust, multilayer integration, open data standards, open source software, and social media integration are suggested. Figure 6.8 depicts IoT challenges and solutions to data and citizen-centric smart city governance. Some of the challenges are elaborated in the following sections.

6.4.1   Data Management

Data management plays a vital role in making data and citizen-centric smart city governance successful. Data management includes: gather, aggregate, store, process, analyze data for creation of knowledge Centres (KCs) and finally take right decision and action. It also includes creation of data related governance policies, data management architecture, database management system integration, and data security. In smart city governance scenario, knowledge-based decision and actions are performed. Data generated in smart city governance environment are varying in nature. Data can be categorized as: data type, data size, protected or unprotected data, authorized or unauthorized data, important or menial data, etc. The category depends on the type of city governance service and the contribution it makes in creating Knowledge Centres (KCs). Data in city governance can also be categorized as private, public, and market data. Each of these categories reveals information about individual's details, his/her behaviors toward markets trends, social orientation, etc.

There are static data and real-time data in smart city governance environment. Citizen details, city governance service details, etc. are static. These are stored in large database systems. Real-time data are collected live, periodically to make day-today decisions. Real-time data include weather, pollution rate, preventive health care, traffic update, important events in the area, emergency response, etc. For efficient functioning of smart city governance, both these data are important as they add value to creation of knowledge centres (KCs).

Data management in smart city governance can be made efficient by integrating advanced IoT data analytics. Government can allow individuals, educational institutions, research centers to access its knowledge center for analysis and

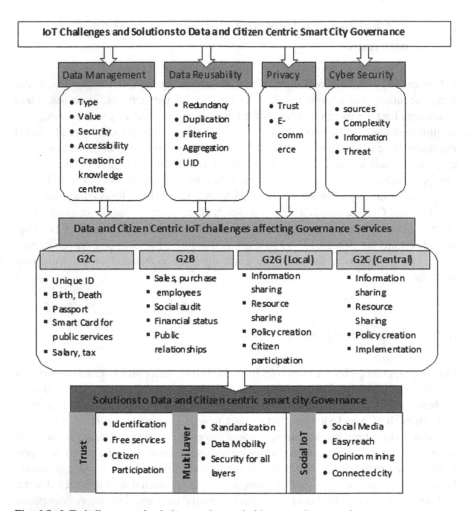

Fig. 6.8 IoT challenges and solutions to data and citizen-centric smart city governance

possible solution faced in smart city governance. In this way, the citizen partici-pation and cooperation will make activities of smart city governance popular and people friendly. Cluster or distributed data center will be helpful in creating knowledge centre with improved efficiency in processing and decision making. At the moment, IoT data looks a bit unstructured which in some sense is hindering mass adoption.

Real-time data need to be carefully normalized. Reliability of data, authenticity of device and data sources, efficient mechanism for sharing and distribution of city information and scalability are still data management challenges in data and citizen-centric smart city governance.

6.4.2   Data Reusability

In data and citizen-centric smart city governance, data reusability is part of data management. When voluminous data is generated data redundancy and duplication are inevitable. When services of smart city governance are many in number, user database will be multiplied for want of efficient data storage and analytics. Data reusability is one method, where the voluminous data can be shrunk. For example, linking smart city governance services like health care, driving license, passport, birth certificate, address, etc. to Unique Identification Number (UID) can merge all these service details. All departments of the government and their service records can be merged under single UID for each citizen. In this way, data reusability in smart city governance can be usefully achieved.

6.4.3   Identity and Privacy

One of the main reasons why IoT technology smart city governance has not been successful among citizens is that citizens have doubts about identity and privacy. Identity and privacy preservation are essential components of smart city governance. Especially, when it comes to services of smart city governance like online financial transactions, individual preferences, healthcare details, details of energy, water consumption, etc. Trust and confidence are essential components of these services. Privacy in commerce, health care, digital communications, financial matters, education, and many other areas can be viewed as trusted interactions between two parties. Personal identity and the ability to authenticate and protect it are issues in the design and delivery of personalized services in smart city governance. Service Oriented Architecture (SOA), Information-centric System (ICS) and Capability-based Access (CBA) are efforts to address the challenges of identity and privacy.

Anonymization is another attempt to manage identity and privacy. However, there are two main challenges for anonymization in IoT environment. One is the difficulty related to anonymization of data during data collection process. Another is the risk of re-identification of the individual from the aggregation of anonymized data. IoT environment for smart city governance relies heavily on cloud platform to store user data, process and retrieve information, where cloud provider is mostly considered trusted. Identity and privacy preservation is a great challenge when the deployment is large.

6.4.4 Cybersecurity

Cybersecurity in data and citizen-centric smart city governance is a big challenge for citizens, government officials, ICT managers and business houses. Networks continue to collect vast amounts of data from an increasing number of sources. This has serious impacts on the social, political, and economic undertaking of governance. Security has taken renewed importance associated with increasing dependence on massive database. Cybersecurity in smart city governance has to protect communication networks, individuals, organizations, systems, and infrastructure from fraud, errors, hackers, and attacks. These attacks may hamper service delivery and effective management of smart city governance services. According to the 2013 Symantec Internet Security Threat Report, 22% of targeted attacks are aimed at governments and energy utility companies, while government and healthcare institutions are the target of 24% in identity breaches [16]. In this regard, Fig. 6.9 explains the relationship between connectivity, complexity, and information.

IoT environment for large data and citizen-centric smart city governance consists of hyper-connectivity, hyper-complexity, and hyper-information. These components also bring hyper-vulnerability to IoT environment. Cybersecurity is an important issue across all layers of the IoT network. Sensing devices, communication network, data and service management (cloud, big data, knowledge centre) and applications (users) need to be secured from unauthorized users. The most common attacks on smart city governance are Denial of Service (DOS), sinkhole attack, tunnel attack, phishing, evesdropping, man in the middle attack, identity theft, etc. The vulnerability increases with large deployments. Cybersecurity in smart city governance can be improved by developing fault tolerant networks, cyber resilience systems and context-aware self-healing networks.

6.4.5 Trust

Data and citizen-centric smart city governance is basically built on trust. Currently, trust is emphasized more on online business transactions in smart city governance. Breach of trust can bring disastrous effect on the IoT network. Communication in smart city governance procedures frequently requires clear and unambiguous identification of the citizen and the public entity involved before the commencement of relations, otherwise, the operation cannot be carried out. Without the relevant relations, citizens are restricted to the simple unauthorized services.

Fig. 6.9 Hyper-vulnerability

There are many issues relating to trust deficit in IoT environment such as lack of standardization, deployment of IoT products without proper security mechanisms in place, private ownership of telecommunication networks and compromise on security to maximize profit. In data and citizen-centric smart city governance, respect for privacy, security, and legal rights need to be emphasized. For this reason, the authorities are obliged to respect in principle that the user should be free to opt for one out of a number of qualified providers. In fact, smart city governance services should be made available free of charge to citizens regardless of their income or specific knowledge [17]. In democracy, elected representatives act in the best interests of the people on behalf of the people. The power, credibility, and authority of government emanate from citizens and are rooted in trust, so governments are sustained only as long as citizens are minded to sustain them.

6.4.6 Multilayer Integration

The efficiency of data and citizen-centric smart city governance can be improved by multilayer integration. We discussed in Sect. 6.4.5 that lack of standardization is a trust deficit as well as security issue in IoT environment. So integration of all layers and adding security mechanism at each layer can secure data and citizen-centric smart city governance model from security threats. The type of security mechanism may differ from layer to layer. For example, the constrained nodes at the sensing layer need to be secured through lightweight cryptographic techniques but this approach will not be sufficient for data and service management layer. This layer needs strong cryptographic techniques. Likewise, the processing capacity of systems at data and service management should be higher than other layers.

Multilayer integration can also help a new node in the IoT network to join and leave without affecting the network. The issue of scalability is also met with multilayer integration. Multilayer integration helps in easy movement of data through all the layers of the network.

6.4.7 Social Media Integration

Social Media like Facebook, Whatsapp, Twitter, and many more are gaining popularity in smart city scenario. Increasing use of smartphones, easy and cheap access to internet has made social media growing day by day. Citizen's interaction with one another by social media is increasing enormously. In fact, live content of what happens in the city spreads virally in short time. This impacts the way citizens perceive and respond to initiatives of smart city governance.

Figure 6.10, gives the details of leading social websites and their increasing growth for years 2013, 2014, and 2015 [18]. People from all walks of life interact with one another in a casual way sharing texts, images, audio, and videos. Topics ranging from education, health, politics, stories, jokes, help messages, alerts, etc. are constantly posted by people. Social media can be of great help for smart city governance. Citizens can post positive messages, feedbacks, suggestions, solutions, etc. to smart city governance initiatives. In a way, social IoT can become a handy tool to strengthen data and citizen-centric smart city governance services. Citizen input is essential to representative democracy and government needs to focus on openness, transparency, and participation. Engaging the citizens online might enhance feelings of being consulted and listened to. There are many successful stories around the world, where citizens effectively used social media to organize people's movements and forced governments to change policies.

From a user perspective, social connectedness of families and friends instill interest and confidence than technological connectedness. The user engagement in social networking sites can bring awareness about IoT technology for smart city governance. In the coming years, research directions in IoT should consider the bundle of information obtained through social media in smart city scenario for governance.

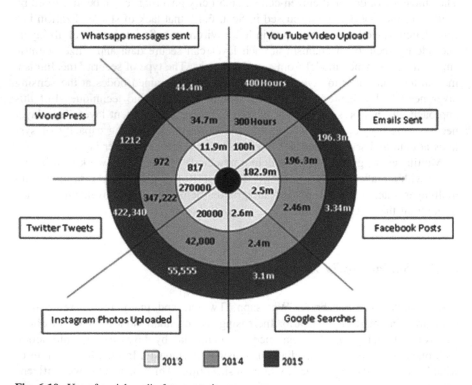

Fig. 6.10 Use of social media for smart city governance

6.5 Quality Indicators of Smart City Governance

IoT technology has much to offer for smart city governance but it needs to meet the challenges. The challenges are: lack of interest in government personal toward digital governance, lack of digitizing of government data and process, low computer literacy rate of citizens, lack of smart city governance infrastructure and privacy and security concerns of citizens. However, IoT is here to stay and so the IoT technology for smart city governance needs fresh ideas. In this section, we suggest quality indicators for data and citizen-centric Smart city governance. Figure 6.11 depicts the various quality indicators that are further explained below.

6.5.1 Efficiency

Efficiency is an important quality indicator of smart city governance. IoT is defined as anytime, anywhere, and anyhow. So delivery of smart city governance services must be round the clock, time-bound, with minimum error, timely intervention to identify or anticipate impending problems, increase in the scale of output and better

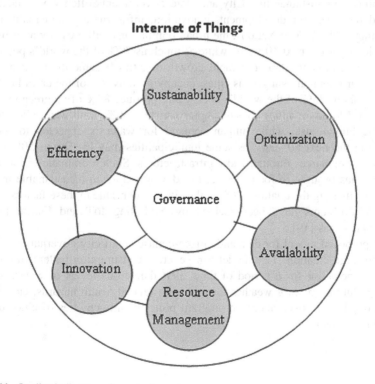

Fig. 6.11 Quality indicators of smart city governance

coordination between all parties of the government due to sharing of knowledge Centre (kc). In short, citizen's welfare is met in a well-organized manner through the use of IoT technology.

6.5.2 Innovation

Innovation is another quality indicator of smart city governance. Smart city governance services need to be delivered with innovation, which will captivate the imagination of citizens. Innovative methods of collecting data, easy Graphical User Interface (GUI) for users, simple Internet access to governance services, secure gateways for financial transactions, incentive-based approach to popularize smart governance are some ways by which we can assess the quality of innovation.

6.5.3 Availability and Sustainability

Two other quality indicators of data and citizen-centric smart city governance are availability and sustainability. City and state governments often work under constrained resources for development, innovation, infrastructure, and maintenance. According to the United Nations, the urban populations will grow by an estimated 2.3 billion over the next 40 years, while as much as 70% of the world's population will live in cities by 2050. The rapid growth of cities became the main driver of global environmental changes, as cities, occupying only 2% of the earth landmass, consume about 75% of the world's energy and produce 80% of its greenhouse gas emissions. Moreover, cities consume approximately 60% of all water allocated for domestic human use, while human demand for water is expected to increase six-fold in the next 50 years, as some municipalities may lose up to 50% of precious water resources through leaky infrastructures. Such a dramatic expansion of the cities has brought to focus the need to develop cities in a sustainable manner, while also making the quality of life in the cities better. Due to these factors, a wide range of problems have been tackled by exploiting IoT and Future Internet (FI) technologies [19].

Our proposed model for data and citizen-centric smart city governance is based on knowledge creation. This model can generate consumption pattern of citizens, consumer behavior for a period of time, alert dangerous levels of water, air and sound pollution, monitor weather forecast with related health hazards, etc. Hence, knowledge-based governance can program policies and activities of cities toward sustainable growth.

6.5.4   Management of Resources

Correct use of natural, human, financial, and technological resources is another quality indicator of smart city governance. Resources in this world are always scarce. So management of resources would mean: Using right resource, at the right place, at the right time, and at the right amount. Modern consumer behavior of citizens based on likes and dislikes cause a lot of waste. Quality indicators will analyze the type of resource available, the amount of resource needed, which resources are utilized maximum and which are underutilized. Toward sustainability, whether resources can be interchanged, etc. can be looked into if related data is available.

6.5.5   Optimization

Automation and digital intervention are aimed at optimization. It is an important quality indicator for smart city governance. Cisco says, "Of the overall $4.6 trillion, cities around the globe that harness so-called killer apps might potentially realize a total of $1.9 trillion through improved energy efficiency in buildings, utility tracking, and highway toll management". Defense agencies around the world might achieve up to $1.5 trillion in value over the next decade by capitalizing on shared communication systems and enhanced information sharing [20]. Federal civilian agencies worldwide could realize as much as $472 billion in savings and efficiencies through better disaster relief, fleet management, and cybersecurity. More than two-thirds of the value at stake for the public sector will come through the enhanced citizen-centric communications that IOE offers, said Cisco [21]. Majority of these benefits will be delivered by data-centric approach to smart city governance. To cite an example, Barcelona has moved most of its citizen service to a virtual environment that uses video and collaborative technologies to give citizens 24/7 interactive access to city government and has implemented an IOE-based approach to water management and smart parking.

6.6   Conclusion and Future Challenges

IoT technology and environment has made many things possible such as smart city services, smart and safer transport, automation of industries, context-aware lighting systems, etc. But smart city governance is not given due importance. Use of IoT to transform government's relationship with citizens, businesses groups, NGOs, and other arms of government are the focus of data and citizen-centric smart city governance. Data and citizen-centric smart city governance is also expected to curtail corruption, provide transparency, deliver convenience to citizen welfare activities, improve revenue, reduce cost, provide innovation, and provide sustainable future. All of these are possible because of knowledge-based approach of smart city governance.

There are many IoT challenges to data and citizen-centric smart city governance. These challenges are for our future research. Preconditions for smart city governance are: (a) City government in good working order, (b) Functioning governance processes, (c) Availability of resources, (d) Consensus on drivers for digital governance and (e) Political support and leadership. Government stakeholders include citizens, businesses, government employees, government ministries, department and agencies, union leaders, community leaders, politicians, and foreign investors [22]. First, smart city governance services can be started with government departments and ministries, which are easily assessable. Next, launching of smart city governance projects involve detailed study of existing applications. This will encourage local and central governments to develop public domains linking existing databases.

Multilayer integration is important in smart city governance to maintain coherent data integration. Setting up Knowledge Centers(KCs) for various services of smart city governance will add value to service delivery. Launching computer literacy programs to the government personnel will assist seamless transfer of information between offices in both center and local government. The information flow can be made fast by setting up dedicated quality communication networks for the government sector. To get more input for smart city governance services, establish links with worldwide institutions engaged in similar activities. Getting advice from the leading IT organizations will be helpful to formulate strategies. Developing One-Stop Shop (OSS) and giving One-Click link (OCL) will enable the citizen to avail the single window services in smart city governance. Involving citizens with computing skills will be an advantage to smart city governance projects [23]. Establishing information kiosks at public places such as shopping centers, post office, railway station, libraries, and selected STD/ISD booths will increase the IoT penetration rate. Social Media data also need to be integrated with data acquisition by sensors for smart city services like transport logistics [24]. IoT technology has much to offer for data and citizen-centric smart city governance.

References

1. Aggarwal CC, Ashish N, Sheth A (2013) Chapter 12. The internet of things : a survey from the data-centric. Manag Min Sens Data 383–428. https://doi.org/10.1007/978-1-4614-6309-2_12
2. Atzori L, Iera A, Morabito G (2010) The internet of things: a survey. Comput Netw 54(15): 2787–2805. https://doi.org/10.1016/j.comnet.2010.05.010
3. Al-Fuqaha A, Guizani M, Mohammadi M, Aledhari M, Ayyash M (2015) Internet of things: a survey on enabling technologies, protocols, and applications. IEEE Commun Surv Tutor 17(4):2347–2376. https://doi.org/10.1109/COMST.2015.2444095

4. Mahmood Z (ed) (2016) Connectivity frameworks for smart devices: the internet of things from a distributed computing perspective. In: Computer and communications and networks, Springer, pp 307–329. https://doi.org/10.1007/978-3-319-33124-9
5. Piro G, Cianci I, Grieco LA, Boggia G, Camarda P (2014) Information centric services in Smart Cities. J Syst Softw 88(1):169–188. https://doi.org/10.1016/j.jss.2013.10.029
6. Albino V, Berardi U, Dangelico RM (2015) Smart cities: definitions, dimensions, performance, and initiatives. J Urban Technol 22(1):3–21. https://doi.org/10.1080/10630732.2014.942092
7. Odat A, Khazaaleh M (2012) E-government challenges and opportunities: a case study of Jordan. Int J Comput Sci Issues 9(5):361–367
8. Gupta V, Sharma A (2012) E-governance in India: problems, challenges and prospects. Res J Econ Bus Stud 1(9):50–54
9. Palanisamy R (2004) Issues and challenges in e-governance planning. Elect Gov: An Int J 1(3):253–272. https://doi.org/10.1504/EG.2004.005551
10. Gershenfeld N, Krikorian R, Cohen D (2004) The internet of things. Sci Am 291. https://doi.org/10.1038/scientificamerican1004-76
11. McKinsey Global Institute (2013) Disruptive technologies: advances that will transform life, business, and the global economy, McKinsey Global Institute, May, 2013
12. Komninos N, Tsarchopoulos P, Kakderi C (2014) New services design for smart cities. In: Proceedings of the 2014 ACM international workshop on wireless and mobile technologies for smart cities—WiMobCity'14, Feb 2016, pp 29–38. https://doi.org/10.1145/2633661.2633664
13. Kolsaker A, Lee-Kelley L (2008) Citizens' attitudes towards e-government and e-governance: a UK study. Int J Public Sect Manag 21(7):723–738. https://doi.org/10.1108/09513550810904532
14. Chin WS, Kim HS, Heo YJ, Jang JW (2015) A context-based future network infrastructure for IoT services. Procedia Comput Sci 56(1):266–270. https://doi.org/10.1016/j.procs.2015.07.207
15. Sarrayrih MA, Sriram B (2015) Major challenges in developing a successful e-government: a review on the Sultanate of Oman. J King Saud Univ—Comput Inf Sci 27(2):230–235. https://doi.org/10.1016/j.jksuci.2014.04.004
16. Evans D (2011) The internet of things—how the next evolution of the internet is changing everything. CISCO white paper, April, pp 1–11. https://doi.org/10.1109/IEEESTD.2007.373646
17. Symantic (2013) Symantec internet security report 2013, pp 15 and 91. https://symnatec.com/security-response/publications/trreatreport.jsp?inid=us_ghp_thumbnail_13tv_2013
18. Electronic Government: Design, Applications and Management by Ake Gronlund, Idea Group Publishing, 2002, ISBN 1-930708-19-X, pp 11–12
19. Hernandez-Ramos JL, Pawlowski MP, Jara AJ, Skarmeta AF, Ladid L (2015) Toward a lightweight authentication and authorization framework for smart objects. IEEE J Sel Areas Commun 33(4):690–702. https://doi.org/10.1109/JSAC.2015.2393436
20. Theodoridis E, Mylonas G, Chatzigiannakis I (2013) Developing an IoT smart city framework. In: IISA 2013—4th international conference on information, intelligence, systems and applications, pp 180–185. https://doi.org/10.1109/IISA.2013.6623710
21. Mittal P, Kaur A (2013) E-Governance—a challenge for India. Int J Adv Res Comput Eng Technol (IJARCET) 2(3):1196–1199
22. Nahrstedt K, Lopresti D, Zorn B, Drobnis AW, Mynatt B, Wright HV (2016) Smart communities internet of things. In: arXiv Preprint arXiv:1604.02028, pp 1–9
23. Accenture (2009) From e-Government to e-Governance. Inst Health Public Serv Value (2):98. https://doi.org/10.1111/j.1748-5991.2007.00004.x
24. Djahel S, Doolan R (2015) A communications-oriented perspective on traffic management systems for smart cities: challenges and innovative approaches. Surv Tutor 17(1):125–151. Retrieved from http://ieeexplore.ieee.org/xpls/abs_all.jsp?arnumber=6857980

Chapter 7
Smart City Surveillance at the Network Edge in the Era of IoT: Opportunities and Challenges

Ning Chen and Yu Chen

Abstract Taking advantages of modern information and communication technologies (ICTs), smart cities aim at providing their residents better services as well as monitoring unexpected changes of city activity patterns. The globally rapid urbanization is proposing various inevitable issues, one of which is smart and efficient surveillance in urban areas. With ubiquitously deployed smart sensors, city mobility can be recorded all the time resulting in tons of urban data in every second. For smart city surveillance, identifying anomaly changes is always of high priority since changes in normal urban patterns may lead to remarkable events or even disasters. However, just like finding a needle in the sea, it is difficult for the surveillance operators to obtain meaningful information from the collected big urban data. Moreover, changes especially in emergent situations require quick decision-making with rather low latency tolerance to prevent a big loss. Therefore, all the issues are propelling researchers to seek new computing paradigms other than cloud computing which is powerful but suffers relatively high latency and bandwidth overconsumption. Connected environments like Internet of Things (IoTs) build a platform for connected smart devices to collaboratively share data and provide plentiful computing resources at the edge of network. Fog computing enables data processing and storage at the network edge which is promising to reduce the bandwidth consumption as well as making smart city surveillance more effective and efficient. This chapter provides a holistic vision about smart city surveillance and fog computing paradigm including the concepts, applications, challenges, and opportunities. A case study of urban traffic surveillance is presented to highlight the concepts through a real-world application example.

Keywords Smart city surveillance · Internet of things (IoTs) · Fog computing
Cloud computing · Edge computing · Urban surveillance · Urbanization
Governance

N. Chen · Y. Chen (✉)
Department of Electrical and Computing Engineering,
Binghamton University, Binghamton, USA
e-mail: ychen@binghamton.edu

© Springer International Publishing AG, part of Springer Nature 2018
Z. Mahmood (ed.), *Smart Cities*, Computer Communications and Networks,
https://doi.org/10.1007/978-3-319-76669-0_7

7.1 Introduction

Among various research domains of smart cities which aim at making our cities smarter and more sustainable, the topic of smart city surveillance is still challenging in terms of efficient information fusion, timely abnormal events detection and quickest correct response. Within the connected Internet of Things (IoTs), urban data are acquired from densely deployed digital sensors, however, these abundant data can become vital and significantly useful only when information and patterns of our cities are efficiently extracted. Anomaly events in our cities can not only result in harmful consequences like monetary loss, but also lead to ending innocent lives. Therefore, facing the open issues proposed by nowadays smart cities, it is significant for the researchers to explore novel solutions for smart city surveillance.

Fog computing, based on IoT environments, is recognized as the extension of cloud computing. It is a novel computing platform that utilizes countless smart devices at the network edge enabling data storage and processing at the proximity of end users. Unlike cloud which centralizes storage and computation, Fog computing is more suitable for latency-sensitive applications which require fast data processing for accurate decision-making. Therefore, the fog computing paradigm opens up new research opportunities for smart cities developers and researchers.

In this chapter, concepts, architectures, current research progress, and research issues regarding smart city surveillance and fog computing paradigm are discussed. Furthermore, this chapter focuses on the advantages and potential applications of fog computing for smart cities research domains. In addition, smart urban traffic surveillance is adopted as a case study to prove the feasibility and effectiveness of IoT-enabled fog paradigm after which future research directions will be discussed as well.

The organization of this chapter is as follows: in Sect. 7.2, concepts, current research progress, and open issues regarding smart city surveillance are discussed; Concepts of fog computing are introduced in Sect. 7.3 in which potential applications of fog computing in smart cities and a thorough comparison between cloud and fog paradigm is presented as well; in Sect. 7.4, the smart urban traffic surveillance as a case study is reported to prove the effectiveness and efficiency of fog computing in smart city surveillance; Potential future research directions about fog computing in smart city surveillance are discussed in Sect. 7.5; at the end, Sect. 7.6 concludes this chapter.

7.2 Smart City Surveillance

The unprecedented development of the IoTs and global urbanization make the concept of smart cities achievable and conceivable [1]. Worldwide urbanization not only enhances the living qualities for resident, but also comes up with critical pertinent urban issues. Air pollution, high energy consumption, traffic violations, urban criminals, and even human-caused disasters, none of them are trivial and will even turn to unacceptable big tragedies. Smart cities, utilizing ubiquitous smart infrastructures and advanced ICT, aim at making our cities more comfortable and sustainable. Various researches about smart cities have been conducted with significant innovation and progress, however, there still exist a lot of open issues to be dealt with. This section starts with the overview of concepts of smart cities and smart city surveillance. Then, the current research progress is presented in detail, after which existing open issues about smart city surveillance are discussed.

7.2.1   Concepts

Before giving a clear definition of smart cities, let us look at some statistical numbers. According to the statistics of United Nations World Urbanization Prospects report [2], in 2014, 54% of the total population of our world have been concentrated in urban areas and this number will be 66% in 2050. Among a number of critical issues introduced by the fast urbanization progress, urban transportation may highlight the impact. The Centre for Economics and Business Research [3] reported that a 50% rise of direct or indirect annual monetary loss caused by traffic congestion will be witnessed in the next 16 years in United States if no further measures are taken for current situations. Besides the impressive money loss, traffic accidents leading to fatal consequences are of significance as well. According to the report from World Health Organization [4], in 2015, the total number of worldwide road accident deaths becomes 7.25 million per year. However, the big money loss or accidental deaths caused by traffic accidents are merely the tip of an iceberg of the issues that cities are confronted with. Therefore, all these urban issues are propelling researchers to seek innovative and effective solutions.

In recent years, the number of smart devices increases drastically and digital sensors are deployed ubiquitously. The smart infrastructures and advanced communication techniques lead to the concept of IoT and enable the development of smart cities. Smart devices, from personal laptops to smartphones, to even smaller embedded sensors, are not only acting as data collectors, but also collaboratively share real-time monitoring data with each other. With densely deployed smart sensors, the pulse of cities is digitally recorded in real time. Leveraging the cloud computing paradigm, big urban data will be processed to unveil underlying patterns of cities, which will significantly improve the decision-making process for city operators or urban planners.

While there are plenty of reported research efforts dealing with the issues in the domain of smart cities, there is still not a consensus definition of smart cities. According to a definition of smart cities as provided in [5] that suggests a holistic vision, a smart city *is a system integration of technological infrastructure that relies on advanced data processing with the goals of making city governance more efficient, citizens happier, business more prosperous, and the environment more sustainable.*

According to the above definition, the core of smart cities is the urban residents. The advanced data acquisition and processing techniques are the essential parts. Figure 7.1 illustrates a typical architecture for a smart city.

As shown in Fig. 7.1, the smart city architecture consists of four layers. The bottom layer is the data sensing layer. As a result of increasing number and category of smart devices, various types of urban data become available at the network edge for further analysis. Apart from conventional data collected from deployed digital sensors, residents as end users are sharing their personal data through social media or other approaches. Hence, a variety of urban data including trajectories, texts, photos, and videos make the concept of smart cities feasible by extracting city activity patterns leveraging the big data. The second layer of the smart cities architecture is the data storage layer. After various urban data are collected, they will be stored at varying locations using different formats. There are a lot of research efforts in this domain addressing the data management issues at this layer. Through these approaches, urban data can be stored either at the edge of network or at the centralized data centers to assist efficient information fusion. In other words, benefiting from IoT platform, smart devices at the data sensing layer can both be the data producers and data storage depots. Another option is to send the collected data to remote cloud data centers for storage. This approach potentially causes higher communication network bandwidth consumption. The third layer is the data mining

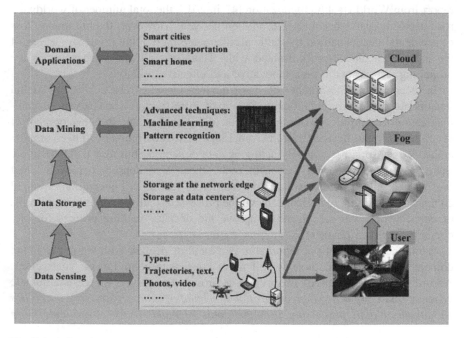

Fig. 7.1 A four-layer smart city architecture

layer where the urban data is processed in data centers or by decentralized devices. A wide variety of advanced data mining techniques such as machine learning are utilized in this layer to recognize urban activity patterns for different service purposes. The top layer is the domain application layer. Analytical outcomes resulting from data mining layer are applied to provide residents better services in various areas, including but not limited to smart grid, smart transportations, smart medicare, smart home, smart surveillance, and more. All these layers work together to improve the living qualities of people in the smart cities.

The right part of Fig. 7.1 depicts the computing paradigms applicable in smart cities. End users at the network edge are data providers as well as the data consumers. A new computing paradigm named fog computing is inserted between end users and cloud layer. Fog computing is inspired by the concept of IoT. Smart devices with computing capability at the edge can serve as fog computing nodes. Besides data sensing, part of data storage and data mining tasks can be migrated to this layer despite cloud centers conduct the same jobs. A more detailed introduction to fog computing and a comparison between cloud and fog paradigm is presented in the next section.

Smart city surveillance is one of the smart city application domains aiming at discovering, locating and dealing with anomalies occurred in urban environments. Tremendous urban data within certain time and space scale not only make it feasible for urban operators to achieve a comprehensive understanding of the urban activity patterns over a certain period, but also provide the opportunities to recognize anomaly situations, especially in dealing with emergencies. The timely detection of the occurrence of anomaly is not trivial and it may result in serious consequences.

Situational awareness (SAW) is essential to smart surveillance and it requires urban planners to maintain a holistic understanding of the cities [6]. Moreover, SAW entails efficient information fusion of diverse formats of urban data. For example, if a fire alarm suddenly breaks out, decisions regarding how to deal with this emergency should be different based on weather, surroundings and what is burning, because burning chemical materials could lead to fatal results. Obviously, in smart cities, especially in dealing with emergent situations, a fast and comprehensive SAW is mandatory for decision-making to avoid fatal consequences. Therefore, quick detection of anomalies, awareness of situations, and precise decision-making are essential to make smart cities sustainable.

Anomalous events in smart cities may cover a wide range, from individually abnormal activities, like suspicious unauthorized payment different from regular credit card activities in records, to citywide anomalies such as driving violations or unexpected events of city power systems. In Sect. 7.2.2, current research progress about smart city surveillance is introduced.

7.2.2   Current Research Progress

Conventional research efforts dealing with surveillance issues mainly focus on video surveillance of crowds or vehicles, but the concept of smart city surveillance indeed is targeting at more aspects of the city. Due to the limited space, the introduction to the state-of-the-art research progress mainly focuses on anomaly detection and smart traffic surveillance applications.

Anomaly Detection

Anomaly detection has been widely used in a variety of smart city applications such as credit card fraud detection, network security, military monitoring tasks, etc. Behaviors are considered anomalous when they are different from certain predefined normal patterns and they may potentially lead to violation of regulations, unauthorized access to valuable information, or harmful consequences to properties or even human being. It becomes more challenging to monitor a wider, more complex, and dynamic urban area. With an overwhelmingly large amount of data, conventional methods cannot satisfy the requirements. For instance, earlier research has shown that human operators are very likely to overlook some anomaly patterns that occur with rather low probability but are similar to normal ones. In addition, the cost of human resources is high. Hence, more efficient approaches for anomaly detection are needed.

Many algorithms have been developed for anomaly detection [7]. They considered mainly four categories of anomaly detection techniques: classification-based, density-based, clustering-based, and statistical-based anomaly detection techniques. In classification-based algorithms, classifiers are trained by labeled dataset telling them what abnormal behaviors are. Different features of normal and abnormal data instances are learned by classifiers that will be applied to process newly collected datasets. Neural networks (NN), support vector machine (SVM), and Bayesian networks are typical algorithms of this category. The assumption in density-based approaches is that the abnormal data instance occurs far from its neighbors and the normal behaviors are distributed with higher densities. Clustering-based anomaly detection algorithms are similar with density-based algorithms; the difference is that clustering techniques aim to cluster data sets into several groups. The statistical approaches always assume a mathematical probability distribution of data instances in advance with which prior probability can be calculated to infer the anomalies. In all the aforementioned approaches, an empirical threshold is used to define the boundary between normal and abnormal behaviors or patterns in smart cities.

Smart Surveillance Application

Traffic surveillance has been a hot research topic in intelligent transportation systems (ITS) [8]. There are three levels in ITS architecture: vehicle recognition, vehicle tracking, and behavior analysis. Vehicle behavior recognition is the highest level in an ITS. Utilizing the spatial-temporal information of vehicles obtained from vehicle detection and tracking techniques, vehicle behaviors can be learned at current time point or predicted for the next time point extensively based on mathematical models. Anomaly detection plays a critical role in the research area about vehicle behavior understanding. The earlier traffic anomalies can be identified, the better opportunity there is to prevent bad consequences such as fatal vehicle accidents resulting from speeding driving or heavy traffic jam.

For example, a hierarchical clustering framework has been proposed to classify vehicle trajectories [9]. The pairwise similarities are computed, based on which anomaly trajectories are determined. Unfortunately, the computational complexity is very high and this method is not suitable for online real-time data analysis. Their method is reported to be robust to noise and can find the anomalies in real time. Similarly, there is a two-stage online inference model for traffic pattern analysis and anomaly detection [10], which models the vehicle trajectories with both regional and velocity information. Gaussian model and hidden Markov model are utilized to infer the trajectory patterns and violations. This method includes model learning and online clustering phases and the experimental results have verified the effectiveness of this approach.

Other than normal pattern learning based methods, some alternative approaches were developed to detect traffic anomalies. For instance, a Sequential Hausdorff Nearest-Neighbor Conformal Anomaly Detector [11] was introduced for online learning and sequential anomaly detection in trajectories. It is an unsupervised learning process. The experimental results are encouraging. However, it still needs the model pretraining.

Innovative technologies such as cloud computing reduce the processing time, which in turn makes real-time, online detection feasible. In a study from the system level perspective, a wide area motion imagery (WAMI) is divided into equally subareas each of which is processed by a container in cloud computing architecture [12]. The container processing the region of interests (RoI) is allocated with more computational resources to achieve pseudo real-time target tracking. This type of divide-and-conquer strategy is also adopted to build a confabulation model to recognize abnormal vehicle events [13], in which a partition strategy is designed to divide wide area into subareas. There are 97 features of each vehicle extracted for training and testing and five types of abnormal events are defined. The reported experimental results are of satisfactory performance and showing the feasibility of the proposed approach.

Other than video-based vehicle tracking, there are also research efforts trying to recognize the anomalous motion patterns of human crowds [14]. Researchers propose a hybrid approach of unsupervised K-means clustering and hidden Markov models. By this proposed method, crowds can be effectively recognized if they are in the abnormal state.

7.2.3 Challenges

Although various approaches are proposed to tackle the issues existing in smart surveillance, there are still some challenging problems in this research domain, as discussed below:

- *Algorithms*: Currently machine learning (ML) techniques are the mainstream trend to detect abnormal events. The ML-based approaches typically require sufficient data sets for training and the "normal" patterns have to be predefined to detect anomalies. However, these requirements sometimes put constraints on the applications as well. It is difficult to obtain sufficient training data sets in practice and it is, if not impossible, very challenging to build a comprehensive pattern database that defines all possible normal or abnormal patterns. Therefore, new algorithms are desired that are able to facilitate operators to be aware of anomalies without depending on the expensive training.
- *Efficient information fusion*: tremendous amount of urban data can be collected in real time, which is the foundation for smart city surveillance. These data are highly heterogeneous in terms of data source, format, quality, etc. To acquire and maintain efficient SAW and precise decision-making, efficient data fusion is mandatory. In addition, a holistic understanding of our cities necessitates the fusion of multiple data processing outcomes across a wide area of application domains involving multiple surveillance tasks.
- *Bandwidth consumption*: utilizing omnipresent sensors and smart devices, citywide urban mobility can be recorded. One of the consequences is that there are tons of data generated every day. How to transfer such a massive size of data is a significant concern. Cloud computing paradigm has been widely recognized as the preferred platform. To users at the network edge, there is enormous amount of data to be transmitted to remote data center for processing. While the powerful data centers are ideal for batch data processing tasks, the transferring will put heavy workload to the communication networks. Actually, most data sets are only of local significance, sending them all to cloud are squandering communication resources. Therefore, more work is expected to be conducted to distinguish the use of surveillance data to relieve the pressure on bandwidth consumption.
- *Response time*: while the cloud computing paradigm is powerful to process big data, the communication delay is a big concern in latency-sensitive surveillance tasks, especially in emergent situations where online, real-time data processing and instant decision-making are required. In fact, in some extreme situations like disaster recovery, a reliable communication network may not be available at all.

7.3   Fog Computing

Cloud computing is attractive to both industrial users and academic researchers for several reasons: with cloud computing, capital outlay becomes unnecessary for businesses and maintenance cost can be significantly lowered down since hardware or software resources are provided by cloud instead of the local resource deployment. Cloud centers provide excellent data storage and computing capabilities. However, the round-trip latency resulted from data transmission to and from cloud centers is a hindrance for delay-sensitive applications such as smart city surveillance. The IoT connects ubiquitously deployed smart devices at the network edge together, such that services and applications are enabled locally at the edge of the network. Under this context, the cloud paradigm is not the universal solution in the IoT era anymore.

The basic concept of fog computing is not new. It was studied under the umbrella of cloudlets, mobile cloud, etc. But it has attracted more and more attention as the IoT become pervasive. As the extension and complement of cloud paradigm, the fog computing supports data storage and processing at the network edge. Unlike cloud that is high in the sky, fog stays close to the ground. In this section, fog computing-related concepts, applications and benefits are presented.

7.3.1   Concepts and Architecture

Fog computing is a *distributed computation paradigm that leverages the huge number of heterogeneous devices deployed at the edge of network, which are connected and collaborate with each other by sharing computation, storage and communication functionalities.*

With this definition, another similar terminology is edge computing. In fact, some researchers do not consider them as two different technologies [15], although some people emphasizes that the fog computing focuses more on infrastructure while the edge computing focuses more on the deployed smart devices. In this chapter, we regard these two concepts as the same and use them interchangeably.

Due to the unprecedented increasing amount of smart devices at the network edge as well as their computational capabilities, the smart devices play multiple roles, they function as data collectors, surplus data storage, and data processing units. Accordingly, the fog computing paradigm is considered as a computing platform that brings computation and storage from centralized cloud centers to the work site at the network edges, which inspires innovative services to end users and improves the quality of user experiences especially for the latency-sensitive applications.

Figure 7.2 shows the basic architecture of a fog computing implementation. At the bottom layer are end users within a working area. The fog layer is inserted between the end users and the cloud centers and consists of a variety of computing

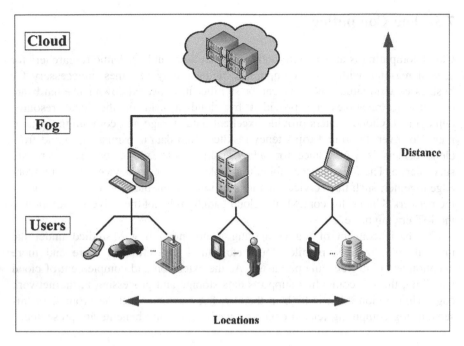

Fig. 7.2 Fog computing paradigm architecture

nodes. Comparing with the cloud scheme, the fog computing layer stays closely with end users and utilizes a group of smart devices at the network edge as computing nodes. Personal laptops, smartphones, cloudlets, or even smart routers can potentially be functioning as fog nodes. While smart devices produce urban data, they are capable of storing and processing data as well. Therefore, with the fog computing paradigm, urban data can be computed on-site, which reduces the bandwidth usage since only globally significant data will be transferred to data centers. The cloud platform is still necessary in the architecture. After the processing done at the fog layer, important metadata can be sent to the cloud center for archival purpose or further analysis for long-term traffic pattern analytics.

The definition and the illustration of computing architecture of the fog computing above have shown that comparing with the cloud, the fog computing based scheme is a better match to smart city surveillance tasks in terms of instant decision-making and the reduction of load on communication networks. However, another important feature of the fog computing paradigm lies in the high heterogeneity in the computing resources at the network edge. Different from powerful cloud data center, not only each individual node possesses weaker computing capability, the management of the entire fog cell is also more complex because of dynamic and heterogeneous environments.

Table 7.1 illustrates a more detailed comparison between the cloud and the fog scheme. With these unique characteristics, the fog computing paradigm is

Table 7.1 Comparisons between fog and cloud computing paradigms

Attribute	Fog computing	Cloud computing
Ubiquity	Fog nodes present higher availability since an enormous amount of smart devices at the network edge have the potentials to be adopted as computing nodes	Cloud centers are located remotely from the network edge
Latency	Fog presents low latency since computing resource are close to users	Higher latency comparing with fog scheme due to the round-trip communication time
Heterogeneity	Fog nodes are heterogeneous because of the utilization of various types of smart devices at the network edge	Normally cloud resources are deployed according to the requirements from users and the computing nodes are deployed of similarity and are provided as clusters
Computing capability	Fog layer mainly consists of smart devices at the network edge which are regarded as of normal computational capability	Cloud centers present powerful computational capabilities
Dynamicity	Fog computing resources are dynamic	Cloud computing resources stay within cloud data centers
Bandwidth consumption	Fog nodes could be connected using local area network which will reduce the Internet bandwidth consumption	Transmitting all the urban data to cloud centers by Internet and other communication networks present high bandwidth usage

considered more suitable for the applications with the requirement of low latency and real-time response. Furthermore, due to different computing capabilities and targeting tasks, the fog and cloud schemes are mutually complementary with each other.

7.3.2 Applications and Ongoing Efforts

The fog computing paradigm facilitates the delay-sensitive applications with minimum response latency and instant decision-making capabilities, which are essential in urban scenarios especially for the emergent situations. A number of research works have discussed potential smart city applications that can leverage the fog computing platform.

- *Connected Vehicles* [16]. The concept of connected vehicles proposes an ideal platform for improving user experience in vehicles and traffic surveillance. On this platform, not only vehicles are connected, but also vehicles and roadside units communicate with each other. With its inherent advantages, the fog is ideal for connected vehicles by providing real-time applications like safety information or entertainment content delivery.

- **Mobile Big Data Analytics** [17]. At the edge of network, tons of urban data are produced every second. Without suffering the communication delay, Fog platform provides on-site big urban data processing services. Because not all urban data are globally important, applying fog computing can efficiently reduce the bandwidth consumption.

- **Smart Grid** [18]. Fog computing provides an environment in which data collected from smart meters in smart grid can be preprocessed. Furthermore, fog nodes act as a bridge between raw data and the data centers. Smart grid can achieve better performance with the facilitation of the fog paradigm.

- **eHealth and Smart Home** [19]. In smart homes, residence data will be collected by devices embedded in the environment, i.e., wearable digital sensors. Data are processed locally in the fog layer to provide personalized services in smart home applications. eHealth is one kind of services in smart homes. Patients at home wear digital sensors or other wearable devices for health condition monitoring. Health data will be preprocessed first by personal services and then decision can be made whether the data should be sent to remote hospitals. Utilizing Fog platform, personal health monitoring service at home is seamlessly connected with remote service providers.

There are more potential applications that the fog computing will improve the performance, but only several representative applications are listed here due to the limited space. What must be emphasized here is, although fog presents some unique advantages in a lot of scenarios, it does not replace cloud computing totally. Instead, fog and cloud are complementary with each other for better improvement. Given the inherent benefits and potential applications in the fog computing paradigm, a variety of research has been explored:

- A fog computing solution is proposed for advanced metering infrastructure in smart grid [20]. A user-friendly interface is developed and the proposed model is verified on a proof-of-concept testbed.

- A virtualized and decentralized fog-based emergency architecture was proposed to improve the smart living environments [21]. In this scheme, resources in the pool are managed by a dynamic resource service.

- The fog computing concept has been leveraged to improve the in-vehicle data processing [22], which achieves the goal of real-time processing by building virtual machines within the vehicles to facilitate on-site data processing tasks.

- The fog computing scheme has also been utilized for face identification and resolution in IoTs [23]. A prototype is proved to be effective through experimental studies and it shows significant reduction of computing overhead.

Besides the efforts focused on the fog-enabled applications at the network edge, there are also research conducted in terms of the resource provisioning and architecture of fog computing. For example, a conceptual system to provision the computing resources of fog has been suggested, which treats the resource provisioning as an optimization problem to optimally reduce the application delay [24]. Some researchers consider the fog layer as a suitable platform to improve the data delivery service and they use Stackelberg game theory to build a hierarchical data center architecture consisting of both the fog and cloud schemes [25]. In addition, there is a fog-enabled orchestration scheme was introduced for on-site applications and services [26], which is still in conceptual proof phase with some early experimental results reported.

7.3.3 Open Issues and Discussion

In spite of the unique advantages of the fog computing paradigm, there still exist a number of open issues waiting for further explorations by researchers. The major research challenges in the fog computing are listed as follows [17, 27]:

- *Resource provisioning and management*: the fog nodes consist of a large number of heterogeneous smart devices. Not only the demands from different applications are variants, but also the computational resources provided by fog nodes are changing constantly. To obtain a satisfied quality of service, latency, dynamic and mobility must be taken into consideration.
- *Computation capability limitation*: although in the fog computing paradigm, fog nodes are ubiquitously available because of the increasing number of smart devices, the computational capabilities of fog nodes are not as powerful as cloud centers. How to ensure the quality of service is a relatively big concern. Additionally, the variant computational capabilities make synchronization an issue as one task may be divided into multiple jobs and each of them is sent to one fog node for processing.
- *Interface and programmability*: like other commercial service providers, the complexity and technical details are expected to be transparent to end users. In fog computing paradigm, the challenging questions such as how to discover computation resources and how to configure the fog nodes and other technical details should not confuse the users. An easy-to-use interface should be provided to ensure that users can migrate their works to fog nodes simply and obtain the outcome feedback timely.
- *Standardization*: there is still not a uniform standardization for fog computing. Cloudlets, close-user servers, and personal smart devices are all well-qualified candidates to be considered as fog nodes. Therefore, a uniform standardization is very critical to address the issues like how to bill fog computing users, how to attract people to share their smart device resources as fog nodes or how to configure the fog services.
- *Privacy and Security*: as mentioned above, personal smart devices can be utilized as fog nodes. How to ensure the privacy and security of personal information becomes a big challenge. In a fog, computational resources may be shared with third parties. In addition, on the user side, how to ensure the privacy

and security of software or application results is also a concern as the task is outsourced to fog nodes.

As discussed in Sect. 7.2, there are a lot of challenges in smart city surveillance, which aims at identifying anomalies occurring in normal patterns. On one hand, in the big data era, it is not practical to monitor cities all the time merely by human operators. Furthermore, monitoring tasks are extremely tedious because anomaly events occur with low probability and human operators can be unaware of changes under the flushing of big urban data. On the other hand, smart city surveillance tasks will present restrict requirements about processing time and decision-making delay since earlier anomalies are identified, greater opportunities there will be to prevent damages or disastrous consequences. Hence, conventional monitoring by human beings and resorting to cloud techniques cannot meet the challenges posed by smart city surveillance tasks.

Because of its unique advantages, the fog computing has been recently identified as an ideal platform for smart city surveillance. Utilizing fog paradigm, big urban data can be processed at where they are produced, which in turn significantly reduces the response time. Moreover, fog and cloud platforms cooperate with each other to form an integrated computing architecture in which fog can preprocess the collected data to provide services as well as discard redundant data.

7.4   Case Study

In this section, a smart traffic surveillance project is introduced as a case study that validates the feasibility and effectiveness of the fog computing. Urban traffic surveillance has been an important research topic in recent years. Driving violations especially speeding cause fatal consequences both to drivers and innocent people like passengers and pedestrians. In traffic surveillance tasks, it is necessary to process traffic data with low latency and to make decisions instantly.

7.4.1   Surveillance Scenario

Figure 7.3 presents the traffic surveillance scenario in which end users are identified as police officers. A drone is adopted to monitor the traffic on road. The real-time traffic video stream is sent back to the on-ground remote controller connected with a tablet, which displays the traffic videos to end users. The goal of this smart traffic monitoring system is to identify vehicles of interests and use a tracking algorithm to lock them down. Since it incurs high overhead and resource-wasting to track every vehicle in video frames, only vehicles of interests are identified and tracked. In this study, only anomalous vehicles that behave differently from others are selected as tracking targets.

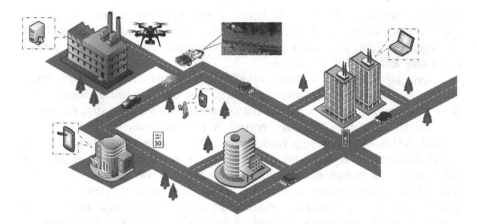

Fig. 7.3 Smart traffic surveillance scenario

The tablet that displays traffic video possesses limited computational capability. The smart traffic surveillance tasks entail quick data processing and decision-making to prevent traffic incidents. Therefore, collaborative processing among multiple devices in the fog cell is critical in this architecture. One fog node is a laptop in the police car. The video is offloaded to that laptop where our anomalous vehicle identification algorithm will be applied. Once anomalous vehicles are identified, each of them is sent to different fog nodes for tracking. As shown in Fig. 7.3, smart devices near the monitoring scene like personal laptops, smartphones or servers are potential fog nodes. Utilizing fog computing, the expensive multiple vehicles tracking function is achieved on top of single target tracking algorithm. Each fog node tracks one anomalous vehicle only.

The tracking results are transferred back to users once the fog nodes have completed the processing tasks. End users will utilize the anomaly identification and tracking results to make decisions about driving violations. In this way, the fog computing platform enables the smart traffic surveillance architecture to collect traffic data, process them, and obtain the feedback in real-time to handle the driving violations on roads. Afterwards, traffic monitoring results can be stored in fog nodes which integrate together with cloud centers to share valuable traffic data for long-term analytics.

7.4.2 Anomaly Vehicle Identification

When real-time traffic video is obtained, information of all vehicles in each frame needs to be extracted. However, it is impractical to track every vehicle and calculate their information like speed and acceleration, especially when there are a lot of vehicles on the road and only limited fog processing resources are available.

Therefore, anomaly vehicles are identified at first and then tracking algorithm is applied to lock them down. It is reasonable in that driving violations occur with low probability and only anomalous vehicles are worth tracking. This strategy saves a lot of time and computing resources.

In previously reported anomaly vehicle detection work, the similarity-based clustering or k-nearest neighborhood approaches are often applied. However, all of these machine learning techniques require sufficiently large training data sets, which is nontrivial in practice. Moreover, normal or abnormal patterns need to be pre-defined, which means pre-built models can only detect what is defined. In real world, however, it is infeasible to define every possible pattern in advance. Additionally, the trained models from these approaches will present poor adaptations when migrating them to different test scenarios. Considering these constraints, a novel approach is proposed by reconsidering the anomaly vehicle detection as a change point detection problem. Based on the fact that most of vehicles on roads obey the regulations, other than defining normal and abnormal behaviors in advance, this approach focuses on only detect vehicles behaving differently from others.

The anomaly vehicle detection algorithm is based on multidimensional singular spectrum analysis (mSSA). The basic SSA algorithm has been proved for its effectiveness for one channel time series change point detection [28]. In this case study, mSSA algorithm considers multiple characteristics of vehicles to examine if there are differences from others. Corresponding to each characteristic of an individual vehicle, i.e., speed, a time series is created. A trajectory matrix is formulated at first and then the singular value decomposition (SVD) process is conducted. After performing SVD, only the most significant principal components are reserved, based on which the time series is reconstructed. At last, for each channel, the average of all the vehicles is calculated, which is considered as the benchmark of the vehicles' behavior. The benchmark is used to determine whether a vehicle's behavior is identified as anomalous one by comparing the distance from the benchmark. For each individual vehicle, distances of multiple channels are summarized into an indicator with different weights. If the distance exceeds an empirical threshold, this vehicle will be considered as an outlier. Essentially, instead of looking for changes temporarily in one time series as what the basic SSA method does, here the anomalous vehicles are identified by detecting the differences in the spatial pattern. Further detailed explanations and more strict mathematical proof can be found in [29].

To evaluate the mSSA-based anomaly vehicle detection algorithm, a public data set named next generation simulation (NGSIM) was adopted. NGSIM [30] is a public data set for various traffic analysis. A subset from NGSIM traffic data has been extracted with 50 frames, each of which consists of 35 vehicles. In the testing data set, there are four types of vehicle trajectories, two of which are anomalies. The number of total vehicles and abnormal vehicles in each frame was modified for performance evaluation.

Figure 7.4a presents the computing time on a laptop, just like the laptops carried in a police car. The configuration of the laptop is as follows. The processor is Intel

I7-6820HQ, the memory is 32 GB, and the maximum processing frequency is 2.7 GHz. As shown in Fig. 7.4a, as the number of total vehicles increases from 5 to 35, and the percentage of abnormal vehicles maintains 20%, the computing time grows from 15 to 98 ms. The vehicle trajectory information is obtained every 0.1 s in the NGSIM testing data sets. Therefore, the algorithm is able to meet the requirement of real-time performance.

Figure 7.4b shows the receiver operating characteristic (ROC) curve. The total number of vehicles maintains 35 and the number of anomaly vehicles is ten. Actually, ten anomalies out of 35 in total is quite a high percentage that could be unlikely happen in real life. Here, such an extreme setting is adopted to demonstrate the performance of the algorithm. As shown in Fig. 7.4b, corresponding to the detection rate of 100%, the false alarm rate stays below 30%, which presents a tolerable false detection rate.

Figure 7.4(a, b) shows the feasibility and effectiveness of the mSSA-based algorithm. This anomalous vehicle detection approach is lightweight, it can be implemented on a single laptop and process traffic data in a real-time manner. In

Fig. 7.4 **a** Experimental results—processing time on a laptop. **b** Experimental results —ROC curve

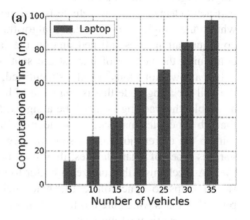

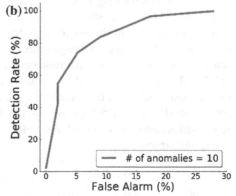

addition, this method is in a plug-and-play style, which does not require any training data.

7.4.3 Fog-Based Multiple Vehicle Tracking

After anomalous vehicles are identified, tracking algorithms are applied to lock them down for more information. Intuitively, multiple target tracking algorithm is the option. Due to the limited computational resources of fog nodes, however, multiple target tracking algorithms are too expensive to meet the requirement of real-time tracking performance. They are very complex and consequently they are very time-consuming. Taking the challenges resulted from complicated environment like occlusion and shadows into account, today's multi-target tracking algorithms would not be able to perform robustly. On the contrary, single target tracking algorithms are simpler and more reliable. They are able to track the target in real time. Therefore, a fog-based multiple vehicle tracking architecture was built using a single target tracking algorithm.

Each detected anomaly vehicle is assigned to one fog node that is available, on which the single target tracking algorithm is implemented. The one-to-many communication is established among the laptop and other nodes. Video frames containing the vehicle of interest are sent to the fog node with uni-cast scheme. When a new anomalous vehicle is identified, the job scheduler on the laptop checks the cell for a fog node that is available to handle a new task. Once there is a node available, the tracking task will be assigned to it. If there is not any node available, the job scheduler may choose to identify an ongoing job with low priority, terminate the current job, and assign the new task to it. Since fog nodes can be of various types of smart devices, they may possess different computational capabilities. A mechanism that utilizes a buffer to store current video frame is introduced, which helps to synchronize the heterogeneous nodes by slowing down more powerful nodes which are too fast for processing and discard the fog node which is too slow for this tracking task.

In the experimental study, a *L1* tracker using accelerated proximal gradient approach is adopted as the single target tracking algorithm. It has been proved to be effective to address the challenges raised by complicated environment and it can achieve real-time tracking performance [31]. This tracking algorithm is selected to validate the effectiveness of the Fog-based architecture. Four fog nodes are utilized to track four vehicles at the same time, and the traffic video is recorded over a local surface road. Figure 7.5(a–c) present the tracking results, which shows that the fog-based architecture can track multiple vehicles concurrently in real time without losing the targets.

The performance of the fog-based target tracking platform is compared with the cloud. Amazon EC2 Cloud web services are used for testing. Two data centers of Amazon EC2 Cloud are selected, one is located in Virginia which is nearer to our location and the other one is located in Oregon.

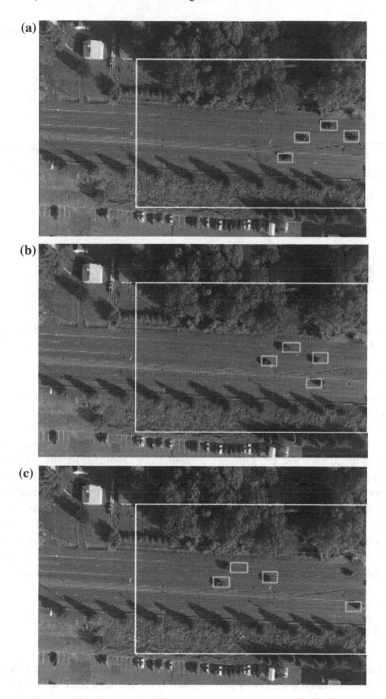

Fig. 7.5 a Multiple vehicle tracking in fog—tracking result at t_1. **b** Multiple vehicle tracking in fog—tracking result at t_2. **c** Multiple vehicle tracking in fog—tracking result at t_3

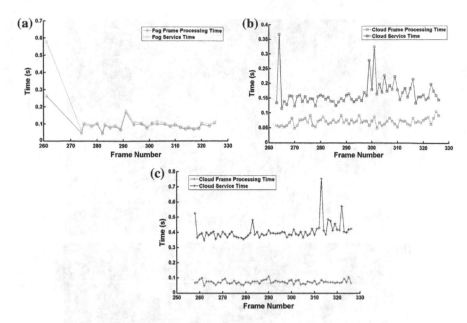

Fig. 7.6 **a** Comparison between fog and cloud platforms—local fog. **b** Comparison between fog and cloud platforms—cloud in Virginia. **c** Comparison between fog and cloud platforms—cloud in Oregon

Figure 7.6(a–c) illustrate the experimental results comparing the performance of fog and cloud computing. Two parameters are used for comparison. The first one is processing time, which is the computing time that each tracking task cost in fog or cloud. The second is service time, which represents the elapsed time from when the task is assigned to when the processing results are obtained. Ideally, if the computing capabilities are the same, the gap between processing time and service time is the round-trip delay. From left to right in Fig. 7.6, there are experimental results of implementing multiple target tracking on our fog platform, the cloud center in Virginia and the cloud center in Oregon. Obviously, the cloud centers suffer very large round-trip delay while the fog-based platform only meets ignorable communication latency. Actually, sometimes the round-trip delay could be even larger when the Internet connection is not stable or the network is heavy-loaded.

7.5   Discussion

The case study discussed in the last section has demonstrated that fog computing paradigm facilitates the smart city surveillance at the network edge with low latency and real-time performance. Consisting of multiple heterogeneous devices, fog platform provides data storage and computing resources at the network edge. Due to the inherent characteristics, fog computing is more suitable for smart city surveillance tasks, which prioritize quick information fusion and instant decision-making. However, there are still a number of open issues worth more research efforts:

- **What is/are the killer application(s) in fog?** Fog computing nodes consist of various types of smart devices at the edge of network. Comparing to cloud centers, inherently the fog cell possesses less computational capabilities and the architecture can be dynamic due to the join/leave of mobile devices. So far, it is still unclear to the algorithm developers, system designers and field practitioners that what applications or functions are uniquely the best stakes in the fog computing paradigm. Without a clear vision, the fog computing will be considered at most as an extension of its powerful big brother, cloud computing.
- **How do we use fog computing efficiently?** While pervasively deployed fog nodes are conveniently accessible to end users, it is nontrivial to take full advantages of the complex, heterogeneous platform. There are a lot of questions yet to be answered and quite a few challenging issues, here is an incomplete list: elastic node churn, dynamic controller churn, location-variable aware applications, perishable and unpredictable service demand, and updating, predicting and maintaining the network latency and dynamic routes in different granularity as well as the softwarization issues including cooperation among different east–west controllers, cross-layer collaboration, controller placement, mobility and latency control, controller scalability, and control reliability [32].
- **Where is the boundary between fog and cloud?** With their own unique characteristics, fog and cloud paradigm complements each other. Therefore, for smart city surveillance tasks, the cooperation between fog and cloud must be taken into account. What part of tasks should be placed into fog and what should be implemented in cloud are critical. Therefore, when implementing smart city surveillance applications on a fog platform, developers must consider what kind of application should be migrated from cloud to fog in consideration of the limits of fog scheme.

7.6 Conclusions

In this chapter, the challenges in smart city surveillance are presented. Huge amount of urban data collected in different formats as well as the requirement of real-time information fusion and decision-making are necessitating fresh solutions for smart cities. Cloud computing cannot meet the strict requirements in delay-sensitive surveillance application in mission critical tasks. As the complement of cloud, the fog computing enables data storage and processing much closer to end users and is identified as a more appropriate computing paradigm for urban smart surveillance applications. A detailed discussion about the difference between fog and cloud is presented as well as the potential applications of fog computing.

A fog-based smart traffic monitoring architecture is discussed as a case study, which shows that fog computing is promising in modern urban surveillance applications. The experimental comparisons between the fog and cloud are conducted. With fog paradigm, the tracking result will be sent back to end users in real time with almost ignorable delays. However, using cloud paradigm, the data transmission between the network edge to cloud centers brings significant latencies which could be more severe from further cloud centers. Therefore, the experiments show that for latency-sensitive smart city surveillance applications, the fog computing becomes more suitable in terms of latency.

At the end, the research challenges of the fog computing in smart city surveillance are discussed. A lot of academic and industrial efforts in the fog computing have been conducted, but there is still a list of open issues to be solved to make the fog computing paradigm more effective and practical for smart city surveillance applications. It is critical for researchers to consider about the boundary between the fog and cloud and how to solve the issues from fog like dynamicity and heterogeneity. We hope this chapter will inspire more active research, discussion, and collaboration in this rising field.

References

1. Chen N, Chen Y, Ye X, Ling H, Song S, Huang C-T (2017) Smart city surveillance in fog computing. In: Advances in mobile cloud computing and big data in the 5G Era. Springer, Berlin, pp 203–226
2. UN (2014) World urbanization prospects 2014. https://esa.un.org/unpd/wup/publications/files/wup2014-highlights.Pdf. Accessed 13 Feb 2017
3. Research Center for Economics and Business (2014) 50% rise in grid lock costs by 2030. https://www.cebr.com/reports/the-future-economic-and-environmental-costs-of-gridlock/. Accessed 13 Feb 2017
4. WHO (2015) Global status report on road safety 2015. http://www.who.int/violence_injury_prevention/road_safety_status/2015/en/. Accessed 13 Feb 2017
5. Yin C, Xiong Z, Chen H, Wang J, Cooper D, David B (2015) A literature survey on smart cities. Sci China Inf Sci 58(10):1–18
6. Chen N, Chen Y, You Y, Ling H, Liang P, Zimmermann R (2016) Dynamic urban surveillance video stream processing using fog computing. In: 2016 IEEE second international conference on multimedia big data (BigMM), 2016. IEEE, pp 105–112
7. Chandola V, Banerjee A, Kumar V (2009) Anomaly detection: a survey. ACM Comput Surv (CSUR) 41(3):15
8. Tian B, Morris BT, Tang M, Liu Y, Yao Y, Gou C, Shen D, Tang S (2015) Hierarchical and networked vehicle surveillance in ITS: a survey. IEEE Trans Intell Transp Syst 16(2):557–580
9. Fu Z, Hu W, Tan T (2005) Similarity based vehicle trajectory clustering and anomaly detection. In: IEEE international conference on image processing, ICIP 2005. IEEE, pp II-602
10. Jeong H, Yoo Y, Yi KM, Choi JY (2014) Two-stage online inference model for traffic pattern analysis and anomaly detection. Mach Vis Appl 25(6):1501–1517

11. Laxhammar R, Falkman G (2014) Online learning and sequential anomaly detection in trajectories. IEEE Trans Pattern Anal Mach Intell 36(6):1158–1173
12. Wu R, Liu B, Chen Y, Blasch E, Ling H, Chen G (2015) A container-based elastic cloud architecture for pseudo real-time exploitation of wide area motion imagery (WAMI) stream. J Signal Process Syst 1–13
13. Chen Q, Qiu Q, Wu Q, Bishop M, Barnell M (2014) A confabulation model for abnormal vehicle events detection in wide-area traffic monitoring. In: 2014 IEEE international inter-disciplinary conference on cognitive methods in situation awareness and decision support (CogSIMA), 2014. IEEE, pp 216–222
14. Andersson M, Gustafsson F, St-Laurent L, Prevost D (2013) Recognition of anomalous motion patterns in urban surveillance. IEEE J Sel Topics Signal Process 7(1):102–110
15. Shi W, Cao J, Zhang Q, Li Y, Xu L (2016) Edge computing: vision and challenges. IEEE Internet Things J 3(5):637–646
16. Bonomi F, Milito R, Zhu J, Addepalli S (2012) Fog computing and its role in the internet of things. In: Proceedings of the first edition of the MCC workshop on mobile cloud computing, 2012. ACM, pp 13–16
17. Yi S, Li C, Li QA (2015) Survey of fog computing: concepts, applications and issues. In: Proceedings of the 2015 workshop on mobile big data, 2015. ACM, pp 37–42
18. Okay FY, Ozdemir S (2016) A fog computing based smart grid model. In: 2016 international symposium on networks, computers and communications (ISNCC), 2016. IEEE, pp 1–6
19. Stantchev V, Barnawi A, Ghulam S, Schubert J, Tamm G (2015) Smart items, fog and cloud computing as enablers of servitization in healthcare. Sens Transducers 185(2):121
20. Yan Y, Su WA (2016) fog computing solution for advanced metering infrastructure. In: Transmission and distribution conference and exposition (T&D), IEEE/PES, 2016. IEEE, pp 1–4
21. Nikoloudakis Y, Panagiotakis S, Markakis E, Pallis E, Mastorakis G, Mavromoustakis CX, Dobre C (2016) A fog-based emergency system for smart enhanced living environments. IEEE Cloud Comput 3(6):54–62
22. Kopetz H, Poledna S (2016) In-vehicle real-time fog computing. In: 2016 46th annual IEEE/IFIP international conference on dependable systems and networks workshop, 2016. IEEE, pp 162–167
23. Hu P, Ning H, Qiu T, Zhang Y, Luo X (2016) Fog computing-based face identification and resolution scheme in internet of things. IEEE Trans Ind Informatics 13:1910
24. Skarlat O, Schulte S, Borkowski M, Leitner P (2016) Resource provisioning for IoT services in the fog. In: 2016 IEEE 9th international conference on service-oriented computing and applications (SOCA), 2016. IEEE, pp 32–39
25. Zhang H, Xiao Y, Bu S, Niyato D, Yu R, Han Z (2016) Fog computing in multi-tier data center networks: a hierarchical game approach. In: 2016 IEEE international conference on communications (ICC), 2016. IEEE, pp 1–6
26. Wen Z, Yang R, Garraghan P, Lin T, Xu J, Rovatsos M (2017) Fog orchestration for internet of things services. IEEE Internet Comput 21(2):16–24
27. Vaquero LM, Rodero-Merino L (2014) Finding your way in the fog: towards a comprehensive definition of fog computing. ACM SIGCOMM Comput Commun Rev 44 (5):27–32
28. Mohammad Y, Nishida T (2017) On comparing SSA-based change point discovery algorithms. In: 2011 IEEE/SICE international symposium on system integration (SII), 2017. IEEE, pp 938–945
29. Chen N, Yang Z, Chen Y, Polunchenko A (2017) Online anomalous vehicle detection at the edge using multidimensional SSA. In: The 3rd IEEE INFOCOM workshop on smart cities and urban computing (SmartCity 2017), 1 May 2017
30. Department of Transportation ITS Joint Program Office (2017) New data sets from the next generation simulation (NGSIM) program are now available in the research data exchange. http://www.its.dot.gov/press/2016/datasets. Accessed 15 Feb 2017

31. Bao C, Wu Y, Ling H, Ji H (2012) Real time robust l1 tracker using accelerated proximal gradient approach. In: 2012 IEEE conference on computer vision and pattern recognition (CVPR), 2012. IEEE, pp 1830–1837
32. Gebre-Amlak H, Lee S, Jabbari A, Chen Y, Choi B, Huang C, Song S (2017) MIST: mobility-inspired software-defined fog system. In: The 2017 international conference on consumer electronics (ICCE), cloud computing track, Las Vegas, NV, USA, 8–11 Jan 2017

Chapter 8
Big Energy Data Management for Smart Grids—Issues, Challenges and Recent Developments

Vidyasagar Potdar, Anulipt Chandan, Saima Batool
and Naimesh Patel

Abstract Urban areas suffer from tremendous pressure to cope with increasing population in a city. A smart city is a technological solution that integrates engineering and information systems to assist in managing these scarce resources. A smart city comprises several intelligent services such as smart grids, smart education, smart transportation, smart buildings, smart waste management and so on. Among all these, smart grids are the nucleus of all the facilities because these provide sustainable electrical supply for other smart services to operate seamlessly. Smart grids integrate information and communication technologies (ICT) into traditional energy grids, thereby capturing massive amounts of data from several devices like smart meters, sensors, and other electrical infrastructures. The data collected in smart grids are heterogeneous and require data analytic techniques to extract meaningful information to make informed decisions. We term this enormous amount of data as big energy data. This book chapter discusses progress in the field of big energy data by enlisting different studies that cover several data management aspects such as data collection, data preprocessing, data integration, data storage, data analytics, data visualisation and decision-making. We also discuss various challenges in data management and report recent progress in this field. Finally, we present open research areas in big data management especially in relation to smart grids.

Keywords Smart city · Smart grid · Big energy data · Data management
Smart meter · Energy data management · Data lifecycle · Data preprocessing
Data collection · Data integration · Data storage · Data analytics
Data visualisation · Decision-making

V. Potdar · S. Batool (✉)
Curtin Business School, Curtin University, Perth, Australia
e-mail: saima-batool@live.com

A. Chandan
National Institute of Technology, Agartala, India

N. Patel
Safeworld Systems Pvt Ltd, Ahmedabad, India

© Springer International Publishing AG, part of Springer Nature 2018
Z. Mahmood (ed.), *Smart Cities*, Computer Communications and Networks,
https://doi.org/10.1007/978-3-319-76669-0_8

8.1 Introduction

The increasing population of the world, limited available resources, and improved lifestyles compel the world economy to think about the intelligent management of the available but scarce resources. This issue is more dominant in an urban area because the urban population is increasing more rapidly as compared to the rural areas because of better job opportunities, better lifestyles and more accessible facilities. This exponential increase in the population of cities all over the world has put pressure on the limited resources available within cities. Increasing pollution, lack of proper transportation facilities, inadequate medical facilities and unreliable electrical supply are some of the major areas which are under tremendous pressure due to rising population. In this context, information and communication technologies (ICT) can resolve many of these challenges, and help the city administration to fulfil the needs of its citizens with optimal utilisation of existing infrastructure. Integration of ICT and fast computational technologies can transform a city into a smart city which will become more functional, better managed and more eco-friendly.

Smart cities refer to a holistic collection of advanced services and facilities, which include smart grids, smart transportation, smart administration, smart agriculture, smart education and smart homes. Among all these, the smart grids are the most critical because smart cities require reliable and sustainable electricity supply to run all technology-based services and failure of smart grids can bring the smart cities to a standstill. Hence, the development and management of the smart grids is of paramount importance in the smart city.

Smart grid management includes demand-side management, renewable energy management, fault management and electrical infrastructure management. All these management activities rely on the vast amount of data captured at different data points (e.g. smart meters, sensors, transformers) in the grid. This data is massive and managing such a significant amount of data is not an easy task for the utility operators. Hence, the utilities face various challenges. This chapter discusses these challenges and provides associated solutions.

In the next section, we present a brief history of power grids. Section 8.3 outlines the difference between traditional grids and smart grids. Sections 8.4 and 8.5 present the big data characteristics of the smart grid, and the various processes for data management. Section 8.6 lists the data management issues in the smart grid. The next section covers the recent technological developments in data management. Finally, we list open research issues in Sect. 8.8 followed by conclusion in Sect. 8.9.

8.2   History of Power Grids

Back in 1882, the first electrical network came into existence when Thomas Edison designed and commissioned the DC electrical network at Pearl Street of New York City with one generator and a few hundred bulb loads. As this network was relatively small compared to the present day electrical networks, it did not generate so much data, and hence it was easy to manage and analyse. With the advancement of the electrical networks, demand and generation both increased and at this same time, the dependency on electrical energy increased at a rapid pace. People began using more and more electrical equipment which vary from watt to kilowatts. Governments also promoted the use of electrical energy because the electricity is generated far away from the city centre that resulted in less pollution in contrast with the other energy source like petroleum products used in vehicle, which is one of the major cause for pollution in the cities. With the continuous increase in demand and supply of electrical energy, there was a rapid growth of associated power data that accumulated in the traditional grid that helped in load forecasting. Limited data sources in the traditional grids made it easier to handle the captured data.

With the increase in load and demand, the power industries which started as regulated industries started to move towards the unregulated industries. Deregulation in the power industry resulted in a generation company, a transmission company and a distribution company. As a result, data management was also segregated across all the three entities because they handled their data separately. Hence, data analysis took longer times in traditional grids.

Rapidly rising load and competition in the energy market coupled with increased computational load led to the adoption of SCADA systems (Supervisory Control and Data Acquisition) for optimal and efficient utilisation of the power grid. Generation and transmission industries began the technological shift, but the distribution side did not adopt these changes so rapidly.

From the data and intelligence perspective, the traditional grid had various drawbacks, such as there was an only one-way data flow, the limited scope of demand-side management, and difficulties in the integration of renewable sources. Such limitations prompted the power industries to become smarter by further integrating ICT to the grids, which eventually led to the smart grid. The smart grid evolved to solve these problems, but it also introduced new challenges from data management perspective, such as security and privacy, data storage and real-time data analysis. Although adoption of smart grids brought several challenges, it also solved the various existing problem to make the grid more efficient, robust and intelligent.

8.3   Traditional Grids to Smart Grids

Smart grids introduced several layers of intelligence into the traditional electrical grids and paved the way for realising the vision of the smart city. Traditional grids primarily focussed on generating and distributing electricity, without considering other aspects like reliable power supply, effective demand-side management, consumer engagement in energy management and integrating renewable energy sources into the grid. All this became possible with smart grids because the smart grids introduced advanced sensing capability throughout the network including the distribution side and the customer end.

Traditional grids mostly collected primitive data in limited quantities, such as load data, voltage data, and current data. Such data was either analysed manually or using low-end analytical tools. Hence, the analysis output was error-prone and slow. Further, the analytics was only limited to load forecasting, fault detection, and fault location.

Smart grids entirely changed this scenario by capturing real-time data at numerous data points throughout the grid thereby storing an enormous amount of data for intelligent analytics. We refer to such data as big energy data and it includes data such as smart meter data, sensor data, weather forecast data, consumer behaviour data, and power quality data and so on. Proper analysis of such data provided advanced intelligence to the grid thereby assisting the decision-makers to make informed decisions. Decision-makers could now assess the health of the grid remotely. They could identify faults, gather relevant information about the fault location and add renewable energy sources on-demand to cover the generation loss. The big energy data captured in the smart grid coupled with real-time analytics helped smart grids to evolve and become self-aware and introduced self-healing capability to keep the grid running and become more reliable electric grid.

Smart grids used big energy data captured from various sources in solving various smart grids issues. Real-time analysis of big energy data generated signals for the end users for efficient demand management in peak periods. Big energy data analytics help the utility for identifying and removing faulty networks and restore the grid back to full functionality. However, the introduction of advanced technological functionality also brought various challenges in smart grids, especially from the data perspective, such as data security, consumer privacy, big data management, data analytics, cost of managing big energy data, cost of storage and efficient retrieval and so on. Hence, there is an urgent need to find a solution for these challenging issues in smart grids. This chapter investigates these challenges, solutions and open research directions in the forthcoming sections.

8.4 Big Data Characteristics of Smart Grids

Smart grid big data is, in general, characterised by volume, velocity, variety and value of such data. Volume refers to the size of ever-increasing data. Velocity refers to the speed of such data generation. Variety reflects the heterogeneous nature of data gathered from diverse sources. Gartner proposed these three 'V's to describe big data elements. Gantz and Reinsel [1] proposed the fourth 'V' to the list, i.e. Value. Value refers to the identifying and extracting hidden data patterns within the data. Analysing big data leads to discoveries that provide actionable insights to take strategic actions. In the context of smart grids volume, velocity, variety and value provide beneficial information that the power companies can use to improve the overall operational effectiveness of the smart grids.

Volume

The transition from traditional grids to smart grids brings a lot of benefits and opportunities to the consumer as well as to the utilities operators. However, it also brings various challenges for the energy sector. One of the significant challenges is the amount of data captured from a smart meter, sensor, consumer behaviour and weather forecast to predict the energy generation from the renewable source. The size of big energy data can be in terabytes or even in petabytes. One terabyte of storage is equivalent to 1500 CDs. Overall this massive amount of data becomes a considerable challenge for the utility companies to store, manage and analyse it. For example, if we consider 1 million smart consumers in the network and the frequency of data collection from smart meter being 10 min, it equates to 144 instances of data collection per consumer per day or 144 million collections in total. Further, if the size of the data is 5 kB, then the daily data collection is massive. The first challenge is the enormous volume of such data. Big energy data is smaller than social media data (e.g. YouTube or other media platforms). However, it still poses challenges for the energy sector, specifically to storage and processing of the big energy data [2]. Volume can be relatively easy to manage because storage is very cheap. However, the challenge lies in the efficient and real-time processing of such high volumes of data for analytics and accurate real-time insights and to comply with business requirements.

Velocity

This characteristic refers to the rate/speed with which data generation happens in smart grids. As mentioned earlier, if data collection frequency is every 10 min, it will generate large volumes of data in a very short span. Within smart grids, several sources can generate real-time data. These sources are smart meters, sensor data, voltage data, power quality data, distributed energy resources (DERs) data, and event-related data. In smart grids, data collection speeds can vary from sub-seconds (e.g. status of an infrastructure, e.g. transformers) to few minutes (smart meters). The gathered data has to be transmitted in a given period (time-value of information) to ensure that the data is useful. The data has to be at the right place at the right time to make the right decisions. Hence, velocity is a combination of data collection and data transmission. The network has to be robust to handle such high-volume and high-velocity data storage and data transfer.

Variety

Variety in big energy data refers to the data gathered from heterogeneous sources like sensors, actuators and smart meters. Data which can be structured, semi-structured or unstructured introduces variance. In the smart grid ecosystems, there exists data that belongs to each of these categories. For example, data from smart meters is structured data. Structured data is stored in a relational database and can be programmed to answer queries. Weather data or web services data used in smart grids for making energy demand forecast is an example of semi-structured data [3]. XML or extensible markup language is used to communicate semi-structured data because it uses data tags that can be read by machines. Unstructured data in smart grids could be textual data gathered at call centres that manage customer service or an existing knowledge base used for decision-making. For data management entities in smart grid, the real challenge lies in managing such heterogeneous data and use of these heterogeneous data to make the smart grid more effective and efficient.

Value

This is the most critical characteristic of big energy data because data is only valuable when it provides useful insights that can be used to make informed decisions. Value extraction happens by exploring the data to discover hidden patterns using different techniques [4]. Big data can be valuable in providing such insights if the data is acquired, processed and analysed correctly. For example, in smart grids, different sensors and power infrastructure send large volumes of real-time data to a central control station for processing and analysis [1]. Such data can be used to improve energy forecasts, predicting the load on the grid, and capacity planning.

Veracity

Veracity refers to the quality of data. Traditionally data quality is measured using several measures such as accuracy, timeliness, reliability, consistency, accessibility, relevancy, believability and security. A complete list of data/information quality dimension can be found in [5]. In the context of big data, veracity is sometimes also referred to as data validity or data volatility. For smart grid operations, veracity is very critical because decision-makers should trust the data to make a confident decision regarding smart grid operations [6]. In a complex network like the smart girds, achieving veracity can be challenging because of the heterogeneity of data sources. Similarly, smart grids also suffer from partial data problem when the data available for analysis is limited or incomplete because consumers are unwilling to share data due to privacy or security concerns or physical limitation of the transmission networks. Such scenarios reflect the importance of veracity in big energy data [6].

8.5 Smart Grids Data Management

The proliferation of smart grids and prosumer participation in producing and consuming energy has resulted in enormous data management challenges for power generation and power distribution companies. Governments and power distribution companies around the world realise the challenge of managing big data generated by the energy sector. Figure 8.1 outlines the energy data lifecycle from data collection to strategic decision-making.

8.5.1 Data Collection

Data collection is the first step in smart grid data management, which involves capturing data from several sources in the smart grid [7]. The most common and well-known source of data originates from the advanced metering infrastructure (AMI) that captures data from smart meters installed at end-user premises. Smart meters typically gather energy consumption data every 10–15 min and relay it back to the central control centre. These 10-min intervals translate to 144 messages from one smart meter per day. Depending on the population of a given location, this data

Fig. 8.1 Energy data life cycle for smart grids

can quickly escalate in size. For example, Sydney, Australia has a population of around 4 million. Australian Bureau of Statistics latest data shows 1,855,753 dwellings in Greater Sydney [8], which means on each day, 267,228,432 messages are sent to the central control station. That is a massive amount of data just from one source, which is the smart meter. There are other sources of data in a smart grid network, such as, sensor data, voltage data, power quality data, control devices, mobile terminals, metadata, DERs data, event-related data (e.g. breakdowns, voltage loss), reliability data, operating system data, grid equipment data, historical data and third-party data. Other than this, smart grids rely on weather data to forecast demand and trigger on-demand renewable energy generation along with fault detection and user energy consumption forecasting [3, 9]. Other than weather data, numerous other sources of big data (e.g. mobile phones, electric vehicles, connected thermostats, real estate data, and customer energy behaviour profiles) integrate with smart grids to provide forecasting and prediction services [10].

Geographic information systems (GIS) also play a critical role in smart grids. Data from GIS sources can provide valuable information that can be used in decision support systems because it provides local geographic information [11–14]. GIS systems can help to identify solar farm locations [14], electrification of rural areas [15] and many other applications in smart grid deployments. It is equally essential in offering visualisation of the overall grid including locations of prosumers, DER, power lines, generation facilities and distribution facilities [9]. Since data is collected from so many different sources, using several different devices and platforms, it gives rise to several challenges such as cleansing, proper integration and storage. The following subsections cover these critical aspects in more detail.

8.5.2 Data Preprocessing

This phase refers to a number of stages; the main ones are discussed below.

Cleaning

In smart grids, data is acquired from several sources as discussed earlier. On many occasions, this data is inaccurate, meaningless and incomplete. Filtering such impure data is essential before running any analytical algorithms. Data cleansing refers to such filtering processes [16]. Data cleaning constitutes five distinct steps. The first step defines and determines the faulty data; next step is to search and identify the faulty data; then correct the error; document it, and modify the entry process to limit future data errors [17]. Data cleaning is an important process to fix any preprocessing errors as well as to keep the data consistent. During the cleaning process, various points should be considered such as data format, completeness and its rationality to minimise errors during analysis. In smart grids ecosystem, data cleaning is used before forecasting generation from PV systems and deciding the dynamic tariff rate [18].

Redundancy Elimination

Data redundancy refers to surplus data, which can be neglected during the transfer and analysis process. Identifying redundant data is the first step [19] because such redundant data does not add any further value during the analysis stage. It more likely increases the processing time and requires additional storage. Eliminating the redundant data at the source reduces the associated transfer cost and results in energy savings [20–22]. There will also be savings in storage space. Data compression, data filtering, data aggregation and redundancy detection are some techniques to reduce the size of data and assist in transmission. However, there are some disadvantages of redundancy elimination such as increased computation burden to compress and decompress the data.

Repeated Data Deletion

Smart grids capture a massive amount of data, but there are also instances of repeated data. Such repetitions occur due to system errors or hardware or software malfunctions. Hence, before sending such data for analysis, these repeated data instances need to be deleted to reduce storage and transmission cost. In smart grids, the rate of data capture is enormous and hence any savings at the source level directly impact associated activities such as analytics and backups. Further, identifying repeated data instances provides clues on the potential error points within the system that needs attention. Fixing such errors increases the reliability of the smart grid.

8.5.3   Data Integration

Big energy data consists of a variety of data collected from various sources like sensor data, load data and smart meter data. Since the collected data originates from different sources, it is not uniform and poses a significant challenge for the energy companies when analysing data. Hence, before beginning any data analysis, the data should be appropriately integrated [23]. For example, integrating the load data and the weather forecast data will help the utility to forecast energy demands and optimise utilisation of the renewable energy source under uncertainty [24–26]. In such situations, the data may be in different formats, which needs formatting to a standard format before analysis. In distribution side of smart grids, different service providers use different types of smart meters, each running different software, and following a proprietary storage format. Such inconsistency becomes a massive problem for the transmission and generation companies when trying to utilise such data [3, 22]. There are several big data analytics tools available in the market that can streamline data integration. However, their performance varies depending on the data inputs. One solution to the data integration issue is standardisation. Standardisation will help in longer term when all the smart meters (new and legacy) and other smart grid infrastructure could talk to each other and share data seamlessly [27]. Another solution for this problem can be a mediator software which can convert the data and maintain uniformity. There are several big data analytics tools available in the market that can streamline data integration. However, their performance varies depending on the data inputs. In the distribution side of the smart grids service-oriented architecture (SOA) can be utilised for data integration purposes, which makes data transmission and data integration easier and flexible. Enterprise service bus (ESB) and common information models (CIM) are some examples of SOA realisations [9].

8.5.4 Data Storage

Data storage in smart grids can be described as the keeping data safely and securely at a particular location that can access speedily, efficiently, and reliably [28]. In the traditional grids, historical data is saved for load forecasting purposes and does not require excessive storage space. However, in smart grids, other than historical data there are also other data instances requiring storage for effective demand management using renewable energy sources [29]. Another important aspect of the data storage is the input/output data speed because there is a need for real-time data analysis in smart grids. So, energy data storage must have two essential features: one is powerful data access interface system to speed up data transfer, and the other is large and reliable storage space to store a variety of data. Smart grids can use existing storage mechanisms available for big data storage such as direct attached storage (DAS) and network storage. These data storage systems are organised into three parts: first part stores the data on a disc array, second is the connection and network subsystem which is responsible for the connection between two discs and servers, and the last part is the management software to share data between various others servers. Another method used for data storage purpose is distributed file system (DFS) like Google's GFS, Hadoop's HDFS and Taobao's TFS, which is cheaper and provides higher performance [30]. DFS allows sharing of resources among multiple users [31]. Additionally, NoSQL databases such as MongoDB, Cassandra, also provide efficient mechanisms to store massive big energy data.

8.5.5 Data Analytics, Mining and Knowledge Discovery

Smart grids gather a massive amount of data regularly. Such data is analysed to discover different patterns of usage within the smart grid [29]. Several different kinds of analysis are performed on smart grid data such as customer behaviour analysis [2, 32], load analysis [33], state analysis [34], operation analytics [35], fault analysis [36], and signal analytics to achieve various aims. We classify such analysis into two broad categories based on the response time required for data processing. In the first category, response time is not very high, and some examples include load analysis for long-term demand forecasting and consumer behaviour analysis. In the second category, response time is very fast, and some examples include real-time analysis of smart meter data for real-time price forecasting, identifying and analysing fault to segregate faulty part from a healthy part of the smart grid. In smart grids, the big data are in present in a variety of forms, and there are various data which need scaling like transformer voltage data and current data. Analytical tools used for the analysis of big energy data need high robustness, high scalability, high-velocity and fault tolerance features. Choice of analytical tools is a very critical aspect of big data analysis from the utility perspective. Proper analytical tools extract value from the raw data which will be beneficial for electrical industries as well as the utility [37]. For smart grids, the real-time processing tools like Splunk and Storm used for analysis provide fast execution time, fault tolerance capability and parallel computational ability. Hybrid processing tools provide another option for the data analysis in smart grid, where high execution time is not required. For example, Apache Flink and Spark are just two of the analytical tools that can be used for batch processing as well as real-time processing.

8.5.6 Data Representation and Visualisation

Data visualisation is the next step after data analysis. Visualisation assists the decision-makers in understanding the analysis because it provides analytical results in forms of visual representations like graphs [38, 39]. The insights gained from visualising results are more efficient than reviewing pure numbers. It provides visible patterns which help to identify sources of concerns and sources of opportunities. A decision-maker can make effective decisions by visual interpretation of data than textual or numeric forms. Hence visual representation is significant. Visual data representation is equally essential to the end consumer because it shows the consumer their usage patterns, which is fundamentally important because such information will initiate a behaviour change that is beneficial to both the utility and the consumer. There are several visualisation tools and techniques available in the market that the utilities and consumers can use to visualise smart grids. For example, use of 2-D and 3-D visualisation tools to present the load forecast, user load consumption, generation from the renewable source and power quality. The visualisation of weather forecast can help prosumer and prosumer community to maintain their generation and demand. Higher dimension visualisation is possible with tools like Scatter diagram and Andrew curve. Since the smart grids concept is directly related to end user, the visualisation needs to be straightforward and appealing. Tableau is one such expressive tool to visualise the data intuitively. GIS software such as ArcGIS, QGIS, MapInfo, GRASS, gvSIG and Maptitude are good alternatives for visualising smart grid data on the maps [39].

8.5.7   Real-Time Decision-Making

Real-time, automated and independent decision-making is one of the critical features of the smart grid that distinguishes it from the traditional grid [40]. As mentioned in a later section, data analysis paves the way for decision-making. Smart grids operators take critical decisions in real time based on the analytics data secured from the analytics engine. Important decisions like real-time pricing, on-demand renewable generation, estimating capacity constraints, forecasting demand and provisioning real-time supply are some examples that require real-time decisions [40, 41]. The ability to make real-time decisions improves the reliability of the smart grid thereby increasing consumer confidence in the technology [42]. With the help of real-time analysis, it is easier to find the faulty sections in the smart grids and take corrective actions to restore the grid back to complete functionality, thereby reducing the loss of revenue and further boosting consumer confidence. Several real-time demand response (DR) algorithms available in the literature facilitate timely and accurate decision-making. On a broader context, integration of electric vehicles with smart grids introduces further challenges requiring real-time decision-making such as charging and discharging allocations [43].

8.6   Data Management Issues in Smart Grids

In smart grids, data collected from various sources have supported to take intelligent decisions within a short span of time. Big data support the utility as well as the consumer to save energy, utilise the resource, active participation of the consumer, better interaction between the end user and utility. However, on the other hand, the massive data collected from different sources bring numerous challenges for the utility to manage. The following subsections describe these challenges.

8.6.1   Standards and Interoperability

The smart grid consists of different type of devices, networks, management software like SCADA and a variety of data. There are various communication devices and technologies used in the background of the smart grid. The communication system and devices in smart grids have a different feature, different communication speeds, different processing speeds and distinct data transfer mode like parallel, series. Thus, data transfer becomes an onerous task for this devices. So, there is a need for interoperability mechanism, which will make the smart grids more flexible and efficient. There is also need for open standardisation for better interpretability and to establish the secure and sustainable smart, which will also be future ready. Some of the standardisation used in smart grids include IEEE 1815, IEEE 2030.5, IEC 61850, IEC 61850-90-7, etc.

8.6.2 Big Energy Data Volumes

Another challenge faced by the utility agencies is the management of massive data in smart grids. As the data captured in the smart grids are enormous, handling this data is not an easy task for utility. To store this massive amount data requires a large storage space. Due to lack of infrastructure and limited skilled workforce, the utility faces hard time to handle and utilise this considerable amount of data. Proper management of the data collected from the users helps to manage the demand and the active participation of the end user. End users should be educated on the workings of the smart meter to understand the signals displayed on the smart meter. Such education will ensure maximum participation of end users in data management and its proper utilisation.

8.6.3 Reliability and Scalability

Data reliability and data scalability are two significant data quality attributes. These attributes are essential to place trust in the data that will be useful for taking critical decisions; it will also enable scaling as the system grows in the future. In smart grids, heterogeneous sensors capture data from different electrical infrastructure, which raises the questions, how to ensure that the data capture is reliable? Hence, reliability becomes a significant challenge for the smart grid operations because the entire forecasting and fault management system rely on this data. The fundamental assumption that this data is reliable needs to be proved. The next issue is that of scalability. Once the operations of the smart grid start using reliable data, they need it consistently to fine tune the forecasts, and this relates to data scalability issue, raising the question, how to ensure that data is captured consistently in the future.

8.6.4 High Bandwidth

The high bandwidth issue relates directly to the management of massive data volumes because data transfers to central control stations require bandwidth. With the rising volumes of data capture, this has become a significant concern. We provided an example in Sect. 8.5.1 that showed the complexity and massive volumes of big energy data in Greater Sydney area. There are two approaches for data transfer—wired and wireless. Wireless is preferred option because of its ease of implementation. However, its drawback is constrained bandwidth. Hence, data compression and data aggregation techniques are employed to manage bandwidth efficiently. However, on some occasions, valuable data may be ignored during compression or aggregation process, which will affect the future forecasting results.

8.6.5 Security and Data Privacy

Ensuring data security and privacy in smart grids is critical because a smart grid is the backbone of any smart city. Smart grids and smart meters collectively generate various data instances that have privacy and security concerns. From personal user privacy perspective, the end consumers will only trust the technology if they know that their data is secure and does not impact their privacy. Such consumer sensitive data needs to be securely transmitted to prevent privacy breaches. From a security point of view, consider a scenario, where a hacker manipulates the sensor data. If the smart grid relies on this hacked data to make future predictions for energy demands, it will be a total failure, thereby, paralysing the entire economy. So, for secure and safe data transfer, all the data must be encrypted before transferring it.

8.7 Recent Developments in Data Management for Smart Grids

This section describes the recent progress in the field of smart city data management addressing the challenges described earlier.

8.7.1 Data Collection

Data collection is the first step in data management. Recent progress in this area has addressed some of the issues like standards, interoperability, security, privacy, reliability, scalability and high bandwidth transmission. For examples, authors in [7] proposed a secure, efficient and scalable data collection protocol to transfer data from source to the power operator in a hierarchical manner. The data collectors or relay nodes can validate the integrity of the data and transfer the data upwards, but they do not have access to the data itself. The proposed solution is optimised for time-efficient data collection. Since the data is not accessible to the DC, several third-party services can provide a number of value-added services, e.g. outsourcing data collection to a third-party DC, or use the cloud for data storage and processing before sending it to the central control station. The proposed solution adopted a heuristics algorithm with good approximation because of the intractable nature of the given problem. Data collection from security and privacy perspective is investigated by some researchers including [44, 45]. Some existing research is focused on data collection for a network that is not hierarchical [44, 46, 47]. These studies developed lightweight message authentication scheme for smart grid data communication considering privacy [46–48]. From a storage perspective, some studies have investigated how to reduce storage when establishing multiple sessions with source devices/sensors [49]. One approach is to use long-term shared keys to save space [49], but such an approach is not applicable to hierarchical data collection structure as reported in [7]. Further, many studies assume that the data collecting devices or DCs are trusted, however, in many cases these devices may be compromised by adversaries thereby severely impacting the quality of data collection. Ensuring privacy and security during data collection using homomorphic encryption approach are studied by several researchers. However, homomorphic encryption is computationally expensive and may drain the battery power from the DCs rapidly [50, 51]. A recent study investigated smart meter data reporting strategy to optimise the performance of the communication network [52]. Here, three strategies are reported to improve the performance of TCP-based communication in IEEE 802.11s networks. Further, [53] addressed the scalability and security aspects and [54] studied cloud-based data management. Here, a three-layered fog-based architecture is proposed to develop a scheduled DCF algorithm to upload data from the sensors to the cloud. Overall, we notice that research has progressed significantly to address the critical research issues from a data collection perspective.

8.7.2 Data Preprocessing

A recent study has compared and concluded that data generated from smart grids is equivalent to big data generated from social media platforms [55]. Data preprocessing involves data cleaning, data aggregation, redundancy removal and repeated data deletion. Several papers discuss data aggregation aspect such as [51, 56–59]. Majority of the research on data aggregation focusses on privacy preservation. Data aggregation assists in anonymising data to ensure privacy preservation. Rather than transmitting data received from each DC, the aggregator combines relevant data and forwards it to the control centre. For example, when the DC received data from the smart meter, it may include data about the customer, customer location, amount of consumption, type of smart meter, usage patterns and so on. Some data instances may result in privacy concerns, e.g. customer location or usage patterns. Such data may offer fine-grained demand forecasting or estimation. However, a reasonable quality forecast is achievable without such information. Hence, data aggregation assists in resolving such privacy issues by selectively deleting some data and aggregating the rest to achieve multiple objectives such as privacy preservation, reducing storage and reducing transmission bandwidth. Data aggregation is also used for preserving data integrity [59], for data security [51, 60], for ensuring scalability [61], for lossless transmission [62], as well as plain aggregation without considering security [63, 64]. Some recent survey articles have thoroughly investigated data aggregation [65]. Data aggregation from home area network perspective is reported in [66]. The location of data aggregators or data aggregation point (DAP) is an important aspect of network planning and manually identifying DAP is time-consuming and laborious [67]. A linear programming optimisation problem is solved to optimise the cost and select a mix of wired and wireless technology [67]. Overall, we observe that the research has progressed considerably to address the critical research issues from a data preprocessing perspective, especially data aggregation and redundancy removal.

8.7.3 Data Integration

The smart grid is a combination of traditional grid and information and communication technology. So, the integration of heterogeneous data is of paramount importance in smart grid data management. Several researchers have done numerous studies to resolve the issue in data integration. In [23], authors proposed a system to integrate heterogeneous data based on metadata mining algorithm and IEC standard. The author used various static and dynamic rules to design main structure of rules to design the decision support system which is a part of Dynamic ETL system. Such methods provide guidance on big energy data integration.

8.7.4 Data Storage

Smart grids capture a large number of heterogeneous data from various sources. Storing and accessing such data at a rapid rate is necessary for the smart grid. Researchers have proposed various architectures for data storage in smart grids. In [68], a SMACK-based platform, which is a combination of kappa and lambda architecture, is presented for data storage in microgrids. Whereas in [69], authors used a graph storage for storing the data in smart grids. They proposed an automatic migration of database from Resource Description Framework (RDF) to graph storage system. This migration increases the access speed of data by reducing the answer to queries. Moreover, the data storage happens on the same node that probably had the answers to the same queries. They used the general graph model and generic query language which make this approach independent of graph database management systems. The data management in smart grids is essential because most of the analysis happens in real time. Smart grids can use the existing data storage methods and tailored it to their needs.

8.7.5   Data Analytics, Mining and Knowledge Discovery

Data analysis in smart grid achieves various objectives like demand-side management, fault detection, self-healing, consumer privacy and network security. Numerous researchers proposed several solutions for managing and analysing big energy data. A distributed data analytics processing approach is proposed in [28]. In this approach, the authors used machine learning algorithm for local processing and decision-making of data to save network bandwidth, and decrease the service delays. For the realisation of this topology of the local processor in the smart grid, they also included a central processor which is responsible for the communication between the local processing units. This mixed approach helps in reducing the overall cost of data processing. In contrast, a support vector machine (SVM), and HBase database platform are used for big energy data analytics [70]. They have utilised LibSVM for data analytics purpose to forecast the load considering some environmental factors. Another important aspect of data analysis is consumer privacy. In [71], authors have presented various kernel-based methods to analysis the consumer smart meter data. Altogether, there are methods available for data analytics in smart grids but need more research which includes the all aspect of data analysis in one.

8.7.6   Data Representation and Visualisation

Pictorial and graphical representation of analytical data has a substantial impact on decision-makers when studying visual patterns. Most of the work done on smart grid big data management presents the extract of analysis in the graphical method. For example, 3D histograms are used to represent the real-time power consumption data [72]. This 3D histogram shows the difference between energy consumption as total consumption in particular area but is unable to obtain information about the distribution of the whole area. The GPS data can represent the real-time power consumption as a heat map, where the real-time data changes are observed, but they are not as easy to interpret as a 3D histogram. With GIS, it is straightforward for the power industries to map the data on geographical maps and make it easier to understand the data and support in taking the critical decision in smart grid management. An efficient visualisation system for the data collected from the smart meter is essential in decision-making [39]. The use of open source GIS software (QGIS) in combination with CIM helps to visualise the smart data more effectively and efficiently. Overall, there is progress in the field of data visualisation and representation but more need to be done to make the presentation more user-friendly so that user is engaged and participates in the smart grid.

8.7.7 Big Energy Data Management in Smart Cities

In [73], authors discussed energy management issues in smart cities. They have presented extensive reviews on planning and operation model of the energy management in smart cities by categorising it in five main areas: generation, storage, infrastructure, facilities and transport. Their studies indicate that the DG (distributed generation) will continue to be the main focus area of research in smart grids and another important research area to be explored in future is improving energy-efficiency with a better device, advanced control system and DR management in future smart cities. Furthermore, the authors also proposed a methodology to design an improved energy model for smart cities. Within this model, there are a number of components that heavily rely on high-quality data such as energy demand data, performance parameters, geolocation data such as wind speed, rainfall and historical and real-time energy prices. Hence, managing data becomes backbone for a reliable and operationally efficient smart grid.

8.7.8 Renewable Energy Data Exchange

Renewable energy source plays an important role in smart cities and integration of these DERs is crucial in smart grids which forms the fundamental energy base of smart cities. In [74], the authors discussed standardisation and protocols for interconnection among sensor, controller, energy sources and load in smart grids. Such standardisation improves data exchange and data communication, which is critical in smart grids. It also discussed at length about the power quality improvement by optimal placement and utilisation of DERs in the distribution network of smart grids. It also described various protocols for information exchange in smart grids which are essential for a reliable power supply to smart cities, as the standard protocol of interconnection and communication are indispensable for reliable and self-healing distribution network. The proposed architecture is designed using security, quality, reliability and availability architecture, thereby ensuring data protection and redundancy.

In [75], authors studied the smart grid systems installed in various cities across the globe, by understanding the smart grid technologies and its modelling. They also studied the features of smart grids, when it is connected to a distribution network and its managing capability of active power supplied by distributed energy sources like wind energy, solar energy and fuel cell. They also identified the necessary facilities and investment required for the smart grid development pathway in Australia. Some of the facilities mentioned in [75] are the integration of electricity retailer to facilitate a seamless customer transaction, high penetration of distributed generation and a communications infrastructure with self-healing capability without human intervention. The critical challenge here is ensuring data management.

8.7.9 Big Energy Data Management

In [9], authors describe how to adopt the current big data techniques for big energy data management. They provide an overview of big energy data management and show how big data techniques assist in managing deluge of data generated by smart grid operations. They provide guidelines on the technical requirements, tools and steps for implementing big data for smart grid data management. Cloud-based application for smart grids also generates a massive quantity of data [3]. Such data and its characteristics are thoroughly covered in [3]. The authors also mention additional challenges like data security, data collection, data privacy and governance, integration, sharing, analysis of big energy data and lack of professionals in big data energy analytics.

8.7.10 Big Energy Data Management in Developing Nations

In [76], authors discussed the development of smart grid in developing nations such as India, China and Brazil. They segregated developing nation into two main groups, pioneer developing nations and developing nations. China, India and Brazil have actively spent significant efforts to develop future smart grids, by starting several pilot projects. Different strategies were adopted in such countries to make future smart grid successful. These include investigation if smart grid is needed, the impact of government backing and funding, promoting and driving test projects, and building capacity with renewable energy sources. One of the elements to accelerating smart grid in developing nations was to focus on information system architecture and data management system for two-way communication in smart grids [77]. Data management tools can assist smart grid operators to use the fine-grained information to manage the smart grid, predict power surges and take remedial actions in real time. Such data management architectures should be interoperable with existing power systems as well as future power systems. Interoperability is also crucial when integrating with smart cities information systems [77]. Relevant data can be used for offering customer friendly services such as billing system using mobile phone technology. Renewable energy sources and batteries, which cope with the increase in energy demand due to its inherent modular nature, form one of the key components of smart grids of the future. The hybrid renewable energy systems rely on intelligent control systems that use NASA surface meteorology and solar energy data to estimate the demand and select an appropriate mix of hybrid solution.

8.7.11 Energy Data Policy and Regulations

In [78], Lee et al. presented a brief review of smart grid industry in some pro-
gressive nations. They mentioned about Taiwan government's energy policies, and
the objective of the policies are energy savings, sustainable supply, strengthen
sustainable energy options, control carbon emission, and work towards zero carbon
economy, and these objective can be fulfilled only by modernising the grid. They
analysed current practices taking into consideration the nation's procedures, regulations and strategies. Finally, authors recommended some changes to the law
governing the greenhouse gas reduction need to be updated, implementation of
critical technologies for future development, invest more in research and development and manufacturing engineering. On the data management side, they proposed the use of data warehousing for predicting demand. Authors in [79] discuss
development policies and challenges faced by European smart grids that are supported by the European Union. The key challenges faced by the European countries
in the development of smart grid are system integration, customer involvement,
legal hurdles and technology development. From the integration perspective, different systems need to be able to share the data with each other to ensure seamless
operation. Data storage and decentralised data distribution and management are
critical elements to ensure successful operations [79]. In comparison, Di Santo et al.
in [80] presented an analysis of policy and regulation in Brazil towards the
development of smart grids. However, the authors stated that full-scale implementation would take decades because it needed policies, legal framework, smart
power sector, smart customers and ongoing funding. However, several pilot projects are going on in Brazil. In this study, they mention one of the technical barriers
being the data models along with the metering infrastructure and standardisation of
communication protocols. Data concentrators are used to capture consumer consumption data in real time and used for prediction and billing purposes.

8.7.12 Big Energy Data Originating from Consumers

Ponce et al. in [81] discussed the key factors involved in adopting the smart grids
technology from end-user perceptions. End users are a critical component of the
smart grid because they offer distributed energy source and participate in
demand-side management. The authors used signal detection theory (SDT) to
capture the consumer's perception of the smart grid technologies. A didactic smart
grid system is used to capture the consumer perception with different scenarios. In
addition to SDT, authors also used fuzzy approaches to capture the consumer
perception. The result of their study showed the conservative behaviours of the
consumer due to lack of confidence in smart and intelligent technologies. Such
behaviour of the end user limits the smart grid performance in real scenarios.

Another study from the user perspective is a cloud-based data management platform for smart grids [82]. The proposed system manages data collection, analysis, storage and visualisation. It outlines several challenges associated with data management such as security, reliability, interoperability and heterogeneous data fusion. Another application of user side analytics is a framework for increasing energy savings [83]. The proposed architecture has three layers—data collection layer, analytics layer and web portal. The analytics layer uses a metaheuristics forecasting system along with dynamic optimisation algorithm to predict energy consumption. In [84], the authors provide a thorough review of residential DR systems for smart girds, focussing on load balancing techniques and information and communication technology to assist in DR. One of the challenges is the non-responsiveness of customers to DR programs. Minor changes to the pricing signals have shown no response from customers. At times, it is believed that the customers do not understand the pricing systems and hence do not respond. These findings show that even with the best available data set, the system may fail or behave unexpectedly.

Another important aspect of smart grids is demand-side management and DR program. DR aims to manage the requisite demand without increasing overall capacity. Offering DR to residential customers along with industrial/commercial customers creates new challenges. Authors in [84] provide a thorough review of DR systems (including load management) for residential consumers. They list the challenges faced by a utility which becomes a roadblock for widespread of DR program to the residential user on a large scale. Among these challenges, the paramount issue was the mutual dependence of energy consumption cost among a different group of energy user which is known as the externality effect. Externality effects refer to the unfair price rise during the peak periods when a small group of consumers consume a significant amount of energy leading to energy shortages and subsequent price rise. They have recommended an adaptive consumption-level pricing scheme (ACLPS) in which the consumer paid electricity charge for their actual consumption thus this scheme overcome externality effect.

8.8 Open Research Directions

In this chapter, we discussed data management aspect of smart grids. We identified the characteristics of smart grid data, data management challenges and the key steps involved in data management. There are open research issues that need resolution. This section summarises these issues.

8.8.1 Secure Data Sensing and Communication Challenges

Securing smart grid data is of paramount importance to ensure proper functioning of the grid. Data should be secured when it is captured, temporarily stored on devices, transmitted over the network and permanently stored at the control centre. There are many open research directions in smart grid data security such as developing lightweight algorithms for data compression or data aggregation, techniques for partial or complete data aggregation, methods for aggregation on the fly, data format for secure transmission, redundant storage strategies and backup plans for archival [51]. Security profiles should be assigned based on the importance of the data. For example, non-critical applications such as meter data collection should have a different security status compared to fault detection [85, 86].

8.8.2 Bad Data Detection Challenges

In the data cleansing section, we mentioned the challenges in managing bad data [16–18]. In many cases, for smart grids, such data poses a massive problem because several information systems are interconnected, and the data flow through each of these systems. Polluted data should be detected early and fast to prevent the pollution infiltrating into other systems. Hence, detection becomes a critical research challenge that requires immediate attention. Bad data also enters the systems when an attacker launches an attack by purposely injecting false or incorrect data. From a security point of view, it is a critical challenge because incorrect data will lead to incorrect decision-making, e.g. excessive energy generation or low tariffs. Either way, bad data has a significantly negative impact on smart grid operations, and hence it should be dealt with extreme caution [87–89].

8.8.3 Cost Optimisation Challenges

One particular area of interest in smart grids is studying the cost of data management. There are several general studies on the cost of data centres and how to cost-effectively manage large data centres. However, specific studies on data management cost of smart grids are missing in the literature. The smart grid is such a complex network and data being one of the most important elements of the smart grid ecosystems; it seems obvious to study this problem and hence this is one significant open research direction.

8.8.4 Quality-of-Service Challenges

The smart grid is a complex network of heterogeneous devices transmitting different types of data at varying intervals with different levels of urgency. Quality of service aspect becomes critical during data transmission. If the captured data reaches the destination in time, it is valuable for other systems. However, network congestion and other factors can introduce delay resulting in poor quality of service. It may even introduce errors or result in complete loss of data, which can become a major concern as it may result in suboptimal power quality if it corrupts the smart meter data or impacts the data centre if the air cooling systems fail. Therefore, the need and urgency for developing QoS frameworks are paramount. The research challenges within this include: (1) identifying and agreeing upon QoS metrics for data acquisition, transmission, storage and security, (2) defining and enforcing service level agreements, and (3) methods to monitor and implement QoS strategies [90].

8.8.5 Data Reliability Challenges

Data reliability during sensing and data transmission using constrained bandwidth need systematic analysis. Several recent studies in big energy data look at data reliability and data transmission [91–94]. Inspecting reliability challenges from an architectural point of view is fundamental. There are several independent algorithms proposed in the literature that addresses data reliability. However, a holistic and a consolidated architectural approach is required to understand and implement reliability mechanisms within the smart grids to make it a 'super smart grid' [92]. Such an architecture should consider the fault tolerance levels of different sub-components in the smart grid while devising a strategic approach to address data reliability. Reliability should be scaled geographically as well as temporally to ensure reliable data capture each time.

8.8.6 Visualisation Challenges

Visualisation tools are designed to improve human cognitive abilities by assisting in rapidly categorising interesting patterns from big energy data [95]. Visualisation also helps to improve human understanding of enormous data sets such as the big energy data, aids in errors and outlier detection, provides thorough insights and enables timely and accurate hypotheses formulation [96]. Numerous researchers have studied visualisation from different perspectives such as techniques and methods, the speed of data processing [97], user-friendly visualisation query engine [98], GIS-based techniques for real-time data integration [11], visualisation of unstructured temporal data [99], the focus-on-context technique [100], and tree-maps for hierarchical data visualisation [101]. In the future, the volume of data is set to rise tremendously, and a fraction of such data will be tagged [102]. There is an immediate need for innovating techniques that can represent data intuitively to aid human cognition and assist in real-time and informed decision-making. Next generation visualisation frameworks are needed to handle this problem. The current visualisation challenges are its ability to handle heterogeneous data formats in real time, the speed of rapid changes to visualisation queries, the capability to manage huge data sets which are typical for big energy data and effective presentation of data.

8.8.7 Data Integration Challenges

Smart grid data originates from diverse sources like sensors, actuators, transformers and other electrical and computing infrastructure that forms part of the smart grid ecosystem. Such data needs to be integrated with other data sources to provide situational awareness and assist in decision-making. Thus, it becomes necessary for such data to be seamlessly combined in real-time to provide necessary data to the central control station. Data semantic approaches need to be investigated to address the data integration challenges. Gathered data needs to be semantically tagged to facilitate interoperability among different data sources. Semantic technologies can solve big energy data integration problems. For example, the nature of big energy data can be studied from an integration perspective, the value of data originating from different sources may be different, and the structure of different data may be different. Hence, integrating needs to happen spatially and temporally. Schema-level mapping approaches should be further investigated to address the upcoming challenges of big energy data.

8.9 Conclusion

The smart grid is a core infrastructure of a typical smart city. Smart grids have the intelligence to manage the electrical energy supplied in very efficient and effective way. This intelligence has come through the adoption of computational technology to plan and execute electrical energy demands. Smart grids generate large volumes of data, and hence the data analysis and data management are a critical aspect of smart grids. This book chapter presented a detailed review of big energy data management in smart grids by describing various steps required for processing the heterogeneous big energy data. It also covered various challenges and issues faced by the user and the utility in smart grids big energy data management. We discussed recent developments in this area and enlisted open research directions in this field.

References

1. Gantz J, Reinsel D (2011) Extracting value from chaos. IDC IView 1–12
2. Tushar W, Zhang JA, Smith DB et al (2014) Prioritizing consumers in smart grid: a game theoretic approach. IEEE Trans Smart Grid 5:1429–1438
3. Zhou K, Fu C, Yang S (2016) Big data driven smart energy management: from big data to big insights. Renew Sustain Energy Rev 56:215–225. https://doi.org/10.1016/j.rser.2015.11.050
4. Chen M, Mao S, Liu Y (2014) Big data: a survey. Mob Netw Appl 19:171–209. https://doi.org/10.1007/s11036-013-0489-0
5. Knight S, Burn J (2005) Developing a framework for assessing information quality on the world wide web. Informing Sci 8:159–172
6. Aman S, Chelmis C, Prasanna V (2014) Addressing data veracity in big data applications. IEEE, pp 1–3
7. Uludag S, Lui K-S, Ren W, Nahrstedt K (2016) Secure and scalable data collection with time minimization in the smart grid. IEEE Trans Smart Grid 7:43–54
8. Australian Bureau of Statistics Dwelling Type (2017) Greater Sydney. In: Id Popul. Experts. http://profile.id.com.au/australia/dwellings?WebID=250. Accessed 1 Nov 2017
9. Daki H, El Hannani A, Aqqal A et al (2017) Big Data management in smart grid: concepts, requirements and implementation. J Big Data 4:13. https://doi.org/10.1186/s40537-017-0070-y
10. Fehrenbacher K (2012) 10 ways big data is remaking energy. https://gigaom.com/2012/01/29/10-ways-big-data-is-remaking-energy/. Accessed 1 Nov 2017
11. Li X, Lv Z, Hu J et al (2015) XEarth: a 3D GIS Platform for managing massive city information. IEEE, pp 1–6
12. Farhangi H (2010) The path of the smart grid. IEEE Power Energy Mag 8
13. Domínguez J, Amador J (2007) Geographical information systems applied in the field of renewable energy sources. Comput Ind Eng 52:322–326
14. Sánchez-Lozano JM, Teruel-Solano J, Soto-Elvira PL, García-Cascales MS (2013) Geographical information systems (GIS) and multi-criteria decision making (MCDM) methods for the evaluation of solar farms locations: case study in south-eastern Spain. Renew Sustain Energy Rev 24:544–556
15. Amador J, Domínguez J (2005) Application of geographical information systems to rural electrification with renewable energy sources. Renew Energy 30:1897–1912
16. Cody R (2017) Cody's data cleaning techniques using SAS. SAS Institute
17. Chu X, Ilyas IF (2016) Qualitative data cleaning. Proc VLDB Endowment 9:1605–1608
18. Sagiroglu S, Terzi R, Canbay Y, Colak I (2016) Big data issues in smart grid systems. IEEE, pp 1007–1012
19. Zhang N, Yang X, Zhang M, Long K (2016) RMI-DRE: a redundancy-maximizing identification scheme for data redundancy elimination. Sci China Inf Sci 59:089301
20. Xie S, Chen Z (2017) Anomaly detection and redundancy elimination of big sensor data in internet of things. ArXiv Prepr ArXiv170303225
21. Lee K, Kim D, Shin I (2017) Improving throughput in wireless networks using redundancy elimination. IEEE Commun Lett 21:160–163
22. Chen W, Zhou K, Yang S, Wu C (2017) Data quality of electricity consumption data in a smart grid environment. Renew Sustain Energy Rev 75:98–105
23. Guerrero JI, García A, Personal E et al (2017) Heterogeneous data source integration for smart grid ecosystems based on metadata mining. Expert Syst Appl 79:254–268
24. Taieb SB, Huser R, Hyndman RJ, Genton MG (2016) Forecasting uncertainty in electricity smart meter data by boosting additive quantile regression. IEEE Trans Smart Grid 7:2448–2455

25. Jurado S, Nebot À, Mugica F, Mihaylov M (2017) Fuzzy inductive reasoning forecasting strategies able to cope with missing data: a smart grid application. Appl Soft Comput 51:225–238
26. Alahakoon D, Yu X (2016) Smart electricity meter data intelligence for future energy systems: a survey. IEEE Trans Ind Inform 12:425–436
27. Neumann S, Wilhoit F, Goodrich M, Balijepalli VM (2016) Everything's talking to each other: smart meters generate big data for utilities and customers. IEEE Power Energy Mag 14:40–47
28. Ahsan U, Bais A (2017) Distributed big data management in smart grid. IEEE, pp 1–6
29. Qiu RC, Antonik P (2014) Big data for smart grid. Smart Grid Using Big Data Anal Random Matrix Theory Approach 485–491
30. Mosaddegh A, Cañizares CA, Bhattacharya K, Fan H (2017) Distributed computing architecture for optimal control of distribution feeders with smart loads. IEEE Trans Smart Grid 8:1469–1478
31. Cao Z, Lin J, Wan C et al (2017) Hadoop-based framework for big data analysis of synchronised harmonics in active distribution network. IET Gener Transm Distrib 11 (16):3930–3937
32. Park C-K, Kim H-J, Kim Y-S (2014) A study of factors enhancing smart grid consumer engagement. Energy Policy 72:211–218
33. Eltantawy AB, Salama MM (2014) A novel zooming algorithm for distribution load flow analysis for smart grid. IEEE Trans Smart Grid 5:1704–1711
34. Weng Y, Negi R, Faloutsos C, Ilić MD (2017) Robust data-driven state estimation for smart grid. IEEE Trans Smart Grid 8:1956–1967
35. Moradi MH, Eskandari M, Hosseinian SM (2015) Operational strategy optimization in an optimal sized smart microgrid. IEEE Trans Smart Grid 6:1087–1095
36. Jiang H, Zhang JJ, Gao W, Wu Z (2014) Fault detection, identification, and location in smart grid based on data-driven computational methods. IEEE Trans Smart Grid 5:2947–2956
37. Diamantoulakis PD, Kapinas VM, Karagiannidis GK (2015) Big data analytics for dynamic energy management in smart grids. Big Data Res 2:94–101
38. Srinivasan D, Reindl T (2015) Real-time display of data from a smart-grid on geographical map using a GIS tool and its role in optimization of game theory. IEEE, pp 1–6
39. Stefan M, Lopez JG, Andreasen MH, Olsen RL (2017) Visualization techniques for electrical grid smart metering data: a survey. In: Proceedings of the 2017 IEEE third international conference on big data. Computing service and applications (BigDataService)
40. Yu M, Hong SH (2016) A real-time demand-response algorithm for smart grids: a stackelberg game approach. IEEE Trans Smart Grid 7:879–888
41. Siano P (2014) Demand response and smart grids—a survey. Renew Sustain Energy Rev 30:461–478
42. Colson CM, Nehrir MH (2013) Comprehensive real-time microgrid power management and control with distributed agents. IEEE Trans Smart Grid 4:617–627
43. Akhavan-Rezai E, Shaaban MF, El-Saadany EF, Karray F (2016) Online intelligent demand management of plug-in electric vehicles in future smart parking lots. IEEE Syst J 10:483–494
44. Liu N, Chen J, Zhu L et al (2013) A key management scheme for secure communications of advanced metering infrastructure in smart grid. IEEE Trans Ind Electron 60:4746–4756
45. Uludag S, Zeadally S, Badra M (2015) Techniques, taxonomy, and challenges of privacy protection in the smart grid. In: Privacy in a digital, networked world. Springer, Berlin, pp 343–390
46. Fouda MM, Fadlullah ZM, Kato N et al (2011) A lightweight message authentication scheme for smart grid communications. IEEE Trans Smart Grid 2:675–685
47. Bekara C, Luckenbach T, Bekara K (2012) A privacy preserving and secure authentication protocol for the advanced metering infrastructure with non-repudiation service. Proc ENERGY

48. Abbasinezhad-Mood D, Nikooghadam M (2017) An ultra-lightweight and secure scheme for communications of smart meters and neighborhood gateways by utilization of an ARM Cortex-M Microcontroller. IEEE Trans Smart Grid

49. Kim Y-J, Kolesnikov V, Kim H, Thottan M (2011) SSTP: a scalable and secure transport protocol for smart grid data collection. IEEE, pp 161–166

50. Yukun N, Xiaobin T, Shi C et al (2013) A security privacy protection scheme for data collection of smart meters based on homomorphic encryption. IEEE, pp 1401–1405

51. Li F, Luo B, Liu P (2010) Secure information aggregation for smart grids using homomorphic encryption. IEEE, pp 327–332

52. Saputro N, Akkaya K (2017) Investigation of smart meter data reporting strategies for optimized performance in smart grid AMI networks. IEEE Internet Things J 4:894–904

53. Saranya P, Ponmagal R (2016) Secure and scalable sensor data access network with delay tolerance. Wireless Commun 8:202–206

54. Wang T, Zeng J, Lai Y et al (2017) Data collection from WSNs to the cloud based on mobile Fog elements. Future Gener Comput Syst

55. Aiello M, Pagani GA (2014) The smart grid's data generating potentials. IEEE, pp 9–16

56. Uddin F (2017) Energy-aware optimal data aggregation in smart grid wireless communication networks. IEEE Trans Green Commun Netw 1:358–371

57. Groat MM, Hey W, Forrest S (2011) KIPDA: k-indistinguishable privacy-preserving data aggregation in wireless sensor networks. IEEE, pp 2024–2032

58. Rottondi C, Verticale G, Krauss C (2013) Distributed privacy-preserving aggregation of metering data in smart grids. IEEE J Sel Areas Commun 31:1342–1354

59. Li F, Luo B (2012) Preserving data integrity for smart grid data aggregation. IEEE, pp 366–371

60. Jin H, Uludag S, Lui K-S, Nahrstedt K (2014) Secure data collection in constrained tree-based smart grid environments. IEEE, pp 308–313

61. Karimi B, Namboodiri V, Jadliwala M (2015) Scalable meter data collection in smart grids through message concatenation. IEEE Trans Smart Grid 6:1697–1706

62. Bartoli A, Hernandez-Serrano J, Soriano M et al (2010) Secure lossless aggregation for smart grid M2M networks. IEEE, pp 333–338

63. Niyato D, Wang P (2012) Cooperative transmission for meter data collection in smart grid. IEEE Commun Mag 50

64. Shao S, Guo S, Qiu X et al (2014) Traffic scheduling for wireless meter data collection in smart grid communication network. IEEE, pp 1–7

65. Dhasian HR, Balasubramanian P (2013) Survey of data aggregation techniques using soft computing in wireless sensor networks. IET Inf Secur 7:336–342

66. Yan Y, Qian Y, Sharif H (2011) A secure data aggregation and dispatch scheme for home area networks in smart grid. IEEE, pp 1–6

67. Tavasoli M, Yaghmaee MH, Mohajerzadeh AH (2016) Optimal placement of data aggregators in smart grid on hybrid wireless and wired communication. IEEE, pp 332–336

68. Pinheiro G, Vinagre E, Praça I et al (2018) Smart grids data management: a case for cassandra. In: 14th international conference on distributed computing and artificial intelligence. Springer, Berlin, p 87

69. De Virgilio R (2017) Smart RDF data storage in graph databases. In: Proceedings of the 17th IEEE/ACM international symposium on cluster, cloud and grid computing. IEEE Press, pp 872–881

70. Yang H, Li P, Masood A et al (2016) Smart grid data analysis and prediction modeling. In: 2016 international conference on progress in informatics and computing (PIC). IEEE, pp 541–544

71. Arora S, Taylor JW (2016) Forecasting electricity smart meter data using conditional kernel density estimation. Omega 59:47–59

72. Zhou Y, Li P, Xiao Y et al (2016) Smart grid data mining and visualization. In: 2016 international conference on progress in informatics and computing (PIC). IEEE, pp 536–540

73. Calvillo CF, Sánchez-Miralles A, Villar J (2016) Energy management and planning in smart cities. Renew Sustain Energy Rev 55:273–287. https://doi.org/10.1016/j.rser.2015.10.133
74. Ruiz-Romero S, Colmenar-Santos A, Mur-Pérez F, López-Rey Á (2014) Integration of distributed generation in the power distribution network: the need for smart grid control systems, communication and equipment for a smart city—use cases. Renew Sustain Energy Rev 38:223–234. https://doi.org/10.1016/j.rser.2014.05.082
75. Haidar AMA, Muttaqi K, Sutanto D (2015) Smart grid and its future perspectives in Australia. Renew Sustain Energy Rev 51:1375–1389. https://doi.org/10.1016/j.rser.2015.07.040
76. Fadaeenejad M, Saberian AM, Fadaee M et al (2014) The present and future of smart power grid in developing countries. Renew Sustain Energy Rev 29:828–834. https://doi.org/10.1016/j.rser.2013.08.072
77. Welsch M, Bazilian M, Howells M et al (2013) Smart and just grids for sub-Saharan Africa: exploring options. Renew Sustain Energy Rev 20:336–352. https://doi.org/10.1016/j.rser.2012.11.004
78. Lee AH, Chen HH, Chen J (2017) Building smart grid to power the next century in Taiwan. Renew Sustain Energy Rev 68:126–135
79. Iqtiyanillham N, Hasanuzzaman M, Hosenuzzaman M (2017) European smart grid prospects, policies, and challenges. Renew Sustain Energy Rev 67:776–790
80. Di Santo KG, Kanashiro E, Di Santo SG, Saidel MA (2015) A review on smart grids and experiences in Brazil. Renew Sustain Energy Rev 52:1072–1082
81. Ponce P, Polasko K, Molina A (2016) End user perceptions toward smart grid technology: acceptance, adoption, risks, and trust. Renew Sustain Energy Rev 60:587–598
82. Sun Y-Y, Yuan J-J, Zhai M-Y (2016) Cloud-based data analysis of user side in smart grid. IEEE, pp 39–44
83. Chou J-S, Ngo N-T (2016) Smart grid data analytics framework for increasing energy savings in residential buildings. Autom Constr 72:247–257
84. Haider HT, See OH, Elmenreich W (2016) A review of residential demand response of smart grid. Renew Sustain Energy Rev 59:166–178. https://doi.org/10.1016/j.rser.2016.01.016
85. Wang W, Lu Z (2013) Cyber security in the smart grid: survey and challenges. Comput Netw 57:1344–1371
86. Tan S, De D, Song W-Z et al (2017) Survey of security advances in smart grid: a data driven approach. IEEE Commun Surv Tutor 19:397–422
87. Kosut O, Jia L, Thomas RJ, Tong L (2010) Malicious data attacks on smart grid state estimation: attack strategies and countermeasures. IEEE, pp 220–225
88. Xie L, Mo Y, Sinopoli B (2011) Integrity data attacks in power market operations. IEEE Trans Smart Grid 2:659–666
89. Xie L, Mo Y, Sinopoli B (2010) False data injection attacks in electricity markets. IEEE, pp 226–231
90. Sooriyabandara M, Ekanayake J (2010, December) Smart grid-technologies for its realisation. In: IEEE international conference on sustainable energy technologies (ICSET) 2010. IEEE, pp 1–4
91. Wang Y, Li W, Lu J (2010) Reliability analysis of wide-area measurement system. IEEE Trans Power Deliv 25:1483–1491
92. Moslehi K, Kumar R (2010) A reliability perspective of the smart grid. IEEE Trans Smart Grid 1:57–64
93. Yan Y, Qian Y, Sharif H, Tipper D (2013) A survey on smart grid communication infrastructures: motivations, requirements and challenges. IEEE Commun Surv Tutor 15:5–20
94. Tonyali S, Akkaya K, Saputro N et al (2018) Privacy-preserving protocols for secure and reliable data aggregation in IoT-enabled smart metering systems. Future Gener Comput Syst 78:547–557
95. Card SK, Mackinlay JD, Shneiderman B (1999) Readings in information visualization: using vision to think. Morgan Kaufmann Publishers, San Francisco

96. Ware C (2012) Information visualization: perception for design. Elsevier
97. Zhu J, Zhuang E, Fu J et al (2016) A framework-based approach to utility big data analytics. IEEE Trans Power Syst 31:2455–2462
98. Liu H, Guo J, Yu W et al (2016) The design and implementation of the enterprise level data platform and big data driven applications and analytics. IEEE, pp 1–5
99. Ma K-L, Stompel A, Bielak J et al (2003) Visualizing very large-scale earthquake simulations. In: 2003 ACM/IEEE conference on supercomputing. IEEE, pp 48–48
100. Lamping J, Rao R, Pirolli P (1995) A focus + context technique based on hyperbolic geometry for visualizing large hierarchies. In: Proceedings of the SIGCHI conference on human factors in computing systems. ACM Press/Addison-Wesley Publishing Co., pp 401–408
101. Johnson B, Shneiderman B (1991) Tree-maps: a space-filling approach to the visualization of hierarchical information structures. In: Proceedings of the 2nd conference on Visualization '91. IEEE Computer Society Press, pp 284–291
102. Tam NT, Song I (2016) Big data visualization. In: Information science and applications (ICISA) 2016. Springer, pp 399–408

Chapter 9
Risks and Challenges of Adopting Electric Vehicles in Smart Cities

Vidyasagar Potdar, Saima Batool and Aneesh Krishna

Abstract Oil prices and increased carbon emissions are two of the key issues affecting mainstream transportation globally. Hence, EVs (Electric Vehicles) are becoming popular as they do not depend on oil, and the GHG (Greenhouse Gases) do not contribute to GHG emissions. In fact, their integration with smart grids makes them even more attractive. Although EV adoption is becoming widespread, three groups of challenges need to be addressed. These challenges are associated with EV technology adoption, integration of EVs and smart grids, and the supply chain of EV raw materials. Regarding the EV technology adoption, the risks and challenges include EV battery capacity, drivers' range anxiety, the impact of auxiliary loads, EV drivers' behavior, EV owners' unwillingness to participate in the V2G (Vehicle-to-Grid) program, economic barriers to adopting EVs, difficult EV maintenance, EV performance mismatch between the lab and the real world, need for government regulation, lack of charging infrastructure such as not enough charging stations, and expensive batteries. There are additional challenges concerning the integration with the smart grids such as system overload, high-cost investment in V2G technology, load mismatch, and unmanaged recharging of EV batteries. Finally, there are challenges regarding the consistent supply of the raw materials needed for EVs. This chapter examines these risks and challenges, suggests solutions and provides recommendations for future research.

Keywords Electric Vehicles · EV · EV adoption · Smart grid
EV integration · V2G · EV supply chain · Renewable energy · Power grid

V. Potdar (✉) · S. Batool
School of Information Systems, Curtin University, Perth, Australia
e-mail: Vidyasagar.Potdar@cbs.curtin.edu.au

A. Krishna
Department of Computing, Curtin University, Perth, Australia

© Springer International Publishing AG, part of Springer Nature 2018
Z. Mahmood (ed.), *Smart Cities*, Computer Communications and Networks,
https://doi.org/10.1007/978-3-319-76669-0_9

9.1 Introduction

The Electric Vehicles (EV) industry is one of the fastest growing industries in today's world, where reducing oil dependence and managing carbon emissions are top priorities [23]. EVs are the best green alternatives to the traditional transport mode. In simple terms, an electric vehicle consists of a battery pack, a power cord, and a plug. Electric vehicles were initially made operational in the nineteenth and twentieth century, but low oil prices, long driving range, and low prices of traditional vehicles led to their decline [7].

These days, the aim is to have electric vehicles with batteries that can be recharged using renewable energy sources (RESs) such as solar power, which integrates EVs with the smart grids. A smart grid is "an electric power grid that intelligently responds to all the components with which it is interconnected including suppliers, consumers, to deliver electric power services efficiently, economically and sustainably" [6]. Furthermore, EVs can be used to store excess electricity when demand is low, and production is high and can supply power back to the smart grid when supply outstrips demand [12]. However, a sudden increase in the number of electric vehicles could also cause undesirable congestion and voltage problems in the grid.

Sales of EVs are on the rise around the globe due to their efficiency and potential to operate as a distributed energy source as well. In the year 2015, more than 800,000 EVs were sold in the United States alone [23] and it is estimated that the Japanese purchased 600,000 EVs. Subsequently, Europe and China followed the trend by buying 200,000 electric vehicles [23]. Nevertheless, the overwhelming rise in the growth of electric vehicles has resulted in many challenges, problems, uncertainties, and risks. We group these problems into three categories: (1) challenges related to smart grids, (2) challenges related to electric vehicle adoption, and (3) challenges related to a consistent and reliable supply of raw materials required for the manufacture of EV parts such as batteries.

First, from the smart grid perspective, these problems include system overload, power losses, line reliability, renewable energy generation, EV drivers' behaviors, and fluctuations in smart grid, which are caused by unmanaged recharging of EV batteries [23].

Second, from the adoption perspective, the driving of EVs at high speed with an auxiliary load such as air conditioning (AC) and heating is also considered to be a significant risk [32]. Long recharging time and short driving range are two of the main deterrents to the adoption of electric vehicles as a mainstream transport system at the moment [32]. Likewise, frequent charging G2V (Grid-to-Vehicle) and discharging V2G cycles can wear out the batteries and shorten battery life [24]. Moreover, EV drivers' attitudes are another important aspect of risk associated with electric vehicles. For example, "driving range anxiety" is one of the risks associated with EV driver behavior. Participating in V2G program depends on driver attitude, as it will cause uncertainties regarding smart grid operations or energy consumption of electric vehicles. Furthermore, due to the lack of a proper charging infrastructure, the demand and supply of electricity estimations by EV aggregators, can have discrepancies leading to load mismatch [37]. Figure 9.1 shows the workflow of EV aggregators and integration of EVs into the smart grid. Renewable energy sources are also one important part of the smart grid.

Finally, the third key risk concerns the availability of a reliable supply of the raw materials required for the ongoing manufacture of EVs. Some electric vehicle components such as batteries use rare earth materials, which are difficult to source and limited in supply. Hence, the recycling of such materials is necessary; however, such recycling also carries its own set of risks and challenges.

This book chapter discusses the main risks and challenges associated with the adoption of electric vehicles in smart cities and its impact on the smart grid, viz.: EV adoption challenges and EV supply chain issues.

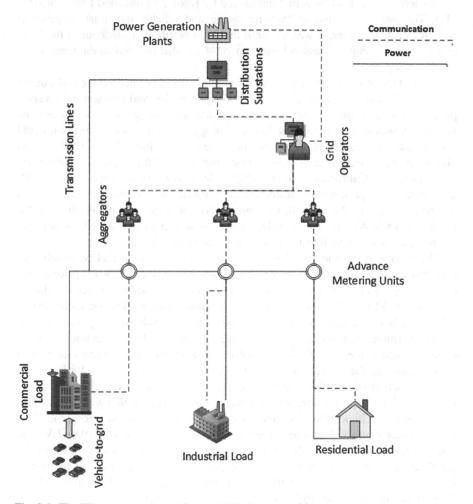

Fig. 9.1 The EV aggregators' workflow and EVs in smart grid

9.2 History of Electric Vehicles and Smart Grid

The first electric power generation plant was constructed by Edison Electric Illuminating Company of New York in 1881 [6]. The need for communication within the power grid arose when the company began to grow and expand. So, communication via telegraph line was introduced in the late 1800s. In the late 1950s, analog computers and communication were used to implement the concept of the automatic grid control. With the advent of digital computers, power stations started utilizing them in their operations in the 1960s. By the early 1980s, micro-processors were integrated into power system devices. Subsequently, by the 1980s, Unix replaced minicomputers [6]. This development resulted in the dominance of digital computers that were run on LAN (Local Area Network) in substations [6].

The term "smart grid" was first introduced by Khoi, Begvoic, and Damir in 1997 [31]. The authors referred to "Self-managing and reliable transmission grid" as SMART grid. However, it was not until the 2003 North East blackout in the USA that it became popular. Massoud Amin in 2004 [6] also referred to the term Smart Grid, in his paper.

The history of smart grid and electric vehicles would be incomplete without the invention of solar energy panels. In 1955, Chapin, Fuller, and Pearson built a solar panel with nine 30 mm diameter cells to provide solar energy to a local telephone network. It was soon realized that this technology was not cost-effective and could only be used for very specific applications, i.e., in satellites [7]. In 1982, due to climate change concerns caused by the burning of fossil fuels, the first solar plant was opened in California with 1 MWp (Mega Watt Peak) capacity [7]. The advancements in photovoltaic technology continued, and eventually, it achieved a record efficiency of 24.7% with the introduction of monocrystalline silicon cells, producing 15 MWp [7]. This development in solar technology paved the way for the integration of RESs into the power grid via Smart Grids.

The history of electric vehicles goes back to the nineteenth and twentieth century, but they did not become successful commercially due to low oil prices, long driving range and relatively low cost of conventional gasoline-powered vehicles [7]. From 1832 to 1839, the first electric-powered carriage with non-rechargeable primary cells was developed by Robert Anderson [38]. Subsequently, in 1856 and 1881, DC (direct current) electric motor and rechargeable battery technology were enhanced; hence, the first DC electric motor was developed and the first electric taxi also appeared on the road in 1897 [38]. However, the EVs did not last for long with the introduction of gasoline-run vehicles in 1908. These were followed by the invention of the electric starter which replaced the hand crank that was used to start a gasoline-run vehicle [38]. As mentioned earlier, due to low oil prices, the EV's short distance range and long recharge time led to its decline, and by 1935, EVs had disappeared [38]. A few decades later, the carbon emissions produced by gasoline-run vehicles had increased, oil dependence led to a renewed interest in EVs [38]. Figure 9.2 outlines the EV adoption challenges, risks involved, its integration into the smart grid, and EV supply chain issues.

EV Adoption Challenges & Risks	Range Anxiety
	Auxilliary Loads
	EV Battery & Charger Issues
	The impact of Motorist attitude on Battery Switching Stations
	Lack of Charging Infrastructure
	EV Performance: Real World Versus Lab Conditions
	The Economic Barriers
	Electric Vehicles and Government Regulations
	Risky Maintenance Of Electric Vehicles
EV Integration in Smart Grid Challenges & Risks	Smart Grid System Overload
	Load Mismatch In Smart Grid Energy Distribution
	Unmanaged Charging of Electric Vehicles
	EV Motorists' Attitude towards Charging Electric Vehicles
	Failure in Smart Grid Functionality
	Unpredictability in V2G and G2V Services
	V2G Service: An Expensive Investment
Electric Vehicles Supply Chain Challenges	Irregularity in Supply of Rare Battery Materials
	Waste Management of Utilised EV Batteries

Fig. 9.2 EV adoption and integration in smart cities challenges and risks

9.3 Electric Vehicles (EV) Adoption Challenges

Despite the effectiveness of the electric vehicles, their adoption has always been challenging due to battery defects, range anxiety of the EV driver, auxiliary loads such as AC, battery cost, lack of charging infrastructure, etc. This section explains the risks and challenges associated with the widespread adoption of EVs.

9.3.1 Range Anxiety

Range anxiety is the term used to describe the fear experienced by drivers that the electric vehicle may not have sufficient charge to reach the final destination [3]. Range anxiety and recharging time are the main barriers which prevent electric vehicles from becoming a part of mainstream transportation fleets [32]. Drivers suffering from range anxiety consider that the remaining EV charge is not enough to reach their destination. Currently, electric vehicles have a range of about 100 miles on a single charge and take hours to recharge compared to a conventional gasoline vehicle [3], that covers more miles and involves no waiting period to refuel.

Solution

While range anxiety leaves customers unsatisfied and is an economic barrier to EV adoption, there are several solutions that can adequately address the issue of range anxiety.

First, fast DC charging is considered a useful technique for decreasing lengthy recharge time and increasing the range when driving on highways between cities [32]. The EV infrastructure planners should take into account that different driving patterns have different energy and recharge demands; hence, the proper and dynamic planning of recharging infrastructure for EVs can help reduce range anxiety.

Second, for estimating correct energy consumption and drivable range, a mathematical vehicle model can be used, which can predict "real road" driving energy consumption and drivable range [32].

Third, the problem of range anxiety can also be solved by developing nationwide charging stations, although this is not possible without government incentives or a public–private partnership [13].

Finally, a network route choice model can be employed to reduce range anxiety. This model uses an algorithm to select the shortest optimal path for EV drivers. However, such models are not mature enough, and can be further extended by considering the departure time choice and duration of stay at a charging station [1].

Likewise, series, parallel, and series–parallel charging configurations can also enhance the driving range using highly efficient electric motors [38]. Some EV manufacturers even offer free rental cars for "local excursions" beyond the EV range, to reduce range anxiety to some extent [9].

9.3.2 Auxiliary Loads

Auxiliary loads significantly affect the energy consumption of electric vehicles, thereby reducing their range. First, in city driving conditions high auxiliary loads cause battery drain, which leads to a reduced EV driving range [15]. In summer, when the AC is used, the driving range drops by 17.2–37.1% (under simulation conditions). Similarly, due to heating requirements in winter, the range varies from 17.1 to 54.1% (under simulation conditions) since EVs uses PTC (Positive Temperature Coefficient) heaters [40]. Second, the impact of auxiliary loads such as AC and heating is yet to be examined when the electric vehicles are driven at highway speeds [32]. Finally, the effect of auxiliary loads in a lab environment and on real roads varies considerably. Under ideal conditions such as minimum auxiliary loads and with the help of RBS (regenerative braking system), EV manufacturers can achieve low energy consumption and long drivable range, but this ideal outcome is different when EVs are driven on highways between cities [32].

Solution

One solution to the problem of reduced range and high-energy consumption due to auxiliary loads is a heat pump in winter to heat EVs. This can add up to 7.6–21.1% to the driving range by having a larger heating CoP (coefficient of performance) [40]. A heat pump has a vapor compression cycle, which is responsible for both cooling and heating. Moreover, it has a 4-way valve that reverses the direction of refrigerant flow. Its CoP is also 1% higher than PTC heaters. Besides, the accurate evaluation of the heating and cooling loads of EVs can significantly reduce the energy consumption of the AC system [40]. Similarly, an appropriate energy management strategy for cooling purposes can reduce the overall energy consumption. Hence, instead of the ON/OFF approach, a suitable energy management plan can regulate the energy consumption [14].

Another solution is the proposed design of a system configuration that can clutch the AC compressor motor with the help of a traction shaft through braking intervals [15]. This mechanism not only lightens the weight of the EV but also reduces energy consumption as well.

9.3.3 EV Battery and Charger Issues

One of the biggest barriers to the adoption of EVs is its battery technology and its associated drawbacks. The current battery configuration of EVs has low energy density, which affects the driving range of the vehicle [38]. Many battery technologies and configurations have been introduced over time for increasing the efficiency of EVs [38].

In this section, we describe three challenges associated with EV battery technology, viz,: Battery Type, Battery Cost, and EV Chargers.

9.3.3.1 Battery Type

EV battery technology needs much improvement, and it has to come a long way to achieve this goal. A suitable EV battery should have high energy density, high power density, should be lightweight, inexpensive, safe, and durable [38]. Energy density refers to the capacity of a battery to store energy. A high energy density battery can store more energy, and hence a device can be kept charged for a longer period. Similarly, power density refers to the speed of charging; hence, a high power density battery will charge faster compared to a low power density battery. As far as the battery's life cycle is concerned, this is the number of "complete" charge/discharge cycles before its capacity drops to less than 80%. That is, if a battery is discharged to 60% and charged to 80%, then this is not a complete charge/discharge cycle. The percentage may vary depending on battery type. Hence, a battery with a short life cycle is not considered a sound option for EVs.

Next, the memory effect of battery refers to a condition in which the battery remembers its last discharge rate and will not deliver more than that (even in a new charge/discharge cycle). In other words, the battery "remembers" how much of its capacity was consumed the last time and will, therefore, not deliver more than that. Due to improvements in battery technology, the memory effect is no longer a problem.

Discharge rate refers to the rate at which a battery uses/releases its energy. A high-discharge-rate battery is not suitable for EVs since the battery cannot be utilized for extended periods of time while it is being charged.

There have been numerous EV battery technologies; we have categorized them into the three types as described below:

- Lead–acid battery: The first battery type used for EVs is the lead–acid battery. These batteries comprise lead electrodes and acid that generates electricity. However, these batteries have low energy density, are heavy, and the electrolytes' level needs frequent inspection. Further, they are not environment-friendly [38].
- Nickel battery: This second type of battery is made of nickel and is considered to be more mature and has relatively higher energy density [38]. However, some of its drawbacks include: poor charge/discharge efficiency and high self-discharge rate; i.e., its power density is low. In addition, nickel-based batteries also suffer from the memory effect and poor performance in cold weather [38].
- Lithium–Sulfur (Li–S), Zinc-Air (Zn-air), and Lithium-Air (Li-Air) battery: The third category of batteries uses various battery technologies like Lithium Sulfur (Li–S), Zinc-Air (Zn-air), and Lithium-Air (Li-Air) battery [38]. Among them, Li–S has high energy density and low cost due to the low cost of sulfur.

Examining them individually, Li–S has a short life cycle and high-discharge rate. Whereas, Zn-Air can be the "potential" future candidate for EV battery technology because its "theoretical/in-lab experiments" show high energy density of 1700 W/kg, which is comparable to the conventional internal combustion engine [38]. However, the major drawback of a Zn-Air battery is its low power density and short life cycle. Moreover, it is still in the prototype stage and unavailable commercially. This is the same case with Li-Air, which is in the prototype phase as well and is not commercially available to date [38]. Refer to Table 9.1 for further comparison of the different battery types.

Solution

Further research is being conducted to improve these battery types since they may be able to extend the EV driving range [38]. Further, to ensure the good performance of electric vehicles, many subsystems are being installed within the battery system, such as a battery management system and proper thermal management system [11].

Table 9.1 Various battery types and their capacities (adopted from [38])

Battery type	Energy density (W/kg)	Specific power (W/kg)	Lifecycle	Self-discharge (% per month)	Memory effect
Lead Acid	35	180	1000	<5	No
Ni–Cd	50–80	200	2000	10	Yes
ZEBRA	90–120	155	>1200	<5	No
Li-Ion	118–250	200–430	2000	<5	No
Zn-Air	460	80–140	200	<5	No
Li–S	350–650	–	300	8–15	No
Li-Air	1300–2000	–	100	<5	No

9.3.3.2 Battery Cost

The high cost of batteries is another EV issue, which prevents it from becoming a market success. Limited driving range, high battery cost, lengthy battery charging time, uncertain battery life, heavy weight of EV batteries, and battery safety are some of the major limitations of EV battery technology [9]. Hence, research should be conducted to develop a high-performance and less-expensive battery technology [9].

Solution

It is predicted that the battery costs will decrease by 70% by 2025, which will then encourage EV adoption as the energy density will be high [9]. This can be seen in the case of Lithium-Ion batteries (Li-Ion), the cost of which has decreased significantly due to their increasing usage in mobile phones and laptops [22].

9.3.3.3 EV Chargers

Most common EV chargers are unidirectional which makes it difficult to integrate them into the smart grid. However, a bidirectional EV charger can solve this problem [38]. It is expected that in the future "super fast" DC chargers will be available in homes that will significantly minimize the charging time [30]. This development may lessen the load on the smart grid and increase the battery life cycle.

Solutions

To solve the problem of EV charger, more research is needed to improve this area addressing EV battery technology as well.

9.3.4   Impact of EV Driver Attitude on Battery Switching Stations

EV driver attitude can affect the effectiveness of the battery switching stations [3]. Battery switching stations can be used instead of battery charging stations to reduce range anxiety. Battery switching stations stock standardized fully charged batteries that EV drivers can easily swap to continue their journey. Figure 9.3 shows the working mechanism of the battery swapping stations. U.S. and European battery suppliers and Tesla are already utilizing this method of EV recharge that provides instant charge to EVs [5].

Comparing conventional petrol stations with battery switching stations, we realize that in traditional vehicles, we have only petrol, gas, and diesel options, so most vehicles support any of these three fuels. But with battery, there will be several types (refer to Sect. 9.3.3), configurations, energy density, power density, etc., so the battery switching stations will have to accommodate a large variety of batteries and sometimes they may run out of one type, which may create the problem of EV driver anxiety.

Solutions

Smartphone applications designed by battery switching stations, will allow EV driver to monitor available battery varieties. They can even reserve batteries ahead of time to swap their depleted batteries. This can save a lot of time and solves the range anxiety problem by providing a communication platform between the battery swapping stations and the EV driver [9]. This enables the driver to drive beyond the normal vehicle driving range [3].

However, this may create additional problems for the battery swapping stations because they may need to stock many more batteries to serve their customers, particularly if some customers do multiple swaps in a day. This problem can be handled in several ways. The alternatives are: limit the number of swaps done per day; impose an additional tariff for every successive swap within the same day; impose some form of penalty for exceeding the daily limit, etc. However, we need to consider which of these solutions are practical because, as suggested in [3], imposing penalties may discourage people from adopting EVs.

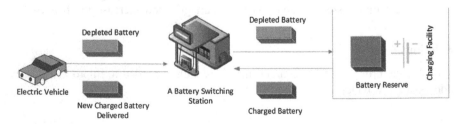

Fig. 9.3 Battery switching station in action

Another problem associated with battery swapping stations is the unavailability of certain types of batteries at all times. As swapping stations may not have a sufficient supply of charged batteries of different types at all times, it may become difficult for them to serve all their customers/EV drivers.

9.3.5   Lack of Charging Infrastructure

Lack of charging infrastructure is the deciding factor in the EV adoption. In this section, we summarize the challenges associated with establishing an efficient charging infrastructure and strategies to manage it.

9.3.5.1   Insufficient Recharging Stations

Insufficient recharging stations are another factor related to EV adoption since customers will be frustrated if they cannot find a convenient recharging station when driving. In addition, it can also lead to range anxiety. Likewise, there are relatively fewer recharging stations along intercity or interstate highways.

Solution

These problems can be solved by constructing a "dense" network of charging stations [13] or integrating EV recharging facilities into traditional fuel stations. Installing recharging stations along highways can further encourage potential customers to invest in electric vehicles. Recent research has shown that innovative entrepreneurs are constructing fast DC-charging stations along highways [32]. This concept is being realized with the "Electric Highway" being designed for the southwest regions of remote Western Australia that will join the city of Perth with several country towns [32].

9.3.5.2   Importance of Standardized Charging Equipment

Lack of standards with respect to the charging devices is another barrier to EV adoption, though standards are being developed.

Solution

A recharging system with compatible recharging components such as couplers and communication protocols should be standardized for all charging stations' operators. This will enable the customers to recharge from any station without worrying about different operators [9]. This will be a very important step to ensure EV drivers are confident that all charging stations can recharge all types of batteries.

9.3.5.3 Need for Smartphone Applications

EVs drivers have to make an effort to identify their nearest charging stations, determine their charging needs, and select an optimized charging plan. This requires a lot of manual effort, and the process can be time-consuming. This is a critical challenge since it can deter customers from adopting EVs.

Solution

One way to resolve this issue would be to use a smartphone application that can assist EV drivers to locate charging stations near them and thereby ease their anxieties. Moreover, such application can even match EV driver driving needs with the existing charging programs and offer the facility to make reservations as well [9]. Such an application can also assist in the integration of EVs into the smart grid which also requires communication for demand-side management (DSM) [30].

9.3.5.4 EV Charging Parking Lots

Lack of EV charging parking lots is another problem in its smooth adoption. Since EV is not adopted by large number of customers yet, hence not enough EV charging parking lots are constructed. One of the ways to promote EV is to build numerous EV charging parking lots for customer facility.

Solution

EV parking lots are presented as one of the most suitable solutions for strengthening and organizing a reliable charging infrastructure. As [9] points out, 90% of the time, vehicles are parked either at home or workplace. Hence, building a charging infrastructure (which includes construction of EV parking lots at public places like shopping centers, schools, and offices) can significantly assist EV drivers as they would not have to wait for extended EV recharge periods [24].

In the same way, EV solar parking lots are not dependent on smart grid and produce no GHG emissions [24]. Moreover, it has been suggested that EV parking lots owners (landowners) should also be subsidized the same as the EV owners, the manufacturers, and the owners of recharging station [9, 24]. This strategy may encourage landowners to give up their land for solar parking lots to encourage EV adoption, since environmental as well as economical concerns are the motives behind EV adoption.

9.3.6 EV Performance: Real World Versus Lab Conditions

Lab conditions and real-world conditions differ to a great extent when it comes to EV performance. Real-world conditions like extreme weather, tire friction that is affected by factors like auxiliary loads, vehicle speed, and driving patterns, can significantly alter the estimated EV lab performance results. As [32] points out, the differences between real-world conditions and lab conditions with regards to energy consumption and drivable range of EVs are greater in comparison with the test results of conventional vehicles.

Solutions

To solve problems in EV performance and load mismatch, a "vehicle mathematical model" is proposed in [32] that can predict real-world energy consumption of EVs.

9.3.7   The Economic Barriers

There are various economic barriers to adopting electric vehicles as mainstream means of transportation. This section identifies the financial obstacles impeding the widespread adoption of EVs.

9.3.7.1   High Price of EVs

Due to the high cost of EV batteries (refer to Sect. 9.3.3) and lack of an EV charging infrastructure (refer to Sect. 9.3.6) electric vehicles are expensive at the moment. Consequently, the high upfront cost of EVs is one of the significant economic barriers preventing their large-scale adoption [25].

The high initial cost is a significant financial barrier to the widespread adoption of EV [28]. The payback period for purchasing an electric vehicle is between 6 and 8 years, which is longer than the 5 years an owner would usually hold on to a conventional car [9]. The high price of electric vehicles should be decreased to make them affordable. This single step can make a great contribution to reducing carbon emissions in the environment. Another financial consideration is the uncertainty regarding the resale value of an EV. Compared to conventional gasoline-run vehicles, the resale price of EVs is unknown due to the unstable EV market [9].

Solution

To make EVs more affordable, governments around the world are making efforts to offer tax credits and exemptions, tax reductions, and direct subsidies [9]. Governments could also decrease sales tax in order to reduce the cost of electric vehicles since EV adoption is essential to reduce carbon emissions [9]. Furthermore, cutting subsidies on petroleum products can also encourage customers to switch their interest to EV adoption as petrol would become expensive. Leasing can be another option for promoting EVs [9]. In the same way, research suggests that by 2030, the difference between ICV (Internal Combustion Vehicles) and EVs will be much less, making EVs much cheaper. Also, the UK Committee on Climate Change has estimated that EVs will be affordable "during" 2020. This cost-effectiveness will result in high EV uptake by 2030 and early 2040 [22]. The EV's operational costs can be further decreased by V2G participation since this generates revenue [25].

9.3.7.2 Expensive Installation of Charging Station

Another economic challenge is that recharging stations are expensive to establish with no guarantee of a profitable return on investment. An average charging station installation costs $5000–$15,000 US dollar. The price may increase if additional construction and electrical work are needed such as setting step-up transformers, drilling, trenching, etc. [9].

Solutions

Government and the private sector should collaborate to form new business models that can make the installation of charging stations less expensive since the increase in the number of charging stations can attract potential customers.

9.3.7.3 Costly EV Charging

Costly EV charging is another economic problem. There are different types of charging stations, i.e., level-1, level-2, and fast DC charging. Level-1 charging can charge 2–5 miles per hour, whereas, level-2 charging can charge 10–20 miles per hour. Lastly, the fast DC charging can charge up to 180–240 miles per hour [13]. Compared to the level-1 charging, which costs around $15,000–$18,000, a DC-charging station can cost from $65,000 to $70,000. It is evident that investment in EV infrastructure is quite costly at the moment. Further, every EV driver's consumption needs are different; hence, an "optimal control policy" should be in place that enables the selection of the best charging option [13].

Solution

The costly EV charging problem can also be solved if renewable energy resources are used to charge EVs. One study [24] estimates that a solar parking lot can charge 75–100% of electric vehicles, depending on the solar power exposure of the parking lot. The EV batteries when integrated into the smart grid can also act as intermittent RESs as they can store energy [16]. By improving the charging infrastructure for electric vehicles, it can become the mainstream transportation medium with financial benefits for the customer, and benefits for the environment.

9.3.7.4   Customer Mindset

Customer mindset or preferences play a significant role in the adoption or rejection of a new technology. Automobile manufacturers have stated that it is challenging task to make this "transition" because customers still do not desire to use fully electric vehicles [28].

Taking EV prices into consideration, even if policy makers are successful in closing the gap between costs of conventional vehicles and EVs, a customer may still consider EVs as "inferior" to conventional gasoline vehicles [26]. Consequently, this "behavioral risk" is an obstacle to EV adoption. In terms of V2G participation in smart grids, many users are not interested in returning energy to the grid and receiving incentives. However, if customers' mindsets can be changed, their engagement with EV technology can reach "high levels", thereby promoting EV adoption [28].

Solution

To avoid this risk, awareness programs about the environmental benefits of using EV should be regularly arranged in an attempt to change the customer's mindset. In addition, automakers should improve every aspect of the EV including battery technology, driving range, and cost of acquisition and maintenance to ensure its competitiveness with conventional vehicles. In addition, EVs should be designed in such a way that customers' behaviors and lifestyles should not have to change [28]. Furthermore, EV hardware should be designed so that EV owners are not required to put extra effort into determining the "optimal rates" for recharging their EVs [28].

9.3.7.5   Limited or Under Investigated Risk Mitigation Policies Regarding EV Charging Setup

In a previous section, the risks and challenges related to the charging infrastructure were explained. However, no risk mitigation plans were described. Although there is ongoing research into affordable and technically advanced charging mechanisms, there are limited studies on risk mitigation policies [8] although these risks are related to power loss, fluctuations in smart grid and even failure to integrate electric vehicles in the smart cities, and are therefore significant.

Solution

Risk mitigation policies for the integration of EVs into smart grid need to be further researched and implemented.

9.3.7.6 Delayed Recharging and EV Sales Decrease

When EV drivers leave their electric vehicles at a charging station, they expect to return to a fully charged vehicle. But depending on the battery size, energy density, charging time, and type of charging station the vehicle may or may not charge fully. This risk is outlined in [13], where a customer returns to a partially charged vehicle. In this situation, the customer will surely be unsatisfied and may not trust the capability of charging stations and aggregators for their subsequent charging needs, thereby affecting the sales of EV in the future.

Solution

One of the ways to improve EV sales is by addressing the social, economic, behavioral, cultural, and infrastructural barriers to EVs adoption [28]. Research suggests that to mitigate these risks, optimal control policies for charging stations should be introduced [13]. There is research focusing on battery and charging infrastructure improvement; however, [28] concludes that much more research and discussion is needed to overcome the socio-technical barriers to EV adoption.

9.3.7.7 Electric Vehicles' Competition with Plug-in Hybrid Vehicles

Plug-in hybrid vehicles are becoming popular among customers due to their reliance on a fuel tank. If plug-in hybrid vehicles are widely adopted, then solely electric vehicles and their chargers will not be fully utilized [26] resulting in slow infrastructure provisioning. The major drawback of plug-in hybrid vehicles is that they are not environment-friendly and contributes to GHG emissions.

Solution

EV manufacturers and promoters may highlight this point in awareness programs in an attempt to increase EV sales.

9.3.7.8 Lack of Partnership between EV Stakeholders

An active partnership between all stakeholders of EVs (such as automakers, charging providers, charging regulators, etc.) is necessary to resolve many of the challenges and risks identified earlier. As [26] asserts, different stakeholders can play a different role in strengthening the EV market. They also suggest that some utilities can educate the masses on the benefits of EV.

Solution

To solve this problem, all the EV stakeholders ideally need to communicate and cooperate with each other and find ways to promote EVs since any single stakeholder cannot make EVs a successful business solution alone [18].

9.3.8   Electric Vehicles and Government Regulations

Government policies can play a critical role in EV adoption. The issue that is preventing governments from initiating EV adoption policies is the "indirect network effects". This is when customers are waiting for a sufficient number of charging stations to be built before purchasing EVs, and investors are waiting for an adequate customer base before they make significant investments [26].

Solution

Governments should promote and subsidize EV adoption to meet air pollution reduction and climate change goals [26]. One good example is the US where 11,600 public charging stations have been installed. A quarter of these charging stations are located in California, but these cater for only 4–6% of the overall EV drivers' needs (in California) [26]. Hence, it becomes evident that with government's investment and policy intervention, the EV adoption market challenges can be overcome. However, there are many hurdles in achieving this aim such as the absence of incentives for the owners of charging stations [13].

To promote the development of a vast network of charging stations, governments should give special incentives to investors, by establishing "state of the art" business models [9]. Furthermore, for strengthening the EV market, an improvement in the EV charging mechanism is required, such as building aggregated distribution networks, distribution lines, and cables and transformers [9].

9.3.9   Risky Maintenance of Electric Vehicles

Hazardous maintenance is another critical challenge to the widespread adoption of EVs. According to research, lifting EVs with traction batteries is the most dangerous maintenance activity. Furthermore, there is the hazard of mechanics receiving electric shocks when repairing EVs. Moreover, the welding of various parts of electric vehicles is rated as high-risk maintenance activities [20]. Also, silent EVs are unsafe for cyclists and pedestrians [20].

Solution

One way to address the noiseless feature is to have a "sound setup" installed in EVs to warn people when EVs are approaching [19, 20]. In the future, we may even see new technology to warn cyclists and pedestrians such as mobile devices that vibrate to detect approaching EVs.

9.4   Electric Vehicles Supply Chain Challenges

There are two issues regarding the EV supply chain problems: unreliable supply of
rare earth battery materials; and waste management of used EV batteries. These are
discussed below.

9.4.1   Irregularity in Supply of Rare Battery Materials

EVs integrated into smart grids can be used for storing energy generated by RESs
such as wind or solar. Hence, it becomes a vital area of research to determine the
reliability of electric vehicles' supply chain. As [2] points out, if we depend on the
electric vehicles as a storage source, then we must assess the uncertainty regarding
its cost and supply chain, particularly when rare earth materials are used in its
manufacturing. These materials include dysprosium, neodymium, terbium, euro-
pium, and yttrium, which are used in EV batteries and motors. Consequently, if
these materials are not available in a timely and uninterrupted manner, then this will
seriously affect EVs and their consumers, and the smart grid.

Solution

One way to resolve this issue is to design EV batteries and motors that are less
dependent on rare earth materials [2]. In addition, research also suggests recycling
or reusing EV components that contain rare earth materials. Reusing is preferred to
recycling due to its lower cost [2].

9.4.2   Waste Management of Used EV Batteries

With the increase in sales of electric vehicles, there is a growing concern about
waste management for end of life (EoL) EV batteries. In California alone, when a
fleet of electric vehicles uses 200 kg of batteries that have a life cycle of 7–
10 years, it produces waste of about 620,000–890,000 metric tons per year [10].
This battery waste has severe impacts on humans, the environment, and wildlife and
should be disposed of in a suitable manner.

Solution

We now describe two technologies to reuse EV batteries that have reached their
EoL:

- First, "Hydrometallurgy" is a recovery method that can recover lithium, alu-
  minum, and other high-value materials from batteries [10]. These recovered
  materials can be used to manufacture new batteries, saving the cost of supply of
  new materials, and decreasing the EV battery's contribution to waste.

- Second, "Pyrometallurgy", focuses on recovering high-value materials from the Lithium-Ion based batteries such as nickel–cobalt, nickel hydride, and copper [10]. However, the economic feasibility of these two methods is a consideration.

Another solution is to form partnerships with suppliers or nations that can guarantee a continuous supply of these raw materials. Flexible contracts should be signed between auto manufacturers and battery materials suppliers under "supply uncertainty" conditions [2].

9.5 EV Integration with Smart Grid: Challenges and Risks

Smart grid is the future of an efficient electrical supply. Its benefits include the generation of electricity by integrating RESs, reliability and improved quality, control over electricity prices, decreased peak demand, and lower carbon emissions. The increasing popularity of EVs makes it suitable for integration into smart grid because of its energy storage and V2G, V2V, and V2H (Vehicle-to-Home) capabilities.

A V2G service can be described as the control and management of EV loads by the EV aggregators by communicating between EVs and the smart grid. This technology utilizes energy from the "EV community" and returns it to a power grid. In the same way, V2V technology refers to a local community where EV charging and discharging takes place among EV owners. Moreover, V2H technology is essential since EVs not only utilize energy but this energy can also be consumed by a domestic power network [29]. Figure 9.4 shows the V2G, V2V and V2H framework.

Despite EVs' environmental benefits and services for the smart grid, it can affect smart grid's performance as well. This section highlights the challenges of EV integration into the smart grid and presents possible solutions to overcome these challenges.

9.5.1 Smart Grid System Overload

The integration of EVs can impose an extra load on the smart grid. While the EV charging is in progress, it can have numerous effects on the smart grid like undesirable congestion and voltage problems in the smart grid distribution network [12]. This situation may worsen if numerous EVs are charging from the smart grid. In 1993, it was predicted that even a "low-level EV penetration" could lead to new peak loads if the load is not distributed in off-peak periods [12]. So, it became evident that without proper load management strategies or smart charging solutions such as "ChargeIQ" [30] EV integration into the smart grid can lead to smart grid

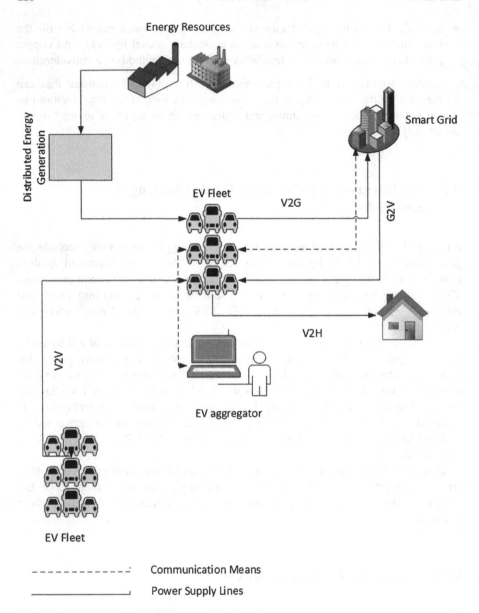

Fig. 9.4 V2V, V2G, and V2H smart grid framework

failure. Here, smart charging solutions refer to the strategies and mechanisms that manage efficient charging of all entities attached to the smart grid [30]. This is where V2G services become necessary to supply energy to the grid, otherwise, it will become a "traditional load" on the smart grid [12], not a resource.

Solution

Many load management algorithms have been proposed for efficient EV charging via the grid. For example, an optimal EV charging algorithm can minimize the impact of power loss and load factor in a distribution network [12]. In addition, the city of Amsterdam combines old grid architecture with smart grid architecture to meet the recharging needs of high average EV diffusion [8].

9.5.2 Load Mismatch in Smart Grid Energy Distribution

The "load mismatch" is also one of the challenges, which can affect the functionality of the smart grid and EV charging. An underestimated EV charging load can negatively affect the functionality of the smart grid. For example, random EV driving activities can cause a difference between actual EV load and estimated EV load [37]. The load mismatch problem can cause problems for EV aggregators (EV charging service providers and regulators) in scheduling the load and minimizing the EV charging cost for customers [37].

Solution

To decrease the EV charging prices and load mismatch risk, a "risk aware day-ahead scheduling framework" is proposed in [37]. This framework is based on day-ahead EV recharging prices and statistical information about EV owners' random driving activities. Further research is needed to counter load mismatch and EV performance estimation since the accurate load and performance prediction can prevent many problems such as high EV charging costs, fluctuations, power loss, branch congestion, etc., in the smart grid. Hence, by successfully addressing this challenge, the transition to EVs will be facilitated.

9.5.3 Unmanaged Charging of Electric Vehicles

An unmanaged EV charging refers to the situation where an EV is connected directly to a smart grid distribution network without any coordination. Normally, EV fleet operators or EV aggregators act a regulatory bridge between the EV fleet and the smart grid. However, without EV aggregators, EV charging will be unmanaged; this can lead to peak congestion problems, power losses, and voltage drop [12]. Another impact of unmanaged charging includes interruption during peak time, resulting in node voltage exceeding the estimated range [36]. Consequently, unplanned charging can lead to inefficiency, instability, and high cost to the grid [39].

Solution

While unmanaged charging can lead to grid instability, a handful of proposed solutions have attempted to manage EV charging in the smart grid. Research has shown that in G2V schemes, controlled charging of EV batteries has positive impacts [18]. For example, efficiently scheduled EV charging programs can prevent these adverse network effects [36]. As trials in the UK demonstrated, 72% of EV owners charge their vehicles during off-peak periods, that is, after 9 p.m. This controlled charging of EVs results in discount rates for power consumption [22].

Another solution for managing EV charging is "smart charging". According to [30], smart charging can manage the different preferences and needs of grid operators and EV owners. In addition, it can also solve the power management problems in the smart grid. The research listed "ChargeIQ" as an example of a smart charging company in Australia. On the other hand, different charging programs with variable pricing can vary the level of safety risks and power loss. For example, when uncoordinated charging with constant price occurs, it causes higher peak-valley difference and larger power loss and safety risks [36]. Hence, an improved TOU (time of use) program can reduce the peak-valley difference, and the safety of a distribution network increases significantly [36].

There are three main EVs aggregator's control strategies for managed EV charging: (1) centralized control of EV fleet operator; (2) transactive control of EV fleet operators; and (3) price control of EV fleet operators:

- Under the centralized control of EV fleet operator, the fleet operator requires all information regarding EV battery model, its driving pattern, grid constraints, and electricity prices in order to program a suitable charging schedule for EVs [12].
- The transactive control of a EV fleet operator refers to the control strategy enabling EV owners to update their charging information/needs depending on prices of electricity. Here, EV owners do not make this change by themselves. A lot of information exchange takes place between EVs and EV fleet operators before any decision is made [12].
- The *price control* by the EV operator depends on the reaction of EV owners to varying prices of electricity. This control strategy for charging is based on TOU pricing or dynamic pricing [12].

Issues with EV Fleet Operator Control Strategies

Each EV fleet operator/aggregator control strategy has its advantages and disadvantages. For instance, a centralized control method is good for security. On the other hand, the transactive control method gives independence to EV owners to some extent, but due to a frequent exchange of information, it poses a security risk. At the moment, the price control method is considered a suitable option for EV owners [12]. It also reduces charging during peak demand time, since the price of electricity during this period is relatively high compared to the low demand/valley demand periods.

9.5.4   EV Drivers' Attitude Toward Electric Vehicles Charging

EV drivers' behavior regarding the recharging of their EVs has various impacts on smart grid functioning, since data shows that EV drivers charge their vehicles during peak demand hours which can jeopardize grid functionality [8]. On the other hand, drivers' behavior can affect the number of vehicles connected to the grid, since no real-world data can assume the time and duration that an EV will stay connected to the grid [4]. Subsequently, the current charging standard for EVs is 1-phase charging with maximum load capacity of 4 KVA, which increases the recharge time and becomes a huge disadvantage for EV drivers; whereas, EV drivers expect a charging technology with a 3-phase charging system with a maximum load capacity of 12 KVA. Hence, these expectations can increase smart grid vulnerability to potential risks [8]. Therefore, EV drivers' behavior in terms of charging and recharging their EVs should change to prevent these risks.

Solution

EV driver behavior should be changed to avoid such impacts; for this purpose, they can be encouraged to charge their EVs during off-peak periods. For instance, reward points or some monthly incentives on EV recharge tariff could be offered to change the attitude of EV drivers toward charging/discharging programs in the smart grid. However, these incentives and pricing mechanisms should be designed to encourage EV adoption [8]. In addition, "reasonable price incentive mechanism" [36] can channel the charging/discharging behavior of EV owners/adopters. Consequently, the peak load can be shifted and safety risks can be reduced in the smart grid.

9.5.5   Unwillingness to Participate in V2G Programs

Another aspect of EV driver behavior that influences the functionality of the smart grid is the EV driver's unwillingness to participate in V2G (discharging) programs. As mentioned earlier, EVs can also store electricity which can be utilized when the smart grid is experiencing peak demand. However, EV owners' unwillingness to participate in V2G technology can be a "social barrier" in this program [38]. The main reason for the unwillingness of EV owners to participate in V2G services is that they perceive that this service offers much less value than the smart grid. Further, participation in V2G also leads to battery degradation, thereby increasing the rate of battery depreciation [18]. Battery degradation occurs due to frequent charging/discharging cycles. Similarly, [34] also points out that very few incentives are offered to EV owners for participating in V2G programs.

Solution

To attract EV owners to the V2G program, an incentive-based energy management policy should be introduced [38]. The economic return to EV owners can also be increased if the V2G service is utilized for load reduction [34]. The researchers expect that this will eventuate if EV owners participate in V2G services in large numbers. In addition, [18] points out that reducing the battery degradation rate and improving the battery lifecycle can increase EV owners' participation in V2G services.

Moreover, EV adoption significantly reduces carbon emissions, thereby not adding to environmental pollution. With a partnership between government and the private sector comprising all stakeholders in the "EV community", including EV owners and the transportation industry, the transition can be made to emission-free transportation [9]. Hence, EV owners will appreciate their significant role and participate in V2G programs to make this transition successful.

Awareness programs could be offered to EV drivers to educate them on the "wise" use of EV charging facilities. This will not only benefit the EV aggregators and smooth integration of EVs into the smart grid, but can also make EV recharging affordable for EV drivers [9]. According to [8], "A lot of research needs to be done regarding recharging behavior of EV adopters."

9.5.6 Failure in Smart Grid Functionality

When a large number of EVs are integrated into to the smart grid, it causes grid functionality failure such as voltage drop, fluctuations, branch congestion, power loss, etc. The reason for the grid functionality failure is the uneven distribution of electricity to an area due to the demand for EV energy. Consequently, the uneven distribution of expected energy requirements for EVs can lead to grid failure since a lower capacity grid can face a high-energy demand from electric vehicles. The problem gets worse when load availability is based on "unbalanced geographical distribution" [8].

Another cause of grid functionality failure is the advancement in auxiliary load management like the integration of heat pumps, which can affect the energy consumption needs of EVs and hence affect the functionality of the smart grid [8].

Solution

To solve this problem, a "load shifting" mechanism has been introduced, that shifts certain amounts of energy demands (or loads) to other time periods requiring lower energy [19]. This load management strategy can help manage the load fluctuations in the smart grid. For the long term, risk mitigation policies should be introduced since grid failure in "early EV diffusion" period can have a negative impact on the potential EV driver base [8]. Another way to solve the smart grid failure problem is DSM, which is the concept of load management in the smart grid. Demand response is one of its methodologies to counter smart grid load management issues. In this system, the energy consumers in the smart grid such as electric vehicles owners respond to the change in electricity prices by making changes to their routine "energy consumption" patterns [19].

In [8], a model is presented to identify the risks associated with grid functionality and reliability caused by the integration of EVs and renewable energy supply. Finally, technological development in smart grids, economic improvement in electricity infrastructure, improvement in the implementation of V2G technology, incentives to change customers behavior can, to a great extent, mitigate the risks associated with grid functionality [8].

9.5.7 Unpredictability of V2G and G2V Services

Uncertainties regarding EV charging are a critical issue in maintaining reliable grid functionality. Some uncertainties that can create problems for smart grid functionality are: rounding estimated charging time, forecasting error in energy consumption, charging equipment failure, EV absence and failure on the part of EV aggregators [35]. Subsequently, when a large number of EVs joins the smart grid, it creates uncertainties about their energy consumption needs and the response of the smart grid. The uncertainty in the number of EVs entering the smart grid can destabilize the operation of the distribution network [36].

On the other hand, it is an advantage that EVs can act as a storage source of smart grid and at the same time return surplus energy to the smart grid as a V2G service. However, the reliability of the V2G service is uncertain since EV serves both the power system and the transportation sector simultaneously [35].

Solution

In order to resolve uncertainty issues of EV integration into the smart grid, an "operational risk assessment" procedure can measure the possibilities and uncertainties in this situation [36]. Similarly, a risk assessment method for a distribution network is introduced in [36] to predict future conditions. In addition, the research suggests that increasing the reliability of EV aggregators can reduce EV charging uncertainties. On the other hand, V2G technology needs "serious" efforts to improve it on the financial and technological front before deploying it commercially [30].

9.5.8 V2G Service: An Expensive Investment

V2G service implementation requires high investment to upgrade the power grid. So, it is not economically "viable" to implement V2G without high-cost investment in EV batteries [18]. In addition, improvement in hardware and software (related to EVs, aggregators, and smart grid) is essential to implement the V2G technology. Next, to participate in the V2G program, each EV has to have a bidirectional battery charger. A high-end bidirectional battery charger has a sophisticated controller and high-tension cabling which demands a high safety requirement. Finally, due to regular bidirectional V2G cycles, power loss increases, and becomes significant when it involves a large fleet of electric vehicles [29]. Furthermore, if issues with EV batteries are not addressed (for participating in V2G service), then it will have severe effects on EV chargers and battery [38]. Subsequent charging and discharging cycles can wear out the battery, causing battery degradation and the need for new replacement batteries. This practice can increase the operational costs of V2G and EV batteries as well.

Solution

However, the possibility of a decrease in prices of EV batteries can be expected soon. The cost of Li-Ion batteries has decreased at a rate of 14% annually. For example, in 2007, $1000 was charged per kWh, but in 2016, the battery price decreased to $300–$700 per kWh [24]. Hence, it is expected that the prices of EV battery will continue to decrease in future to compete with conventional vehicles. On the other hand, to counter the battery degradation issue, new EV batteries are designed in such a way that battery degradation occurs but without affecting the electric power capability. In addition, further improvements are expected in energy and power capability by the year 2030 [18].

9.6   Research Directions and Future Work

The electric vehicle is not a new concept, after going through different transitional phases and increased awareness about environmental hazards of gasoline vehicles it is becoming popular again. On the other hand, the introduction of the smart grid for electricity distribution has introduced a new research area regarding the integration of electric vehicles into smart grids. In this section, we outline the open research directions and opportunities for future work.

9.6.1   EV Adoption as Mainstream Transportation

Electric Vehicles (EV) technology adoption has many dimensions that need improvement and further research. First, the capacity of electric vehicle aggregators should be extended to take into account the driving pattern of electric vehicles. The design of aggregators should empower the EV drivers. For example, they should be able to select charge and discharge programs depending on their preferences [23].

Similarly, it is advisable to build a forecast model of EV parking lots' power output and EV power requirements that should be linked to the price of charging [24]. In addition, the idea of EVSPL (Electric Vehicle Solar Parking Lot) is significant; however, it is yet to be a commercial success. Thorough research is needed regarding the implementation of EVSPLs on a large scale by studying its commercial and financial feasibility [24].

The establishment of charging stations (electric or solar parking lots) is a most expensive and complex task. Researchers need to research ways of making this task easier. For example, they can propose business models suitable for average investors to set up a charging station. In this regard, we suggest that special research and consultancy firms be established to assist investors in setting up charging stations by producing feasibility and financial reports. Moreover, charging stations have a significant impact on EV adoption challenges. A network of EV chargers has to be deployed, but its establishment requires extensive planning and investment. An investigative research can be conducted to study all technical aspects of this issue [38].

Subsequently, the next innovation in the development of EVs is the advent of automated electric vehicles. By 2030, the traditional transport system will begin to be replaced by automated or driverless vehicles [24]. In fact, one example can be seen in a suburb named South Perth in Western Australia, where "Intellibus" has been introduced. It is an entirely driverless bus with the following characteristics: it is 4.80 m in length, 2.05 m in width, and 2.60 m in height. It can travel at a speed of 45 km/h (maximum) and 20–25 km/h (average). Intellibus weighs 1.8t when vacant, but its gross weight is 3t. Moreover, Intellibus can carry 11 passengers at a time. All possible safety measures are ensured. For example, it has an emergency stop button, emergency braking, power shortage brake, seat belts, etc. The Intellibus route is from Sir James Mitchell Park to Old Mill Road in Perth, Western Australia.

Another Australian example of an automated electric vehicle is a driverless bus at Curtin University in Western Australia [17]. The bus operates on 100% electricity equipped with digital input programming, GPS, and remote sensors. The bus travels within university premises accompanied by a chaperone that monitors the bus's performance and can control the bus manually if needed. Like the Intellibus, it can carry 11 passengers and travels at a speed of 45 km/h. These initial trials show the future of driverless electric vehicles in Australia and the potential for future automated transportation. Hence, the design and functionality of EVSPLs have to be reviewed [24].

Moreover, if car manufacturing companies are heading to automated electric vehicles, a legal framework should also be crafted. For example, if a road accident occurs, there should be a clear set of rules to identify the responsible party. Hence, the investigation of the legalities associated with automated EVs is another important research direction. For example, the autonomous electric vehicles depend on customer's information. This information may include personal details of customers, their destinations, traveling routes and patterns, the frequency of travel, etc. There is a concern about the use and access of this information in terms of cybersecurity. Consequently, it may cause route alteration. So, a security model can also be implemented to avoid this situation. Regarding the future implementation of automated EVs, this research area is of great importance.

Subsequently, a network route choice model for EVs intended to alleviate range anxiety has already been introduced, but it does not consider the parameters of traffic congestion, departure time choice, duration of stay at charging stations, etc., which should be taken into account to enhance this model [1]. Consequently, this future research area could help to reduce the range anxiety.

EV driver behavior plays an important role in the adoption and success of EVs not only in the market but in terms of their integration into the smart grid. EV drivers can take advantage of charging facilities like battery swapping stations and drive-above range. Even though penalties can be imposed for this behavior, there is a risk that this will turn away potential customers. Hence, substantial research is required on regularizing the EV drivers' behavior when they are availing themselves of EV charging facilities.

Regarding suggestions for successful EV adoption, the lack of an effective charging infrastructure poses a big challenge. While sustainability of the EV market is expected, the lack of a charging infrastructure can halt this development. However, this challenge could be overcome by: building enough charging stations, installing standardized charging equipment, developing EV charging Smartphone applications, investing in EVSPLs and decreasing the costs of EVs and battery recharging.

Without a reduction in the economic barriers to EV adoption, it is impossible for the EV industry to grow. In order to address the financial barriers, government and EV stakeholders should collaborate to promote the EV's economic and environmental benefits. In addition, changing customers' mindset for considering EV as a sound competitor to gasoline vehicles and establishing EV risk mitigation policies are two possible ways of ensuring the market success of EVs. In contrast, the risky maintenance of EVs is an underrated challenge. A decent effort should be put into investing in safe ways of repairing and maintaining EVs. Instead of human mechanics being used for repairs and maintenance of EVs, special robots could be used for these services.

Similarly, like the smart grid, the EV aggregator utilizes a set of software and hardware to function. Another vast area of research is the development of a set of IT solutions/software to manage the EV charging infrastructure. As we suggested earlier, a mobile app can be designed to locate charging stations near a customer's current location. In addition, this app could be used to check various varieties of EV batteries and their availability.

To reduce the price of EVs and the recharging cost, solar panels can be included in the EV design. Solar panels can generate electricity directly for EVs. Since EVs can store energy, they can be used to return energy to the grid and can be utilized for household energy needs as well. This setup can also reduce smart grid system load since EVs will no longer be dependent on the smart grid for their energy needs.

A media awareness program can be launched to increase public awareness of the hazards of pollution and the benefits of electric vehicles. In addition, government,

EV manufacturers, and promoters could fund this program. The government sector can also promote EV adoption by introducing special electricity rates for EV drivers. This attracts potential customers and decreases the transport sector's dependence on oil.

Like traditional car financing schemes, EV financing programs can also be introduced to make the purchasing of EVs much easier. This step will make the EV market stable to some extent.

9.6.2   Successful EV Integration into Smart Grid

The integration of the EV into smart grid is an integral feature since, in addition to being energy consumers, EVs can be used for energy storage. However, there are still several challenges and risks that need to be considered for its successful integration into the smart grid.

First, due to charging/discharging cycles in V2G programs, the bidirectional batteries start to deteriorate. Hence, further research should be done to explore battery durability. In addition, another research direction is to study innovative ways to prolong battery life [24]. Next, with the high penetration of EVs into smart grid with its existing battery technology, concerns arise about battery cost and its durability. Recent researches have shown good performance of Lithium-Ion batteries for this scenario [21]. Hence, future research can be conducted to find an efficient, cheaper and durable battery type which should be most suitable for V2G programs [21].

Second, EVSPLs can be integrated into smart grid. Many researchers have already researched this area and provided much theoretical knowledge. Now it should be implemented and the necessary devices should be developed [24]. To overcome charging needs of EV consumers, extensive charging infrastructure and stable V2G connectivity are required in order to deliver all the environmental benefits of EVs [27]. Moreover, simplifying and improving the components which will connect with the EV and smart grid infrastructures such as telecom and power grid is a vital step in the integration of EVs into smart grid [27]. This simplification idea could be another area of research for researchers to "simplify" EV integration into the smart grid. Even though smart charging has solved many problems, there are still several hurdles such as system load on the smart grid when the capacity of the grid is less than the EV's energy demand. Currently, research is being conducted to resolve this issue [27]. According to research, the V2G EV technology has the potential to assist the smart grid to utilize the "irregular" RESs [27]. Increasing the energy storage capacity of EVs in order to store renewable energy by means of an EV-charging infrastructure such as EVSPLs and returning it to the grid can fulfill the energy needs of the smart grid. Hence, working on efficient V2G "distribution" algorithms is a vital area of research.

Third, grid behaviors such as voltage drops are inevitable, so integrating RESs into the smart grid should be considered as well [21]. Consequently, studying these variable grid behaviors is an essential research area.

Fourth, another research area is to find other energy storage options for smart grid apart from V2G technology. Even though a V2G technology (with the aid of EV aggregators) can regulate voltage and frequency challenges, peak power control, power support in case of emergency and reduces smart grid operating cost but, other storage technologies should also be researched for a sustainable and reliable operation of smart grid [21].

In addition, since EV aggregators use different control strategies to manage EV charging in the smart grid, investigating these control strategies, proposing new ones and improving the existing control methods are potentially rewarding research areas. For instance, centralized control needs more research in building those business models that can enable frequent communication between EV owners and EV fleet operators [12]. In addition, in order to ensure the market success of the transactive control, an "automated negotiation device" can be installed in EVs which will conduct the communication between EV fleet operators [12]. Finally, price control can be improved by proposing price-elastic models to ensure efficient grid performance and best EV output [12]. Testing these control strategies with real-time parameters is another research area that can consider battery and gird dynamics while implementing the mentioned EV fleet operator control strategies [12].

Further, new models should be researched to make EV aggregator operations more intelligent [33]. Subsequently, further research in the areas of cybersecurity and avoidance of communication delays should be conducted to ensure the efficient and secure operation of the V2G framework [21].

In order to address the uncertainties associated with the EV charging and V2G, many scheduling programs are being introduced. However, EV risk factors such as an error in energy forecasting or damage to the charging equipment, etc. (refer to Sect. 9.5.2) are not mentioned in these algorithms [35]. A future research work is to take these uncertainties into consideration for continuous smart grid operations. Likewise, EV aggregators' improvement programs can also be investigated to increase EV reliability.

Finally, integrating the interests of EV owners, ancillary services demanded by transmission system operators and distribution system operators is the new trend for improving the smart charging solutions [12]. This research area can be a catalyst in making EV integration in the smart grid a reliable option for transport electrification and the designing of smart cities.

We propose the introduction of a gaming strategy in which reward cards can be issued to those EV owners who have maximum participation in V2G programs. They can utilize these reward cards to receive discounted rates on recharging EVs or even for buying additional batteries. These research findings are currently being published.

9.6.3 Steps Toward Reliable EV Supply Chain

To ensure the uninterrupted functionality of the grid, all of its economic, environmental, social, and technical challenges and risks should be identified and evaluated. The EV battery supply chain is one of those underrated challenges that will undoubtedly affect the performance and reliability of the EVs and the smart grid in the long run. EV motors and EV batteries contain critical and rare earth materials [2]. Consider a scenario where there are no more supplies of these rare earth materials. The disruption to the supply chain of EVs can lead to grid functionality failure, and hence to the failure of EVs as well. There are two issues regarding the EV supply chain: (1) the uninterrupted supply of rare earth materials required for EV batteries, (2) the recycling or reuse of EV batteries that have completed their life cycle.

In order to have a continuous supply of rare earth materials for EV batteries', there is a need to develop new recycling methods and "multimodal" transportation to support the EV supply chain [10]. After they have been retired from operation, EV batteries can be reused as energy sources. This practice can offset fuel prices and optimize the EV supply chain as well [10].

Another research area to investigate is the EV supply chain risk management in regards to EV manufacturers and EV battery owners, which will help to mitigate the risks associated with EV storage that may affect electricity consumers [2].

Pyrometallurgy has emerged as a suitable option for the recovery of valuable battery material. However, if the amount of extracted cheap materials is greater than the more valuable materials, then the extraction process may not be effective [10]. A similar recovery mechanism can be investigated to extract and distinguish between valuable and non-valuable battery materials. In addition, Hydrometallurgy is another mechanism for recovering EV battery material, but due to its high operating cost "and operational complexities", it cannot be fully implemented commercially [10].

An investigative study can be started to create, identify, and compare different recycle and reuse methodologies of EV battery materials. It will be beneficial to the environment and can reduce the operation costs of EVs.

In addition, the cost effect of a disruption to the EV supply chain can be mitigated by proper risk management strategies. Such as, if EV battery shortage occurs, fewer batteries will be used to continue V2G services. These frequent charging and discharging cycles cause battery degradation [2]. Battery degradation will increase the price of EV batteries, thereby significantly influencing the EV uptake.

9.7 Conclusion

In this chapter, we reviewed and examined the risks and challenges associated with EV adoption and its integration in smart grid and smart cities. Even though its adoption and integration into smart cities have still a long way to go, the benefits and prospects of this idea are significant.

We identified several EV adoption challenges such as range anxiety, EV driver attitude, lack of charging infrastructure, and economic barriers and tried to find possible solutions in the existing literature. Moreover, we reviewed numerous challenges and risks regarding EV integration into the smart grid that include extra load producing smart grid/system overload, unmanaged EV charging, EV adopters' recharging behavior, grid functionality failure, uncertainties in EV charging/discharging, high investment cost of V2G.

By exploring the literature on risks and challenges of EV adoption and its integration, we have come to the conclusion that EV adoption can be successful through the concerted efforts from all sectors of society. For example, governments, car manufacturers, electric supply companies, technology firms, and customers have to realize the significance of this technology. There is room for improvement in smart grid utilities to make EV integration successful.

References

1. Agrawal SK, Boyles SD, Jiang N, Shahabi M, Unnikrishnan A (2015) Network route choice model for battery electric vehicle drivers with different risk attitudes. Transp Res Rec J Transp Res Board 2498:75–83. https://doi.org/10.3141/2498-09
2. Aguilar S (2015) Electric vehicle (EV) storage supply chain risk and the energy market: a micro and macroeconomic risk management approach. ProQuest Dissertations Publishing
3. Avci B, Girotra K, Netessine S (2014) Electric vehicles with a battery switching station: adoption and environmental impact. Manag Sci 61:772–794. https://doi.org/10.1287/mnsc.2014.1916
4. Bishop JDK, Axon CJ, Bonilla D, Banister D (2016) Estimating the grid payments necessary to compensate additional costs to prospective electric vehicle owners who provide vehicle-to-grid ancillary services. Energy 94:715–727. https://doi.org/10.1016/j.energy.2015.11.029
5. Bonges HA III, Lusk AC (2016) Addressing electric vehicle (EV) sales and range anxiety through parking layout, policy and regulation. Transp Res Part Policy Pract 83:63–73. https://doi.org/10.1016/j.tra.2015.09.011
6. Bush SF (2014) Introduction to power systems before smart grid. In: Smart grid. Wiley, New York, pp 1–53
7. Castro TS, de Souza TM, Silveira JL (2017) Feasibility of electric vehicle: electricity by grid × photovoltaic energy. Renew Sustain Energy Rev 69:1077–1084. https://doi.org/10.1016/j.rser.2016.09.099
8. Eising JW, van Onna T, Alkemade F (2014) Towards smart grids: identifying the risks that arise from the integration of energy and transport supply chains. Appl Energy 123:448–455. https://doi.org/10.1016/j.apenergy.2013.12.017

9. Haddadian G, Khodayar M, Shahidehpour M (2015) Accelerating the global adoption of electric vehicles: barriers and drivers. Electr J 28:53–68. https://doi.org/10.1016/j.tej.2015.11.011
10. Hendrickson TP, Kavvada O, Shah N, Sathre R, Scown CD (2015) Life-cycle implications and supply chain logistics of electric vehicle battery recycling in California. Environ Res Lett 10:14011. https://doi.org/10.1088/1748-9326/10/1/014011
11. Hermann F, Rothfurs F (2015) Introduction to hybrid electric vehicles, battery electric vehicles and off road electric vehicles. Advances in Battery Technologies for Electric Vehicles, pp 3–16
12. Hu J, Morais H, Sousa T, Lind M (2016) Electric vehicle fleet management in smart grids: a review of services, optimization and control aspects. Renew Sustain Energy Rev 56:1207–1226. https://doi.org/10.1016/j.rser.2015.12.014
13. Jiang DR, Powell WB (2016) Optimal policies for risk-averse electric vehicle charging with spot purchases. arXiv preprint arXiv:1605.02848
14. Jiménez-Espadafor FJ, Guerrero DP, Trujillo EC, García MT, Wideberg J (2015) Fully optimized energy management for propulsion, thermal cooling and auxiliaries of a serial hybrid electric vehicle. Appl Therm Eng 91:694–705. https://doi.org/10.1016/j.applthermaleng.2015.08.020
15. Kumar NS, Schier M (2014) Increasing efficiency of ecological vehicles by integrating auxiliary units directly to the traction shaft. In: 2014 ninth international conference on ecological vehicles and renewable energy EVER, pp 1–6
16. Liu L, Kong F, Liu X, Peng Y, Wang Q (2015) A review on electric vehicles interacting with renewable energy in smart grid. Renew Sustain Energy Rev 51:648–661. https://doi.org/10.1016/j.rser.2015.06.036
17. Lloyd E (2017) Curtin's driverless bus, autonomous bus, automated driving technology—Curtin's driverless bus. Curtin University, Perth, Australia. In: Research Curtin. http://research.curtin.edu.au/institutes-centres/driverless-bus/. Accessed 5 Apr 2017
18. Loisel R, Pasaoglu G, Thiel C (2014) Large-scale deployment of electric vehicles in Germany by 2030: an analysis of grid-to-vehicle and vehicle-to-grid concepts. Energy Policy 65:432–443. https://doi.org/10.1016/j.enpol.2013.10.029
19. López MA, de la Torre S, Martín S, Aguado JA (2015) Demand-side management in smart grid operation considering electric vehicles load shifting and vehicle-to-grid support. Int J Electr Power Energy Syst 64:689–698. https://doi.org/10.1016/j.ijepes.2014.07.065
20. López-Arquillos A, Rubio-Romero JC, Súarez-Cebador M, Pardo-Ferreira M del C (2015) Comparative risk assessment of vehicle maintenance activities: hybrid, battery electric, and hydrogen fuel cell cars. Int J Ind Ergon 47:53–60. https://doi.org/10.1016/j.ergon.2015.02.005
21. Mwasilu F, Justo JJ, Kim E-K, Do TD, Jung J-W (2014) Electric vehicles and smart grid interaction: a review on vehicle to grid and renewable energy sources integration. Renew Sustain Energy Rev 34:501–516. https://doi.org/10.1016/j.rser.2014.03.031
22. Newbery D, Strbac G (2016) What is needed for battery electric vehicles to become socially cost competitive? Econ Transp 5:1–11. https://doi.org/10.1016/j.ecotra.2015.09.002
23. Nezamoddini N, Wang Y (2016) Risk management and participation planning of electric vehicles in smart grids for demand response. Energy 116(1):836–850. https://doi.org/10.1016/j.energy.2016.10.002
24. Nunes P, Figueiredo R, Brito MC (2016) The use of parking lots to solar-charge electric vehicles. Renew Sustain Energy Rev 66:679–693. https://doi.org/10.1016/j.rser.2016.08.015
25. Richardson DB (2013) Encouraging vehicle-to-grid (V2G) participation through premium tariff rates. J Power Sources 243:219–224. https://doi.org/10.1016/j.jpowsour.2013.06.024
26. Ryan N, McKenzie L (2016) Utilities' role in transport electrification: promoting competition, balancing risks. Public Util Fortn 154:32–37
27. Simpson A (2009) Environmental attributes of electric vehicles in Australia. Curtin Universty sustainability Institute

28. Sovacool BK, Hirsh RF (2009) Beyond batteries: An examination of the benefits and barriers to plug-in hybrid electric vehicles (PHEVs) and a vehicle-to-grid (V2G) transition. Energy Policy 37:1095–1103. https://doi.org/10.1016/j.enpol.2008.10.005

29. Tan KM, Ramachandaramurthy VK, Yong JY (2016) Integration of electric vehicles in smart grid: a review on vehicle to grid technologies and optimization techniques. Renew Sustain Energy Rev 53:720–732. https://doi.org/10.1016/j.rser.2015.09.012

30. Ustun T (2015) Impact of EV and V2G on the smart grid and renewable energy systems. Veh Grid Link Electr Veh Smart Grid 79:11

31. Vu K, Begouic MM, Novosel D (1997) Grids get smart protection and control. IEEE Comput Appl Power 10:40–44

32. Wager G, Whale J, Braunl T (2016) Driving electric vehicles at highway speeds: the effect of higher driving speeds on energy consumption and driving range for electric vehicles in Australia. Renew Sustain Energy Rev 63:158–165. https://doi.org/10.1016/j.rser.2016.05.060

33. Wang B (2016) Smart EV energy management system to support grid services. Ph.D., University of California, Los Angeles

34. White CD, Zhang KM (2011) Using vehicle-to-grid technology for frequency regulation and peak-load reduction. J Power Sources 196:3972–3980. https://doi.org/10.1016/j.jpowsour.2010.11.010

35. Xu NZ, Chung CY (2015) Uncertainties of EV charging and effects on well-being analysis of generating systems. IEEE Trans Power Syst 30:2547–2557. https://doi.org/10.1109/tpwrs.2014.2362653

36. Yang J, Hao W, Chen L, Chen J, Jin J, Wang F (2016) Risk assessment of distribution networks considering the charging-discharging behaviors of electric vehicles. Energies 9:560. https://doi.org/10.3390/en9070560

37. Yang L, Zhang J, Poor HV (2014) Risk-aware day-ahead scheduling and real-time dispatch for electric vehicle charging. IEEE Trans Smart Grid 5:693–702. https://doi.org/10.1109/tsg.2013.2290862

38. Yong JY, Ramachandaramurthy VK, Tan KM, Mithulananthan N (2015) A review on the state-of-the-art technologies of electric vehicle, its impacts and prospects. Renew Sustain Energy Rev 49:365–385. https://doi.org/10.1016/j.rser.2015.04.130

39. Yu Z (2017) Large scale charging of electric vehicles: technology and economy. Ph.D., Cornell University

40. Zhang Z, Li W, Zhang C, Chen J (2017) Climate control loads prediction of electric vehicles. Appl Therm Eng 110:1183–1188. https://doi.org/10.1016/j.applthermaleng.2016.08.186

Part III
Examples and Case Studies

Chapter 10
Rising of Yokohama, Keihanna, Kitakyushu, and Toyota Smart Cities in the Land of the Rising Sun

Somayya Madakam, Rajesh M. Holmukhe and Siddharth Tripathi

Abstract Quality of Life (QoL) in the cities of Japan is slowly deteriorating because of several factors including high global migration, urban densities, pollution, crime, and government inefficacy. In addition, the inability to meet the high demands for public utilities by the city government officials exacerbates the situation. Hence, through the development of advanced Internet of Things (IoT) and new business models, corporate giants like Hitachi, Toyota, Cisco, International Business Machines (IBM), Microsoft, Nippon, and Accenture are looking into new urban solutions such as development of *Smart Cities* to resolve the related urban issues. The objectives of building a Smart City are to provide improved Quality of Life (QoL), economic development, environmental balance, and efficient governance. These cities are the nodal points for civic services like security, health care, electric power, potable water, good houses, and good administration. Hence, the emphasis of smart cities is on 24 × 7 urban operational efficiency and the ease of citizens' life. In this light, this chapter discusses 360° views of global smart city projects with respect to connotation, designing, deployment of IoT, and other sustainable approaches for a better urban life. By way of studying existing models, this chapter also explores four Smart City projects in Japan including Yokohama, Keihanna Eco City, Kitakyushu, and Toyota Smart City.

S. Madakam (✉)
Information Technology Area, FORE School of Management, B-18, Adhitam Kendra, Qutab Institutional Area, New Delhi 110016, India
e-mail: somayya@fsm.ac.in

R. M. Holmukhe
Electrical Engineering Department, Bharati Vidyapeeth Deemed University College of Engineering, Satara Road, Pune 411043, India
e-mail: rajeshmholmukhe@hotmail.com

S. Tripathi
Marketing Group, National Institute of Industrial Engineering (NITIE), Vihar Lake, Mumbai 400087, Maharashtra, India
e-mail: siddharthtripathi.nitie@gmail.com

© Springer International Publishing AG, part of Springer Nature 2018
Z. Mahmood (ed.), *Smart Cities*, Computer Communications and Networks,
https://doi.org/10.1007/978-3-319-76669-0_10

S. Madakam et al.

Keywords Smart cities · Digital cities · Internet of things · IoT
Yokohama · Toyota · Keihanna · Kitakyushu · Quality of life
Sustainability · Security · Urbanization

10.1 Introduction

Japan, the third-largest economy in the world, is home to some of the world's largest metropolitan cities. Japan is renowned for its rich heritage and vibrant culture. It is also well-known as the Land of the Rising Sun. Besides, it is a nation recognized for its technological expertise. Its industrialization, software, hardware products and services, technological advancements, and management style are world renowned. It has also set several milestones in its journey toward efficient, citizen-friendly, and environment-friendly urbanization. Life in urban Japan is superconvenient with fantastic public transport, great shopping, and wonderful service, which is why Japan is one of the globally acknowledged developed countries today. However, the Quality of Life (QoL) in Japanese cities is slowly deteriorating given the challenges of high global migration, urban densities, pollution, and governance drawbacks. In addition, the high demand for public utility services is not being met by the city government officials. Other issues include energy shortage due to economic growth and an aging population due to declining birth rate and increasing life expectancy. Since the Great East Japan Earthquake in March 2011, energy shortage became an even more serious problem due to the loss of electricity generated by the nuclear power plants. Nuclear pollution in Japan is also one of the areas of concern, but unless one lives in the immediate neighborhood, the effects are limited. Despite increasing efforts to develop new energy sources such as solar and wind power, it will take some time before the Japanese are able to make up for the loss of nuclear power. In addition, the price of crude oil has continued to creep upwards and will inevitably lead to increased pressure on the supply and demand for energy throughout the world [1]. The electric power systems of many industrialized nations are challenged by the need to accommodate distributed renewable generation, increasing demands of a digital society, growing threats to infrastructure security, and concerns over global climate disruption [2]. Hence, given the current global scenario, Smart Cities with their energy-efficient systems can be the answer. Smart cities are capable of providing sufficient civic services for even migrated people, self-assisted automated devices to aged people and other Quality of Life services. In the section below, relevant academic literature regarding the Internet of Things (IoT) technologies in the constitution of Smart Cities has been outlined. Later in the chapter, we explore smart city projects relating to six of the Japanese cities.

10.2 Literature Review

"Smart Cities" have become the new catchword in every corner of the world, including developed countries in the continents of Europe and United States. Similar to the developed countries, the developing countries are also planning the upgradation of their cities to Smart Cities to provide Quality of Life to their citizens. The retrospective studies on Smart Cities point out that while this concept was born way back in 1992 under the name of Digital Cities, the term "Smarter Planet" only appeared during the economic crisis of the year 2008, when it was given global recognition by International Business Machines (IBM). Since 1992 researchers, academicians, architects, and practitioners working for new digital urban models and authored and published several scripts on "digital cities" in peer-reviewed journals, magazines, and other bibliographies.

In these publications, smart cities have been referred to using different names like wired cities, Internet cities, cyber cities, connected cities, intelligent cities, i-cities, and ubiquitous cities, to name but a few. Giffinger, Mitchell, and Somayya (e.g., [4, 12]) are some of the authors who are major contributors in this upcoming field through their research work, though their focus has largely been on how citizens are availing better services via computer and other allied electronic devices. Today, the concept of smart cities has been upgraded as it aims to resolve urban glitches of all hues using technologies.

As various authors have outlined, the concept of smart city emerged during the last two decades as a fusion of ideas about how information and communication technologies could improve the functioning of cities, enhancing their efficiency, improving competitiveness, and providing new ways in which problems of poverty, social deprivation, and poor environment might be addressed [3]. This area of research owes its roots to multidisciplinary fields like urban studies, information technology, civil engineering, computers, sociology, environment, economic, and electrical engineering to name a few. In one word, it is sprouting from all the grounds that have evolved since the inception of human civilization. Defining Smart Cities is rather difficult because of its interdisciplinary nature, with several definitions being propounded. However, most of the definitions underpin the importance of smart technologies. These technologies and their deployment are nothing but Internet of Things. The next subsections discuss state-of-the-art research on Internet of Things and Smart Cities using Microsoft Excel point and the web of science analytics (clarivate analytics).

10.2.1 Internet of Things

The new built-in environments of urban spaces are uniting with the so-called advanced technologies Internet of Things (IoT). The beauty of IoT technologies is that they can be embedded with any physical objects irrespective of whether they are living or nonliving. With the help of IoT even the city roads, transportation, hospitals, schools, security, trees, pipes, dust, and many more things can be connected to the Internet for better operational efficiency. Hence, IoT is the tool for making cities smart, ensuring 24/7 automation. IoT technologies connect every physical object to the Internet for self-identification, automating them, and helping in their monitoring and controlling. These technologies and related software tools include Radio-Frequency Identification (RFID), Electronic Product Code (EPC), IPv6, Quick Response codes (IPv6), sensors, actuators, cloud, Big Data Analytics, Geographical Information Systems (GIS), Geographical Position Systems (GPS), Artificial Intelligence (AI), web 3.0, and Hypertext Markup Language 5 (HTML5). Several converted Brown Field Cities like Hong Kong, Bangkok, Singapore, New York, London, Copenhagen, and Vienna have already mounted these IoT technologies for their city operational smartness.

Giffinger et al. [4] characterize Smart Cities with six charms including Smart Economy, Smart Environment, Smart Mobility, Smart People, Smart Governance, and Smart Life. The Smart cities are the cities that think, talk, and do the things on behalf of the urban citizens. In fact, Smart Cities are driving the national economy. Many new Smart Cities have been planned from scratch, such as the Wave City (India), Meixi (China), and Songdo (South Korea). Smart cities are playing an increasingly important role in the sustainable economic development of a determined area. Smart cities are considered key elements for generating wealth, knowledge, and diversity, both economically and socially [5]. However, the plantation or conversion process of new cities will take a long period. The development of Smart Cities requires an enormous number of IoT deployment and special designing for responsible usage of natural resources like water, soil, and energy. The IoT is expected to substantially support the sustainable development of future Smart Cities [6]. It has been initiated by the business corporates through technical support and adopting cities in order to grab long-term business over the competitors' entire globe.

The term "Internet of Things", was coined for the first time by Kevin Ashton in 1999 at the Auto-ID Center in Massachusetts Institute of Technology (MIT), USA ([7–11]). The IoT technologies have also been called the technological GOD [12] as its abundant potential for information gathering, omnipresence, capabilities of data processing, monitoring, and controlling of things or events in the domain of the cyber-physical systems makes it rather God-like. IoT technology has also been named the Web of Things [13–15]. In the same year in 1999 when this term was coined, Prof. Neil Gershenfeld from MIT published his book titled "When the Things Start to Think" which addresses the IoT principles. Kevin Ashton, David Brock, and Sanjay Sharma [7] together set up an Auto-ID Center in MIT and invented the most prominent technology EPC. These were the basic steps in the IoT technology evolution. Since then, over a period, it has received ample attention from researchers, academicians, corporate people and developers, hardware and software producers, and service providers. However, one should acknowledge that this concept has been floating since long, for there in the 1980s in Carnegie University, programmers developed a coffee vending machine linked to the Internet. Also, the RFID-related technology existed since the Second World War

[16–19]. The Electronic Product Code (EPC) and Radio-Frequency Identification (RFID) technologies were developed to connect the physical objects to the Internet for identification and logistics purposes. However, development of the IoT has been primarily driven by the needs of large corporations that stand to benefit greatly from the foresight and predictability afforded by the ability to follow all objects through the commodity chains in which they are embedded [20].

The Smart Grid is also one of the Internet of Things technologies. Smart grid and metering systems allow monitoring, managing of the entire life cycle of power generation, transmission, distribution, and consumption. Consumers traditionally do not have control over their exact consumption of electricity but are now empowered to manage and track their own consumption. A smart grid is an electrical grid which includes a variety of operational and energy measures including smart meters, smart appliances, renewable energy resources, and energy-efficient resources. This new paradigm shift potentially creates enormous savings for consumers and also for multinational power companies.

10.2.2 Review of Literature on IoT

The IoT has become an attractive research topic, in which the real entity in the physical world becomes a virtual entity in the cyber world, and both physical and digital entities are enhanced with sensing, processing, and self-adapting capabilities to interact through special addressing schemes. For the review of existing literature, we referred to a total of 70 research articles. Only the articles published during 2009–2016 were considered for the review process; which were selected randomly from both open-access and closed access databases. Refer to Fig. 10.1.

The text mining software, Microsoft Excel, was used for developing the database and for text analysis. The author with the maximum number of publications is Madakam and Ramachandran [12] with 6 publications to his credit. Also, the publication statistics show that in 2012, 14 articles were published on IoT, 12 in 2011, and also 12 in 2015. It is noticed that from 2009 onwards, the importance of IoT appears to increase, that means from 2012 onwards, IoT applications seem to have increased in our daily life. The IoT connects the physical world objects/things with the virtual world of Internet, for identification, automation, monitoring, and controlling of the things [21–23]. This technology can, thus, touch all the disciplines of human life including home science, biology, environment, medicine, pharmacology, manufacturing, and engineering. In addition, logistics, transportation, governance, defence, education, business, media, and mining can also require IoT. Given its manifold applications for day-to-day life, tremendous IoT technological products and services are mushrooming. Multinational companies are paying fat pay cheques to the technology experts for designing, coding, development of hardware, software, and networking products and services.

There are sometimes particular products that can be embedded in other technologies in order to bring about operational efficiency. Despite being popularly thought of

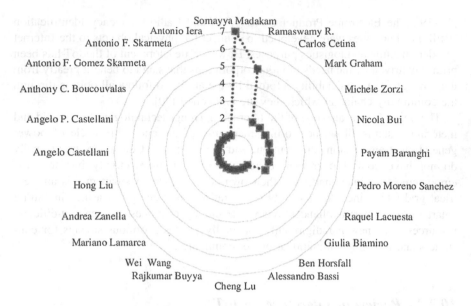

Fig. 10.1 Top 30 authors on IoT applications from 70 selected articles

as being limited to sensors and RFID, IoT technologies also include the existing software including existing operating systems like Windows, Linux, SuSE Linux, Macintosh, Ubuntu, Android, Sun Solaris, Unisys, CP/M, upcoming Urban Operating Systems. Even electronic hardware devices including computers, laptops, servers, tablets, and smartphones are included under the banner of IoT. The utility software including Bluetooth, Wi-Fi, ZigBee, EPC, barcode, QR codes, IPv4/6, microcontrollers, sensors, actuators, social media, 4G/5G, AI, robotics, Ambient intelligence, web 3.0, Big Data Analytics, and Clouds are also part of IoT-related technologies.

These technologies help to improve the quality of human life with respect to public utility services, home automation, education, good governance, manufacturing process, defence services, and health care in a big way. Several of these technologies are already well-known in public. Using these technologies even earthen things or objects like table, chair, curtain, window, fridge, washing machine, clothes, glasses, etc., can be connected to Future Internet (FI). Even the dust, mountains, rivers, lakes, and forests can also get connected to Wi-Fi or Local Area Network for monitoring and security from potential threats. IoT can, therefore, help objects interact with humans.

Europe, Singapore, Korea, Japan, and China are more proactive in developing these IoT technologies for the betterment of urban life. They have several collaborative projects in designing hardware, software, and networking products. Some of the projects are working on IoT architectures and their interoperability. Many corporates, firms, universities, and organizations have a common understanding in developing IoT products like IPSO (Internet Protocol for Smart Objects). Last, but not least, the issue of security of devices and data is a real concern. IT corporate giants are in the line of developing better, high-standard security software. Even international cyber laws are coming into practice for data security. Best applications of IoT are Smart Cities. The following subsection explains the smart cities connotes and their global developments scenario.

10.2.3 Smart Cities—The Global Scenario

It is generally accepted that more than half of the world's population lives in urban areas [24, 25]. We are living in an urban age where the world's urban population has grown from 220 million to almost three billion, which will show an increment of additional 3 million till 2050, continuing a trend that has been accelerating since the late 1980s. United Nations (UN) forecasts show that in 2050, more than 70% of the world's population will be living in cities. According to "Smart City: Smart Strategy" report dated on June 21, 2012, by Jin-Hyeok Yang (KC Smart Service-KT Corporation), the world is now urbanized and the percent of the population living in cities is depicted in the above diagram. Hence, it is not a surprise that many nations in the world have started exploring the Smart City concept. They have adopted various technologies such as installing wireless networks, implementing e-government initiatives by providing access to city departments and website development, integrating public transportation with intelligent transportation systems or developing ways to decrease their carbon footprints, and reduce the number of recyclables that are consigned to the trash heap. The development in new cities is badging themselves as smart. Many future IoT technologies will help in the building of Smart Cities. To enhance efficiency of Smart Cities' subsystem components, several IoT technologies need to be deployed. One of the first applications of IoT will be Smart Cities [26]. As the Internet and other relevant technologies have continued to develop and mature since a decade after beginning of the twenty-first century, a number of solutions from market giants such as Cisco, IBM, and others have emerged that have made IoT a feasible option for a good number of modern cities and metropolises today [27]. For the deployment of IoT technologies, many global standard organizations are working for global standards interoperability. These international standards are related to hardware, software, and networking products; and solutions are being embedded into city's physical objects aiming at the Future Internet. Besides, global legal standards are also being used in setting up a process.

Smart city concept in various countries is rapidly being adopted. Masdar, a township located outside Abu Dhabi is being developed by General Electric (GE) as the world's first carbon-neutral city; In Paredes, Portugal, Microsoft is wiring an energy-efficient city. Dongtan in the Yangtze Delta is being developed by Arup as a smart green eco-town, and in Songdo in South Korea, Cisco is building a town wired at all levels [28]. In India, about 100 new Smart Cities are being developed from the scratch or while 500 cities will be rejuvenated and developed into smart cities, in keeping with the Prime Minister's vision. Lavasa Smart City near Pune, India has been planned as a sustainable city. One more example is the Gujarat

International Finance Tech City near Ahmedabad, which is a good illustration of uplifting International Financial Services of India in the coming years. China is not lagging behind in the race having already set into motion more than 300 Smart City projects. In the USA, research on Smart Cities has also evaluated relevance in smart urban development, in fighting urban sprawl used as an approach to assess the role of psychological and cognitive attitudes toward Information and Communication Technologies (ICT) in reducing extent of the digital divide, which is verified on the field to confirm whether concrete actions can be taken against such a digital divide in poor urban areas [29–32].

The Smart City ideas are driven by the technology-based corporates, which are promoted in the forums. Led by strong business models for these companies, the idea is sold at city, state and national levels, making it politically agreeable, even to the extent of making it the political agenda in most of the countries across the world, especially in Europe, United Arab Emirates, and Saudi Arabia, and Asian countries including China, Malaysia, Singapore, Korea, India, and Japan. In Japan, the Ministry of Economy, Trade and Industry (METI) has invested a lot in an increasing number of smart city projects since 2010. The promotion of smart energy initiatives is now one of the goals established by the fourth energy strategic plan. Figure 10.2 lists some of the global smart cities which show the built-in cities process including Lavasa (India), Sao Paulo (Brazil), UNAM (Mexico), Skolkova Technopolis (Russia), and Hwaseong Dongton (S. Korea).

Fig. 10.2 Strategies that make your city smarter (adopted from [42])

10.2.4   Review of Literature on Smart Cities

The Web of Science database search showed over 12,000 journals and 1,48,000 conference proceedings across the engineering, sciences, social sciences, arts, and humanities streams, reporting high-quality research catering to several areas of interest. It links between relevant research using the cited references and explore the subject connections between articles that are established by the expert researchers working in any field. The web of science database enables to examine the list of references cited by a particular author, or conversely, to find articles that cite a particular work. The indexes can be searched topic-wise, author-wise, source title-wise, and address-wise, too. Refer to Graphs 10.1 and 10.2. Here, the web of science database was accessed in April 2017 for the analysis of research articles on Smart Cities, accessing 4832 records in this research area. The summary is as follows:

Results found: **4832**
Sum of the Times Cited: **13934**
Sum of Times Cited without self-citations: **10357**
Citing Articles: **10608**
Citing Articles without self-citations: **9163**
Average Citations per Item: **2.88**
H-Index: **48**

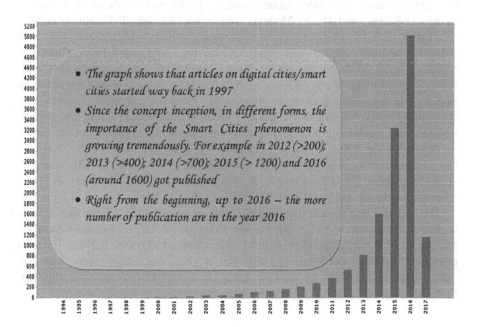

- *The graph shows that articles on digital cities/smart cities started way back in 1997*
- *Since the concept inception, in different forms, the importance of the Smart Cities phenomenon is growing tremendously. For example in 2012 (>200); 2013 (>400); 2014 (>700); 2015 (> 1200) and 2016 (around 1600) got published*
- *Right from the beginning, up to 2016 – the more number of publication are in the year 2016*

Graph 10.1 Articles published per year

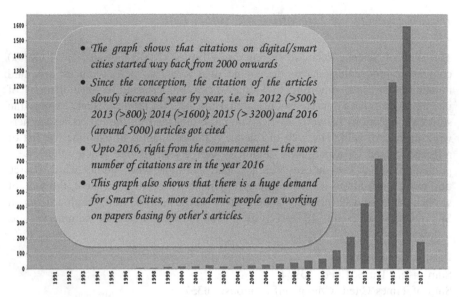

The graph shows that citations on *digital/smart cities started way back from 2000 onwards*

- *Since the conception, the citation of the articles slowly increased year by year, i.e. in 2012 (>500); 2013 (>800); 2014 (>1600); 2015 (> 3200) and 2016 (around 5000) articles got cited*

- *Upto 2016, right from the commencement – the more number of citations are in the year 2016*

- *This graph also shows that there is a huge demand for Smart Cities, more academic people are working on papers basing by other's articles.*

Graph 10.2 Citations per year

Web of Science subject-wise publication database analysis on smart cities yields the information that Engineering Electrical and Electronics stream had the maximum number of 1521 articles with a percent share of 31.478%. This is followed by Computer Science and Information Systems (936) with a share of 19.371%, Computer Science and Theory Methods (881) with 18.233%, Telecommunications (739) with 15.294%, Computer Science—Interdisciplinary Applications (409) with 8.464%, Computer Science—Hardware Architecture (396) with 8.195%, Computer Science—Artificial Intelligence (358) with 7.409%, Urban Studies (324) with 6.705% and Energy Fuels (301) with 6.229%. The subject-wise categorization implies that the planning of smart cities is an interdisciplinary subject including computer science, electrical, electronics, environment, urbanization, economics, business, and much more. Similarly, author-wise, the decreasing order of number of publications is as follows: Jara A.J. (19), Alba E. (18), Dustdar S. (17), Zhang Y. (16), Zhang J. (14), Foschini L. (14), Anthopoulos L. (14), Liu Y. (13), Wang Y. (12), Magedanz T. (12), Corradi A. (12), Solanas A. (11), Nesi P. (11), Marsal-Llacuna M. (11), and Li J. (11).

The analysis also reveals that the USA has the largest share of research articles with 736 publications and a percentage share of 15.232%; followed by Italy (670) with 13.866%, China (579) with 11.983%, Spain (400) with 8.278%, England (299) with 6.188%, and Germany (229) with 4.739%. India lags behind with 205 publications and a share of 4.243%. Japan is at the 11th position in this list. Publications aside, Japan is deeply involved in developing Smart Cities.

10.3   Rising Trend of Smart Cities in Japan

The U.S., European nations, and South Asian countries like China, Japan, and Singapore are driving dedicated Research and Development initiatives and implementing smart city technologies and applications, with the primary aim of addressing current urban problems such as energy shortages, traffic congestion, inadequate and poor urban infrastructure, health and education [33]. Smart Cities are a booming market in the EU and Japan. The growing economic importance of cities and the necessity of addressing environmental issues require the development of local solutions for energy management [34]. The World Bank once said that across Japan, a number of cities offer "world-class and unique 'best-practice' experiences and solutions" on a variety of challenges and additional cities are expected to be added in future. Many Smart City projects in Japan are concentrated on renewing social infrastructures through Internet of Things technologies. Among infrastructural attributes, an introduction of Smart Grid technology is the first priority. Due to the scarcity of electricity power that followed right after the Fukushima nuclear accident, energy efficiency in Smart Cities has become a necessity. The Feed-In Tariff (FIT) system was introduced in July 2012 to expand renewable energy generation for sustainable livelihood. However, the cities in Japan are relatively "smart". For instance, electricity grids in Japan are stable and system average interruption duration is the lowest among major nations. Yet, to further improve the functions of cities, from emission reduction point of view, the government has initiated the "EcoModel City" program since 2008, by selecting six cities with a range of population, geography, and industry backgrounds including Japan's four major Smart Cities. The Japanese version of the so called "smart city" exists in a post-fossil fuel world. Alternative sources like the sun, wind, and nuclear power have been harnessed in mass quantities. That power is then distributed to buildings, homes and electric cars connected to each other through "smart grids," which monitor usage throughout the network to maximize efficiency. Japan designated 23 urban areas as eco-towns by 2005, but unlike their European counterparts, these towns focused on developing industrial parks, introducing earth-friendly technologies, and promoting environmental methods such as integrated waste management, the three Rs (Reduce, Reuse, and Recycle), growing consumerism, and energy conservation [35].

Smart grids represent one of the most significant evolutionary changes in energy management systems as they enable decentralized energy systems, the use of large-scale renewable energy as well as major improvements in demand-side-management. Japan is one of the pioneers in smart grid deployment. The Japanese model is characterized by a government-led, community-oriented, and business-driven approach with the launch of four large-scale smart community demonstration projects [36]. Smart houses and buildings in Japan do take measures for energy saving such as installing Building and Energy Management System (BEMS), Light-Emitting Diode (LED), and rooftop solar panels. The Japanese concept of smart buildings tends to focus on connecting household appliances to

ICT system via mobile telephone. These measures, however, largely remain cosmetic, lagging behind European levels. Especially in the context of integrating renewable energy into smart building management, Dutch companies have useful experiences to share. Smart Cities in Japan, an Assessment of the Potential for EU–Japan Cooperation and Business Development report begins by outlining the Smart City policy and actors in Japan, before considering different types of projects in Japan and abroad and comparing them with international standards. The report also identifies key sectors of possible cooperation between EU and Japan and assesses potential obstacles to these opportunities. The European Union and Japan have launched a two-and-a-half-year program that aims to provide cities with a cloud-based platform to link government data with the IoT technologies. Called CPaaS.io (City Platform-as-a-Service–integrated and open), the platform will link technologies like the IoT, virtual and cloud computing and big data, analytics with open government data and linked open data, in order to enable a multitude of different applications. The project is being coordinated by the Bern University of Applied Sciences in Europe, and by the YRP Ubiquitous Networking Laboratory in Japan. In Japan, smart cities are largely funded via subsidies from The Ministry of Economy, Trade and Industry (METI). The smart cities market here, which stood at around ¥1.12 trillion in 2011, is expected to grow to ¥3.8 trillion by 2020. METI also invests in Japanese business involvement in smart cities globally. The next subsections discuss Yokohama, Keihanna, Kitakyushu, and Toyota smart cities.

10.3.1 Yokohama—Smart City

The city of Yokohama, just southwest of Tokyo, is the site of a social and infrastructure experiment to create a smart city for the rest of the world to imitate. Yokohama Smart City Project is shortly referred to as YSCP. Yokohama Smart City Project (YSCP) is one of the largest scale smart city experiments in Japan. This city is an initiative to establish overseas expansion of Japan's smart grid technology. In April 2010, the Ministry of Economy, Trade and Industry selected Yokohama Smart City Project as a Next Generation Energy Infrastructure and Social System Demonstration Area (NGEISSDA) and was about to finish by end of the year 2014 [37, 38]. The results of the experiment, during the period up to the Financial Year 2014, were utilized for even larger scale community planning. Yokohama Smart City Project covers specifically three areas in the Yokohama City: Minato Mirai area as 21st District (Central); Kanazawa Green Valley; and Kohoku New Town. The total Yokohama Smart City Project combining these three areas is around 60 km with a population of circa 420,000 in 1,70,000 households. The YSCP was set up in collaboration with the private sectors including Accenture, Toshiba, Tokyo Gas, Nissan Motor, Meidensha, Panasonic, and Toden, and much more to implement successful solutions for the project. The project (Fig. 10.3) deals with the introduction of renewable energy, energy management of households, buildings, local communities while last but not least, is the next-generation electric vehicles systems. The YSCP primarily aims to establish a social system with 30% CO_2 emissions reduction, testing with Wide-Area Energy Management (WAEM) and Demand Response (DR) systems. Wide-Area Energy Management combines three subsystems: (1) Community Energy Management System (CEMS); (2) Home Energy Management System (HEMS); and (3) Building Energy Management System (BEMS). M/s. Toshiba is mainly responsible for CEMS, BEMS, and HEMS for condominiums and houses. One of its solutions is to introduce an Automatic Demand Response (ADR) system for condominiums, where Toshiba air conditioners installed in each unit connected to a CEMS that serves as a central control system providing control based on factors. Toshiba is also implementing its new SCiB batteries in 2000 electric vehicles for this project. The rechargeable batteries feature superior safety and quick charging performance with a longer life

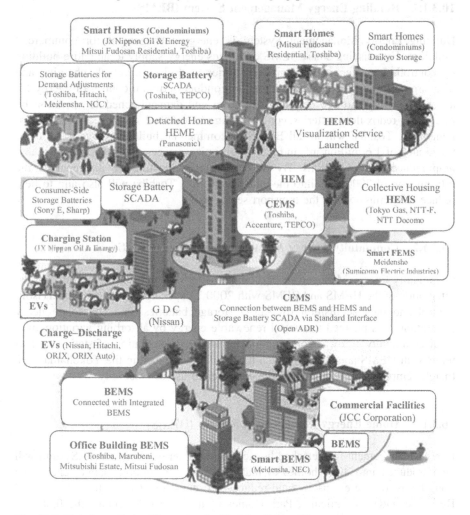

Fig. 10.3 Yokohama Smart City project by Toshiba Corporation

and higher efficiency. New Toshiba air conditioning has been installed in each unit, which will be connected to CEMS; the central control system will be controlled according to the status of power consumption for optimal operation. The plans call for control equipment to be introduced in the autumn of 2012 to enable the Demand Response system to be launched in April 2013. It is also planned to conducting automated settings for charging and discharging based on photovoltaic output, electric consumption, electric vehicle usage patterns, etc., by integrating HEMS, BEMS with EV data center. Additionally, it is aimed to make peak cuts by creating a system that combines batteries and high-speed chargers and by coordinating it with CEMS; also, one can regularize the territory's electricity feed.

10.3.1.1 Building Energy Management System (BEMS)

Building Energy Management System is energy management for commercial buildings. Establishing smart BEMS optimizes energy supply to an entire building by controlling co-generators, storage batteries, and electric vehicle charging and discharging infrastructure. It is planned to conduct optimum control of energy for an entire factory through peak cut operation and demand schedule operation by integrating redox flow batteries, concentrating photovoltaic systems, and gas engine generators. Toshiba will install BEMS in commercial buildings covering a combined area of 1.6 million m^2, in order to optimize power consumption control and help reduce CO_2 emissions. By developing an infrastructure that enables the introduction of 2000 EVs into the entire area, M/s. Toshiba will also aim to help reduce CO_2 emissions in the transport sector too.

10.3.1.2 Community Energy Management System (CEMS)

Community Energy Management System provides system stabilization through the integration of the HEMS and BEMS with 2000 EVs, charging stations, supervisory control and data acquisition (SCADA) storage batteries, and PV solar energy generation. It is planned to control renewable energy by absorbing variations in a local community's power consumption through the integration of stationary batteries with HEMS and BEMS, which have been introduced in the Yokohama area, thereby empowering consumers to make efficient use of electricity.

10.3.1.3 Home Energy Management System (HEMS)

Energy management for detached houses. Home Energy Management System will be introduced into 4000 homes to make power consumption visible, encourage households to save electricity, and reduce CO_2 emissions (20%) through Demand Response (DR). In particular, Park Homes Okurayama will become the first condominium to introduce a Demand Response system. Realizing visualization of energy consumption and demonstrating the DR function integrated with CEMS by integrating power generators such as solar cells and fuel cell batteries, storage batteries with home electric appliances such as air conditioners.

10.3.2   Keihanna—Smart City

Kansai Science City, also called the Keihanna Science City (Keihanna Smart City), was set up in 1978 as the second oldest science city after Tsukuba Science City in Japan. In "Keihanna Eco-City Next Generation Energy Society System" inspection project, which was carried out in Keihanna Science City (Kyoto), a demand response analysis was performed by three Japanese companies including MHIMS. It is a new city, planned out as a national project to serve as a center of culture, learning, and research; in fact, it is a new cultural capital intended to open paths into the future. For the demand response analysis of transportation, electric vehicle users received notification of when and where to charge EV in accordance with target values for power demand. Specifically, EV users could choose three levels of power supplies from quick chargers to normal chargers. Peak saving of electricity was exercised by advising users not to charge when the supply–demand was extremely high. They have collected and analyzed the charging data from each charger, and gathered the information for organizing and optimizing the configuration of charging infrastructures. In the Keihanna smart city project, approximately 700 households participated. These were divided into four groups, each receiving a different level of information regarding their electricity consumption. Included study variables were basic consumption, Time-of-Use pricing (TOU), Critical-Peak-Pricing (CPP), and energy consultation. These were combined with demand reduction opportunities, which included financial incentives. Energy savings for the Time-of-Use pricing group were 7% in summer and 14% in winter. The Critical-Peak-Pricing group, on the other hand, saw 7% in winter and 33% in summer. The analysis shows that much of the variation correlated with times when people were at home and were able to take advantage of DR opportunities [39]. The main objectives of the constitution of Keihanna Smart City are (1) For the establishment of a community with a next-generation cycle in place, including CO_2 reduction and efficient use of renewable energy, (2) Through effective use of IoT and without sacrificing Quality of Life, establish people's "Eco-Awareness and Behaviour" and develop a sustainable "Eco-Cycle", (3) Develop Smart Community as a feasible operational community to ensure its sustainability.

The Keihanna Smart City is home to a large number of company laboratories and other research institutes, and possesses high technological and communication capacity, the Advanced Telecommunications Research Institute International and the Kansai-kan of the National Diet Library. In addition to its research institutes, universities, companies, and other institutions, Kansai Science City is proceeding with a large-scale housing development, making it the ideal location for testing and verifying the outcomes of research on advanced IoT technologies and new social systems in cooperation with residents. Making full use of this environment, the project seeks to develop a Community Energy Management System that will minimize CO_2 emissions without affecting Quality of Life for residents, aiming for the construction of next-generation energy-efficient societies.

10.3.3 Kitakyushu—Smart City

The Kitakyushu city is one of two designated cities in the Fukuoka Prefecture, Japan, together with Fukuoka, with a population of just under 1 million people. Kitakyushu City offers unique experiences of a city that has completely transformed itself in terms of environmental sustainability. The inception of Smart City project of Kitakyushu was in the year 2010. To receive Ministry of Economy, Trade and Industry subsidies that amount to ¥126.5 million, initially, the above four pilot cities focused on improving the Quality of Life and showcasing innovative technologies. However, after the 2011 earthquake, there was a paradigm shift to work toward reducing energy consumption and improving energy efficiency. Some areas of success include demand response programs, which reduced energy consumption during peak period by 20% in the Kitakyushu smart city.

Effective smart communities do so by applying a hub approach that connects people with the information and technology to drive improved quality of life, innovation, and better choices. The Kitakyushu Smart Community Project, outlining a vision of the optimum form for community energy management, will seek to create the appropriate social structures for a low-carbon society by innovating lifestyles, business styles, and urban planning styles. A smart community is a new lifestyle designed to provide sustainable growth and encourages healthy economic activities that reduce environmental burden while improving the quality of life of the residents [40]. Japan's Smart Community initiatives are government-planned social security systems, which focus on regional energy management systems and lifestyle changes under such energy supply structure [41]. By means of the establishment and operation of a customer energy management system called Smart Community Center or the Community "Setsuden-sho," the project aims to establish mechanisms for citizens and companies to think about and participate in the process of energy distribution. This implies that the Kitakyushu smart city has worked to promote energy saving with the creation of new energy sources as a part of its measures to fight global warming. In response to electricity shortages, soaring power bills and other problems following the Great East Japan Earthquake, the city decided to take on some responsibility for ensuring a stable supply of low-priced energy, in order to support citizens' lives and industrial activities in the urban regions. In fact, ensuring stable supply of low-priced energy has become a key component of the smart city's growth strategies. In addition, other initiatives will include preparation for the large-scale introduction of next-generation vehicles and their linkage with public transport. The outcomes of the operational experiments in the Higashida area will be extended to other areas of the City of Kitakyushu, for example to the Jono district in Kokurakita Ward, which is being newly developed, and from there to the rest of Japan and the world. Thus, the city of Kitakyushu is transforming from a brownfield project to a sustainable smart city of the future. The renewable and energy-efficient technologies will definitely light up the lives of all the Kitakyushu residents.

10.3.4 Toyota—Smart City

In Toyota city, local resources like human, materials, and technology are being used effectively and efficiently. The city is working on the Public–Private Partnership (PPP) model for smart community development. Refer to Fig. 10.4. To *follow the standards of tomorrow* is the motto of Toyota Smart City. Toyota foresees a low-carbon society, promoting the use of new, IT/IoT-based smart power grids for more stable supply and energy conservation. In Toyota City, several verification trials are underway, based on the idea of developing "Smart Mobility and Energy Life in Toyota City (Smart Melit)", where people and vehicles can coexist better than anywhere in the world. This is an experimental project promoted by METI to try out systems for low-carbon societies [1].

The Toyota smart grid includes the recharging of next-generation environment-friendly cars (Plug-in Hybrid Vehicles and EV); it also includes "smart houses" being developed by Toyota Housing. The Toyota Smart Center is a

Fig. 10.4 Smart Mobility Park

system that links vehicles, homes, and information, and enables integrated control of energy data and information; trials of the system have been conducted over smart grids in Toyota City. The Toyota Smart City project focuses on the use of heat and unused energy as well as electricity. It has a high demand response with more than 70 homes and 3100 Electrical Vehicles. Through this project, houses that contain an IT network of electrical appliances and other household equipment, solar panels, household storage batteries, onboard automobile storage batteries and other devices can develop household power leveling and optimized energy usage [41].

The Toyota Smart Mobility Park in Fig. 10.4 is a next-generation charging station based on a vision for a near-future society; it is equipped with chargers and batteries fueled by solar and wind power for use in various ways of charging next-generation environment-friendly vehicles such as PHVs and EVs, as well as other electric-powered means of mobility. Through collaboration with the Toyota Smart Center Energy Management System, Toyota Smart Mobility Park addresses the needs brought on by mobility diversification and will function as a hub that manages energy used for transportation and supports future car-sharing systems. In Toyota Smart Community, residents enjoy their lives while working for energy sharing and peak shifts. Already, smart devices and energy management have achieved reductions in carbon dioxide emissions by roughly 70% and decrease in peak electrical power demand by 40%, under certain conditions.

Health monitoring system that acquires, saves, and utilizes human health information by using an onboard equipment has been deployed. Driving modal shift, supporting vulnerable road users, and creating a vibrant community is also being achieved. So the Toyota Smart City is the sustainable society.

10.4 Conclusion

This book chapter explains the concepts of both smart cities and the embedded Internet of Things technologies in order to bring about operational efficiency in the new urban development and management models. Shift toward Smart Cities will certainly resolve the urban issues of transportation, security, governance, public utility services, old age, urban migration, and other environmental challenges throughout the world. This chapter has focussed upon energy efficiency systems of smart homes, smart meters, smart grid, PHV, and electric vehicles based on DR mechanisms; it has also discussed in detail the renewable energy resources like solar, wind, tidal, and others. The limitation of this study is that apart from those outlined above, other IoT technologies have not been discussed in detail. It may be stated that the future Yokohama, Keihanna, Kitakyushu, and Toyota Smart Cities will definitely become full-fledged sustainable smart cities with the collaboration of Accenture, Toshiba, Tokyo Gas, Nissan Motor, Meidensha, Panasonic, Toden, and several other global IT/ITeS plus telecom multinational companies. The future Internet of Things technologies will definitely provide the required energy efficiency to the Land of the Rising Sun.

References

1. Tamai H (2014) Fujitsu's approach to smart cities. Fujitsu Sci Tech J 50(2):3–10
2. Brown MA, Zhou S (2013) Smart-grid policies: an international review. Wiley Interdiscip Rev: Energy Environ 2(2):121–139
3. Harrison C, Tan D, Morris D (2010) Skinput: appropriating the body as an input surface. In Proceedings of the SIGCHI conference on human factors in computing systems, ACM, April, pp 453–462
4. Giffinger R, Fertner C, Kramar H et al (2007) Smart cities—ranking of European medium-sized cities. Vienna University of Technology, Vienna, Austria
5. Castro M, Jara AJ, Skarmeta AF (2013) Smart lighting solutions for smart cities. In: 27th international conference on advanced information networking and applications workshops (WAINA), IEEE, March, 2013, pp. 1374–1379
6. Vlachea P, Giaffred R, Stavroulaki V, Kelaidonis D, Foteinos V, Poulios G, Demestichas P, Somov A, Rahim Biswas A, Moessner K (2013) Enabling smart cities through a cognitive management framework for the internet of things. Commun Mag IEEE 51(6):102–111
7. Ashton K (2009) That 'internet of things' thing. RFID J 22(7):97–114
8. Sundmaeker H, Guillemin P, Friess P, Woelfflé S (2010) Vision and challenges for realising the internet of things. Cluster of European research projects on the internet of things, European Commision, 3(3), 34–36
9. Haller S (2010) The things in the internet of things. In: Poster at the, Tokyo, Japan, 2010
10. Weber RH (2010) Internet of things–new security and privacy challenges. Comput Law Secur Rev 26(1):23–30
11. Gubbi J, Buyya R, Marusic S, Palaniswami M (2013) Internet of things (IoT): a vision, architectural elements, and future directions. Future Gener Comput Syst 29(7):1645–1660
12. Madakam S, Ramachandran R (2015) Barcelona smart city: the Heaven on Earth (internet of things: technological God). ZTE Commun 13:3–9
13. Atzori L, Iera A, Morabito G (2010) The internet of things: a survey. Comput Netw 54 (15):2787–2805
14. Bandyopadhyay D, Sen J (2011) Internet of things: applications and challenges in technology and standardization. Wirel Pers Commun 58(1):49–69
15. Pintus A, Carboni D, Piras A (2012) Paraimpu: a platform for a social web of things. In Proceedings of the 21st international conference companion on World Wide Web, ACM, April, pp 401–404
16. Hicks P (1999) RFID and the book trade. Publ Res Quart 15(2):21–23
17. Garfinkel SL, Juels A, Pappu R (2005) RFID privacy: an overview of problems and proposed solutions. IEEE Secur Priv 3:34–43
18. Roberts CM (2006) Radio frequency identification (RFID). Comput Secur 25(1):18–26
19. Heidrich J, Brenk D, Essel J, Schwarzer S, Seemann K, Fischer G, Weigel R (2010) The roots, rules, and rise of RFID. Microw Mag IEEE 11(3):78–86
20. Lianos M, Douglas M (2000) Dangerization and the end of deviance: the institutional environment. Br J Criminol 40:261–278
21. Atzori L, Iera A, Morabito G (2009) The internet of things: a survey. Comput Netw 54 (15):2787–2805
22. Kortuem G, Kawsar F, Fitton D, Sundramoorthy V (2010) Smart objects as building blocks for the internet of things. Internet Comput IEEE 14(1):44–51
23. Uckelmann D, Harrison M, Michahelles F (2011) An architectural approach towards the future internet of things. Springer, Berlin, pp 1–24
24. Dirks S, Keeling M (2009) A vision of smarter cities: how cities can lead the way into a prosperous and sustainable future. IBM Institute for Business Value, New York, p 8
25. Dirks S, Gurdgiev C, Keeling M (2010) Smarter cities for smarter growth: how cities can optimize their systems for the talent-based economy. BM Institute for Business Value. Accessed 12 Sept 2016

26. Gea T, Paradells J, Lamarca M, Roldan D (2013) Smart cities as an application of internet of things: experiences and lessons learnt in Barcelona, In: 2013 seventh international conference on innovative mobile and internet services in ubiquitous computing (IMIS), IEEE, July, pp 552–557
27. Boulos MNK, Al-Shorbaji NM (2014) On the internet of things, smart cities and the WHO healthy cities. Int J Health Geogr 13(10)
28. Batty M (2012) Smart cities, big data. Environ Plan B: Plan Des 39(2):191–193
29. Partridge HL (2004) Developing a human perspective to the digital divide in the 'smart city'
30. McAllister LM, Hall HM, Partridge HL, Hallam GC (2005) Effecting social change in the 'smart city': the West End connect community project, pp 1–16
31. Bronstein Z (2009) Industry and smart city. Dissent 56(3):27–34
32. Caragliu A, Del Bo C, Nijkamp P (2009) Smart cities in Europe. J Urban Technol 18(2): 65–82
33. Lee JH, Phaal R, Lee SH (2013) An integrated service—device—technology roadmap for smart city development. Technol Forecast Soc Change 80(2):286–306
34. Clarisse PHAM (2014) Smart cities in Japan. In: An assessment on the potential for EU-Japan Cooperation and Business Development, Tokyo
35. Brendan B (2012) After the nuclear disaster. Japan considers a green future. Solutions 3.1: 99–103. Web, 5 Nov 2012
36. Mah DNY, Wu YY, Ip JCM, Hills PR (2013) The role of the state in sustainable energy transitions: a case study of large smart grid demonstration projects in Japan. Energy Policy 63:726–737
37. DeWit A (2014) Japan's rollout of smart cities: what role for the citizens? スマートシティーが公開されるなか、 日本の市民の役割とは. The Asia-Pacific J 11(24-2)
38. Clarisse PHAM (2014) Smart cities in Japan. An assessment on the potential for EU-Japan Cooperation and Business Development, Tokyo
39. RP Siegel (2015) Japan smart cities project wraps up with impressive results, 2 Oct 2015. http://www.triplepundit.com/2015/10/japan-smart-cities-project-wraps-impressive-results/. Accessed 3 May 2016
40. Tastuno S (1986) The Technopolis strategy: Japan, high technology, and the control of the twenty-first century. Prentice Hall Press, New York
41. Ling APA, Kokichi, S, Masao M (2012) The Japanese smart grid initiatives, investments, and collaborations, arXiv preprint arXiv: 1208.5394
42. Cohen B (2017) Strategies-that-make-your-city-smarter. Available at https://www.slideshare.net/Ray1961/20131218. Also published in Technology, Business

Chapter 11
A Business Model for Digital Services for Smart Cities in India

Chandrakumar Thangavel and Parthasarathy Sudhaman

Abstract Today, more than ever, the challenge of the cities is to bring the digital experience to the citizens. Innovative digital cities that use technology in terms of advanced infrastructures, platforms, and e-services helps to provide more efficient urban services, improve the quality of life of citizens, and meet the present and future needs of the city in economic, social and environmental perspectives. It guarantees efficiency, effectiveness, and sustainability. Such cities, also known as Smart Cities, are a future reality for municipalities around the world. These cities will use the power of ubiquitous communication networks, highly distributed wireless sensor technology, and intelligent management systems to solve current and future challenges and create exciting new services. In this chapter, we propose a sustainable business model to implement the Smart City digital services. The proposed model aims to accelerate the process of urbanization, reduce the urban development problems such as food safety, urban crime, traffic jams, traffic accidents, etc. The chapter also discusses the importance of updating digital service for a smart city in order to promote innovation in e-services.

Keywords Digital service · Smart city · Information city · Ubiquitous city
Security · Internet of things · IoT · E-services

11.1 Introduction

The term "Smart City" was coined in the early 1990s to illustrate how urban development was now turning toward technology, innovation, and globalization [12]. A "Smart City" is an urban region that is highly advanced in terms of overall

---

C. Thangavel (✉) · P. Sudhaman
Department of Computer Applications, Thiagarajar College of Engineering,
Madurai, Tamilnadu, India
e-mail: t.chandrakumar@gmail.com

© Springer International Publishing AG, part of Springer Nature 2018　　263
Z. Mahmood (ed.), *Smart Cities*, Computer Communications and Networks,
https://doi.org/10.1007/978-3-319-76669-0_11

infrastructure, sustainable real estate, communications, and market viability. It is a city where information technology is the principal infrastructure and the basis for providing essential services to residents and governance mechanisms for city officials.

In a Smart City, economic development and activity are sustainable and rationally incremental by virtue of being based on success-oriented market drivers such as supply and demand. This benefits all including citizens, businesses, the government as well as the environment. Other terms that have been used for similar concepts include *cyberville, digital city, electronic community, flexi city, information city, intelligent city, knowledge-based city, MESH city, telecity, ubiquitous city,* and *wired city.*

The concept of smart cities originated at the time when the world was facing one of the worst economic crises. In 2008, IBM began work on a *smarter cities* project as part of their Smarter Planet initiative. By the beginning of 2009, the concept had captivated the imagination of various nations across the globe.

The concept of Smart City embraces several technologies and devices depending on the meanings of the word *smart*, e.g., smart roads, smart grids, smart governance, etc. Many definitions of Smart City exist, but no one has been universally acknowledged as complete [7]. A major hurdle in having a complete definition is the ambiguity of meanings attributed to the word *smart*. Our literature review about Smart City and Digital City has been carried out using the methodological model proposed by vom Brocke et al. [37].

We can also see that Digital City also embraces several meanings of "smart", such as virtual city, cyber city, wired city, ubiquitous city, and so on [22, 29–31]. Moreover, Digital City is sometimes considered as a Smart City based on ICT infrastructures, because one of the most important technologies used to support Smart City strategies is ICT [6]. Therefore from this analysis, it appears that Digital City is the most recurrent terminology linked to the meaning of Smart City. Smart cities initiatives also require innovation in business models namely new ways through which the private and public sector generate and distribute economic value.

Cities are built on the three pillars—*Infrastructure, Operations,* and *People.* In a Smart City, not only is each one of these pillars infused with intelligence, but more importantly the pillars work in an interconnected and integrated fashion to utilize resources efficiently. The literature search process never comes to a definitive end [27].

In the rest of this chapter, we first outline the concepts and definition of Smart City and discuss the Components and Framework of Smart Cities and Digital Services in Sects. 11.1 and 11.2. Then, in Sect. 11.3, we provide a Business model for digital service in India. Section 11.4 presents a brief summary.

11.2   Smart City

11.2.1   Definitions

A Smart City is an urban region that is highly advanced in terms of overall infrastructure, sustainable real estate, communications, and market viability. It is a city where information technology is the principal infrastructure and the basis for providing essential services to residents. In a Smart City, economic development and activity are sustainable and rationally incremental by virtue of being based on success-oriented market drivers such as supply and demand. This benefits citizens, businesses, the government as well as the environment. The concept of smart cities was first originated when in 2008, IBM began working on a "smarter cities" project as part of their Smarter Planet initiative. By the beginning of 2009, the concept had captivated the imagination of various nations across the globe. Peoples' strong inclination toward it generated both positive and negative effects at a global level [2, 25]. Several papers discussed the meaning of and the concept behind the word *smart* (in particular the paper of Hollands [17] and the IBM report [16]). Smart City appears to be a broad concept including many aspects of urban life, such as urban planning, sustainable development, environment, energy grid, economic development, technologies, social participation, and so on [29].

11.2.1.1   Smart City Definitions

The UK Department of Business, Innovation and Skills considers smart cities a process rather than as a static outcome, in which increased citizen engagement, hard infrastructure, social capital, and digital technologies make cities more livable, resilient, and better able to respond to challenges. A major hurdle in definition is the ambiguity of meanings attributed to the word *smart* and, therefore, to the label *Smart City*. For this reason, other synonymous terms include Digital City, Wired City, Knowledge City, and Green City, which often link together technological informational transformations with economic, political, and sociocultural change [6, 17, 35].

The British Standards Institute defines it as "the effective integration of physical, digital and human systems in the built environment to deliver sustainable, prosperous and inclusive future of its citizens" [5]. The Indian Government defines Smart City in the following way: "Smart City offers sustainability in terms of economic activities and employment opportunities to a wide section of its residents, regardless of their level of education, skills or income levels." Smart Cities Council defined a Smart City as the "one that has digital technology embedded across all city functions." IBM defines a Smart City as "one that makes optimal use of all the interconnected information available today to better understand and control its operations to optimise the use of limited resources."

Table 11.1 Smart city definitions

Source	Definition
Courtney Humphries, Boston Globe [18]	A *wired, sensor-filled streetscape that uses cloud computing and sophisticated software* to transform cities into intelligent machines that adapt to people's lives and steer behavior. The ultimate vision is a city that is hyper-efficient, easy to navigate, and free of waste and which is *constantly collecting data* to help it handle emergencies, disasters, and crime [18]
Anthony Townsend, New York University [36]	A city where *information technology* is being incorporated into services that affect urban problems [36]
Gridaptive Technologies, transportation and power systems manufacturer [14]	A technology term that is inclusive of *smart grids, smart meters, intelligent transportation, buildings, and other smart infrastructure* that make up technologically innovative cities [14]
Colin Harrison, IBM [15]	A city that has "*Urban Systems models* that are capable of helping citizens, entrepreneurs, civic organizations, and governments to see more deeply into how their cities work, how people use the city, how they feel about it, where the city faces problems, and what kinds of remediation can be applied" [15]
Boyd Cohen, Fast Company Co. Exist [4]	A broad, integrated approach to improving the efficiency of city operations, the quality of life for its citizens, and growing the local economy [4]

There is no single consensus definition of a Smart City, but there is some general agreement that a Smart City is one in which information and communication technology (ICT) facilitates improved insight into and control over the various systems that affect the lives of residents [3, 24]. Table 11.1 lists a range of other definitions, with the ICT elements highlighted in italics.

The list, although not comprehensive, shows near unanimity about the central role of ICT in developing a smart city. The last entry is a notable exception, being more focused on the efficiency and quality of life.

11.2.2   Components of a Smart City

The Smart City concept illustrates how urban development is now turning toward technology, innovation, and globalization [12]. Others have suggested that the phrase's popularity rose out of the "Smart Growth" movement of the late 1990s, which advocated improved urban planning. Advocates suggested the use of information technology to meet urban challenges in the new global knowledge economy. In the past decade, the phrase has been used by various technology companies (e.g., Cisco, IBM, and Siemens) for the application of complex

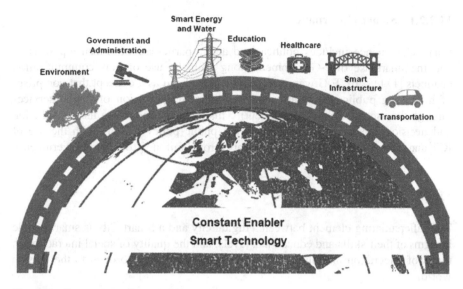

Fig. 11.1 Components of smart cities

information systems to integrate the operation of urban infrastructure and services such as buildings, transportation, electrical and water distribution, and public safety [15]. Figure 11.1 shows the components of a Smart City [20].

In recent years, the ICT infrastructure such as broadband infrastructures, wireless sensor networks, Internet-based networked applications, and open platforms were spread more and more in order to work together to form the backbone of a large intelligent infrastructure [28]. It is through the use of Internet-based infrastructures, that the e-services supply regarding health care, energy, education, environmental management, transportation, mobility, and public safety has begun to spread among citizens. At the same time, mobile phones have become more accessible for everybody (not only for businessmen but also for each citizen) evolving in technologically sophisticated products able to use the Internet access point and to supply intelligent services to the users. The accessibility to the Internet in urban life has become easier and more popular [20, 21]. The newness is that the city increases its cooperation with the surrounding territory in physic and virtual terms in order to build an arena, where people in communities can share knowledge, experience, and mutual interests [34]. Many authors observe that this scenario supports more and more the concept of Digital City as a wired city based on the Internet in which it is possible to provide public and private services to create socioeconomic value for customers, citizens, and the civil society [8]. Therefore, the Internet diffusion is one of the main drivers of interest regarding the Digital City concept. The following subsections discuss some of the core features and requirements of a smart digital city.

11.2.2.1 Smart Governance

Smart Governance includes political and active participation, citizenship services and the smart use of e-Government along with the use of new communication channels [1, 11, 26]. E-Government can be considered as a concept that comprises of improving public governance and providing the provision of public services through the use of ICT (e-Government). This includes improving the consultation and decision-making processes, improving public policy making with the use of ICT and incorporating more critical agents throughout the process (e-Government).

11.2.2.2 Smart Citizen

The differentiating element between a digital city and a Smart City is smart people in terms of their skills and educational levels, and the quality of social interaction in terms of integration and public life along with their ability to open to the outside world.

11.2.2.3 Smart Education

A key element in the development of cities is having a major presence of well-educated citizens in the city. It is important to design digital development plans in classrooms that primarily focus on closing the digital divide promoting the digital skills of teachers and incorporating the new generation of digital learning resources. Virtual education offers many benefits such as reduced costs, flexible hours, and greater interaction.

11.2.2.4 Smart Energy

The variable nature of power generation from renewable energy sources requires that networks, generation, and consumption are connected in an efficient and intelligent way. The power supply has been governed by the consumption-oriented generation model. Since power would be generated increasingly from renewable energy sources in the future, it is necessary that we move to a model based on principles of smart power generation, smart power grids, smart storage, and smart consumption.

11.2.2.5 Smart Technology

Smart City technologies are being developed to address a range of issues including energy management, water management, urban mobility, street lighting, and public safety. These innovations are underpinned by general developments in areas such as wireless communications, sensor networks, data analytics, and cloud computing.

11.2.2.6   Smart Mobility

Smart mobility aims to improve operational efficiency through linking traffic road information, the vehicle condition, real-time data acquisition, and integration of urban traffic capacity, thus achieving a smooth flow of traffic running with RFID automatic toll collection technology and other data gathering instruments.

11.2.2.7   Smart Infrastructure

Smart infrastructure designs contain many small-scale networked elements that serve a multitude of uses, rather than one single guiding purpose for their existence. For example, urban community garden plots provide food for urban dwellers as well as serves as stormwater management systems. Cities need to accurately measure current conditions and model the future. Sensors and technological controls embedded within new and retrofitted urban designs could monitor existing conditions and provide real-time feedback in case modifications are needed.

11.2.2.8   Smart Building

Smart buildings deliver useful building services that make occupants productive (e.g., illumination, thermal comfort, air quality, physical security, sanitation, and many more) at the lowest cost and environmental impact over the building lifecycle. Smart buildings are connected and responsive to the smart power grid, as they interact with building operators and occupants to empower them with the next level visibility and actionable information.

11.2.2.9   Smart Health Care

Smart health care is the application of new technologies in ways that affect health care. These include diagnosis monitoring patients, including the management of organizations involved in these activities. Use of new technologies would help citizens enjoy a number of online medical services including key services such as requesting an appointment online or the possibility of having a digital record.

11.3   Digital Services in Smart Cities in India

In the context of Smart Cities, a major part of the success of development of these depends on the use of a virtual *metaphor of city*, because the use of appropriate navigation metaphors can help to make the structure of modern information systems easier to understand and, therefore, easier to use [10].

The Government of India launched the Smart Cities Mission (SCM) in June 2015 with the objective to promote sustainable and inclusive cities that provide core infrastructure and give a decent quality of life to its citizens, a clean and sustainable environment, and application of *smart* solutions. The focus is on sustainable and inclusive development and the idea is to look at compact areas, create a replicable model which will act like a lighthouse to other aspiring cities. The Smart Cities Mission is meant to set examples that can be replicated both within and outside the Smart Cities, catalyzing the creation of similar Smart Cities in various regions and parts of the country. As the data network has evolved, society has also changed in ways that have enabled and accelerated the use of data. People who have grown up with computers and the Internet, often termed as digital natives, make up an increasing proportion of the workforce and society at large. Because they are more comfortable with ICT and mobile technologies, they tend to accept and even demand that it be integrated into their lives [33]. Also, partly because of an aging population that is less mobile and less demanding of space than it was when it was younger, the trend is for a growing fraction of people in the U.S. and also globally to live in urbanized areas [2]. These urbanized areas offer greater opportunities for the creation and use of data as multiple people and systems interact more frequently than in more rural areas [23, 29, 32]. Within the SCM, *Digital India* is a programme to transform India into a digitally empowered society and knowledge economy. The vision of Digital India is centered on three key areas as follows:

- Digital Infrastructure as a utility to every citizen
- Governance and services on demand
- Digital empowerment of citizens.

These vision areas focus on providing the following:

- Providing a cradle-to-grave digital identity that is unique, lifelong, online, and authenticable to every citizen
- Providing mobile and online bank accounts enabling citizens' participation in digital and financial space
- Ensuring services availability in real time from online and mobile platforms.

In India, the Internet habitual consumers are rapidly increasing, and this is only set to escalate in the future. India's Internet user base is estimated to reach 550 million by 2020 with a penetration of approximately 40%, a significant increase from the current 35%. The youth have the highest adoption rate of technology. With every third person in India being a youth, India will witness an incredible pace of Internet growth. Figure 11.2 shows Internet users growth in India [19].

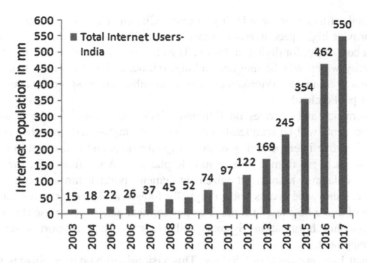

Fig. 11.2 Internet users' growth in India

Two thousand were characterized by widespread of the Internet all over the world, not only in business or academic context but especially in everyday life. The adjective "smart" identifies devices that combine telephony and computing: smartphones have high-speed data access by Wi-Fi and mobile broadband in order to supply in real-time digital services to their users and, at the same time, to improve their quality of life [13, 38]. This kind of study includes all papers which investigate on the Smart/Digital City phenomena within its real-life context in order to verify the empirical applications of theoretical concepts [39].

11.3.1 Overview of Digital India

A good governing body requires a good communication platform to communicate with the stakeholders efficiently. Communicating with the citizens has been a big challenge for the government of India with widespread geography, massive population, and enormous linguistic and cultural diversity. The way of communication has changed a lot from postal and telegraph era to print and broadcasting media to the era of Digital Communication. The efficient way to communicate with the citizens of the world's largest democracy with a population of 1.2 billion is only possible by connecting with everyone on a digital platform. Though India is considered as the IT powerhouse of the world, there is a huge digital divide [27].

The Digital India initiative is a dream project of the Government to transform India into a digitally empowered society and knowledge economy. It is centered on three vision areas:

- Digital Infrastructure as a Utility to Every Citizen: The government is planning to provide high-speed internet connectivity to 250,000 g panchayats, which will be a core utility for digital inclusion. The citizens will be provided with a digital identity which will be unique, lifelong, online, and valid. There will be easy access to common service centers and a shareable private space for every citizen on a public cloud.
- Governance and Services on Demand: Under this vision, all the government departments will be seamlessly integrated with high-speed optical fiber, which will improve interoperability of these organizations and will result in real-time service delivery from online or mobile platform. Apart from this, the government is planning to make all citizen entitlements portable through cloud for easy and country-wide access and to digitally transform the services for improving ease of doing business in India. The government also plans to use the power of Geographic Information Systems (GIS) for decision support systems and development.
- Digital Empowerment of Citizens: This vision is to empower citizens through digital literacy and universal access to digital resources. e.g., all documents/ certificates to be available on the cloud and in Indian languages. Government also wants to provide collaborative digital platforms for participatory governance e.g. MyGov website for crowdsourcing ideas.

The three vision areas further encompass nine themes or *pillars* of Digital India. Some of these are presented in Fig. 11.3. The Digital India initiative covers many important projects like National e-Governance Plan, National Knowledge Network, National Optical Fiber Network, digital cities, etc., which will help in digital inclusion in the country and empower the citizens to eradicate the digital divide.

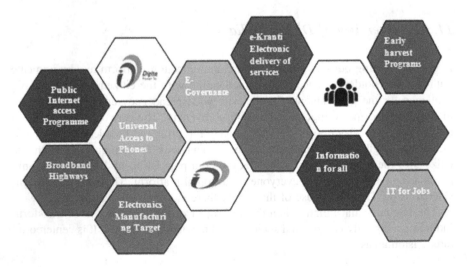

Fig. 11.3 Nine Pillars of Digital India project (adopted from [9])

11.3.1.1 Digital Cities of India

The list of 20 smart cities out of the 98 shortlisted for the Smart Cities Mission (SCM) was released in March 2017 by the Government of India. These 20 cities will be the first to receive funds, thus kick starting the process of developing them into "smart cities". The next 2 years will see the inclusion of the remaining 40 and 38 cities respectively. As mentioned earlier, a Smart City is an urban region that is highly advanced in terms of overall infrastructure, sustainable real estate, communications, and market viability. It is a city where information technology is the principal infrastructure and the basis for providing essential services to residents. There are many technological platforms involved, including but not limited to automated sensor networks and data centers.

Of the 98 cities and towns that 5 years down the line will graduate into smart cities, 24 are capital cities, another 24 are business and industrial centers, 18 are culture- and tourism-influenced areas, and 5 are port cities and three are education and healthcare hubs. The list of the first 20 smart cities in India, as part of the Smart Cities Mission are as follows:

1. Bhubaneswar, Odisha
2. Pune, Maharashtra
3. Jaipur, Rajasthan
4. Surat, Gujarat
5. Kochi, Kerala
6. Ahmedabad, Gujarat
7. Jabalpur, Madhya Pradesh
8. Visakhapatnam, Andhra Pradesh
9. Solapur, Maharashtra
10. Davangere, Karnataka
11. Indore, Madhya Pradesh
12. New Delhi Municipal Corporation
13. Coimbatore, Tamil Nadu
14. Kakinada, Andhra Pradesh
15. Belagavi, Karnataka
16. Udaipur, Rajasthan
17. Guwahati, Assam
18. Chennai, Tamil Nadu
19. Ludhiana, Punjab
20. Bhopal, Madhya Pradesh.

11.4 A Business Model for Digital Services
for Smart Cities

The smart cities concept is based on replicating this data process across multiple systems delivering exponentially greater benefits with fuller deployment across service areas. There are significant benefits to be realized from the network effect, as data, technology, and people are joined together and this exponentially magnifies the potential benefits, impact, and value that can be delivered. Investment in digital technologies and improved data management alone will not, however, deliver the Smart City. Cities need to consider the strategic intent, governance/service delivery models and their approach to stakeholder engagement if they are to secure the maximum impact from their investments.

In the current research, a Smart Cities Business Model has been developed to meet the objectives set out in the background section of this chapter. The Model shown in Fig. 11.4 adapts existing models and frameworks in this field. The model remains compatible with these models but is designed to walk cities through the process of clearly identifying next steps and investment and resources required to realize their ambitions.

The proposed business model may be used to develop a city with digital services for open information to all, IRCTC (Indian Railway and Catering Services) E-Market place, E-Trade, Digital Signature, Digilocker, etc.—these being the major

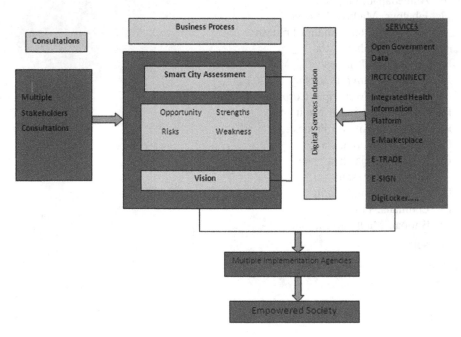

Fig. 11.4 Business model for digital India Smart City

digital services in India. This model helps the government and public sectors to include digital services in the cities with various business perspectives. With the consultation of stakeholders, the digital services can be monitored and assessed with risks and strengths. It will help to make a city smarter in the empowered society. The model outlines three maturing levels namely: consultation, assessment, and digital services, which lead to an optimized Smart City digital services approach. The business process in the model deals with the assessment of the digital services in the smart cities with its strength and weakness. The definition and the vision of a Smart City are already discussed in an earlier section. It outlines that a maturing Smart City digital service business model will increasingly plan and deliver services with an interconnected system. This system approach is enabled by increasing the use of data and digital technologies to transform governance and multiple implementation agencies. The model identifies these as a dimension that a Smart City must invest in and commit to as part of its intent. The ultimate vision is of a Smart City with digital services that strategically manages multiple systems as a city-wide level and through increased transparency, openness, and shared accountability creates an innovation system that improves outcomes and enhances city competitiveness.

Let us take an example of MobiKwik, who are partners with Bhopal smart city initiative, for payments. Bhopal Plus facilitates government–citizen engagement and collaboration, as a step toward the national smart cities mission. The tie-up will enable residents of Bhopal in paying taxes and bills for utility services such as electricity and water, digitally with the help of MobiKwik. Bhopal Plus also provides a platform to apply for birth and death certificates, marriage registration, and register complaints on civic amenities. This association is in line with the vision to support Digital India and the government's smart cities initiative. MobiKwik and Bhopal Plus together would be incentivizing users to do online transactions, which would further give impetus to the Digital India campaign. The partnership aims to bring better payment experiences for our users across the city. MobiKwik and Bhopal Municipal Corporation would be incentivizing digitally paying users with 5 per cent cashback on bill payments. MobiKwik has over 55 million users on its platform and currently powers payments for IRCTC, NHAI, GSRTC, Meru Cabs, Big Bazaar, MakeMyTrip, Zomato, PVR, Shop Clues, Myntra, Pepperfry, and many other organizations. With the help of third-party consultants, stakeholders, and the smart city vision, digital services for the people will be easily assessed and it will help to improve cities to be smarter.

Existing city development process across India involved preparation of city development plan and master plan. This plan laid a greater emphasis on the spatial aspects and regulations with a view to align the infrastructure of the city for its development. It adopted a resource-based approach for the planning and development of the city with a vision to achieve social equity and sustainability.

Developing business models of smart cities has of late attracted much attention. Use of bullet trains, metros, aerotropolis, eco-city, eco-towns, etc., speak volumes about the ways new business models are being evolved as innovative business propositions. In general terms, a Smart City is typically characterized by heritage, architecture, esthetics, ecology, lifestyle, etc. This apart, the current focus is directed toward improvement of essential services, economy with a focus on employment generation, transportation, health care, education, municipal and social security, civil services, etc. Many countries and cities have taken lead in these domains; including the unique selling propositions in international business terms (viz., as tourist destinations; high-tech cities, commonwealth heritage centers, ports and harbors, Olympic stadium, etc.).

Presented below are some of the illustrative international business models of smart cities; carefully chosen to represent different continents of the world as case studies.

11.4.1 City Development Model in India—Organic Versus Inorganic Growth

Organic Growth Model:

Here, we have existing agglomeration of people and city services are planned as per the needs of the people. Many Indian cities are very old, and that makes it hard to initiate new developments without impacting daily lives of citizens. In this context, challenges include [33]:

- Development of the city is always citizen focused, without holistically considering the impact on the industry
- City tend to develop mostly in the outer periphery.

Examples include cities of Delhi, Mumbai, Varanasi, Kolkata, and Chennai.

Inorganic Growth Model:

Here, an industry is first developed; the city then develops as per the requirements of the industry. Most of the citizen needs are catered to after the industry has been established and industry has attracted a sizeable population. Challenges include:

- Lacks holistic nature of planning for both citizens and industry
- Lack of focus leads to ancillary industries being set up much later in the city lifecycle.

Examples include cities of Jamshedpur, Pune, Bangalore, Gurgaon, and Hyderabad.

11.5 Conclusion

A Smart City strives to optimize operations in real-time to maximize operational efficiency and effective governance. The application of modern analysis and processing techniques to the streams of data flowing around a city offers the prospect of using predictive techniques to intervene in the functioning of a city to prevent problems and to improve efficiency. IBM's Journal of Research and Development in 2010 offered the following definition of a Smart City: *an instrumented, interconnected and intelligent city*.

Smart cities evolve toward a strong integration of all dimensions of human intelligence, collective intelligence as well as artificial intelligence within the city. At the core of Smart Cities is strong infrastructure, seamlessly connected and coordinated. The key infrastructure pillars comprise of transportation, power, integrated utilities, urban development, resource management, IT-based connectivity. In a Smart City, these basic infrastructure pillars form the foundation that supports building blocks like sustainability, inclusiveness, and convergence. All aspects of daily life like education, health, connectivity, waste-management, basic utilities, upkeep, and upgrade of civic services and functions are accessible through on a single platform driven by IT. The focus and aim is to deliver a happier lifestyle through integrated solutions, innovation, and technology.

Computer simulation, modeling, and visualization tools will be central to interpreting and understanding the mass of data generated by the Smart City, allowing the relevant public authority to coordinate their services and interact with its residents and businesses. In particular, smartphone applications are already central to the Smart City, with many cities already testing applications to allow citizens to report littering, anti-social behavior, etc., via cameras on their phones, with the relevant city authority sending back a message when the problem is resolved. GE, for example are developing games linked to smart meters which enable children to drive energy-saving behavior by competing with friends and neighbors. Integrated into and supporting this infrastructure is a parallel ICT infrastructure of increasing numbers of sensors picking up data to be stored on servers. The data is accessed by city authorities, the energy provider, businesses, and residents increasingly via the "Cloud" which enables all parties to concurrently analyze and share data. Increasingly people will want to consume data wherever they are, and whole-city Wi-Fi will become all the more important in supporting the Smart City and "Smart Citizen".

Key to creating a step change in the sustainability of cities is *smarter grids*. One of the biggest challenges for cities is its energy infrastructure. In addition to needing to revolutionize the way we produce and distribute energy so as to meet climate change targets, the pressures of growing city population increases energy demand, and the need for greater resilience from national electricity grids. Smart grids seek to manage peak energy demand to reduce the need to build more capacity through new power stations. Smart grids also incorporate distributed and micro renewable energy (solar PV, combined heat and power, wind turbines, etc.) thereby supporting the transition to a lower carbon energy mix. Smart grids require communication between users and suppliers of electricity meaning that energy transmission infrastructure (substations, gas pipes, etc.) need to be improved to allow data to be captured and transmitted.

Dealing with waste in a Smart City will require, at a basic level, the facilities to collect, sort, and recycle household and business waste. There are also an increasing number of "up-cycling" projects that take waste streams and turn them into more valuable products (a good example are Freitag bags made from truck tarps, used car safety belts, and used inner tubing of bicycle tires). Businesses of this kind can be supported by the development of hub facilities where similar businesses can share costs and innovate together.

Collaborative data platforms can provide city planners and developers information on a wide range of city information to assist with smarter planning. Real-time information on traffic, land use, building typologies, demographic data, socioeconomic data, environmental data, infrastructure systems, and flood risk zones present new opportunities for much more intelligent spatial planning of city growth and infrastructure. This is increasingly important in the context of sustainable urban development, which is increasingly resulting in mixed-use neighborhoods.

The self-assessment process requires cities to consider their maturity and identify future investment across these dimensions at a city-wide level. To add granularity to this analysis, investment planning is also undertaken on a sector-specific or "domain" basis (such as public transport, energy, water, waste, health, finance, and economy). Cities are asked to reflect on the findings from domain-specific analysis identifying synergies, gaps, and integrated actions.

References

1. Al-Hader M, Rodzi A (2009) The smart city infrastructure development and monitoring. Theor Empir Res Urban Manag 2(11):87–94
2. Caragliu A, Del Bo C, Nijkamp P (2011) Smart cities in Europe. J Urban Technol 18(2):65–82
3. Chourabi H, Nam T, Walker S, Gil-Garcia JR, Mellouli S, Nahon K, Pardo TA, Scholl HJ (2012) Understanding smart cities: an integrative framework. In: 45th Hawaii international conference on system sciences, IEEE Xplore, pp 2289–2297
4. Cohen B (2012) What exactly is a smart city? Fast Company Co.Exist. 19 Sept 2012. Available at: http://www.fastcoexist.com/1680538/what-exactly-is-a-smart-city
5. Cooper HM (1988) Organizing knowledge syntheses: a taxonomy of literature review. Knowl Soc 1:104–126
6. Dameri RP (2013) Searching for Smart City definition: a comprehensive proposal. Int J Compu Technol 11(5):2544–2551 (Council for Innovative Research)
7. Dameri RP, Rosenthal-Sabroux C (2014) Smart city, progress in IS. Springer, Switzerland
8. Dameri RP (2012) Defining an evaluation framework for digital cities implementation. In: IEEE international conference on information society (i-society), IEEE Xplore, pp 466–470
9. Department of Electronics and Information Technology (2017) How digital India will be realized: pillars of digital India. Available at: http://digitalindia.gov.in/content/programme-pillars

10. Dieberger A, Frank AU (1998) A city metaphor to support navigation in complex information spaces. J Vis Lang Comput 9(6):597–622 (Elsevier)
11. Europe 2020 Strategy from ec.europa.eu/regional_policy/what/europe2020/index_en.cfm
12. Gibson DV, Kozmetsky G, Smilor RW (1992) The Technopolis phenomenon: smart cities, fast systems, global networks. Rowman & Littlefield, Lanham, MD
13. Giffinger R, Fertner C, Kramar H, Kalasek R, Pichler-Milanovic N, Meijers E (2007) Smart cities. Ranking of European medium-sized cities. University of Technology, Vienna
14. Gridaptive Technologies (2012) Smart cities: intelligent transportation and smart grid standards for electrical and lighting management systems. White paper, 2012
15. Harrison C, Abbott Donnelly I (2011) A theory of smart cities. White paper, 2011
16. Harrison C, Eckman B, Hamilton R, Hartswick P, Kalagnanam J, Paraszczak J, Williams P (2010) Foundations for smarter cities. IBM J Res Dev 54(4):1–16
17. Hollands RG (2008) Will the real smart city please stand up? City: Anal Urban Trend, Culture, Theory, Policy, Action 12(3):303–320
18. Humphries C (2013) The too-smart city: we're already building the metropolis of the future— green, wired, even helpful. In: Now critics are starting to ask whether we'll really want to live there. The Boston Globe, May 19, 2013
19. IAMAI-IMRB (2017) Number of Internet users in India could cross 450 million by June: report http://www.livemint.com/Industry/QWzIOYEsfQJknXhC3HiuVI/Number-of-Internet-users-in-India-could-cross-450-million-by.html
20. Ishida T (2000) Understanding digital cities. In: Ishida T, Isbister K (eds), Digital cities. LNCS, vol 1765. Springer, Berlin, pp 7–17
21. Ishida T, Hiramotsu K (2001) An augmented web space for digital cities. In: Proceedings of symposium on applications and the internet, pp 105–112
22. Moutinho JL (2008) Building the information society in Portugal: lessons from the digital cities programm 1998–2000. In: van Geenhuizen MS (ed), Value-added partnering and innovation in a changing world
23. Moutinho JL (2008) Building the information society in Portugal: lessons from the digital cities programm 1998–2000. In van Geenhuizen MS (ed), Value-added partnering and innovation in a changing world
24. Pardo TA, Nam T (2011) Smart city as urban innovation: focusing on management, policy and context. In: Proceeding of the 5th international conference on theory and practice of electronic governance, ACM, New York, pp 185–194
25. Pardo T, Taewoo N (2011) Conceptualizing smart city with dimensions of technology, people, and institutions. In: Proceedings of the 12th annual international conference on digital government research, ACM, New York, pp 282–291
26. ABB Report (2012) Smart cities in Italia: un'opportunità nello spirito del Rinascimento per una nuova qualità della vita. Technical report, ABB
27. Ricciardi F (2010) ICTs in an ageing society: an overview of emerging research streams. In: D'Atri A, De Marco M, Braccini AM, Cabiddu F (eds), Management of the interconnected world. ITAIS, vol 1. Springer, Berlin, pp 37–44
28. Schaffers H, Ratti C, Komninos N (2012) Special issue on smart applications for smart cities —new approaches to innovation: guest editors' introduction. J Theor Appl Elect Comme Res 7(3). (Universidad de Talca, Chile)
29. Schiewe J, Krek A, Peters I, Sternberg H, Traub KP (2008) HCU research group "digital city": developing and evaluating tools for urban research. In: Ehlers et al (eds), Digital earth summit on geoinformatics, pp 239–244
30. Schuler D (2002) Digital cities and digital citizens. In: Tanabe M, van den Besselaar P, Ishida T (eds), Digital cities II: computational and sociological approaches. LNCS, vol 2362. Springer, Berlin, pp 71–85
31. Schuurman D, Baccarne B, De Marez L, Mechant P (2012) Smart ideas for smart cities: investigating crowdsourcing for generating and selecting ideas for ICT innovation in a city context. J Theor Appl Electron Commer Res 7(3):49–62 (Universidad de Talca, Chile)

32. Schuurman D, Baccarne B, De Marez L, Mechant P (2012) Smart ideas for smart cities: investigating crowdsourcing for generating and selecting ideas for ICT innovation in a city context. J Theor Appl Elect Commer Res 7(3):49–62 (Universidad de Talca, Chile)
33. Shriram AB, Pahwa D (2015) Smart cities—what's in it for business?, Grant Thorn ton International Ltd. October 2015
34. Sorrentino M, Simonetta M (2013) Incentivising inter-municipal collaboration: the Lombard experience. J Manag Gov 17(4):887–906
35. Su K, Li J, Fu H (2011) Smart city and the applications. In: IEEE international conference on electronics, communications and control (ICECC), IEEE Xplore, pp 1028–1031
36. Townsend A (2013) Smart cities: big data, civic hackers, and the Quest for a New Utopia. W. W. Norton & Co., New York
37. vom Brocke J, Simons A, Niehaves B, Plattfaut R, Cleven A (2009) Reconstructing the giant: on the importance of rigour in documenting the literature search process. In: ECIS 17th European conference on information systems, pp 2–13
38. Wacker JG (1998) A definition of theory: research guidelines for different theory-building research methods in operations management. J Oper Manag 16:361–385 (Elsevier)
39. Yin RK (2003) Case study research: design and methods. SAGE Publications, Thousand Oaks, CA

Chapter 12
Opportunities for Brazilian Smart Cities: What Is Realistic and What Is not

Lucio Agostinho Rocha

Abstract Smart cities comprise new technologies that contribute to increase in the availability of smart, integrated services to the population and offer new opportunities for collaboration, communication, business, and sustainability. New technologies aim to link up the smart devices and help to increase machine-to-machine communication, Longer Term Evolution (LTE, and mobile telephone service integration. The smart devices and related resources combine together to act as an ecology of interconnected "things". These technologies are offered in short phases and become a part of daily life. However, many related aspects need to be thought over carefully to offer even better service quality to the population. Many authors consider these services a natural consequence of ubiquitous and pervasive computing. In this scenario, in cities, linked services are driven mainly by distinct political, entrepreneurial, business, and financial interests. This chapter considers and aims to discuss the core-related aspects presented in the current literature that make Brazilian smart cities a reality, as well as the main challenges that these cities face.

Keywords Smart cities · Internet of things · IoT · Governance
Sustainability · Brazil

12.1 Introduction

The main goal of this chapter is to look into how Brazilian smart cities can grow more effectively and how the various indicators are being successfully used to support the smart services in these cities. The objective is to perform a survey of these cities and the technologies that are offered or can be offered in a transparent and effective way, despite many political, financial, and social restrictions.

L. A. Rocha (✉)
GPESI Research Group, Software Engineering,
Federal University of Technology—Paraná, Dois Vizinhos, Brazil
e-mail: outrosdiasvirao@yahoo.com.br

© Springer International Publishing AG, part of Springer Nature 2018
Z. Mahmood (ed.), *Smart Cities*, Computer Communications and Networks,
https://doi.org/10.1007/978-3-319-76669-0_12

We believe that this research will prove useful to understand how smart services are offered to the Brazilian population and to highlight what reasons contribute to the delivery of quality services within these cities.

Smart city is a concept, that is fast becoming a reality, that involves much more than just the various technologies. Although there is not a definitive formal definition [1], it is well accepted that smart cities are cities concerned with the use of new technologies and the improvement in their current urban services to accommodate increasing city growth. Smart cities contemplate transportation, technology, infrastructure, sustainability, and governance issues [2]. New urbanization technologies include innovative ways to manage city resources in a sustainable fashion for the entire population. However, nowadays, smart cities can be deemed a natural evolution of the acceptance of new technologies in similar ways to power, gas, or water supply. In order to understand how these technologies affect our daily lives, we can give many examples: parking meters that report availability; cities that manage their resources better; surveillance; real-time traffic jam analysis; transit systems adjustment according to demand; public illumination sensors; Internet hotspots; pets that communicate with embedded devices to inform their location; communication to measure home electric power consumption, urban transport billing, collection of climatic data (weather forecast); and many others. It is observed that the use of new technologies is not obligatory, but to rethink current alternatives for managing and improving urban services.

Smart city concepts describe better practices of public resource usage to offer quality services to the population. This objective is generally attained through the management of operational costs to offer sustainable services [3]. Within this context, the Internet of Things (IoT) is an interesting alternative because it brings up new possibilities to optimize the management of traditional public services, such as the public area maintenance, surveillance, illumination, transport, garbage collection, noise monitoring, traffic jams, energy consumption, and many others. The urban phenomenon is a reality, and the majority of the population is concentrated in cities nowadays [4]. This reality requires special attention to urban management improvement. This topic comes together with the large dissemination of ICT (Information and Communication Technologies) in areas that had not been considered in earlier years: schools and universities, transit management, hospitals, governmental departments, open area surveillance, and many new business opportunities [4]. New technologies will not solve urban management problems completely, but they will offer new mechanisms to minimize the problems and point toward alternatives [4]. ICT frequently offers many affordable services with great availability, precision, broad analysis of big data in a short time, mobility, and many other features that are essential to our lives. In previous decades, no one would have imagined that current services such as telephony, electricity, gas, and running water would be so easily available in our homes. So, it is not an overstatement to imagine that ICT services will become more of a reality to urban populations within the next decades [4].

However, some questions need to be considered to offer quality services to large populations: city halls are managed by mayors with the support of city councilmen and people's representatives. Even with governmental aims, many city halls receive limited governmental resources to invest in many areas of their administration, such as education, security, sports, health, urban infrastructure, personnel wages, and many other areas. Reducing expenses is the major concern of managers at present. In this sense, ICT electronic or e-services are a realistic alternative to improve the sustainability of cities and offer better services at lower costs. However, it is necessary to foster investments to reinforce the base of these services. In this sense, this chapter relates the various aspects to make IoT services accessible in Brazilian cities. There are many aspects: politics, finance, establishment of patterns, communication restrictions, technological aspects, increasing network data link and bandwidth, and others. We propose a discussion on these items illustrating successful case studies where new services are offered to the population. Our objective is to evaluate the reasons that contribute to bring these services with quality to the population.

The remaining chapter is structured as follows. Section 12.2 deals with a set of related works that are significant to the reality of Brazilian cities. Section 12.3 explores the main aspects needed to make new services available to smart cities: collaboration, communication, business, market, and sustainable services. Section 12.4 investigates how Brazilian cities are increasing their service offerings to their populations with new technologies. Section 12.5 concludes this chapter.

12.2 Background

This section provides an overview of new and current technologies that are suitable for smart cities. Recent studies state that up to 2% of the planet is covered by cities that consume 75% of the energy supply and are responsible for high rates of gases that pollute the atmosphere [5]. Also, a high population increase in cities is expected, and in Brazil, this reality is not different. The Brazilian population is aging, and estimated life expectancy for the next decade is about 80 years.

The Brazilian local governments are greatly concerned in improving urban health care to the population. Current governments have implemented a large urban project known as "Minha Casa, Minha Vida" [6] that already offers more than one million homes to the low-income population. To be eligible, future homeowners must meet a number of requirements: a potential familiar candidate must not have made previous loans, must not have any home property, and must have a good credit history. Also, family rents must reach up to BRL 1800.00. This project is a partnership between enterprises, cities, and state governments, which will offer loans to be paid in 120 monthly installments calculated over 5% of family income [6]. However, they are not smart where the best practices of sustainability are concerned. Some authors [5] argue that this infrastructure uses a very basic building material that will give in under inclement weather, the houses are very similar and close to each other, and are not sustainable. It is necessary to rethink this traditional model of housing with similar alternatives that are cost-effective and that offer a new alternative to energy consumption, new mechanisms of sanitation, garbage collection, and human care living infrastructure. Realistic alternatives to low-income families are not the same as those for high-income classes. From this point of view, low-income families are highly dependent on government investment to support any kind of innovation. This is an important consideration, because the majority of the Brazilian population earned about BRL 1226.00 in 2016 [7].

Smart cities should consume less resources, should be less polluting, and less costly to manage [5]. São Gonçalo do Amarante, a city in Ceará state, is an example of a pilot project that has the objective to build a smart city infrastructure to accommodate 20,000 inhabitants. This project is supported by an Italian enterprise and stands on four pillars: architecture, technology, environment, and social inclusion. Innovations include green corridors to minimize inclement weather, cycle paths, pedestrian areas, waste treatment, exploitation of pluvial resources, mobility services, intelligent garbage collection, solar and wind energy supply, air and water quality monitoring, free wireless digital Internet access provided, smart electricity and water supply improvements, security surveillance, smart public illumination, shared gardens, and many opportunities of collaboration with digital media [5].

Many researchers are active in smart city studies in Brazil. Brazilian cities comply with only 50% of reference [8] indicators. The urban system enterprise [9] states that it is possible to classify smart cities according to such indicators. Also, the MCTIC (Ministério de Ciência e Tecnologia da Informação e Comunicação) has expressed interest in providing support to Brazilian smart city projects. In 2012, a project known as "Cidades Digitais" [10] provided 342 cities with fiber optic networks, and investments of BRL 245 million. The goal was to establish fiber optic rings through public organizations and offer free Internet access areas to the population. Also, RNP (Rede Nacional de Pesquisa) actually uses a portion of bandwidth for teaching and research activities. This project continued until 2016 [11] with PAC (Programa de Aceleração do Crescimento) through the project "Minha Cidade Inteligente" [12], which evaluated projects for the implementation of fiber optic networks and other solutions for the improvement of surveillance, security, and public illumination in urban areas. It is a well-known fact that many telephone companies put out many kilometers of fiber optic cables under the roadsides of federal roads in São Paulo state.

However, to the best of our knowledge, there is still no Brazilian legislation for smart cities. Five recent initiatives have gained importance [13]: (a) use of urban public illumination service fees in smart cities projects; (b) reduce annual taxes on connected devices in urban areas, such as IoT sensors and smart phones; (c) use of open connection platforms; (d) private incentives to support innovation projects; and (e) improvement of security rules to avoid DDoS attacks.

Important digital security laws are Act 12.965, known as *Marco Civil da Internet* [14], which deals with Internet users' and service providers' obligations and duties, and Act 12.737 [15] (also known as "Carolina Dieckmann" law), which qualifies cybercrimes and prescribes punishments. On the other hand, there is no Brazilian model to guide how these innovations should be implemented.

A recent research sponsored by the Nokia conducted by Machina Research [16] identified three main paths to making smart cities viable:

- the anchor path is the use of a single mobile application to provide urgent public news, such as heavy traffic, accidents, weather forecast and others, and aggregate new applications in collaborative ways;
- the platform path is about providing a large infrastructure to provide a set of intelligent services;
- beta city is based on the evaluation of many pilot projects before their implementation.

This same research identified best practices used in many successful cases, viz., (a) data traffic open rules and transparency; (b) disclosure of services for governmental and nongovernmental institutions to avoid segregation; (c) offering of benefits from innovations, such as intelligent parking areas, surveillance, green areas, bicycle paths, and many others to the population; (d) scalability of services with security; and (e) transparence and independence in the partnerships for the implementation to reduce dependence on proprietary solutions.

12.3   Brazilian Smart City Indicators

This section explores the main factors that are needed to make new services available to Brazilian smart cities. Many authors use independent practices and methodologies to classify smart cities [1, 2]. So, there is not a consensus about what model is better, but a set of indicators are evaluated to increase the chances of success. In a sense, large enterprises are interested in these indicators to explore new business possibilities. ISO 37120 classifies a city as "smart" when it has "smart" economy, mobility, environment, people, lifestyle, and governance characteristics [1]. We believe that all these indicators are broad and necessary to classify smart services in Brazilian cities. We cannot ignore their existence, because they collaborate with each other. However, in our current research, we are especially interested in investigating "Technology and Innovation" indicators. Based on this assumption, we restrict the explanations of the other indicators because they are out of the scope of our current research. Urban systems [18] define a set of 10 indicators for smart cities including (1) mobility, (2) urbanism, (3) environment, (4) energy, (5) technology and innovation, (6) health, (7) security, (8) education, (9) entrepreneurship, and (10) governance. As an illustration, we summarize in Table 12.1, a group of sub-indicators with common features [1, 2, 9, 17, 18] regarding only the *Technology and Information factor* in Brazilian smart cities. These indicators allow sorting the cities by individual inside indicators as well as by their sum. For example, the city of São Paulo is ranked first because it scored more sum points in all these 10 indicator groups, while Guarapuava city ranks first only for indicator group 4 (Energy) in the energy supply indicator subset.

Table 12.1 Summary of the technology and innovation indicator group

Item/indicator 5—technology and innovation
(5.1) Internet connection bandwidth
(5.2) Optic fiber connection
(5.3) 4G mobile coverage
(5.4) Free high bandwidth
(5.5) Multimedia communication service access
(5.6) Inclusion in the "cidade digital" project

In this chapter, we are interested in investigating the *Technology and Innovation* indicator which is item 5, as proposed by [18], regarding Brazilian cities. This choice does not mean that the other indicators are not relevant, but they are out of the scope of this research. Our considerations, with respect to the items referring to the Technology and Innovation indicator, as shown in Table 12.1, are the following:

- **Internet connection bandwidth**: according to Akamai [19], the average broadband connection bandwidth in Brazil (ADSL, cable modem, and 3G connections) in 2016 was below the global median, reaching about 6.4 Mbps against the global average of 7 Mbps. However, IPv6 implementation increased approximately 11% in 2016. The research also indicated that the average mobile connection broadband speed in Brazil was about 4.7 Mbps, against the global average of 7 Mbps [20].
- **Optical fiber connections:** this is relatively recent when compared to other countries. According to [21], governmental incentives granted to ISPs through BNDES (*Banco Nacional de Desenvolvimento Social*), and FTTx (Fiber To The x) tax breaks, network projects were mainly responsible for making network access to the population possible. Conventional broadband connections are becoming obsolete, and Passive Optic Networks (PON) are being adopted gradually. On the other hand, in contrast to conventional copper wire networks, the fiber optic connection infrastructure is more expensive and, consequently, broadband subscriptions will be more expensive too. In Brazil, only 1.31 million accesses to broadband Internet are done by FTTx, against 25.56 million conventional broadband accesses [21]. Anatel [22] informed that medium-sized ISPs are responsible for maintaining about 2.28 million broadband Internet accesses. These ISPs compete with corporate ISPs that impose client data traffic restrictions. The 2010 Brazilian project "*Plano Nacional de Banda Larga*" (PNBL) did not achieve the expected results [22]. The government has recently relaunched a follow-up program under the name *Regime Especial do Programa Nacional de Banda Larga* (REPNBL) with an investment of over BRL 15 billion in broadband networks. The goal is to offer broadband Internet to 95% of the population and cover 70% of Brazilian cities, with an incredible broadband speed of up to 25 Mbps [22, 23]. Also, there has been several changes in TV subscription, radio broadcast policies, and the "*Marco Civil da Internet*" Act [23]. It is important to bear in mind that most of these initiatives are not driven

to offer free broadband with quality to the population, but by public/private network infrastructure investments to improve commercial services. In 2016, 218 million Internet accesses were reached [22].

- **4G mobile coverage:** this coverage should have been available for the 2014 World Cup host cities, but the initiative is still being implemented by telephony companies and electricity concessionaries at present. These companies use conventional street lamp posts to reduce investments in new infrastructure [24]. According to a report by OpenSignal [25], the current 4G bandwidth average speed is about 19.7 Mbps, but reaches up to 25.6 Mbps with some mobile operators. LTE services are still in progress and their main problem is availability. According to this same report, LTE services failed to be active for more than 60% of the time in tests. Access to LTE services is still limited, but the average latency in tests was about 52 ms.
- **Free high bandwidth:** according to the magazine Exame.com [26], only 57% of the Brazilians have Internet access. Due to the general communications Act 9472/1997 [27], telecommunication companies are authorized to offer Internet services, but no additional services. These additional services are frequently offered by ISPs (e.g., e-mail account, newsletter, credentials (user and password) to access the Internet through the ISP service portal, and others). Most telecommunication companies already offer free Internet access for their clients, but those clients are free to choose free access from other ISPs. Free Internet access is not synonymous with free broadband, because telephone companies charge for telephone line utilization and offer free Internet access as an additional service. Besides, it is well known that free broadband is available in most Brazilian schools, universities, and federal institutions, as well as in many public areas. An important consideration about this assumption is that it is not possible to offer free broadband with little investment in public infrastructure to be able to maintain service quality to a large number of users. If the quality offered is low, people will prefer investing in broadband services in their own homes to using public services. As a consequence, it will imply in wasted government resources to the population. But investments in infrastructure are equally important to offer better broadband services with quality to end users, and the end users will accept/justify the relatively high investments in city infrastructure if they observe a reduction in the cost of their own domestic use and/or improvement in urban quality of life. In part, privatization of telecommunications reduced governmental expenses with telecommunication infrastructure, and the government regulates the infrastructure maintenance and expansion [28].
- **Multimedia communication:** this is defined by Resolution 614/2013 [29]. This document defines multimedia as audio, video, data, voice, image, text signals, and any other type of information. According to this document, multimedia communication enables the transmission, emission, and reception of multimedia information by service provider subscribers. However, the exploration of these services is not free [30] because they are guided toward enterprises and

companies, even radio broadcast in the same edification. The access to these services by the population is transparent, but highly dependent on broadband availability.

• **Inclusion in the *"Cidade Digital"* project:** this project started in early 2013 and was known as the *"Cidades Digitais"* government program [10]. It was included in the PAC , and 262 municipalities with a population of up to 50,000 inhabitants were selected [10]. This program continued in 2016 [11] with financing for the installation of a fiber optic network, offer of e-govern applications, public servant training, and free Internet hotspots in public areas. These projects are aimed at public, state, and municipal entities. Through Decree 8777/2016, the Federal Govern defined the rules for public data disclosure. Nowadays, many public service portals are available on the Internet. However, although these data are available, finding them is no simple task due to the complexity of the search mechanism [31].

12.4 Brazilian Smart Cities—A Case Study

This section investigates how Brazilian cities use technology and innovation for their citizens. Table 12.2 shows the best ranking smart cities as suggested by [18], in terms of technology and innovation indicators. We investigate how ICT technologies are offered and utilized in these Brazilian cities.

We investigated five of the best ranking Brazilian smart cities. We chose these cities because they ranked best in 2016 [18], in terms of the 10 indicators, as mentioned before: (1) mobility, (2) urbanism, (3) environment, (4) energy, (5) technology and innovation, (6) health, (7) security, (8) education, (9) entrepreneurship, and (10) governance. Our methodology is focused on the argument about technology and innovation (Item 5) indicators in these cities.

The other cities present little discrepancies to maintain the rank position between 2015 and 2016, but there are isolated cases where the variation is greater than ten positions.

Rio de Janeiro (RJ)

In 2016, Rio de Janeiro (RJ) was considered the smartest Brazilian city [18, 33]. Within this same context, a recent study from the Inter-American Development Bank [34] indicated some technological requirements for this success case. Since 2009, when it was chosen to host the Olympic Games, Rio de Janeiro experienced one of the greatest urban transformations, and the marketing about it was important to attract new investors. This study realized in association with the Korean Research Institute for Human Settlements (KRIHS) included the experience of the city of Rio de Janeiro in smart city initiatives, focusing mainly on the Rio Operations Center Project (COR). The methodology was based on many areas: field research, site visits, publications, and interviews held with local government representatives.

Table 12.2 Brazilian smart city ranking for the technology and innovation factor

2015	2016	City (State)	2015	2016	City (State)
1	3	São Paulo (SP)	26	33	Santo André (SP)
2	1	Rio de Janeiro (RJ)	27	–	Cuiabá (MT)
3	8	Florianópolis (SC)	28	–	Uberlândia (MG)
4	9	Porto Alegre (RS)	29	31	Manaus (AM)
5	2	Brasília (DF)	30	–	Campina Grande (PB)
6	4	Campinas (SP)	31	29	Barueri (SP)
7	5	Belo Horizonte (MG)	32	30	Juiz de Fora (MG)
8	16	Curitiba (PR)	33	39	Osasco (SP)
9	6	Recife (PE)	34	10	Campo dos Goytacazes (RJ)
10	11	Salvador (BA)	35	–	São José do Rio Preto (SP)
11	13	Fortaleza (CE)	36	32	Piracicaba (SP)
12	20	São Carlos (SP)	37	–	Santos (SP)
13	–	Goiânia (GO)	38	50	São Bernardo do Campo (SP)
14	–	Campo Grande (MS)	39	–	Camaçari (BA)
15	17	Vitória (ES)	40	44	Indaiatuba (SP)
16	12	São José dos Campos (SP)	41	24	São Caetano do Sul (SP)
17	–	Niterói (RJ)	42	–	Rio Branco (AC)
18	15	Belém (PA)	43	–	Palmas (TO)
19	–	Maringá (PR)	44	40	Joinville (SC)
20	–	Ribeirão Preto (SP)	45	–	Maceió (AL)
21	47	Natal (RN)	46	–	Aracaju (SE)
22	–	Santa Maria (RS)	47	36	Canoas (RS)
23	–	Londrina (PR)	48	–	Petrópolis (RJ)
24	46	João Pessoa (PB)	49	–	Cascavel (PR)
25	–	Teresina (PI)	50	–	Pelotas (RS)

Note Cities marked as "–" ranked much lower in that year

The research observed the events monitored, the mechanisms of access, the dissemination of information, and the decision-making process [34]. The study revealed that Rio de Janeiro is a special case where the entire city is monitored by more than 1000 video surveillance cameras, with over 500 dedicated professionals [34]. The dedicated Rio Operations Center registers occurrences in the city in real time in a collaborative manner. The COR building is equipped with workstations, IP phones in wired LAN, CISCO telepresence equipment, internal video wall sectors, the largest one with 10,446-in. screens and others with four, six, and eight screens, video conferencing and sound systems, WLAN wireless network, printer pooling, and other IT devices. COR uses 2 Gbps Internet access links, and the camera signal is transmitted via radio by TCP protocol [34]. On the other hand, many administrative sector urban services, car traffic, bus schedule, school services, and hospital services are monitored in real time. Another important factor is the common use of social media technologies, such as Alerta Rio, Moovit, Waze, Facebook, Instagram, and many others that are intensively used by the population. As to mobility, there are Rapid Bus Transit (BRT), Bus Rapid System (BRS) corridors, and Light Rail Vehicle (LRV) and subway expansion in partnership with the state government. Rio de Janeiro uses a Digital Inclusion Program to grant access to mobile phones, computers, and the Internet [34]. The city's telecommunication network has a fiber optic cable extension of over 480 km. High-speed connections allow for the integration of administrative buildings, including CORs, schools, and hospitals [34]. Now, regarding interactivity and communication, the city uses social networks to discuss and propose public policies to the population. A collection of more than 4000 ideas resulted in two mobile applications widely used by the population: Easy Taxi and Procon Carioca [34]. Unfortunately, Rio de Janeiro is known as one of the most violent cities in Brazil, and these studies did not take into consideration how the high violence rates affect the quality of life of the population.

Brasilia (DF)

Brasília is similar to São Paulo and Rio de Janeiro regarding investments in qualified professionals for the technology areas. Brasilia is the capital of the Brazil and situated in the Federal District. It is an important technology center, featuring a large number of technology enterprises that provide services to other Brazilian regions. The most common smart services are 4G mobile telephone services, large number of research scholarships from CNPq, and a large number of patent filings by its universities and research centers [18]. In 2016, Brasilia had 28% formal employment for higher education professionals [18]. Additionally, the city received one of the major federal investments in research scholarships from CNPq [18]. It has one of the best universities in the country, University of Brasilia (UnB), as well as technologic centers, start-up incubators, and consultants specialized in new enterprises.

São Paulo (SP)

São Paulo city is the capital of São Paulo state and the most important technology and innovation center in the country. São Paulo city is one of the best-known examples of a Brazilian smart city, despite its many urban metropolitan problems. This city offers high-quality communication technologies such as high network bandwidth, LTE technologies and fiber optic networks. Also, there is a large number of public illumination sensors and surveillance devices that have call centers connected to monitoring cameras from the Public Security Department since 2014 [16]. São Paulo has a large number of patents filed at the INPI (*Instituto Nacional de Propriedade Intelectual*), and CNPq (*Conselho Nacional de Desenvolvimento Científico e Tecnológico*) and offers a large number of research scholarships. Another important innovation is the Fab labs projected for many schools as alternative 3D prototyping. Other innovations concern air quality monitoring, vehicle traffic management, shared gardens, and urban mobility [18].

Campinas (SP)

Campinas city is an important research and technology center. It is known in the region mainly for highly educated and qualified professionals. The University of Campinas (UNICAMP) is considered one of the best universities in the country. It is also known for its tradition to attract investments from many international enterprises, such as Lenovo, 3M, IBM, Samsung, and many others. There are important research centers that collaborate with the universities to leverage the quality of research in the region. The most common smart city services are available such as camera surveillance, high network bandwidth, LTE technologies, and fiber optic networks. The city logistics supports large vehicle traffic, a large road network, fiber optic networks, and camera surveillance services [18]. Viracopos International airport is rated one of the best Brazilian airports [32]. The city offers free quality wireless Internet in many public areas. It is well known that Campinas city has many startups and partnerships between academia and private companies.

Belo Horizonte (MG)

Belo Horizonte is the capital of Minas Gerais state. It has mobile telephone companies with 4G support, high rates of multimedia communication utilization, and highly educated technology professionals [18]. The most common smart city technology services available are camera surveillance, high network bandwidth, LTE technologies, and fiber optic networks [18]. Unfortunately, Belo Horizonte is known as one of the cities with the highest violence rates in the country, and its road network and accessibility services are lacking. However, it offers better urban services than the other cities mentioned, such as water supply, waste collection, and urban reforestation. An important consideration is about investments in photovoltaic energy. In 2016, Belo Horizonte received the third major governmental investment in research scholarships from CNPq [18].

12.4.1 Brazilian Smart City Success Factors

Many reasons and success factors contribute toward making smart cities a reality. These include the following:

- Planning, Incentive, Assistance, and Governance: it is important to note that many smart services are provided by private enterprises and it is not clear if the way that these services are offered to the population has been planned. Planning should be supported by governance to define regulatory laws in cooperation between public and private interests. In particular, these cities should encourage fair competition, assistance support to large-scale innovation, monitoring to leverage the quality of these services, and clear billing rules for these new services to avoid speculation;

- ICT technologies: these are important because they open new possibilities for optimizing resource management, but these technologies must be offered to the population with quality;
- Universities, research centers, and government incentives: for new enterprises contribute to the development of these cities;
- Government investment: this must be offered in a transparent way to avoid questions about how they are employed;
- Investment in technology infrastructure: this must be planned for it to evolve with security, efficiency, and sustainability to serve the population;
- Innovation: it is necessary but not sufficient for its own sake because it is allied to other indicator groups. So, integrated planning on how to offer each one of these groups of indicators is necessary.

Furthermore, recent technologies are gradually changing the way that the population uses technology in daily life. As a recent example, Zanella et al. [3] define IoT as a paradigm where electronic devices interact with each other through Internet protocols. In this sense, IoT explores a range of applications in many areas such as home help, health care, energy management, smart grids, traffic management, industry automation, and others. According to these authors, there are some restrictions to its effective use, some of them related to network quality to forward data traffic to tens of thousands of devices. Cisco [35] describes IoT as a set of interactions with conventional technologies. Complementing the latter, the Internet of Everything (IoE) is defined as a combination of processes, businesses, and people [35]. Note that conventional technologies can be incorporated, but they will be highly dependent on high bandwidth quality. Even so, it is possible to optimize conventional network protocols to send smaller amounts of data between end hosts. In this sense, it is possible to use most solutions, such as proxy server, HTTP-based solutions, WAN cloud technologies, HTTP/REST, IPv6, sensors to optimize energy consumption, Ethernet Wi-Fi, and IEEE standards for IoT that embrace web services architectures due to well-documented protocols, for example, XML/W3C, XML Schema, AJAX, and RESTful services.

These technologies can be used to offer tens of billions of new services to smart cities, such as machine-to-machine interaction and Fog networks. One of the most interesting aspects about IoT is its possibility to develop small, dedicated embedded systems at low cost with features similar to those of legacy proprietary systems. These features enable prototyping in a relatively short time. Besides, there are plenty of small IoT devices that are available in several electronic component stores. We highlight that these technologies are already being used in many areas, such as dynamic weather forecast, urban transportation with smart cards, RFID, highway toll automatic billing, and others.

According to [36], only 20% of Brazilian cities with over 200,000 inhabitants have smart public transportation solutions, surveillance cameras, or any kind of public lighting sensor. This same study revealed that São Paulo has near 8 million vehicles. This city has GPS in buses and bus arrival identifiers in many bus stops. There are companies that offer mobile apps for train and subway lines, and current transportation operation status. In a sense, there has been a high wave of mobile apps since the spread of relatively low-cost mobile phones. Most of the users prefer Android Smartphone, but up to 92% of these users have applications from foreign developers [37]. Act 11.196/05 (known as *Lei do Bem*) grants fiscal incentives to technology innovation and research companies. Unfortunately, many of these companies redirect these fiscal incentives to their own internal research, and not to other institutions, such as public universities and other research centers.

The development of technology and innovation in these cities is very similar. At least 30% of the professionals in these cities have higher education [18]. Network infrastructure offers high network bandwidth, and uses 3G, 4G, and 5G technologies. Also, network infrastructure offers high bandwidth fiber optic support. These cities have a large number of patents filing at the INPI, and CNPq grants a large number of research scholarships. Each of these cities promotes their own government projects in partnership with private enterprises and/or nongovernmental initiatives [18].

12.4.2 Other Challenges Facing Brazilian Smart Cities

Although there are many success cases, many factors make the offering of smart services to the general public much difficult. A well-known example is the use of water management best practices to optimize water distribution. It is well known that some large Brazilian metropolitan cities, such as São Paulo and Brasilia, need to reduce water distribution, having adopted water distribution rotation due to a historical drought period in 2015/2016. Also, in that same period, the ONS (National Electrical System Operator) needed to readequate Brazilian electrical distribution due high energy consumption by the population. The main reason was unusually high temperatures, which resulted in high thermal discomfort [38]. Additional energy from thermal power plants was employed during this period, but resulted in an increase in electricity service fees to the population, known as a "red flag" period. Similar considerations can be made about the management of railroads, subway, and highway vehicle traffic. Brazil is a global leader in heavy-duty transport, and metropolitan cities are facing traffic management problems. In a holistic overview, mobile applications can be used to inform road status in real time and help indicate potential points for street expansion, and/or speed reduction to improve vehicle flow.

Another issue is that governments will need to invest more in health services in the short term, which was not planned in earlier decades. Smart cities will obligatorily offer better health technologies to their growing populations. Recently, the social security rules have been changed based on the Brazilians' life expectancy and current social security funds. In short, each employer indirectly pays for part of the employee s' wages to the government, which goes to social security. But this money goes to pay the wages of other current retirees and pensioners. Due to the current political instability, a chain of problems is observed: many companies are closing down, dismissing employees, and failing to pay social security taxes. As a consequence, fewer funds are deposited in the public coffers, and fewer resources are available to pay current and future retirees and pensioners. Another issue that major researches do not consider in smart cities is the higher violence rates in Brazilian metropolitan cities [39, 40] and the social gap [41], i.e., only investing in technology and innovation is not synonymous with improvement in urban quality of life. As a normal condition in growing cities, urban policies to improve the quality of life, health, and education are also necessary to make smart cities a reality. Other direct consequences in growing urban areas are traffic noise and air and water pollution.

Important topics within this context are the substantial initiatives to provide free software to government departments. Since 2005, E-Gov [42], a government project, has sought to modernize public service management. This project includes the automation of public processes and services to citizens via the Internet, for example, vehicle licensing, income tax filing via Internet (known as *Receitanet*), payments of many municipal and federal tributes, urban cleaning, and others. Brazil is also a leader in Latin America on the disclosure of government data, and its prescription is regulated by Statute 8.777 [43]. The Brazilian Open Data Portal [44] makes a very large amount of government data available over the Internet. Regarding public financial institutions, the major examples are Brazilian banks *Banco do Brasil*, and *Caixa Econômica Federal*. These institutions divulge the use of open source software in bank operations publicly [45, 46].

12.5 Conclusion

This last section summarizes comments relating to the current research and final considerations. Recent studies [47] claim that before discussing smart city projects, it is important to think about smart people. It is necessary to adopt a holistic approach that brings solutions together in the urban environment. Strategies must go beyond technology and must be implemented with process management and planning. Smart cities contribute to make urban centers more efficient and to improve the population's quality of life. Hence, participation of the population is essential to effectively implement new services. This same document states that smart cities put citizens at the center of planning and use ICT to better manage public services, and consequently improve human quality of life in urban areas. An actually smart city uses technologies to offer a set of sustainable services. These technologies include land and mobile high-speed broadband connectivity networks, sensors, mobile applications, and many others. The massification of smart phones and mobile wireless networks still faces many challenges, because most Brazilian cities are still on the way to offering better quality broadband services to the population. The Brazilian government has belatedly granted many fiscal incentives to help improve private network infrastructures.

References

1. Benamrou B, Mohamed B, Bernoussi AS, Mustapha O (2016) Ranking models of smart cities. In: 4th IEEE international colloquium on information science and technology (CiSt), Tangier, 2016. IEEE, pp 872–879
2. Afonso RA et al (2017) Brazilian smart cities: using a maturity model to measure and compare inequality in cities. ACM. http://dl.acm.org/citation.cfm?id=2757426
3. Zanella A, Bui N, Castellani A, Vangelista L, Zorzi M (2014) Internet of things for smart cities. IEEE Internet Things J 1(1):22–32
4. Fornetti V (2014) Os Segredos das Cidades Inteligentes. Revista Exame, Brazil, Aug 2014
5. Planet The Smart City (2016) Smart city Laguna. http://smartcitylaguna.com.br/
6. Caixa Econômica Federal (2015) Programa Minha Casa Minha Vida, Entenda como funciona. http://www.caixaminhacasaminhavida.com/programa-minha-casa-minha-vida-entenda-como-funciona/
7. Instituto Brasileiro de Geografia e Estatística (2016) Renda domiciliar per capita. http://www.ibge.gov.br/home/estatistica/indicadores/trabalhoerendimento/pnad_continua/default_renda_percapita.shtm
8. Revista Exame (2016) As 50 cidades mais inteligentes do Brasil em 2016. http://exame.abril.com.br/brasil/as-50-cidades-mais-inteligentes-do-brasil-em-2016/
9. Urban Systems (2015) Connected smart cities apresenta soluções para impulsionar cidades inteligentes no Brasil. http://www.urbansystems.com.br/noticias/ler/29368/connected-smart-cities-apresenta-solucoes-para-impulsionar-cidades-inteligentes-no-brasil
10. MCTI.gov.br (2010) Cidades Digitais. http://www.mcti.gov.br/images/licitacoes/editais-e-avisos-pregao/editais-na-modalidade-pregao/2010/014/EDITAL_14_ANEXO_1.pdf
11. MCTI.gov.br (2016) Tem início a vistoria em municípios do Piauí selecionados pelo programa Cidades Digitais. http://goo.gl/4ntIZX
12. Brasil.gov.br (Web Portal) (2016) Projetos de 172 municípios serão avaliados pelo Minha Cidade Inteligente. http://www.brasil.gov.br/ciencia-e-tecnologia/2016/07/projetos-de-172-municipios-serao-avaliados-pelo-minha-cidade-inteligente
13. Jornal de Brasilia (2016) Frente parlamentar mista é criada para incentivar legislação a favor de cidades inteligentes. http://news.bizmeet.com.br/noticia/frente-parlamentar-mista-e-criada-para-incentivar-legislacao-a-favor-de-cidades-inteligentes, 2016
14. Planalto.gov.br (Web Portal) (2014) Lei nº 12.965, de 23 de abril de 2014. www.planalto.gov.br/ccivil_03/_ato2011-2014/2014/lei/l12965.htm
15. Planalto.gov.br (Web Portal) (2012) Lei nº 12.737. www.planalto.gov.br/ccivil_03/_ato2011-2014/2012/lei/l12737.htm
16. Jackeline C (2016) IPNews, Relatório identifica melhores práticas de 22 cidades inteligentes. https://ipnews.com.br/relatorio-identifica-melhores-praticas-de-22-cidades-inteligentes/
17. Urban Systems (2015) Connected Smart Cities apresenta soluções para impulsionar cidades inteligentes no Brasil. http://www.urbansystems.com.br/noticias/ler/29368/connected-smart-cities-apresenta-solucoes-para-impulsionar-cidades-inteligentes-no-brasil
18. Urban Systems (2016) Ranking connected smart cities. http://www.urbansystems.com.br/
19. Akamai.com (2016) State of the internet/ connectivity—trends report for Q4 2016. https://content.akamai.com/pg8228-q4-2016-soti-connectivity-report.html
20. IDGnow.com.br (2017) Brasil sobe duas posições em ranking de velocidade média da banda larga. http://idgnow.com.br/internet/2017/03/14/brasil-sobe-duas-posicoes-em-ranking-de-velocidade-media-da-banda-larga/
21. João M (2016) Panorama para a expansão de fibra óptica no Brasil em 2016. https://www.cianet.com.br/panorama-para-a-expansao-de-fibra-optica-no-brasil-em-2016/

22. Anatel.gov.br (2016) Fevereiro de 2016 fecha com 25,56 milhões de acessos de banda larga fixa. http://www.anatel.gov.br/institucional/index.php/noticias/1057-fevereiro-de-2016-fecha-com-25-56-milhoes-de-acessos-de-banda-larga-fixa

23. Brasil.gov.br (Web Portal) (2016) Governo prepara atualização do Programa Nacional de Banda Larga. http://www.brasil.gov.br/infraestrutura/2016/03/governo-prepara-atualizacao-do-programa-nacional-de-banda-larga

24. Brasil.gov.br (Web Portal) (2013) Primeira antena 4G do País apresenta solução sustentável. http://www.brasil.gov.br/infraestrutura/2013/03/primeira-antena-4g-do-pais-apresenta-solucao-sustentavel

25. OpenSignal.com (2017) State of mobile networks: Brazil (January 2017). https://opensignal.com/reports/2017/01/brazil/state-of-the-mobile-network

26. Exame.com (2017) App quer oferecer internet gratuita a milhões de brasileiros. http://exame.abril.com.br/pme/app-quer-oferecer-internet-gratuita-a-milhoes-de-brasileiros/

27. Planalto.gov.br (Web Portal) (1997) Lei 9472. http://www.planalto.gov.br/ccivil_03/leis/L9472.htm

28. Teleco.com (2017) Telefonia Móvel no Brasil, o Grande Boom das Empreiteiras. http://www.teleco.com.br/tutoriais/tutorialgpter1/pagina_3.asp

29. Anatel.gov.br (2013) Resolução nº 614, de 28 de maio de 2013. http://www.anatel.gov.br/legislacao/resolucoes/2013/465-resolucao-614

30. Anatel.gov.br (2017) Dúvidas freqüentes. http://www.anatel.gov.br/Portal/exibirPortalPaginaEspecial.do?codItemCanal=1266

31. Gazetaonline.com.br (2017) Teste mostra dificuldade em encontrar dados em sites oficiais. http://www.gazetaonline.com.br/noticias/politica/2016/01/teste-mostra-dificuldade-em-encontrar-dados-em-sites-oficiais-1013920429.html

32. SAC (2015) Secretaria de Aviação Civil. http://www.aviacao.gov.br/noticias/2015/08/passageiros-estao-muito-satisfeitos-com-aeroportos-mais-movimentados-do-brasil/relatorio-geral-1.pdf

33. Connected Smart Cities (2017) Cidades mais inteligentes do País foram conhecidas na manhã desta segunda. http://www.connectedsmartcities.com.br/index.php/cidades-mais-inteligentes-do-pais-foram-conhecidas-na-manha-desta-segunda/

34. Inter-American Development Bank (IDB) (2016) Estudos de casos internacionais de cidades inteligentes: Rio de Janeiro, Brasil. https://publications.iadb.org/handle/11319/7727

35. Cisco Netacad (2017) Introdução à Internet de Todas as Coisas. https://static-course-assets.s3.amazonaws.com/IoE11/PT/index.html

36. TechinBrazil.com (2015) Smart technologies for urban mobility in Brazil. https://techinbrazil.com/smart-technologies-for-urban-mobility-in-brazil

37. TechinBrazil.com (2014) Incentives for mobile app development in Brazil. https://techinbrazil.com/incentives-for-mobile-app-development-in-brazil

38. ONS (2015) Operador Nacional do Sistema Elétrico - Boletim de Carga Especial. http://www.ons.org.br/download/sala_imprensa/BoletimEspecial_20151022.pdf, Oct 2015

39. Julio JW (2016) Mapa da Violência 2016 - Homicídios por Armas de Fogo no Brasil. http://www.mapadaviolencia.org.br/pdf2016/Mapa2016_armas_web.pdf

40. Seguridad, Justicia Y Paz (2017) Metodología del ranking (2016) de las 50 ciudades más violentas del mundo. http://www.seguridadjusticiaypaz.org.mx/biblioteca/prensa/send/6-prensa/239-las-50-ciudades-mas-violentas-del-mundo-2016-metodologia

41. IBGE (2014) Síntese de Indicadores Sociais: Uma Análise das Condições de Vida da População Brasileira. http://biblioteca.ibge.gov.br/visualizacao/livros/liv91983.pdf

42. E-gov (Web Portal) (2005) O que é E-GOV. http://www.governoeletronico.com.br/index.php?option=com_content&task=view&id=19&Itemid=29

43. E-gov (Web Portal) (2017) Brasil está em 8ª lugar no ranking mundial de Dados Abertos. https://www.governoeletronico.gov.br/noticias/brasil-esta-em-8a-lugar-no-ranking-mundial-de-dados-abertos

44. Dados.gov.br (Web Portal) (2017) Portal Brasileiro de Dados Abertos. http://dados.gov.br

45. Software Livre (2017) A migração do CRM da Caixa. http://www.softwarelivre.gov.br/noticias/CAIXA%20CRM
46. Software Livre (2017) Banco do Brasil adota software livre nos servidores. http://www.softwarelivre.gov.br/noticias/BancoBrasil
47. Maurício B et al (2016) The road toward smart cities—migrating from traditional city management to the smart city. https://publications.iadb.org/bitstream/handle/11319/7743/The-Road-towards-Smart-Cities-Migrating-from-Traditional-City-Management-to-the-Smart-City.pdf

Chapter 13
Standards-Based Sustainability Requirements for Healthcare Services in Smart Cities

Sofia Ouhbi, Ali Idri and José Luis Fernández-Alemán

Abstract In Smart Cities, there is a need to reduce overcrowding in hospitals and healthcare institutions, improve the lifestyle of people with chronic disease; promote patient self-management, and independence of patients. All of these can be promoted through connected health services. Current connected health technologies are transforming health care and empowering patients as they are assuming greater responsibility for their own healthcare decisions. This chapter presents connected health solutions to improve healthcare services in smart cities. The aim of the chapter is to present different types and applicationsof connected health services. It also aims to discuss standards related to health informatics. Examples of connected health applications to improve healthcare services for cardiology, obstetrics and blood donation are also presented. Moreover, this chapter presents requirements for sustainable connected health services to improve their large-scale adoption. These requirements are based on the main related software engineering standards, e-health technology standards, and literature and they cover the individual, social, environmental, and technical dimensions of sustainability.

Keywords Smart cities · Health care · Connected health · Requirements
Sustainability · Mobile applications

S. Ouhbi
FIL, Université Internationale de Rabat, Rabat, Morocco

A. Idri (✉)
Software Project Management Research Team, ENSIAS,
University Mohammed V, Rabat, Morocco
e-mail: ali.idri@um5.ac.ma

J. L. Fernández-Alemán
Department of Informatics and Systems, University of Murcia, Murcia, Spain

13.1 Introduction

Smart Cities have the potential to offer advanced healthcare provision to citizens by providing them with connected health services. Connected health can be defined as "the collective term for telecare, telehealth, telemedicine, mHealth, digital health and eHealth services" [1]. In a smart city context, it includes the concept of smart health known also as s-health [2].

Connected health technologies are transforming health care [3] and empowering patients as they are assuming greater responsibility for their own healthcare decisions [4, 5]. In fact, connected health can improve healthcare outcomes by connecting patients with caregivers, and clinicians [6]. They empower people [7, 8], provide an emotional support [9], raise awareness about chronic diseases [10], and improve the access to supportive care [11]. Despite the aforementioned benefits, connected health applications are facing implementation, adoption, and utilization challenges in practice [12]. It is argued that a focus on technology over the formulation of a well-defined value proposition to patients have resulted in many connected health project failures [13]. To promote a large-scale adoption of connected health applications there is a need to promote their sustainability. This chapter presents connected health solutions to improve healthcare services in smart cities. Different types and example of applications of connected health services are presented. Standards related to health informatics and the requirements to achieve sustainability of connected health services are also presented in this chapter.

In the rest of this chapter, we first present the rationale behind the need of connected health in smart cities in Sect. 13.2. Then, we outline the well-known application types of connected health in Sect. 13.3. Section 13.4 presents standards related to health informatics. Examples of fields of application of connected health are presented in Sect. 13.5. In Sect. 13.6, we present requirements to develop/ evaluate sustainable connected health applications. Section 13.7 presents a brief summary.

13.2 Rationale Behind Connected Health in Smart Cities

The widespread adoption of Information and Communications Technology (ICT) has changed the way people deal with information in urban context, which has led to the concept of smart cities. Smart cities can be defined as "cities strongly founded on information and communication technologies that invest in human and social capital to improve the quality of life of their citizens by fostering economic growth, participatory governance, wise management of resources, sustainability, and efficient mobility, whilst they guarantee the privacy and security of the citizens" [2].

One of the areas that are concerned by the concept of smart cities is health care. There is a need to provide advanced assistance and healthcare services within the years to come, especially in densely populated urban areas [2]. Healthcare stakeholders are looking for ways to improve services, reduce costs, and enhance the efficiency of the healthcare system. The ICT revolution offers us the potential to leverage technological innovations to develop proactive connected health to improve healthcare services for smart cities' citizens [14]. Connected health services are efficient tools to improve healthcare services especially, with the advance in the Internet of Things (IoT) and wearable technology [14].

13.3   Applications of Connected Health Services

Self-management of health has been proved to be beneficial to the healthcare sector and to be highly efficient in reducing healthcare costs in populations with diverse chronic diseases [15, 16]. Health records usage has been strongly recommended by healthcare professionals to improve healthcare quality [17]. This section presents two main types of health records, viz., electronic personal health records (EHRs) and personal health records (PHRs). This section also presents a widespread connected health system, which can be considered as the clinical decision support system (CDSS).

13.3.1   Electronic Health Records (HER)

EHRs offer healthcare centers and institutions the possibility to improve the management of their patients' health data. Currently, many physicians are using EHRs to improve healthcare quality and efficiency. A large number of companies have emerged to provide hospitals with the opportunity to adopt EHRs within a healthcare platform proposing different functionalities and services, which achieve certain certification criteria. A healthcare organization or institution in which authorized clinicians can enter and manage a patient's health-related information maintains the EHR.

The usage of an EHR can be tremendously beneficial for a healthcare center, and can lead to the following advantages [18]: potential productivity, financial improvement, quality of care improvement, rapid and remote access to patient information, easier chronic disease management, and improved continuity of care. Many healthcare institutions promote the adoption of EHRs, such as the Health Information Technology for Economic and Clinical Health (HITECH) Act which supports a meaningful usage of EHRs by hospitals and clinicians through Medicare and Medicaid incentive payments to physicians and hospitals [19].

13.3.2 Personal Health Records (PHR)

PHRs are more than just static repositories for patient data; they combine data, knowledge, and software tools, which help patients to become active participants in their own care [20]. PHRs are private applications through which patients may access, manipulate, and keep tracking of their health data [21]. PHRs can include data entered by the patient and/or from other sources such as laboratories, and Electronic Medical Records (EMRs) or EHRs [22].

There are many types of PHRs: USB-based PHRs [23], Web-based PHRs [24], and mobile PHRs (mPHRs) [25]. An mPHR is a mobile application that allows users to access and coordinate their health data through their mobile devices such as smartphones or tablets [25]. The usage of an mPHR can be tremendously beneficial for smartphone users, and can lead to [26]: improve patient engagement, easier chronic disease management, encourage family health management, improve quality of care, rapid access to health information, and improved continuity of care. An mPHR can be very useful for people suffering from a chronic disease such as diabetics or cardiovascular disease [27], especially in emergency cases, where they can access easily their health data, which is available in their smartphones or tablets. A large number of applications have been developed to provide users with the opportunity to choose mPHRs within a mobile platform proposing different functionalities.

13.3.3 Clinical Decision Support Systems (CDSS)

A recent research [28] showed an increased amount of CDSS applications owing to continuing advances in medical informatics technology. CDSS is a type of application that interprets specific patient information that is entered into the system in order to provide assistance in making the most appropriate and safe decisions when providing patient care. According to Osheroff et al. [29], CDSS could be defined as the "act of providing clinicians, patients and other health care stakeholders with pertinent knowledge and/or person-specific information, intelligently filtered or presented at appropriate times, to enhance health and health care."

CDSS aims to increase quality of care, helps to avoid errors and adverse events, improves efficiency and reduces costs. It covers a set of tools to improve decision-making in the clinical workflow, such as computerized alerts and reminders to healthcare providers and patients, clinical guidelines, and diagnostic support [30, 31]. There are two main types of CDSS:

- Knowledge-based CDSS which contains the rules and associations of compiled data in order to be combined with the patient's data and show the results to the user, such as electronic health records (EHRs) [30].

- Non-knowledge-based CDSS which uses machine learning techniques allowing computers to learn from past experiences and/or find patterns in clinical data [32, 33].

13.4 Standards

In order to facilitate the widespread use of connected health, there is a need to implement standardized platforms. This section presents a list of standards related to health informatics. Many international organizations are working on the standardization of connected health applications such as the one listed below. Each one addresses different issues related to connected health technology standards and specifications, e.g., architectures, interfaces, interoperability, accessibility, privacy, security, and internationalization.

- CLSI [34]: Clinical and Laboratory Standards Institute.
- ITU-T/ITU-D [35]: International Telecommunication Union.
- eHSCG [36]: e-health Standardization Coordination Group.
- DICOM organization [37]: Digital Imaging and Communications in Medicine organization.
- OASIS [38]: Organization for the Advancement of Structured Information Standards.
- CEN/TC 251 [39]: European Committee for Standardization Technical Committee 251.
- ISO/TC 215 [40]: International Organization for Standardization's (ISO) Technical Committee (TC) on health informatics.
- CEN ISO/IEEE 11073 committee [41]: Medical device communication standards committee.
- IEC/TC 62 [42]: Technical committee for standards regarding electrical equipment in medical practice.

Figure 13.1 represents a landscape of focal points in the area of e-health information obtained from ISO/TR 20514:2005 [43]. Most of these areas have one or more standards available.

More related standards, and further details on these, can be obtained from the ISO, IEEE, and CEN websites and the other standardization organization websites, such as the following:

- ISO/TR 18307:2001 Health informatics—Interoperability and compatibility in messaging and communication standards—Key characteristics. This standard describes the main requirements related to achieve interoperability and compatibility in trusted health information interchange between software applications and systems in health care.

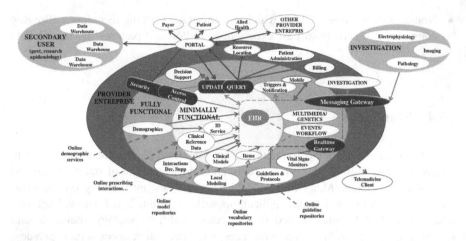

Fig. 13.1 e-health information environment

- CEN/TR 15212:2006 Health informatics—Vocabulary—Maintenance procedure for a web-based terms and concepts database
- EN ISO 21090:2011 Health Informatics—Harmonized data types for information interchange (ISO 21090:2011)
- ISO/TR 20514:2005 Health informatics—Electronic health record—Definition, scope, and context
- ISO/TR 14292:2012 Health informatics—Personal health records—Definition, scope, and context
- ISO/TS 22220:2011 Health informatics—Identification of subjects of health care
- ISO/TS 14265:2011 Health Informatics—Classification of purposes for processing personal health information
- ISO/HL7 27931:2009 Data Exchange Standards—Health Level Seven Version 2.5—An application protocol for electronic data exchange in healthcare environments
- ISO 27799:2008 Health informatics—Information security management in health using ISO/IEC 27002.
- CEN/TR 15640:2007 Health informatics—Measures with which to ensure patient safety as regards health software.

An example of recommendation from standards can be given from ISO/TR 20514-2005 Subsection 3.5.6.3.1.7 on Personal health record [43] that states: *The key features of the PHR are that it is under the control of the subject of care and that the information it contains is at least partly entered by the subject (consumer, patient). There is a widespread misapprehension in the community, including among health professionals, that the PHR must be a completely different entity from the EHR if it is to meet the requirements of patients/consumers to create, enter, maintain, and retrieve data in a form meaningful to them and to control their own health record. This is not correct. There is no reason why the PHR cannot have exactly the same record architecture (i.e., standard information model) as the health provider EHR and still meet all of the patient/consumer requirements listed above. In fact, there is every reason to ensure that a standardized architecture is used for all forms of EHRs (but certainly the ICEHR), to enable sharing of information between them as and when appropriate, under the control of the patient/consumer.*

13.5 Examples of Fields of Applications

Connected health applications have been developed for a wide range of medicine fields. This section presents examples of connected health applications that can advance the quality of services in cardiology, blood donation, and obstetrics fields.

13.5.1 *Cardiology*

Cardiovascular diseases are the leading cause of death throughout the world [44]. Keeping track of the heart rate (HR) can be very important in the prevention and the treatment of cardiovascular diseases [45]. A sudden or major slowing down of a patient's HR, which s/he may detect, can probably indicate a serious heart problem [46]. Moreover, the pulse pressure is an important predictor for coronary heart disease [47]. Heart problems can be better understood by analyzing data from health records [48].

The analysis of the autonomic control of the heart may identify patients at higher risk for sudden cardiac death [49]. The diagnosis of autonomic nervous system (ANS) disorders is of utmost importance as these disorders are associated with a severe disease burden [50]. The ANS *controls the synergistic action of all visceral organs in the human body* [51]. The ANS disorders can lead to several health dysfunctions, such as dysfunctions of blood pressure, heart rate digestion, urinary function, and sexual function [51]. Analyzing patient's health history is essential in the ANS evaluation and can avoid the need for additional testing which may cause a substantial delay in diagnosis [50]. Extra time spent by doctors on the patient's health history is likely to be more profitable than extra time spent on the physical examination [52].

Heart rate can be measured using the fingertip photoplethysmogram signals using camera and flashlight of the user's smartphone. The pulse photoplethysmography (PPG) is based on blood light absorption [53]. This technology has been used in different clinical settings, such as the monitoring of heart rate, blood pressure, cardiac output and respiration [54]. PPG can provide valuable information about the cardiovascular system [55].

Requirements for a mPHR application for cardiology are shown below:

- The mPHR shall have an authentication procedure.

  – The user should be able to access the app using the login (username/password) given by the healthcare center.
  – The user should be able to choose "Remember me" option to skip authentication procedure in future logins.

- The user should be able to visualize his/her profile.

  – The user should be able to read the profile.
  – The user should be able to edit the profile.
  – The profile shall contain personal information: username, password, birth date, height, blood type, and weight.

- The user should be able to visualize the medical record.

  – The user should be able to read the medical record.
  – The medical record should contain the following information: (1) dates, (2) risk factors, (3) exams, (4) ECG, (5) laboratory test results, (6) treating doctor, and (7) diagnosis.

- The user should be able to visualize treatments.

  – The user should be able to read the list of medications and treatments received from the EHR.
  – The mPHR shall display the treatment details: name, period of the treatment, how many intakes and how often to use the treatment per day.
  – The user should be able to share treatments with others using short message service (SMS), email, or social networks.

- The user should be able to visualize appointments.

  – The user should be able to read the appointments fixed by the healthcare workers in the cardiovascular department.
  – The user should be able to call the center to cancel/postpone an appointment.

- The user should be able to enter measurements.

  – The user should be able to enter measurements manually.
  – The user should be able to connect a device to the smartphone with which to measure blood pressure and heart rate.

- The mPHR shall interact with the EHR to receive and send information from and to the server.
- The mPHR shall send an SMS automatically to the treating doctor in case of emergency (high-risk blood pressure and/or heart rate).
- The user should be able to consult help information to manipulate the application.
- The user should be able to have an offline access to the application.

– The user should be able to access the application without the Internet.
– The user should be able to access to the latest received information from the EHR before the Internet connection drops.
– The user should be able to share data via SMS and edit her/his profile offline.

13.5.2 Blood Donation

Blood donation is seen as a noble act as it helps save precious human lives. According to the World Health Organization (WHO), 108 million blood donations take place every year from all types of blood donors (voluntary unpaid, family/replacement, and paid) and 65% of blood transfusions in low-income countries are given to children under 5 years of age [56]. Note that around 50% of blood donations are collected in high-income countries, home to 15% of the world's population [57]. Blood donation is vitally important to the correct delivery of health care. The sufficiency of blood supplies is still one of the major problems of health services [58]. Hospitals and blood donation centers in many countries confront difficulties as regards ensuring a sufficient and safe blood supply [59].

The year 2020 is WHO's target year for all countries to obtain 100% of blood supplies from voluntary unpaid donors. Patients in need are dependent on a constant supply of blood. There is consequently a need to recruit and retain more blood donors, which has traditionally been done using methods such as brochures or videos [60, 61]. New methods have been used to gain attention from blood donors, such as applications to attract more donors and to raise awareness about blood donation.

Blood donation applications are very useful for people in need, particularly in the case of emergencies when it is necessary to identify eligible blood donors. Blood donation applications can help save lives or help volunteers keep records of their blood donation activities. Blood donation applications can provide an insight into and useful information about blood donation types and process. Information on blood donation has been identified as a popular service in smart cities [62].

The following types were identified from the description in the repository of each of the blood donation applications selected from a previous study [63]:

- Find donors. Applications which help the user find donors.
- Find centers. Applications which help the user find centers/hospitals at which she/he can donate blood.
- Records. Applications which record the user's donation history.
- Blood types. Applications which explain information about blood types to the user.
- Blood calculation. Applications which estimate the user's blood type by using the blood types of relatives.

- Related to a center. Applications which provide the user with information related to a center or centers such as blood transfusion services, hospitals, or laboratories.
- Eligibility. Applications which calculate the date on which the user may donate blood based on the date of her/his last donation of blood.
- General information. Applications which provide the user with general information about the blood donation process.

13.5.3 Obstetrics

Pregnancy is one of the health conditions that require meticulous monitoring for both the pregnant woman and the baby, and it extends for a period of 40–41 weeks for normal pregnancies. PHRs for pregnancy are useful for managing and sharing health data with the healthcare providers [64], notably for emergencies by detecting abnormalities on time to prevent severe complications during pregnancy [65]. Therefore, they are supported by obstetricians and gynecologists [66]. The medical information that are stored in the mPHRs for pregnancy cover the pregnant woman's medical history such as her family health history, allergies or immunizations, her obstetrical history such as the contraception or information about previous pregnancies, in addition to health data related to her current pregnancy, so that the pregnant woman keeps track of measurements of the weight, blood pressure, or the waist size [67]. This medical information is easily accessible to health providers and other parties in case of emergencies.

In order to use the mPHR for pregnancy monitoring, the expectant woman should create a profile containing her personal details including: (1) full name, (2) date of birth, (3) marital status, (4) occupation, (5) address, (6) phone number, (7) email, (8) insurance details, (9) family member/partner's contact information. This requirement is crucial for the pregnant woman as in case she needs help she will have someone close to call or contact.

Pregnancy is a critical period in which the pregnant woman needs to keep track of a set of physical body data and measurements in her mPHR for pregnancy monitoring, which are: (1) height; (2) weight. Increased maternal gestational weight gain is associated with increased risks of fetal macrosomia; (3) blood pressure. A high blood pressure may cause severe problems for the fetus and the woman; (4) folic acid. It is very important for the development of a healthy fetus, as it can significantly reduce the risk of neural tube defects; (5) waist size; (6) glucose; (7) temperature; (8) pregnancy symptoms. Tracking pregnancy symptoms such as nausea, vomiting, headache, back pain, etc., is also beneficial in order to avoid complications; (9) heart frequency; (10) fetal height; (11) fetal weight; (12) fetal heart rate; (13) food intake/Diet; and (14) physical activities. Dietary information and physical exercises should be controlled moderately for the pregnant woman.

In addition to her personal profile, the pregnant woman should create a medical profile in her mPHR for pregnancy monitoring, containing health data and her background medical history, as being easily available and useful information for caregivers and other parties in case of emergency. This information is presented as follows: (1) blood group; (2) family health history such as asthma, diabetes, a heart disease, high blood pressure, a genetic disorder, etc.; (3) illness/treatments history; (4) allergies/drugs allergies; (5) medication; (6) surgical history; (7) immunization; (8) social history/lifestyle such as smoking, alcoholism, drug addiction, and tabagism; (9) psychological disorders; and (10) emotional disorders.

The obstetrical history of the pregnant woman and the information related to her current pregnancy are among the main requirements of an mPHR for pregnancy monitoring, as they represent a very important data for health providers to avoid any kind of complications. These requirements are:

- last menstrual period, which helps to calculate the estimated birth date
- estimated due date
- gynecological history, such as gynecological diseases, fertility problems, etc.
- contraception, by identifying the previous contraception method and the date of ceased
- previous pregnancies, by giving information about the mode of delivery, the number of previous pregnancies, the duration of labor, the newborn's sex, the feeding method (e.g., breastfeeding or bottle feeding), abortions, etc.
- pregnancy's complications
- birth plan, by specifying the mobility and position for labor and birth, pain relief, the infant feeding, etc.

13.6   Sustainability of Connected Health Applications

Connected health provides the potential for enhanced reach at a relatively low cost; scalability; time efficiency; and the capacity to provide individual patients including traditionally underserved populations, patients with chronic conditions and consumers all over the world with tailoring and customization [68]. Despite the aforementioned benefits, connected health applications are facing implementation, adoption, and utilization challenges in practice [12, 69]. Developing connected health through the sustainability lens will enable providers to deal with these challenges [70]. Sustainability requirements should be considered at early stages in the software development phase. However, software engineers treat sustainability as a postscript as they are driven by time-to-market pressure and do not have time to apply sustainability guidelines [71].

Recently, research has begun to be undertaken into how to achieve sustainable software also known as green software [72–74]. In fact, achieving sustainability of healthcare systems is one of the objectives of research and innovation financed by the EU [75]. Sustainability is concerned with the economic, individual, social, environment, and technical dimensions which may be positively impacted by connected health applications [76].

To promote a large-scale adoption of connected health applications, there is a need to promote their sustainability. Therefore, there is a need for a requirement catalog, which provides different stakeholders of connected health applications with different requirements set to develop and/or audit sustainable connected health applications. In this section, sustainability is defined as the extent to which an application is adopted and maintained to achieve durability and continuity in use in a given context.

13.6.1 Economic Dimension

Economic sustainability aims to maintain capital assets and added value (interest) assets. Economic sustainability can be taken care of in terms of costs, budget constraints, long-term business objectives, and market requirements [73] among other economic requirements.

Requirements of economic dimension depend on variable factors and they can vary according to the needs of the industry. For this reason, general economic requirements for connected health applications cannot be provided. These requirements are considered as assigned software requirements which mean that they can be changed without changing the code source of the application.

13.6.2 Individual Dimension

Individual sustainability refers to the maintenance of the individual human capital, e.g., health, education, skills and access to services. Individual sustainability can be covered by privacy, safety, security, human–computer interaction, usability, personal health, and well-being [73].

The list of requirements presented below concerns the individual dimension of connected health applications [70]:

1. The software application (app) shall have a positive individual impact

   a. The app shall respect security and privacy of the user

      i. The app shall have an authentication procedure, i.e.,

         1. The user should be able to choose in the app's settings whether to be authenticated or not
         2. The user should be able to access the app using a login or social network account

    ii. The app shall allow the user to manage personal information, such as different countries' specific legislation or regulations regarding user ownership of personal information

  b. The user should be able to edit personal data in the profile
  c. The user should be able to remove personal data from the profile
  d. The user should be able to add personal data to the profile
  e. The user should be able to share personal data from the profile

2. The app shall promote personal health and well-being of the user

  a. The user should be able to consult health recommendations
  b. The user should be able to manage his/her personal health record, e.g.,

    i. The user should be able to edit the health record data
    ii. The user should be able to remove data from the health record
    iii. The user should be able to add data to the health record
    iv. The user should be able to share data from the health record
    v. The user should be able to import data to the health record
    vi. The user should be able to export data from the health record
    vii. The user should be able to back up data from the health record.

13.6.3 Social Dimension

Social sustainability aims to preserve the social capital and preserve services and solidarity of social communities. Social sustainability can be handled via computer-supported collaborative work [73] that aims to strengthening community building and improve community interaction.

    The list of requirements presented below concerns the social dimension of connected health applications [70]:

1. The software application (app) shall have a positive social impact

  a. The app shall promote interaction among users via social networks and/or online healthcare forums
  b. The app shall promote social solidarity among users via a rewards system

2. The app shall be designed for cultural diversity and multilingual use

  a. The app shall adapt its content to the user's language preferences
  b. The app shall be available in different languages, the languages supported and the links for selecting them should be clearly presented
  c. The app shall allow the user to switch between languages at more than one point while using it
  d. The app shall allow the user to choose the language of the video or audio clips

e. The app shall adapt the online help section to the user's language preferences
f. The app shall adapt the human anatomy terminology to user's language preferences
g. The app shall show the text with a correct text-align depending on the user's language preferences (e.g., right align for the Arabic language)
h. The app shall use appropriate formats, units of measurement or currency for international audience
i. The app shall control the advertisements showed to the user to avoid cultural discrepancies.

13.6.4 Environmental Dimension

Environmental sustainability seeks to improve human welfare by protecting natural resources, such as: water, land, air, minerals, and ecosystem. Any system applied in a real-world context is situated within a natural environment which means that it has an impact on the environment [73]. Environmental sustainability can be managed by controlling resource flow: waste management, life cycle analysis, and environment impact assessment [73].

The list of requirements presented below concerns the environmental dimension of connected health applications [70]:

1. The software application (app) shall have a positive environmental impact

   a. The app shall reduce transportation means

      i. The user should be able to find nearby healthcare centers

   b. If the app connects with EHRs, PHRs or third parties, it shall provide users with the possibility to interchange data

      i. The user should be able to send data from the app to EHRs, PHRs or other parties
      ii. The user shall be able to receive data from EHRs, PHRs or other parties

2. The app shall be convenient for frequent use

   a. The app shall use pictures to explain ideas
   b. The app shall use icons to explain its contents
   c. The app shall use graphs to illustrate health data history

3. The app shall connect to other IT resources

   a. The app shall back up data in data repositories, drivers or cloud systems
   b. The app shall connect to social networks
   c. The app shall use device features such as Bluetooth and/or near-field communication (NFC) technologies
   d. The app shall connect with maps repositories to display locations.

13.6.5 Technical Dimension

Technical sustainability: refers to software systems longevity and their adequate evolution with changing surrounding conditions and respective requirements. Technical sustainability requirements include all requirements, which lead to the longevity of a system such as non-obsolescence requirements and the ISO/IEC 25010 [77] quality characteristics (e.g., maintainability, reliability, and transferability). Moreover, energy efficiency is also part of technical sustainability requirements [73].

The list of requirements presented below concerns the technical dimension of connected health applications [70]:

1. The software application (app) shall have a positive technical impact

   a. The app shall easily adapt to future operating system (OS) changes

      i. The app shall respect mobile OS development guidelines
      ii. The app shall be adapted to the mobile OS platform

2. The app shall be energy efficient

   a. The app shall shut down in idle mode
   b. The app shall create different profiles on the same device

3. The user should be able to have an offline access to the app

   a. The user should be able to access the app without Internet connection
   b. The user should be able to edit data offline
   c. The app shall save edited data offline.

13.7 Conclusion

Although, researchers still have to address some significant challenges, connected health has the potential to transform health and social care in the future [14]. This chapter has presented an overview of connected health application types, fields, and related standards. Functional requirements for applications for cardiology and pregnancy in addition to sustainability requirements for connected health have also been presented. The requirements presented in this chapter have been primarily established from the results of literature reviews and analysis of standards related to software engineering and health informatics. These requirements can be applied in different scenarios and adapted to fully capture the needs and constraints of connected health applications development.

This chapter can be useful to requirements engineering researchers and practitioners concerned with the improvement of health care services in smart cities. Moreover, audit organizations or connected health stakeholders can use the requirements presented in this chapter to evaluate and/or audit connected health applications. A checklist can be generated that includes a set of requirements that can constitute the list of items to be checked and can be adapted to the connected health applications to be evaluated.

References

1. Taylor K (2015) Connected health: how digital technology is transforming health and social care. Deloitte Centre for Healthcare Solutions, London
2. Solanas A, Patsakis C, Conti M, Vlachos IS, Ramos V, Falcone F, Postolache O, Pérez-Martínez PA, Di Pietro R, Perrea DN, Martinez-Balleste A (2014) Smart health: a context-aware health paradigm within smart cities. IEEE Commun Mag 52(8):74–81
3. Steinhubl SR, Muse ED, Topol EJ (2013) Can mobile health technologies transform health care? JAMA 310(22):2395–2396
4. Mirza F, Norris T, Stockdale R (2008) Mobile technologies and the holistic management of chronic diseases. Health Inf J 14(4):309–321
5. Norris AC, Stockdale RS, Sharma S (2009) A strategic approach to m-health. Health Inf J 15 (3):244–253
6. DuBenske LL, Gustafson DH, Shaw BR, Cleary JF (2010) Web-based cancer communication and decision making systems: connecting patients, caregivers, and clinicians for improved health outcomes. Med Decis Making 30(6):732–744
7. Ouhbi S, Fernández-Alemán JL, Toval A, Idri A, Pozo JR (2015) Free blood donation mobile applications. J Med Syst 39(5):52
8. Kuijpers W, Groen WG, Oldenburg HS, Wouters MW, Aaronson NK, van Harten WH (2016) Ehealth for breast cancer survivors: use, feasibility and impact of an interactive portal. JMIR cancer 2(1):e3
9. Kim SC, Shah DV, Namkoong K, McTavish FM, Gustafson DH (2013) Predictors of online health information seeking among women with breast cancer: The role of social support perception and emotional well-being. J Comput Med Commun 18(2):98–118
10. Salonen A, Ryhänen AM, Leino-Kilpi H (2014) Educational benefits of Internet and computer-based programmes for prostate cancer patients: a systematic review. Patient Educ Couns 94(1):10–19
11. Swan M (2009) Emerging patient-driven health care models: an examination of health social networks, consumer personalized medicine and quantified self-tracking. Int J Environ Res Pub Health 6(2):492–525
12. Jha AK, DesRoches CM, Campbell EG, Donelan K, Rao SR, Ferris TG, Shields A, Rosenbaum S, Blumenthal D (2009) Use of electronic health records in US hospitals. N Engl J Med 360(16):1628–1638
13. Mettler T, Eurich M (2012) A "design-pattern"-based approach for analyzing e-health business models. Health Policy Technol 1(2):77–85
14. Caulfield BM, Donnelly SC (2013) What is connected health and why will it change your practice? QJM: Int J Med 106(8):703–707
15. Lorig KR, Ritter P, Stewart AL, Sobel DS, Brown BW Jr, Bandura A, Gonzalez VM, Laurent DD, Holman HR et al (2001) Chronic disease self-management program: 2-year health status and health care utilization outcomes. Med Care 39(11):1217–1223
16. Fu D, Fu H, McGowan P, Shen Y-E, Zhu L, Yang H, Mao J, Zhu S, Ding Y, Wei Z (2003) Implementation and quantitative evaluation of chronic disease self-management programme in Shanghai, China: randomized controlled trial. Bull World Health Organ 81(3):174–182
17. Walsh MN, Albert NM, Curtis AB, Gheorghiade M, Heywood JT, Liu Y, Mehra MR, O'Connor CM, Reynolds D, Yancy CW et al (2012) Lack of association between electronic

health record systems and improvement in use of evidence-based heart failure therapies in outpatient Cardiology practices. Clin Cardiol 35(3):187–196

18. American Academy of Family Physicians (2017) http://www.aafp.org/home.html. Accessed Sep 2017

19. Society for Vascular Surgery (ed) (2013) Electronic medical records/Health information technology: background information and resources, SVS Clinical Practice Council

20. Tang PC, Ash JS, Bates DW, Overhage JM, Sands DZ (2006) Personal health records: definitions, benefits, and strategies for overcoming barriers to adoption. J Am Med Inform Assoc 13(2):121–126

21. Señor IC, Alemán JLF, Toval A (2012) Personal health records: new means to safely handle health data? Computer 45(11):27–33

22. Ouhbi S, Idri A, Fernández-Alemán JL, Toval A, Benjelloun H (2014) Electronic health records for Cardiovascular medicine. In: 36th annual international conference of the IEEE engineering in medicine and biology society (EMBC), pp 1354–1357

23. Maloney FL, Wright A (2010) USB-based personal health records: an analysis of features and functionality. Int J Med Inform 79(2):97–111

24. Fernández-Alemán JL, Seva-Llor CL, Toval A, Ouhbi S, Fernández-Luque L (2013) Free web-based personal health records: an analysis of functionality. J Med Syst 37(6):9990

25. Kharrazi H, Chisholm R, VanNasdale D, Thompson B (2012) Mobile personal health records: an evaluation of features and functionality. Int J Med Inform 81(9):579–593

26. Bouri N, Ravi S (2014) Going mobile: how mobile personal health records can improve health care during emergencies. JMIR mHealth uHealth 2(1):e8

27. Chang IC, Hsiao SJ, Hsu HM, Chen TH (2010, June) Building mPHR to assist diabetics in self-healthcare management. In: 7th international conference on service systems and service management (ICSSSM), pp 1–5

28. Castaneda C, Nalley K, Mannion C, Bhattacharyya P, Blake P, Pecora A, Goy A, Suh KS (2015) Clinical decision support systems for improving diagnostic accuracy and achieving precision medicine. J Clin Bioinform 5(1):4

29. Osheroff JA, Teich JM, Middleton B, Steen EB, Wright A, Detmer DE (2007) A roadmap for national action on clinical decision support. J Am Med Inform Assoc 14(2):141–145

30. Romano MJ, Stafford RS (2011) Electronic health records and clinical decision support systems: impact on national ambulatory care quality. Arch Intern Med 171(10):897–903

31. Castillo RS, Kelemen A (2013) Considerations for a successful clinical decision support system. CIN: Comput Inf Nurs 31(7):319–326

32. Berner S (ed) (2007) Clinical decision support systems. Springer, New York, NY

33. Wyatt JC (2000) Decision support systems. J R Soc Med Dec 93:629–633

34. Clinical and Laboratory Standards Institute (CLSI) (2017) http://www.clsi.org. Accessed Sep 2017

35. ITU-T. ITU Telecommunication Standardization Sector (2017) http://www.itu.int/ITU-T/. Accessed Sep 2017

36. eHSCG. eHealth Standardization Coordination Group (2017) www.itu.int/en/ITU-T/studygroups/com16/ehscg. Accessed Sep 2017

37. DICOM. Digital Imaging and Communications in Medicine (2017) http://medical.nema.org/. Accessed Sep 2017

38. OASIS (2017) Organization for the advancement of structured information standards. https://www.oasis-open.org/org. Accessed Sep 2017

39. European Committee for Standardization (2017) CEN/TC 251. http://www.cen.eu. Accessed Sep 2017

40. International Organization for Standardization (2017) ISO/TC 215. http://www.iso.org/iso/. Accessed Sep 2017

41. IEEE 1073 Standard for Medical Device Communications (1998)

42. International Electrotechnical Commission (2017) IEC/TC 62. http://www.iec.ch/. Accessed Sep 2017

43. ISO/TR 20514:2005 (2005) Health informatics—electronic health record—definition, scope and context
44. Pagidipati NJ, Gaziano TA (2013) Estimating deaths from cardiovascular disease: a review of global methodologies of mortality measurement. Circulation 127(6):749–756
45. Verdecchia P, Schillaci G, Borgioni C, Ciucci A, Pede S, Porcellati C (1998) Ambulatory pulse pressure. Hypertension 32(6):983–988
46. Prevention & Treatment of Arrhythmia. American Heart Association (2017) http://www. heart.org/HEARTORG/Conditions/Arrhythmia/PreventionTreatmentofArrhythmia/ Prevention-Treatment-of-Arrhythmia_UCM_002026_Article.jsp#.WWLgPHfMzHg. Accessed Sep 2017
47. Franklin SS, Khan SA, Wong ND, Larson MG, Levy D (1999) Is pulse pressure useful in predicting risk for coronary heart disease? Circulation 100(4):354–360
48. Palatini P (2007) Heart rate as an independent risk factor for cardiovascular disease. Drugs 67 (2):3–13
49. Reynoldson C, Stones C, Allsop M, Gardner P, Bennett MI, Closs SJ, Jones R, Knapp P (2014) Assessing the quality and usability of smartphone apps for pain self-management. Pain Med 15(6):898–909
50. Lahrmann H, Rocha I, Struhal W, Thijs RD, Hilz M (2011) Diagnosing autonomic nervous system disorders-existing guidelines and future perspectives. Eur Neurol Rev 6(1):52–56
51. Struhal W, Russell JW (2014) Autonomic nervous system. In: Atlas of neuromuscular diseases. Springer, pp 291–297
52. Hampton JR, Harrison MJ, Mitchell JR, Prichard JS, Seymour C (1975) Relative contributions of history-taking, physical examination, and laboratory investigation to diagnosis and management of medical outpatients. Br Med J 2(5969):486–489
53. Yoshiya I, Shimada Y, Tanaka K (1980) Spectrophotometric monitoring of arterial oxygen saturation in the fingertip. Med Biol Eng Comput 18(1):27–32
54. Allen J (2007) Photoplethysmography and its application in clinical physiological measurement. Physiol Meas 28(3):R1
55. Gil E, Orini M, Bailón R, Vergara JM, Mainardi L, Laguna P (2010) Photoplethysmography pulse rate variability as a surrogate measurement of heart rate variability during non-stationary conditions. Physiol Meas 31(9):1271
56. World Health Organization: world blood donor day: safe blood for saving mothers (2017) http://www.who.int/campaigns/world-blood-donor-day/2014/event/en/. Accessed Sep 2017
57. World Health Organization: Global database on blood safety. Summary report 2011. http:// www.who.int/bloodsafety/global_database/en/. Accessed Sep 2017
58. Williamson LM, Devine DV (2013) Challenges in the management of the blood supply. The Lancet 381(9880):1866–1875
59. Tagny CT, Owusu-Ofori S, Mbanya D, Deneys V (2010) The blood donor in sub-Saharan Africa: a review. Transfus Med 20(1):1–10
60. France CR, France JL, Kowalsky JM, Cornett TL (2010) Education in donation coping strategies encourages individuals to give blood: further evaluation of a donor recruitment brochure. Transfusion 50(1):85–91
61. France CR, France JL, Wissel ME, Kowalsky JM, Bolinger EM, Huckins JL (2011) Enhancing blood donation intentions using multimedia donor education materials. Transfusion 51(8):1796–1801
62. Ylipulli J, Suopajärvi T, Ojala T, Kostakos V, Kukka H (2014) Municipal WiFi and interactive displays: appropriation of new technologies in public urban spaces. Technol Forecast Soc Chang 89:145–160
63. Ouhbi S, Fernández-Alemán JL, Pozo JR, El Bajta M, Toval A, Idri A (2015) Compliance of blood donation apps with mobile OS usability guidelines. J Med Syst 39(6):63
64. Sayyedi VK (2014) A personal health record module for pregnant women: system development and user adoption study. Master thesis. McMaster University Hamilton, Ontario, p 85. http://hdl.handle.net/11375/13981. Accessed Sep 2017

65. Gibbins J, Thomson AM (2001) Women's expectations and experiences of childbirth. Midwifery 17(4):302–313
66. Shaw E et al (2008) Access to web-based personalized antenatal health records for pregnant women: a randomized controlled trial. J Obstet Gynaecol Can: JOGC 30(1):38–43
67. Idri A, Bachiri M, Fernández-Alemán JL (2016) A framework for evaluating the software product quality of pregnancy monitoring mobile personal health records. J Med Syst 40(3):1–17
68. Ahern DK, Kreslake JM, Phalen JM (2006) What is eHealth (6): perspectives on the evolution of eHealth research. J Med Internet Res 8(1):e4
69. Carroll N (2016) Key success factors for smart and connected health software solutions. Computer 49(11):22–28
70. Ouhbi S, Fernández-Alemán JL, Toval A, Pozo JR, Idri A (2017) Sustainability requirements for connected health applications. J Softw Evol Process (under review)
71. Durdik Z, Klatt B, Koziolek H, Krogmann K, Stammel J, Weiss R (2012) Sustainability guidelines for long-living software systems. In: 28th IEEE international conference on software maintenance (ICSM). IEEE, pp 517–526
72. Erdelyi K (2013) Special factors of development of green software supporting eco sustainability. In: IEEE 11th international symposium on intelligent systems and informatics (SISY). IEEE, pp 337–340
73. Penzenstadler B (2014) Infusing green: requirements engineering for green in and through software systems. In: Workshop on requirements engineering for sustainable systems, pp 44–53
74. Penzenstadler B, Fleischmann A (2011) Teach sustainability in software engineering? In: 24th IEEE-CS conference on software engineering education and training (CSEE&T). IEEE, pp 454–458
75. Horizons 2020 (2017) Health, demographic change and wellbeing. http://ec.europa.eu/programmes/horizon2020/en/h2020-section/health-demographic-change-and-wellbeing. Accessed Sep 2017
76. Ouhbi S, Fernández-Alemán JL, Idri A, Pozo JR (2015, October) Are mobile blood donation applications green? In: 10th international conference on intelligent systems: theories and applications (SITA). IEEE, pp 1–6
77. ISO/IEC 25010 Standard (2011) Systems and software engineering—systems and software quality requirements and evaluation (SQuaRE)—system and software quality models

Index

Numeral
4G, 286, 287, 290, 293
802.11p, 55, 60, 65
802.15.4, 55, 60

A
Actuators, 246, 248
Adoption, 299–301, 309, 310
Advanced metering infrastructure, 183
Agent-based modeling, 4, 5
Agents, 6
Anomaly detection, 158, 159
Applications, 299–302, 309–313
Architecture, 51, 53, 55, 59–64, 66–68
Artificial intelligence, 108, 246, 252
Attribute-based approach, 136
Automatic demand response, 255

B
Bandwidth, 283, 284, 286, 287, 290, 291, 293
Bandwidth consumption, 160
Battery cost, 211
Battery switching stations, 216
Bayesian networks, 158
Behavior analysis, 158
Benefits, 268, 274
Big data, 31, 36, 39
Big data analytics, 164, 246, 248
Big data characteristic of smart grids, 181
Big data management, 177, 180, 193
Big energy data, 180, 194–196
Biometrics, 34
Blood donation, 299, 307, 308
Botnets and Spyware, 43

C
Cardiovascular diseases, 305
CDSS, 301, 302
Cidades Digitais, 284, 288
CIM, 186, 193
Citizen participation, 130
Citizens, 144, 145
Citizen welfare, 131, 132
City, 263–268, 270, 275–278
City governance, 137, 138, 140–145, 148, 149
City government, 129
City management, 128
Client, 13
Cloud computing, 59, 61, 66, 67, 108,
    112–114, 121, 153–155, 159, 161, 163,
    164, 172, 173
Clustering-based anomaly, 158
Clustering framework, 159
Cognitive management framework, 5
Coherency, 110
Communication, 51–57, 59–62, 66–69
Complex organization, 4
Compressor motor, 213
Connected health, 299, 300, 309–313
Connected vehicles, 163
Consumer privacy, 180, 193
Consumer satisfaction, 82
Convergence, 134
Cost reflective pricing, 71, 73, 91

Brazilian cities, 283, 284, 286, 288, 292, 294
Broadband, 286–288, 294
Building units, 16
Business, 264, 265, 274

Critical peak pricing, 71–73, 77, 86, 97
Customer mindset, 221
Cyber threats, 27

D
Data, 301, 302, 304, 305, 308, 311–313
Data aggregation, 140
Data analytics, 132, 138, 141, 180, 185, 193
Data collection, 183, 190
Data integration, 185, 192
Data integrity, 43
Data management, 122, 141, 143
Data preprocessing, 184, 191
Data representation and visualisation, 187, 193
Data reusability, 143
Data security, 180, 191, 195, 198
Data storage, 186, 192
Day-ahead pricing, 71, 73, 89, 98
Demand side management, 71, 97
Design and planning, 29
Digital, 264, 265, 267, 270–272, 274, 275
Digital city, 27, 245
Digital sensors, 154–156, 164
Distributed energy resources, 181, 184, 194
Driving range anxiety, 208
Dwelling units, 10

E
e-business, 110
EcoModel City, 253
Economic, 300, 310
Economy, 285
Edge computing, 161
Efficiency, 54, 59, 133, 145, 147
e-Government, 268
e-health, 164, 299, 303, 304
EHRs, 301, 302, 312
Electric highway, 217
Electricity, 20
Electricity distribution, 73
Electricity generation, 72, 73
Electricity transmission, 73
Electric vehicles, 207, 210, 211, 222–224, 227, 229, 232
Electronic product code, 246, 247
Energy, 265, 267, 268, 277, 278
Energy consumption, 282, 284, 292, 293
Energy data lifecycle, 183
Energy data policy and regulation, 196
Energy management, 84, 115
Energy management system, 253, 255, 256, 258, 260
Enterprise architectures, 54, 55, 173

Enterprises, 283, 285, 287, 290, 293, 294
Environment, 284, 285, 294, 304, 312
EV, 207–225, 227–238
EV battery and charger issues, 213
EV charging station, 216
Event-driven architecture, 111
EV integration, 225, 231, 235, 236, 238
EV parking lots, 218
EV supply chain issues, 209

F
Feed-In Tariff (FIT), 253
Fiber optic, 286
FI or local area network, 248
Fleet operator control, 228
Fog computing, 153, 154, 157, 161–167, 172–174
Fog paradigm, 154, 157, 164, 166, 174
Food management, 107, 111, 115
Framework, 62, 63, 68
Fuzzy techniques, 113

G
Geographic information systems, 111, 184
Global village, 34
Governance, 26, 27, 29–32, 36, 38–41, 46, 153
Governance services, 140
Governmental, 282–286, 288, 293, 294
GPS, 34, 39, 44, 246
Granular radio energy, 121
Grid functionality failure, 230
Grid-to-Vehicle (G2V), 208

H
Health care, 110, 267, 269, 276, 299–301, 308, 311, 312
Health informatics, 300, 303
Heterogeneous, 51–54, 58, 62, 63, 68
Hidden Markov model, 159
Hierarchical structure, 4
History of electric vehicles, 210
History of smart grid and electric vehicles, 210
Holarchy, 7
Holons, 7
Hybrid vehicles, 222
Hybrid V-WSN, 56
Hydrometallurgy, 224, 237

I
ICT-Driven City, 27
Indicator, 284–286, 288
Individual, 299, 309, 310
Individual knowledge, 8

Information and Communication Technology
    (ICT), 26–32, 34, 38, 40, 46, 107, 264,
    266–268, 270, 277, 282, 283, 288, 292,
    294
Information fusion, 154, 156, 157, 160, 173
Infrastructure, 282–287, 293
Intelligent city, 28
Intelligent distributed autonomous smart city, 5
Intelligent system, 110, 119–121
Intelligent Transport System (ITS), 107
Internet, 267, 270, 271, 282, 284, 286–289,
    292, 294
Internet access, 127, 131
Internet of everything, 3
Internet of Things (IoT), 4, 7, 34–37, 39–41,
    43, 59, 62, 66, 67, 107, 108, 111,
    113–115, 122, 153–157, 161, 164,
    243–249, 254, 257, 259, 260, 282–284,
    292
Internet protocol for smart objects, 248
Internet services, 132
Interoperability, 111
Investments, 283, 284, 287, 290, 293
IoT environment, 143, 144
IPv6, 246

J
Japan, 243, 244, 248, 250, 252–254, 257, 258

K
Knowledge centre, 132, 140, 142, 148, 150
Knowledge city, 28

L
Lack of charging infrastructure, 211, 217
Large-scale multi-agent systems, 4
Large-scale multi-agent systems modeling, 3
Lead–acid battery, 214
LED, 253
Legal dimensions, 26
Load management, 84, 85
Load mismatch, 207, 209, 219, 227
LTE, 281, 287, 290, 291

M
MESH city, 28
Metadata, 137
Metamodel, 7
Microgrid, 75, 79
Microsoft, 243, 245, 247, 249
Mitigation policies, 221
Mobile, 302, 313
Mobility, 115, 267–269, 282, 284, 285, 290
Model, 274, 276

Motorist attitude, 216
MPHR, 302, 306, 308, 309
Multi-agent systems, 4
Multimedia, 286, 287
Multiple vehicle tracking, 170

N
Negotiate, 11
Negotiation, 13
Negotiator, 17
Neighbourhoods, 16
Network communications, 29
Neural network, 158
Nickel battery, 214
Normative organizational
    structure, 5
Normative roles, 20

O
Of participatory government, 136
Optimization, 149
Organizational design, 5
Organizational dynamics, 7
Organizational metamodel, 5
Organizational model, 4
Organizational modeling, 3–6
Organizational unit, 7
Organizations, 4

P
PAC, 284, 288
Participating in V2G, 208
Patient, 299, 301, 302, 305
Peak time rebate, 71, 73, 92–95
Peak time rebate pricing, 71, 73
Photovoltaic system, 18
PHRs, 301, 302, 308, 312
Platforms, 263, 267, 270, 272, 278
Positive temperature coefficient, 212
Power grid, 208, 210, 225, 231, 235
PPG, 305
Pregnancy, 308
Pricing mechanisms, 71, 73, 91, 94
Privacy, 59, 119, 143
Privacy and security, 165
Public safety, 122
Pyrometallurgy, 225, 237

Q
QR codes, 248
Quality, 281, 282, 284, 287, 290, 292, 294,
    300–302, 313
Quality indicator, 148
Quality of Life, 243–245, 257, 258

R

Radio-Frequency Identification System
   (RFID), 108
Range anxiety, 211
Rapid urbanization, 26, 33
Rare battery materials, 224
Real time, 56
Real-time decision-making, 188
Real time pricing, 71–73, 77, 81, 97
Recharging stations, 217, 220
RecipeWorld, 9
Recursive hierarchical structure, 15
Renewable energy, 209
Requirements, 299, 300, 309–313
Resource autonomy, 13
Resource provisioning, 165
Resources, 10, 20, 281–284, 287, 292, 294
RFID, 108, 112, 121, 246, 248
RFID tags, 27, 42
Role, 8

S

Safety, 51, 52, 55–57, 60, 61, 68
SCADA, 74, 177, 179, 188
Scholarship, 290, 293
Seasonal pricing, 71, 73, 90, 91
Securing interoperability, 122
Security, 55, 57, 59, 109, 135, 136, 145, 283,
   284, 293
Security and data privacy, 190
Security challenges, 27, 36
Security testing, 39
Self-adapting, 28
Self-sustainability, 3–6, 10, 12–17
Self-sustainable, 4
Semantic web, 108
Sensor, 51–54, 56, 58, 60, 62–64, 68, 246, 248
Server, 13
Service-oriented architecture, 111
Services, 51–54, 56–59, 61–64, 66–68,
   299–301, 307, 308, 310, 311, 313
Singular value decomposition, 168
Signal detection theory, 196
Signal interference, 42
Situational awareness, 157
Smart citizens, 130
Smart city, 3–5, 7, 20, 21, 25, 28, 33, 34,
   51–55, 58, 63, 64, 68, 69, 109, 111, 135,
   137, 153–158, 173, 243–246, 249,
   251–254, 260, 263–266, 268, 275, 277,
   282, 299, 300
Smart city governance, 127, 134

Smart city management, 129
Smart city surveillance, 153–155, 157, 158,
   160–162, 166, 172–174
Smart economy, 246
Smart governance, 246
Smart grid, 5, 71–76, 78, 99, 164, 208, 210,
   225, 227, 230, 235, 247, 253
Smart grid management, 178
Smart grids data management, 183
Smart infrastructures, 155
Smart metres, 108
Smart mobility, 39
Smartphone, 218, 284, 293, 294, 302, 305
Smart self-sustainable human settlements, 4
Smart sensors, 108
Smart technologies, 4
Smart transportation, 52–55, 57, 59
SOA, 111, 113, 115
Social, 263, 265, 268, 275–277, 299, 300,
   310–312
Social media, 145, 146
Society, 267, 270, 271
Software, 299, 302, 309, 313
Solutions, 284, 285, 292, 294
Standards, 299, 300, 303, 304
Standards and interoperability, 188
Support vector machine, 193
Sustainability, 299, 300, 309–313
Sustainability mechanisms, 3, 13, 15
Sustainable energy microsystem, 115

T

Tag cloning, 42
Tag killing, 42
Technical, 299, 313
Technologies, 264, 265, 268, 269, 274, 275
Time of use pricing, 71, 73
Traffic overload, 26
Traffic surveillance, 153, 154, 158, 163, 166,
   167
Transparent governance, 131
Transport management, 116
Trust, 137, 144, 145

U

Ubiquitous city, 27
U-City, 27, 28
Urbanization, 153

V

V2G, 207
V2V, 225, 226

Vehicle tracking, 158, 159, 170, 171
Vehicular Ad hoc Network (VANET), 117
V-WSN, 56, 58–60, 63, 64, 67

W
Warm technology city, 28
Waste management, 224
Web of science, 245, 251

Wide area motion imagery, 159
Wireless, 284, 289, 291, 294
Wireless sensor networks, 112
World energy council, 72

Z
ZigBee, 55, 60, 248

Printed in the United States
By Bookmasters